Paul Joannou & Alan Candlish

PIONEERS
of the
NORTH
the Birth of Newcastle United FC

T0315743

Preface by Alan Shearer OBE.
Foreword by Rowland Maughan (Northumberland FA).

First published in Great Britain in 2009 by The Breedon Books Publishing
Company Limited, Breedon House, 3 The Parker Centre, Derby, DE21 4SZ.

This paperback edition published in Great Britain in 2014 by DB Publishing, an
imprint of JMD Media Ltd

ISBN 978-1-78091-407-7

Printed and bound in the UK by Copytech (UK) Ltd Peterborough

PIONEERS
of the
NORTH
the Birth of Newcastle United FC

CONTENTS

DEDICATION

To the Pioneers who started it all.
They should be remembered.

FOREWORD

BY ROWLAND MAUGHAN
Chief Executive, Northumberland Football Association

It is nearly 130 years since the original Northumberland & Durham Football Association was founded in 1880 at a meeting in Newcastle's Grey Street, at the old Turk's Head Hotel opposite the Theatre Royal. Three years later the two counties separated and the Northumberland Football Association was formed, one of the oldest such affiliated bodies to the FA in the country. A lot has happened in football since then, with the North East becoming a proverbial hotbed of the game.

There has been very little recorded on those early Victorian days and on the pioneer clubs of the region, notably Tyne Association and Newcastle Rangers. I must admit, like many, to knowing little of that era all those years ago, but it is important that we do know how the game developed and who the founders were. Football is so important to many of us here in the North East. It is an insight now to understand how the sport came to the region's heartland of Tyneside from a surprising route – from the great public-schools of England; Eton, Harrow and Charterhouse included.

The formation of the district's premier club, Newcastle United, is understood a little better now that the East End and West End rivalry is related in fascinating detail; however, this history not only looks at the bigger clubs, it also relates how some of our grassroots teams were formed and developed, some of which are still in existence over a century later like Alnwick and Ashington. Some of course have long gone, such as Elswick and Rendel. It also covers the important neighbouring areas of Durham and Teesside.

This book is the first exhaustive record on the subject. Paul Joannou and Alan Candlish have completed a wonderful and comprehensive book. I am pleased that the story has now been told.

**NORTHUMBERLAND
FOOTBALL ASSOCIATION**

PREFACE
BY ALAN SHEARER OBE

Many great football oaks have out of little acorns grown, and 130 years and more ago many of those acorns were taking root all over the North East. In the late 19th century, numerous amateur clubs were springing up in many areas, often in the city suburbs, just as often in small towns and even smaller villages, and all with one common aim – to make the sport of association football great.

Today, the game we know, with all its international media coverage, bears little resemblance to those pioneering days when few devotees of Victorian football could ever have known or even predicted what the future would hold. But it is to those original Victorian visionaries that we owe so much. For it was they who put the wheels in motion towards everything we have in football in the 21st century.

I was fortunate enough, and privileged enough, to play for 18 wonderful years at the top level of English football with Southampton, Blackburn Rovers and, of course, in the final 10 years of my career, my own beloved Newcastle United. But as a youngster I played in two communities which had fostered their own pioneer clubs on Victorian Tyneside, and I came through their descendants so to speak, Wallsend Boys' Club and Cramlington Juniors. I was always aware that, for every major club such as Newcastle United, there were dozens more who may never command national headlines but who mean every bit as much to their fans as Newcastle United do to theirs.

United. That name itself tells a story. For Newcastle United is thus called because of the sort of union in 1892 of two city clubs, Newcastle West End and Newcastle East End, who in turn had their own very different origins rooted deeply in the pioneering years of football in the North East. West End and East End themselves competed alongside clubs with names of charm and mystery in various local leagues, some of which still bear their own proud identities today.

The development of football in the North East is a fascinating story of hope, ambition, dedication and achievement; of brave and driven men who would not be deflected from their targets and who left monumental legacies for their descendants that would establish the healthy foundations of the game for generations to come.

Paul Joannou and Alan Candlish, both Newcastle United supporters and both devoted students of the game, have worked together to tell the full and fascinating story of the North East's football pioneers and at last, after so many generations, to give those pioneers the platform they so richly deserve.

AUTHORS' NOTES & ACKNOWLEDGMENTS

T he subject matter of this account of the *Pioneers of the North* goes back over 130 years. For much of the opening decade of football's origins, factual information is very scarce. Reporting of the sport in local newspapers was at first mixed with the rugby code, brief and devoid of hard information.

Gradually, though, the association code gained column inches, despite conflicting match reports, teams, goalscorers and attendances being frequent in different newspapers. Notes on individual players and officials were scant, with the formal approach then being not to give Christian names and only initials. This all added to the problems of unravelling the past.

Apart from the local Tyneside press, notably the *Daily Journal*, *Daily Chronicle* and *Tyneside Echo*, extensive reference has also been made to contemporary newspapers from other parts of the region, primarily the *Northern Echo*, *Cleveland News*, *North Eastern Weekly Gazette* and *Morpeth Herald*. There were also other good sources of information like rare volumes of the *Northern Athlete* magazine.

Investigation has proved fruitful in other certain quarters, and leads have been tracked to the great public schools and universities of England, whose comprehensive archives have been invaluable in finding out who some of the pathfinders of North East's football were.

The Northumberland FA archive was of noteworthy investigation, especially the few surviving year-books of the era, although hand-written notes contained in the official annals did contain several errors, transcribed over time.

Over many years of research, Newcastle upon Tyne Central Library's Local Studies Department has been a priceless and a core point of inquiry, and their staff are duly thanked. Similarly the Local Studies Departments at Gateshead, Darlington and Middlesbrough libraries, together with the Tyne & Wear Archives Service at the Discovery Museum in Newcastle (where the Northumberland FA archives are housed), have also been an invaluable source of research. Mention must also be made of the excellent archive facilities at the Woodhorn Northumberland Museum in Ashington. Staff at all these locations have shown unfailing courtesy and assistance. Their help is much appreciated.

Acknowledgement is also made to the many authors of books on the North East region which over the years have created a first-class collection for reference. In addition, many historical football volumes covering the English and Scottish game have been reviewed, too many to schedule in a bibliography. Past study of Newcastle United's official minute books from the earliest times has provided much original information, while Jordan Tinniswood's extensive research notes *Before They Were United* were a point of reference, as was *Northern Goalfields Revisited* – the comprehensive *Millennium History of the Northern League* compiled by Brian Hunt. Reference has also been made to Arthur Appleton's *Hotbed of Soccer* – the first comprehensive history of football in the North East.

Illustrative material from this era is extremely rare, actual photographs not arriving into the printed media until much later; however, certain vintage prints and sketches of the North East's footballers have been found, and they give a fascinating insight into that Victorian period.

Several extracts and adaptations from vintage Ordnance Survey maps of Tyneside have been used and adapted to show the location of the pioneering sites of football. The excellent series of OS reproductions published by Alan Godfrey Maps have been invaluable.

The following individuals and organisations have assisted in unearthing facts on the region's Pioneers:

M. Dix, H. Greenmon, R. McBrearty (Scottish Football Museum), J. Edminson, P. Brennan (*www.donmouth.co.uk*), P. Tully (Newcastle United FC), R. Mason (Sunderland AFC), P. Days (Sunderland AFC historian), A. Mitchell, M. Amos MBE, T. Henderson, H. Hollier at WMG, M. Stevens, A. Stephenson (Northumberland CCC), D. Walton (Corbridge historian), D. Dale (South Bank FC and Stockton FC historian), K. Belton (chairman of the Durham Amateur Football Trust), D. Waggott, M. Mardall (Charterhouse School), T. Bowman (Lancing College), J. Ringrose (Pembroke, Cambridge), J. Tarrat-Barton (Eton College), T. Rogers (Marlborough College), F. Colbert & L. Steel (St John's, Cambridge), P. Hoose (Repton School), S. Hill (Malvern College), C. Hopkins (Trinity, Oxford), R. Boddy (Newcastle Preparatory School).

Grateful thanks to Rowland Maughan, at the Northumberland FA, and Alan Shearer for their introductions. Finally to Steve and Michelle at Breedon Books for their willingness to publish this volume.

Paul Joannou (Edinburgh) & Alan Candlish (Newcastle), August 2009.

Chapter 1

A HOTBED IS BORN

'Nothing, of course, happens suddenly. Modern football is the culmination of a long tradition.'
Percy M. Young, 1968

The north-east corner of England, most notably Tyneside and Wearside, has long been regarded as a 'hotbed of football'. These days, supporters of Newcastle United and Sunderland are recognised as some of the most passionate in the country, if not the wider footballing world. Especially so considering that trophy success has been such a rarity in modern times; the Magpies last winning a major trophy in 1969 and the Wearsiders four years later in 1973. Despite this lack of silverware, though, both rivals have flown the flag of the North East region with much pride, fans supporting their respective clubs on Tyneside and Wearside in crowds regularly approaching 50,000 and over. And there have been plenty of hero figures for those thousands to look up to and worship.

While the region has been at the forefront of the English game for a hundred years, with some of football's most celebrated line ups, as the sport first took hold nationally the North East was a late developer in many respects.

Football has long been an important part of the British way of life and is now a civic institution – *the* national sport. The game in this country evolved from the ancient days of the Romans and Normans, through the Middle Ages and Renaissance, the Reformation and Restoration, to the Regency and Georgian periods and then to the Victorians, who organised the sport and laid down the first laws. The game took many forms, and as Percy Young wrote in the seminal *A History of British Football*: 'Nothing, of course, happens suddenly. Modern football is the culmination of a long tradition.' It is, however, difficult to trace football's origins in this country, and even it is more difficut to do with any precision.

We do know that the Chinese played *cuju* as early as the first century BC, and Japan had its version called *kemari*. Neither of these games bore much resemblance to the game that we know today, however, and even these can be pre-dated. It is known that ball games were first played in Egypt as long ago as 1800 BC and there are claims that some form of ball game was played even earlier in ancient China, possibly as far back as 2500 BC, although these may have been linked to religious ceremonies and fertility rites.

The Romans adopted the Ancient Greek game of *episkyros*, which they called *harpastum*. Two teams played on a rectangle of space, striving to take a ball beyond a base-line at either end of the pitch – by using almost any means. Harpastum may have been more a rugby-style of football, the hands being used as well as the feet, and it was noted in one description as being a 'violent exercise', but it was nevertheless an early form of the game as we know it now.

Harpastum was popular in the Roman Army and when they marched to the north of their new province of Britannia around AD 70–80, it is possible that they may have brought the sport with them. It is known that soldiers in the region played many games to while away the time during prolonged, monotonous periods off duty. Archaeological evidence has been found in the North East at Vindolanda and Corstopitum (Corbridge) of various indoor pastimes such as dice games (with gaming boards and counters) and a forerunner of the modern game of draughts *(ludus latrunculorum)*. It is comparatively rare to find archaeological evidence of outdoor activities, although mosaics of hunting scenes and an altar depicting similar events have been discovered, as well as jewellery showing a chariot race.

No documentary or archaeological evidence exists as far as can be ascertained that harpastum was played alongside Hadrian's Wall. But with plenty of Romans in the area, even allowing for the widespread make-up of the legions and their workers, it is possible that one of the origins of the game that is now so fervently followed was indeed played some 1,900 years ago not far from the Tyne. Maybe those Romans who occupied and guarded the northern frontier of their vast empire may have created the first hotbed of football? As noted in *Association Football And The Men Who Made It*, the respected early text on the game: 'Roman cohorts may have planted the seed.'

Newcastle owes its existence to the building of Hadrian's Wall. It was originally the beginning of the wall that was constructed westwards to Bowness-on-Solway (and later extended east to Wallsend). A bridge over the River Tyne, Pons Aelius, was named after the emperor (Titus Aelius Hadrianus) following his visit to his northern province in AD 122. The wall itself was built under the direction of Aulus Platorius Nepos, the Governor of Britain from AD 122–126. The bridge was erected at the very beginning of this period, possibly as early as AD 120, and was guarded by a fort which adopted the same name. The site of the fort was near the current Castle Keep; although initially it was a small settlement in terms of population, certainly smaller than Corstopitum, Vindolanda and Lugulvallium (Carlisle), all of which pre-date the building of the wall. Gradually, however, Pons Aelius grew and by the year AD 200, it is estimated that the population may have been around 1,000.

Later the settlement of Monkchester was developed around the old site of Pons Aelius, and in 1080 when the Normans, under Robert Curthose, the youngest son of William the Conqueror, constructed the 'new castle', the fledgling community was renamed Newcastle. It is possible that Normans brought with them their own version of football *La Soule*, or, as commoners called it, *La Choule.*

This mediaeval contest was often a brutish event, with any roughly spherical object utilised, including animal bladders and hogs heads! Historical research also indicates that even human heads were used on rare occasions – of the English in the north and the Scots in the south!

This rudimentary form of football was played and in the region elsewhere. A wonderful scarce record of early football exists from 1280 in the County of Northumberland, at Ulgham near Ashington, one of the earliest involving football on manuscript in this country. And it shows the game back then could be even fatal. It was

FOOTBALL'S DEVELOPMENT

Timetable of football's evolution

Caju, Kemuri:	BC
Harpastum, around:	100
La Soule, 'Mob football', around:	1100
Public schools playing football, around:	1750
Eton Rules established:	1815
Rugby football code established:	1845
Cambridge Rules established:	1848
Sheffield FC formed:	1857
Sheffield Rules established:	1857
Thring's *Simplest Game* established:	1862
Notts County FC formed:	1862
The Football Association formed:	1863
The *Laws of Football* published:	1863

noted that on Trinity Sunday: 'One Henry, son of William de Ellington, was playing at football with a large number of his friends. In the course of play he ran against David le Keu, who was wearing a knife. The unfortunate Henry impaled himself on the knife and subsequently died.'

Sport, in its various forms, grew throughout the country in the Middle Ages. To appreciate the rudimentary game of football in its true context, it is worth considering Fitzstephen's account of the manner in which London schoolboys indulged themselves in the 12th century (translated by John Stow): 'Every yeare also at Shrove Tuesday...the school boyes bring cockes of the game to their master, and all the forenoone delight themselves in cockfighting. After dinner all the youthes go into the field to play at ball. The schollers of every school have their ball (or staff) in their hands; auncient and wealthy men of the citie come forth on horseback to see the sport of the young men, and to take pleasure in beholding their agilitie.'

So, it is clear that in mediaeval England and Scotland an early form of the game multi-millions now watch around the world was being played. Admittedly, it was a crude contortion of the sport but, in the centuries that followed, the folk of Britain showed a liking for the then often rough and vulgar pastime of chasing a ball. Despite several attempts to kill the game off – by the very highest authority – football evolved from that primitive contest into the sophisticated sporting business we have today.

Much later, in 1690, it is recorded in the eminent early volume *The History of England* by Macauley, that 'letters from Newcastle give an account of a great match at football, which had been played in Northumberland, and was suspected to have been a pretext for a large gathering of the disaffected, i.e. Jacobites'. The legendary record of England went on: 'In the crowd, it was said, were 150 horsemen well mounted and armed, of whom many were Papists.' In the same century a contest at football is recorded in County Durham between a team of butchers and a team of glovers.

The rough-and-tumble game of football did have its problems in those very early days, with the highest authority in the land – the King – taking steps to extinguish the sport. As early as 1314 the Lord Mayor of the City of London banned football on behalf of Edward II, the translation noting, 'for as much as there is a great noise in the city caused by hustling over large foot balls in the fields of the public from which many evils might arise which God forbid: we command and forbid on behalf of the king, on pain of imprisonment, such game to be used in the city in the future'.

Football was again mentioned by Edward III, Richard II, Henry IV and Elizabeth I, all of whom laid down further restrictions as the years moved on. So too did the Parliament of Scotland, which passed a Football Act making the game illegal and punishable by a fine of four pence. In the North East a certain John Wonkell of Durham county was sent to prison for a week in 1579 for playing football on a Sunday.

The lawmakers found football a flourishing activity, in their view distracting the male population from military practise and exercise. There was also an underlying anti-football mindset in certain quarters, especially from the religious faction. The rancorous author of the 16th century, Philip Stubbs, was particularly scathing of football, classing it as 'develyshe pastimes' practised on the Sabbath Day. In his *The Anatomie of Abuses in the Realme of England* published in 1583, he describes the game: 'As concerning football playing, I protest unto you that it may rather be called a frendlie kinde of fyghte than a play or recreation – a bloody and murthering practice than a felowly sport or pastime. For dooth not everyone lye in waight for his adversarie, seeking to overthrow him and picke him on his nose, though it be on hard stones, on ditch or dale, or whatever place soever it be he careth not, so he can have him downe? And he who can serve the most in this fashion, he is counted the only felow, and who but he.'

But all was not bad. Henry VIII actually ordered a pair of football boots in 1526; although soon afterwards scholar Thomas Elyot described the sport as 'nothing but beastlie furie and extreme violence'. In 1615 James I of England was 'entertained' with a 'foot-ball match', and he soon afterwards encouraged Christians to play at football every Sunday afternoon following worship. Thus football survived the earlier Royal attempts to have the amusement extinguished and now had the Court seal of approval and began to flourish.

Until, that is, Britain dabbled with its only period of republicanism during the Commonwealth and Protectorate (1649–60). The Lord Protector, Oliver Cromwell, who was reputedly a keen footballer in his youth, succeeded in imposing a ban on the game (and other sports). Boys caught playing football on a Sunday could be whipped as a punishment. This ban on Sunday football remained in force for over 30 years.

Many passages relating to football are included in various volumes over the decades and centuries, notably even those by Chaucer, Sir Walter Scott and Shakespeare. The Bard's works, particularly, are replete with sporting analogies. One of the key speeches in *Henry V* (Act I Scene II) is Henry's vehement response to the Dauphin's gift of tennis balls. Shakespeare makes a number of references to football, even indicating that a leather case ball was used in the game when he wrote *The Comedy of Errors* in 1593–94. In Act II Scene I, he has Dromio of Ephesus bemoan:

'Am I so round with you, as you with me,
That like a football you do spurn me thus?
You spurn me hence, and he will spurn me hither:
If I last in this service you must case me in leather.'

Shakespeare was also not averse to using football as means of an insult. In *King Lear*, Act I Scene IV, Kent taunts Oswald by calling him a 'base football player'.

Joseph Strutt in *Sports and Pastimes of the People of England* includes a description of early football from 1834: 'When a match at football is made, two parties, each containing an equal number of competitors, take the field, and stand between two goals, placed at a distance of 80 or 100 yards the one from the other. The goal is usually made with two sticks, driven into the ground about two or three feet apart.'

An historic engraving from 1721 showing street football in old England; the mob-style game.

'The ball, which is commonly made of a blown bladder, and cased with leather, is delivered into the midst of the ground, and the object of each party is to drive it through the goal of their antagonists, which being achieved, the game is won.

'When the exercise becomes exceedingly violent, the players kick each other's shins without the least ceremony, and some of them are overthrown at the hazard of their limbs.'

Perhaps this is not 'the beautiful game' that the world knows and loves today, but it bears more than a passing resemblance to it.

Various communities around the region and along the borders arranged what can be termed 'folk football' or, as it has sometimes been described, 'mob football', still traditionally played in some locations even today. These contests were widespread in Britain, from Kirkwall on the Orkney Islands to Torrington in Devon. These took place at Shrovetide and Whitsuntide, or at other public festivals and fairs such as at Easter, Christmas and New Year.

It was a largely chaotic game of hundreds, similar in many respects to *La Soule*, with little to compare it to the modern sport, but football it was, albeit a mix of both the football and rugby codes. Contested usually between rival parts of a town or neighbouring communities, the aim was to get a ball to the opposition's mark, perhaps at one end of the town and maybe either a few hundred yards away from their rival's mark, or indeed two or three miles apart. It was one huge free-for-all, and violence was commonplace, even resulting in loss of life. The game lasted for hours, rather than the now regulation 90 minutes, and the two teams literally battled on and on, almost until exhaustion.

Alnwick and Rothbury in Northumberland hosted such matches, while Chester-le-Street and Sedgefield south of the Tyne did likewise. Many of the towns along the England-Scotland border at places such as Hawick, Duns, Jedburgh and Ancrum featured local battles to get the ball to one end of the town or another as well.

At Rothbury a ball was thrown in the air to set the match going, while in the town of Alnwick the game can be traced back to 1788, and it is noted that the Duke of Northumberland provided prizes and refreshments and dropped a ball from the castle battlements. The contest was played out with goalposts or 'hales' on the pastures below the fortress. In Sedgefield the custom was for a Shrove Tuesday contest, where 'the parish clerk is obliged to find a ball for the use of the townsmen and the country people, who assemble for the purpose of playing a game of football'. At Chester-le-Street a game was played between the 'Up-Streeters' and the 'Down-Streeters' with the aim to get the ball to the opponent's end of the street.

Folk games in the North and in the Borders were still played as the modern contest of football began to take root in an organised way in the Victorian North East. Even now, these festival matches still take place at Alnwick, Sedgefield and at Duns, only a few miles over the Cheviots from Northumberland.

All these early forms of football developed into the beginnings of the game we know today, and in Victorian Britain the nation's principal field sports really took hold; cricket and football in either of its two variants: by using largely the hands – the 'rugby code' – or the feet – the 'association code'.

Ball games first became a focus of stricter control as the country's authorities tried to suppress street free-for-alls. In 1835 Parliament passed the Highways Act which, among other things, provided fines for 'playing at football or any other game on any part of the said highways to the annoyance of any passenger'. Normal working-class citizens faced controls as football in particular was classed as a vulgar and rowdy pastime. Yet as this took place, the opposite end of the social scale found ball games to be more and more of an enjoyable activity. And that move was a key factor to football developing in a structured and considered way.

The game of cricket was played in the 18th century and was fully established by 1800. It was very much an upper-class pursuit. On Tyneside men were playing a degree of organised cricket as early as the 1820s, although not in a sophisticated way as in the south.

During the middle part of the 19th century, the game of football developed from the mob-style bedlam of the people to the educated classes – to the public schools of Eton, Shrewsbury and Rugby as well as Harrow, Westminster, Charterhouse and Uppingham, and to the Universities of Oxford and Cambridge. As one writer put it, 'order out of the chaos resulted'. Organisation followed, although the game was still as rough with much 'hacking' and 'shinning' prevalent, while at the same time a sprinkling of football clubs were established. All, however, were at least 150 miles south from the heartland of the North East. To the north, in Scotland – another 100 miles and more from Tyneside – the game also had early beginnings at some of the many private schools in the country's capital, Edinburgh.

When it came to football, some of these schools and institutions favoured the form of the sport in which the ball could be carried – as at Rugby, Cheltenham and Marlborough – while others preferred a contest where kicking and dribbling with the ball was promoted – as at Eton, Harrow and Charterhouse. Two factions and 'codes' developed; those who preferred a kicking, passing and dribbling approach, and those with a handling and ball-carrying style. At the same time two different shaped balls evolved, spherical and oval.

Eton developed differing ways of playing early forms of football and pupils staged games in the early decades of the 18th century. The Eton Wall Game was played on a narrow strip against a brick wall and is one of the oldest forms of organised football in existence in this country. Alternatively, the Eton Field game is played with a smaller ball that was eventually decided upon for the formal rules of association football and is a bit of a mix of football and rugby, like the Wall Game, although the ball may not be handled.

Charterhouse School started to play football shortly after Eton and Westminster schools in the 1750s. Due to limited space they played an early variety of the game within the cloisters and, as a result, players depended on close dribbling skills rather than long kicks or passes. Harrow did likewise, and as at Eton they had their own distinctive way of playing and still do, known as Harrow Football. Essentially a dribbling game on open fields, handling is allowed from a kick on the volley. Importantly, though, it is played with a round ball and was an organised activity from as early as 1803.

The origins of association football in the North East of England would be to a large extent influenced by old-boys of these very public schools. The Old Etonians, Carthusians

Football in Victorian Britain was far from the sophisticated game we now have, yet football it certainly was, as shown in this early engraving.

and Harrovians as well as the Old Reptonians and Marlburians would become a surprising foundation for the game on Tyneside.

The rugby code was the first of the two groups to cultivate and expand, with a set of rules being established at Rugby school in 1845, and by 1870 there were around 70 clubs playing variations of the rugby game. Organised rugby was played in the North East by the early years of the 1870s. Indeed, the Darlington (Rugby) Football Club was formed as early as 1863.

The 'association code', as it was termed to distinguish from its rugby rival, originated in these public schools of England. And soon, during the 1850s and 1860s, the scholarly institutions began to think about sets of rules to go with their favoured code. Cambridge University and Harrow laid down their own early methods of playing the game, so did other institutions and pioneer clubs, Sheffield in Yorkshire and Turton in Lancashire, as well as Queen's Park in Scotland. Out of several different ways of playing the game, the Cambridge Rules, Sheffield Rules and a version laid out by John Thring, a master at Uppingham, Thring's code, known as 'the Simplest game', became popular.

The formation of the Football Association in 1863 was *the* significant point in the game's development, and the sport was soon to prosper. In October of that year at The Freemason's Tavern in London's Lincoln Inns Field, football's organising and ruling body was created. The Football Association had a focus to generate one set of laws and to bring all the various groups together – to unify the association code. After much debate, the rules were largely consolidated and drafted by secretary Ebenezer Cobb Morley. By the end of the year the new association published their own 'Laws of Football', the very foundation and standard for the world game to follow.

It should be noted, however, that there was still a period of refinement over these laws and some much-heated debate followed over the content, notably between the Football

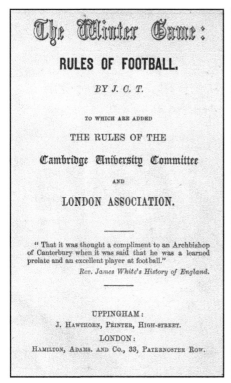

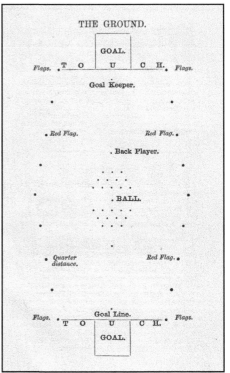

One of the earliest sets of rules of the game was Thring's Code, *The Winter Game*. This published copy incorporated the Cambridge University Rules and the new FA Rules, together with a pitch layout. *(A. Mitchell archive)*

Association and their Scottish counterparts. Queen's Park and later the Scottish Football Association held strong views on how the game should be played as compared to some in England; a passing game rather than the dribbling style was preferred, while there were different interpretations of both the offside and throw-in rules during those early years. Nevertheless, the authority of the FA, as they were to be known, and its laws was far reaching and was quickly laid down.

The Association went on to encourage local bodies to be set up under their banner, with a network of football organisations being created over the coming decade. The game was on its way, and development was rapid in the years leading up to the turn of the century.

As noted, clubs were already being formed by the time the FA had been created. The Sheffield club was founded in 1857 and is still in existence today, while Notts County, the country's oldest professional club, was formed in 1862. Leeds Athletic was formed in 1864, the most northerly club in England at the time by all accounts. Thereafter the association code was quick to develop, especially in the Midlands and North West of England.

In Scotland the rugby style of football held a virtual monopoly prior to the formation of the Queen's Park club in 1867. They produced their own version of the Football

Association's laws of the game and started to spread the game north of the border. There is, however, evidence of football – with the round ball – being played during the early years of the 19th century in Scotland's capital, at the High School of Edinburgh and Edinburgh Academy, before rugby held sway north of the border. An Edinburgh lawyer, John Hope, wrote an association-type set of rules, while there was a New Town club in the capital formed around 1824 (which survived until 1841). Indeed, some in Scotland claim that this club, rather than Sheffield FC, should be recognised as the oldest in the world. But both the FA and FIFA currently identify the Sheffield club with that title.

However, the North East of England – from Teesside through Tyneside to the Scottish border – lagged behind. For much of the century before the Football Association was founded, the sporting pastimes of the people of the region, and on Tyneside in particular, rarely featured a ball. Cricket and rugby were initially minority pursuits. As late as 1850, bloodsports were still popular among all levels of society. Cockpits were commonplace in towns, usually attached to the back of an inn. Contests flourished in certain parts of Newcastle, notably The Crown Inn at Westgate and at Dunston Bank, as well as on Gallowgate. It was noted that 'the sport was in great measure left in the hands of the dregs of society'.

Tyneside life in the mid-1800s in many ways centred on drinking establishments. It was noted in one history of the city: 'There were over 500 pubs or brewery shops in Newcastle; that is, 1 for every 39 families – every 22nd house was licensed to sell drink!'

A SNAPSHOT OF SPORT IN THE NORTH EAST

Fact Box

Reports of sporting activity between January 1870 & December 1873 in the contemporary local press.

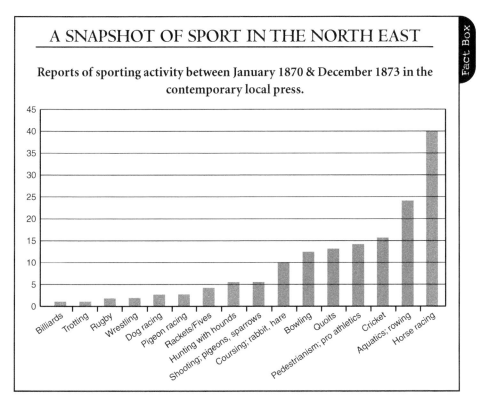

Hunting with hounds, shooting, as well as dog-fighting and bear-baiting also took place, although the latter was all but outlawed by the beginning of 19th century. Bull-baiting was also popular on the Sandhill in Newcastle's old heart. Tangible evidence of this so-called sporting activity from a by-gone era can be seen by visitors to the Castle Keep in the city. In the depths of the fortress they can view a large stone with a metal ring embedded in it. This was a bull-baiting stone. Bulls were tethered by ropes to the ring and were set upon by dogs. Injuries and fatalities were common among the poor animals, and occasionally spectators themselves suffered. This particular stone was last used on Sandhill in 1768 when a young apprentice called Kenslyside Henzill got too close to the action and was badly gored. He later died from his injuries and his death heralded the end of bull-baiting in Sandhill and the stone fell into disuse. It was dug up in 1821 and eventually taken to the castle. It now serves as a gory reminder of sports and pastimes of years gone by. Much of this so-called bloodsport pastime was barbaric yet was still extremely popular until laws were gradually introduced which curtailed the somewhat distasteful activity by the middle of the century, although events still were organised behind closed doors for some while.

Greyhound coursing was highly popular as well, especially in the mining districts. Pigeon shooting took place too, and one match between Robert Richardson (from Pity Me) against Joseph Brown (of Blaydon) in 1872 comprised a contest shooting at 50 pigeons each – with the winner taking £100 – a huge sum at that time. In a challenge of shooting at sparrows – 15 of the poor birds each – in the same year, Joseph Jackson (Elswick) and Henry Rayne (Winlaton) took part in what was a controversial match. With £20 at stake it was found that Jackson was using the wrong size of shot in his gun. Rayne eventually decided to sue the stakeholder, Robert Hutchinson of the Sun Inn in Newcastle's Newgate Street!

Most of the events had big cash prizes and frequently involved gambling, with the stakeholder usually being the local publican. It was a thriving business with large sums wagered. Betting really encouraged more and more events, despite the fact that gaming in a public house was illegal. Indeed, gambling was linked to almost all the North's sporting activities in those years and was just as important as the event itself, if not more so.

During the early and middle part of the 19th century there was a lack of development of places of recreation on Tyneside and in the North generally. Newcastle's Leazes Park was not opened until 1873, while during the decade that followed both Brandling Park and Bull Park were created in the town. The latter was originally located on the corner of Claremont Road and the Great North Road. The Hancock Museum was later built near to the site of the original park which was developed and extended as Exhibition Park for the Royal Jubilee Exhibition of 1887 (although the name Bull Park remained in vogue for many years afterwards). The development of Elswick Park and Heaton Park followed, as did Saltwell Park in Gateshead. Until more parks and venues were established, sport on Tyneside usually took place on the open fields of the Town Moor, the vast open grassland situated then on the outskirts of the town. In addition, for what were at the time very popular water events, the River Tyne was the principal venue.

Horse racing was the first spectator sport to be organised and recorded. Popular with the gentry of the region, the landed families of the North East both arranged and participated in the earliest events. Racing took place on Killingworth Moor just outside Newcastle as early as the 1630s. The venue moved to the Town Moor around 1720, where some records show racing had already taken place on the site. There were other favoured race meetings in the 18th century at Hexham and Rothbury, as well as south of the Tyne in Sunderland. But by far the biggest event was the June meeting at Newcastle when the Northumberland Plate was run. This was first staged in 1833 and, even today, is still now a huge meeting on Tyneside – a northern carnival which at its peak was able to attract crowds upwards of 50,000.

The Town Moor venue was developed, and a lavish grandstand was erected in 1800, but the course was moved to High Gosforth Park during the opening years of the 1880s, with the Northumberland Plate first run there in 1882. Grandstand Road, which runs next to the Town Moor, still marks the area of the old racecourse where the winning post was sited.

Another major event and venue was situated four miles up the Tyne. The Blaydon Races, now such an iconic symbol to Tyneside which has given the region its local anthem, was more than a sporting event. Indeed, it was more of a fair and festival, like the Blaydon Hoppings where lots of sports were played; wrestling, foot races and of course more humorous events like chasing a soaped pig! In 1861, the year before George Ridley's famous comic song was written, the actual horse races were entered in the British racing calendar and were a properly organised hunt meeting. Thousands travelled to the long day out at Blaydon, but it was more a fun-day than a serious sporting occasion like the Northumberland Plate.

There were other popular fairs in the region where sporting activity was prevalent, usually at holiday times, notably Easter and Whitsuntide. A carnival was attached to what became Northumberland Plate 'Race Week' to eventually develop into a Temperance

Horse racing was well supported during the Victorian era in the North East. A lavish grandstand was built on Newcastle's Town Moor racecourse.

Festival, then into the Town Moor Hoppings, which is still an important occasion on the Tyneside calendar, held during the week of the Plate meeting. Now, though, the Hoppings is a fun-fair with little sporting activity. In Charleton's valuable history of the city, published in 1885, it is noted that 'thousands troop there to look at or take part in the foot races, football matches, assault-at-arms, bicycle matches and other sports which are carried on'. There was also an earlier Hoppings at Gallowgate on what is now the doorstep of St James' Park, home of Newcastle United, of course. Long before football was played on the site, a raucous festival occurred nearby, with all sorts of activities played out on the streets and adjacent Town Moor.

Alongside horse-racing, by far the most widespread sport in the region before football came on the scene, was rowing, including both skiff racing and sculling. Staged principally on the River Tyne, perhaps surprisingly now looking back, the spectacle of rowing was hugely trendy in the Victorian North East, with tens of thousands flocking to the banks of the Tyne to watch the races. During the mid-to-late years of the 19th century, Tyneside's rowers took on the world, boasting not only British Champions but also World Champions too in Harry Clasper, Bob Chambers and James Renforth.

At its peak it is recorded that the race days and regatta attracted estimated attendances of between 250,000 and 500,000 for events which usually took place along the Tyne between the High Level Bridge and Scotswood Bridge, a distance of around four miles. The latter audience looks to be somewhat of an exaggeration considering the region's population then, but, even if a more realistic crowd was at the lower end of the scale, it was still a gathering only matched by football at the height of Newcastle United's FA Cup glory when the trophy came back to Tyneside.

An international boat-race on the Tyne in the summer of 1866, as sketched and published in *The London Illustrated News*. Thousands flocked to the river bank.

In *Tyneside Celebrities*, an early text on the region's personalities published in 1873, it is noted that the race day is heralded by a great 'ringing of bells', while shops in the town completely close down and an 'all-absorbing spectacle' is created. It is recorded: 'Men of all cliques, classes and colours are there; Radical and Tory; Quayside merchant and slouching loafer; master and servant; the great white-washed and the great unwashed are there.

'The High Level Bridge and the Redheugh Bridge, each bears seething masses of humanity; the Rabbit Banks on the south, and the ballast mounds on the north, are thronged with anxious spectators, while others crowd amid the foliage of Redheugh Hall.'

The aquatic sport was a professional one, with big prize money for success, equivalent to football wages today. There were national contests, especially with the men of the Thames, an inspiring North versus South contest, as great as any Arsenal versus Newcastle United contest a century later. Again, gambling was a big part of the race event.

The Tyne had become (arguably – along with the Thames) the most important aquatic venue in the world, but rowing also took place on the Wear – especially at Durham – as well as on the Blyth and Wansbeck rivers. Many clubs were created, a mix of amateur and professional, notably the Northern Rowing Club and the Tyne Amateur Rowing Club at Low Elswick and the Albion Club at Dunston. In fact, the Tyne Amateur RC was formed in 1851 because some of the members of Northern Rowing Club had become disenchanted with the overt professionalism that had become prevalent.

The winners of the high-profile individual sculling and skiff races were regarded as heroes – probably the original sporting icons in the region. Harry Clasper was the first to come to prominence around 1837, and he dominated the sport for over 20 years. From Dunston, he pioneered the growth of the water pastime and won Championship races on both the Tyne and Thames. On his death in 1870, crowds estimated at over 100,000 joined the funeral train, and it was noted that 'men with heavy hearts and tear-dimmed eyes stood around the oarsman's grave'. Other members of the Clasper family were prominent on the waters too – it was quite a sporting family.

There were also Bob Chambers of St Anthony's and James Renforth of Gateshead, two more champions and both 'unequalled as oarsmen in their day'. Chambers was nicknamed 'Honest Bob' and was a prodigy of Clasper. He became Champion of England and then Champion of the World in 1863. George Ridley, who was to pen the Tyneside national anthem, *The Blaydon Races*, in 1862, paid tribute to Bob when he won the Championship of England against Harry Kelley when he wrote the ditty:

'O, Ye cockneys all
Ye mun think't very funny
For Bob he gans and licks ye all
An collars all your money.'

Renforth became sculling Champion of the World five years on, in 1868, but sadly he died only three years later at a young age during a race on the Kennebecasis River in New Brunswick, Canada. His last words were: 'What will they say in England?' Another huge

The famous Tyne oarsman Harry Clasper, one of several rowing heroes of the time from the region.

funeral gathering, possibly even bigger than Clasper's or Chambers' (who had died in 1868), took place on Tyneside, such was his popularity. The passing of this trio of sporting legends within a mere three-year period hit Tyneside hard.

There were other notable oarsmen including William Fawcus of Tynemouth and James Candlish of Newcastle, who, after making a name for himself in this country, did much to popularise the sport in Australia. He was a rival, as well as a rowing partner, of Clasper and on occasion defeated Tyne's number one, notably in the Championship of the Tyne in 1851 and when winning the Nottingham Regatta All England skiff event two years later.

Athletics, or more particularly ped-racing, as well as cycling, were two other well-liked sports in the latter half of the century. Again, both activities were largely professional with considerable prize money at stake. Once more wagers were an integral part of the event. Known in 1873 as 'pedestrianism', this form of athletics featured walking and sprint racing and was described as 'one of the most prominent gymnastic pastimes of the North,' with 'Newcastle and Gateshead regarded as great centres around which not only local but national "peds" have radiated'.

As early as 1813 a certain George Wilson was recognised as a celebrity athlete. Remarkably, it was noted that during a time when he was confined in the gaol of Newgate in Newcastle for a debt offence, he 'undertook for the trifling sum of three pounds one shilling, to walk 50 miles in 12 successive hours, within the prison walls'! After that well-publicised episode he went on to complete various feats around the country and became nationally renowned.

Races were held on the Town Moor and later at The Grapes running ground on Westgate Road, as well as at the Victoria Ground, which had a full-sized track and covered stands next to Elswick Lead Works. Both locations were in Newcastle. Subsequently, other venues were created as multi-purpose recreation grounds were established in the region. Crowds were sizable; in November 1872 a gathering of between 14,000 to 20,000 (according to the varying contemporary reports) turned up at the Borough Gardens in Gateshead to see James Davidson (from Jarrow) meet James Talbot (Newcastle) in a quarter-mile race – all for a purse of £100. Davidson won by just over two yards in a time of 52 seconds. Other race venues included Fenham Park Grounds at Nuns Moor and Victoria Gardens in Sunderland.

While cash prizes attracted the crowds, later in the 19th century amateur running began to create an interest, and in 1887 the Newcastle Harriers club was formed. Saltwell Harriers and Elswick Harriers followed, and rapidly clubs were formed all over the North East with ped-racing quickly being replaced by road-running, cross-country events and track-running as we know it today. By then, however, football had largely taken a stranglehold on the sporting mind of the North East.

Racing on two wheels became equally as fashionable during this period. Cycling clubs sprang up over the region, and regular meetings were held from 1870 onwards. Important societies were formed, notably Newcastle's Clarion club. Tynesider George Waller was an early personality, winning the long-distance World Championship in 1879. A cycling track was set-up in Dalton Street, Byker – near to where Newcastle United's pioneers Newcastle East End played for a period. Another track was created at East End's new home, the Heaton Junction Ground a mile away.

Wrestling and Boxing were favourites of the Victorian Geordie too. Indeed, at Pottery Lane, near to Newcastle's elegant Central Station, stood a purpose-built wrestling arena, complete with stands. The site now lies beneath the Redheugh Bridge approach road. Contests also took place on Spital Fields and in 1857 prize money could amount to £140 – a very sizable sum then. A major tournament regularly took place between Northumberland, Cumberland and Westmorland, and it was noted that on occasion 'upwards of 6,000 witnessed the tests of skill and strength'.

Boxing in Newcastle was a respected sport, noted by one commentator during the era to be ranked 'only second to London in the early days'. Bare-knuckle fighting under the

THE SPORTING NORTH EAST

Fact Box

Timetable of sporting popularity

Bowling, from:	1600
Horse-racing, from:	1630s
Athletics, from:	1810
Cricket, from:	1827
Rowing, from:	1830s
Rugby football, from:	1863
Cycling, from:	1870s
Association football, from:	1876

London Prize Ring Rules took place during the first part of the century. These were drawn up in 1743, promulgated in 1839 and significantly revised in 1853. But when these rules were superseded by the first Marquess of Queensberry rules in 1867, bare-knuckle events were driven underground to the hidden dens of Tyneside. The Percy Cottage public house was a noted venue – described as 'rough and tough'. Other pubs in the district held contests too: the Rokeby Arms, Three Tuns and Barley Mow in particular.

As the century moved on through the years there was an increasing demand for more and more entertainment of a sporting nature as the North East's labour force in rapidly growing communities around the rivers Tyne and Wear, as well as in the coalfields, had more leisure time. A five-and-a-half-day working week was generally commonplace by then. Apart from the hugely popular athletics, cycling and aquatics, other participation sports included more gentle activities such as bowling, rackets, golf, tennis and the quaintly titled game of trippet & quoit, also known as knurr & spell.

As far back as Elizabethan Tyneside, bowling is recorded as being a pastime in the region, with a green situated near where Newcastle's St Mary's Cathedral now stands. It was overlooked by a tavern, as it was described, 'from whence the spectators, calmly smoking their pipes and enjoying their glasses, beheld the sportsmen below'. That Forth Bank area was popular for bowling, while another green was sited near Northumberland Street. Later, and also in the heart of Newcastle's town centre, a bowling green could be found at Bath Lane, while greens were much later incorporated into the communities' new parks; at Leazes, Brandling, Heaton and Elswick, as well as at Saltwell in Gateshead.

The Town Moor and Newbiggin Moor became centres for a variant of the bowling contest. The manicured greens were replaced by any piece of rough grass where bowls of different weights were rolled and thrown over varying distances – a sort of shot-put game, known as potshare bowling, which was well-liked by the mining communities of Northumberland. And it was very much a gambling-based sport too. Mackenzie's *History of Newcastle* records contests between pitmen 'who are expert in a species of lofty bowling, with very small stone or iron balls'. In 1872 a challenge match 'across the mile' using 15 oz bowls for a stake of £20 saw Neil Macnally (of St Peter's) take on James Semple (Newburn). The winner was the man who completed the course in the least number of throws. Crowds of over 2,000 were attracted to some bowling contests. It was also noted that 'scarcely a Saturday passes without some trial of skill taking place'.

Rackets, also known as Fives, a squash-like event, was an established game too. In the centre of Newcastle on Newgate Street a fine Racket Court was to be found, complete

Bowling in Newcastle during 1881 as sketched in *The Graphic*; a refined pursuit of Tyneside's gentry.

The game of Knurr & Spell was an unusual Victorian sport; a small ball being hit with a golf-like club.

with a gallery, 'from which spectators may view the progress of the game in the court below'. The building, by all accounts, also had an adjoining billiard-room and an area 'to which gentlemen may retire for refreshment'. But away from this more upper-echelon gentleman's club in Newcastle, it was noted that tournaments were more frequent 'in the pit villages of Northumberland and Durham – Willington and Coxhoe being the principal areas of contest'.

Quoits matches over 10 yards or 20 yards also took place in the mining centres and are recorded in the region as early as the 14th century. Many public houses had quoits pitches nearby, while the principal venues were at the Gateshead Running Grounds and the Fenham Park track, as well as Castle Leazes or on the Town Moor. In the game known as knurr & spell, wooden 'knurrs', golf-ball like spheres, were sprung into the air by a mechanical 'spell' and the aim was to hit them with a 'pommel' – a golf-like club – as far as you could. More locally, a similar game was called trippet & quoit. In 1873 over 1,000 attended within the circle of Newcastle Racecourse to witness a contest for a stake of £100 between George Sutherland and Richard Stewart, two well-known players from County Durham. Sutherland won by five score and 14 yards.

Although golf is now such a widespread game, in the 19th century it was not a common pastime in the region. But there were a sprinkling of clubs. Early golfing centres were established at Alnmouth in 1869 and Newbiggin in 1884, both on the north-east coast. Tyneside and Newcastle lagged behind; not until the 1890s was a course laid out on the Town Moor.

Tennis was more established on Tyneside when, in 1878, the Portland Park Tennis Club was founded in Jesmond. Another club was created on the Grainger estate in 1884 with more clubs following. Both golf and tennis were very much recreational sports for the region's well-to-do middle classes.

The games of cricket and rugby are most closely linked to the development of the association code of football in this country – and it was no different in the North East. Most of the footballing pioneers of the North evolved from either local rugby or cricket teams. Often the same players took part in all three sports. As will be seen, football's roots firmly belong to both rugby and, especially, cricket.

The first cricket club on Tyneside was recorded as early as 1827 in *Tyneside Celebrities*. Newcastle Albion Cricket Club played on the Town Moor, and the Northumberland Cricket Club along with Sunderland Cricket Club (founded as Bishop Wearmouth) were formed in the 1830s, two of the most prominent clubs in the area. The game had been established in England since before 1800, and other early clubs in the North East were based in Durham and Gateshead, with notable sides visiting the area for contests from the middle of the century.

Gosforth Cricket Club was founded in 1864 as Bulman Village Cricket Club at Coxlodge, then a rural community detached from Newcastle. They later became South Northumberland Cricket Club. At the same time other cricket organisations were in existence at Tynemouth, Morpeth, Whitburn, Alnwick and Hexham as well as at Benwell, Whickham, Chester-le-Street and Astley (Seaton Delaval). By 1873 the prominent Northumberland Cricket Club had 'nearly 200 members' with an annual subscription being 'one guinea per member'. Interestingly, among the prominent names associated with the club were 'Nesham' and 'Bramwell'. Both men would later be involved in the development of football – and Newcastle United's pioneers. During this period the major clubs even employed a professional. It is recorded that Gosforth Cricket Club in 1875 paid a certain R. Proctor the sum of 35 shillings (£1.75) per week to both play and coach the side. The following year Charles Anthony was appointed for a similar salary.

Cricket fields were formed around the district, with the major venue being in the heart of Newcastle. The Northumberland Cricket Club field was located at the end of Bath Road near to Ridley Place, now on the site of university and college buildings. In a few years it would also become the principle ground for the fledgling new game of association football. It was a large, first-class arena that held prestigious matches including a three-day drawn contest in 1847 against a celebrated All-England XI. There was also the proverbial Cricketers Arms public house nearby in Pandon Dene below Barras Bridge. The Bath Road ground remained important until 1881 when the site was redeveloped to accommodate a new Dame Allan's School building. The cricketers moved first to Heaton Lane – near to Chillingham Road where Newcastle East End were to play football – then into Jesmond.

Northumberland Cricket Club's ground at Bath Road in Newcastle, near St Mary's Place. St Thomas's Church is in the background. As well as being the centre for local cricket, it was football's principal venue until 1881.

In May of that year the Northumberland County Cricket Association was established and the County Club formed, while the Durham County Cricket Club was created a year later. In July 1882, the Australian Touring XI visited the region – a huge draw for Tyneside. The newly formed County side faced the star-studded Aussies, who were skippered by the famous Billy Murdoch, a great friend of W.G. Grace. Not surprisingly, the Australians won. Murdoch's men helped cricket to flourish, and a number of minor local clubs were dotted all over the North East by the opening years of the 1880s, and many were to expand their sporting activities into the new code of football.

Rugby found a stronghold on Tyneside in the latter quarter of the 19th century, a decade earlier than its rival association code. Records show that the first rugby club in the region was founded at Darlington in 1863; although it was some time before others followed suit, with the Sunderland club being founded in 1870, followed by Durham City (1872), then Percy Park and Stockton in 1873.

Various matches were played in the early years of the 1870s, including Northumberland FC (XIII) versus Durham University (XV), and Northumberland XII versus Darlington XII. The Northern Rugby Club was created as Elswick, formed by the Cail brothers, printers on Newcastle Quayside. They convened a meeting at the Neville Hotel in Newcastle

Rockcliffe were one of the earliest rugby clubs, becoming a most respected side in the North.

A Victorian supporter card depicting Alnwick rugby club. The historic town of Alnwick saw football in both its forms quickly take hold.

during September 1876 to form the club which enrolled 25 members at the outset. They played their early games on the Town Moor opposite the Fleming Memorial Hospital but had difficulties because the field was hired from a horse dealer whose stock covered the ground with manure! Soon afterwards, clubs were formed at Tynedale (1876) and Gosforth (1877), while Ryton, Blaydon and Alnwick Hotspur all started in 1880. The Wallsend club was created a year later and Rockcliffe in 1882.

A great deal of credit for the development of rugby as a popular sport in the North East in the 1870s and 1880s must go to the Cail brothers – and to William and Richard Cail in particular. The latter became the Elswick club's first honorary secretary and treasurer, but it was William who became the driving force for creation of the Northumberland County Rugby Union in 1880. By this time the Elswick club had changed its name to Northern RFC.

The Durham County Rugby Union had been formed in 1876 and joined the English Rugby Union some six year later. The honorary secretary of the Northumberland rugby club, Mr Milvain, sent invitations to the other major clubs in the county to attend a meeting at the Royal Turk's Hotel at the beginning of March 1880, with a view to forming a similar union for Northumberland County. Apart from the Northumberland club itself, representatives also came from Tynemouth, Northern, Gosforth, Tynedale (Hexham) and Percy Park (Tynemouth).

J.F. Ogilvie of the Tynemouth club briefly explained the object of the meeting – to consider whether to form a union from such rugby clubs in the county that were eligible and chose to join. William Cail (Northern) proposed the motion which was seconded by Mr Martin (Tynemouth) that such a club be formed under the title of the Northumberland County Rugby Union Football Club for the management of (rugby) football throughout the county and the selection of representative teams. The motion was carried.

William Cail drew up the first set of rules which were adopted after some slight alterations, and he became the first secretary and subsequently treasurer. He was later to become president of the Northumberland Rugby Union and also an Alderman of the city.

In addition to these main clubs, there were also organised sides made up from the better social class of the district, including clubs known as Bank Clerks, Accountants and one from the College of Physical Science. Similar professions later combined to form the early association football teams in the area, but these did not necessarily evolve into permanent clubs.

The Royal Grammar School in Newcastle also started to play the game. Although the rugby code was not nearly as popular as cricket, it was to have a huge bearing on the evolution of the game of football in the North. The very first contest using the association code was played by men of the rugby persuasion.

As cricket and rugby took a hold in the region during the years leading up to 1880, the regional capital, Newcastle upon Tyne, was already rapidly developing and undergoing a major transformation. The Victorian North East as a whole went through huge changes. The classical improvements of Grainger and Dobson transformed Newcastle, while the industrial innovation of the period also had a gigantic effect.

In 1801 the population of the town (not yet being classed as a city under certain definitions) was a modest 34,092. By 1851 it had jumped to 80,100 and by 1901 to 233,644 with a parallel explosion of its hinterland, especially along the banks of the Tyne itself. It was recorded in one handbook of the area in 1889 that within a radius of a very few miles of Newcastle 'would give double the amount of population contained in the city'.

At the time Queen Victoria was on the throne, Disraeli, Gladstone and the Marquess of Salisbury had spells as Prime Minister. In 1849 the fast-developing railway network of which George Stephenson was such an influence saw Newcastle have a main line link directly to Edinburgh and London. In 1878 local inventor and entrepreneur Joseph Swan

The heart of Newcastle as the century closed; Grainger Street looking towards Grey's Monument.

Newcastle upon Tyne during the 1880s, looking across the Tyne from Gateshead with the High Level Bridge, Swing Bridge, castle and cathedral spire in view. The now famous arched Tyne Bridge was still over 40 years from being constructed.

and Thomas Edison in America (among others) invented the electric lamp. During 1885 the first petrol-driven car took to the road. The modern era, as well as the 20th century, was approaching.

Today, in the 21st century, Newcastle has seven landmark bridges crossing the Tyne at the city centre. Back in 1880 there were only three, and the famous arched masterpiece was almost 50 years from being constructed. Robert Stephenson's High Level Bridge was opened in 1849, the original Redheugh Bridge in 1871 and the Swing Bridge was built in 1876.

Newcastle became a diocese in 1882 and the Church of St Nicholas was given the status of cathedral – and by one criteria, Newcastle became a 'city'. There were no vast shopping-malls, no party-night dens of entertainment and no Metro rapid-transit system. Trams were introduced in 1879, but by the 1890s they were still horse-drawn.

The present-day city suburbs of Benwell, Denton, Gosforth, Kenton and Byker were mere villages at the mid-point of the century, with green fields along the roads leading to Newcastle's outskirts and remnants of the old town wall. But the monumental industrial growth led to a vast development of the community towards the west – to Elswick, Benwell and Kenton – and to the north and east – to Jesmond, Gosforth, Heaton and Byker. There was as an extraordinary building programme as Newcastle expanded with factories, shipyards and workers' accommodation, row after row of new terraced houses and flats spreading far and wide on the slopes of Elswick, Benwell and Byker.

With this background, the association code of football first took hold in the far south of the region, in Cleveland when the Middlesbrough club was formed in 1876. The emerging game moved north to Tyneside when the North East's second-oldest club, Tyne Association, was created in 1877. It was the first embryo. The hotbed was born, and the Pioneers of the North were to soon spread the people's game.

Chapter 2

THE PATHFINDERS –
TYNE & RANGERS

'The members of the Tyne club – sons of leading families in Newcastle and Gateshead who had learnt the game at public-schools – showed the sport for the first time.'
Arthur Appleton, 1960

The date: 3 March 1877; the venue: Elswick Rugby Football club; the occasion: the birth of association football on Tyneside. A few local enthusiasts formed two scratch teams (eight men against nine) and played the first-ever match under association rules in Newcastle. The names of these true pioneers of the game on Tyneside are known, although at the time the sides were rather prosaically named merely as *Team A* and *Team B*, captained by S.N. Challoner and C. Gibson:

Team A: Challoner (S.N.), Bruce, Weeks, Challoner (T.D.), Hodgson, Burnop, Mather, Paxton.

V

Team B: Gibson, Burnett, Clark, Harris, Pringle, Bittleston, Guthrie, Harrison, Ross.

It should not be presumed that the captains of both sides were goalkeepers. It was customary at the time to name the captain first in the team lists. Indeed, in later games, it is recorded that S.N. Challoner, who was to become the first captain of the new Tyne club, played as a full-back. Little is known about this trial game itself, although the names of the goalscorers were faithfully recorded in a 2–0 win for Team A: R.S. Weeks and J. Bruce. More importantly, a number of these sportsmen persevered with the game and ensured that it would grow in popularity.

Many of these players were members of the Elswick Rugby Club, with a number of them playing for either the first team or the second XV. The club had been formed just over six months earlier, in September 1876, at a meeting held in the Neville Hotel, Newcastle, when some 25 members had been initially enrolled. J.A. Mather was captain, and among the rugby players we find the names of Challoner, Bruce, Gibson, Burnop and Harrison. In most cases the Christian names (or even initials) are unknown, although Alfred Harrison, C. Gibson and E. Burnop are exceptions. But this would explain why Elswick Rugby Club allowed the trial association football game to be played on their ground.

Soon afterwards, these sporting pioneers announced that 'a new club has been formed under the name of Tyne AFC in the hopes of inducing the clubs in the area to play'. The 'clubs' referred to in the declared objective were rugby clubs, and Tyne's first match was against such a club, Northumberland Rugby Football Club, three weeks after that inaugural, experimental contest. To be known as Tyne Association, labelling the club distinctly as not a rugby football organisation, they won 2–1, after leading 1–0 at half-time with goals from Cornish and Bittleston. It is only fair to add that, although Tyne played throughout the match with 10 men, the rugby club only had eight in the first half and nine in the second period when latecomer Mulcaster joined in. It is interesting to note that eight of Tyne's team participated in the inaugural trial match:

Tyne: Challoner (S.N.), Challoner (T.D.), Bruce, Harris, Weeks, Mitchell, Gibson, Cornish, Bittleston, Harrison.

V

Northumberland: Hughes, Logan, Fawcus, Dunford, Kyle, Clark, Hunter, Pringle, Mulcaster.

Thus, association football took its first faltering steps on Tyneside. But this was not the first appearance of 'soccer' in the North East; Teesside had beaten Tyneside to the punch, and by a considerable margin. Middlesbrough Association Football Club can claim its origins to a full year before that historic first game on Tyneside, and it is the oldest of the North East's so-called 'big three'.

But even Middlesbrough may not have been the oldest club on Teesside. That accolade may belong to South Bank, whose origins can apparently be traced back to 1868, a mere 14 years after the town was founded. Indeed, the Bankers (as they became known) celebrated their centenary with a challenge match against Leytonstone, then holders of the FA Amateur Cup, at the Clairville Stadium in Middlesbrough during September 1968. It was reported in the *Cleveland News* in December 1881, however, that Middlesbrough were the first club to play the association game in North Yorkshire; there is therefore some doubt about South Bank's claims.

What is undeniable is the fact that South Bank took to the game at a very early date, although they may have played both rugby and association forms of the sport. Other clubs were quickly formed within the town, such as South Bank White Star, South Bank Erimus and South Bank Waterloo, and they played against the likes of North Ormesby, Redcar and Yarm. Admittedly, games were few and far between, probably due to a lack of suitable opponents, and the club played without any recognisable colours, often in full-length pants, buttoned-up shirts and tasselled caps.

The biggest step forward as far as the South Bank club was concerned came sometime later in 1885 when, under the direction of Dr John Glenn, a highly respected and well-known local medical practitioner, a decision was made to merge the South

Bank, South Bank Erimus and South Bank Excelsior clubs into a single entity that would thereafter be known simply as South Bank Football Club.

By this time, however, the Middlesbrough club had been formed and had become pre-eminent on Teesside. According to legend, the Boro (as they became popularly known) were formed over a tripe supper held at the Albert Park Hotel on Linthorpe Road in Middlesbrough on 18 February 1876, although this has now been rejected and replaced by research which indicates the first meetings were held sometime later, during October and November of that year, first in a gym behind the Albert Hotel and then in the Talbot Hotel on the Market Square corner of South Street. Indeed, in recent years the Middlesbrough club has totally denied the tripe supper connection, claiming that 'tripe and football only really mix in Sunderland', yet that colourful story cannot be dismissed totally as it was a popular meal then and could well have been served at either gathering. Recent research has discovered they were actually formed by players of Middlesbrough Amateur Cricket Club, established for some two decades. The new football club played first on the Archery Ground, then at Grove Hill and afterwards on a cricket field off Linthorpe Road.

What is irrefutable is that association football was founded on Teesside before Tyneside; however, while Middlesbrough can trace their roots back to the later months of 1876, the first recorded game was against a local Rugby Union club, Tees Wanderers, on 24 February 1877, although it is possible that the odd game was played before that first reported fixture. The date of this game was just a matter of days before the trial match at Elswick. The game on Teesside was played at the Archery Ground in Albert Park and lasted two periods of 20 minutes each, ending in a 1–1 draw. It seems that it was poor fare indeed and did not impress the handful of spectators who turned up out of curiosity to watch it.

But the coarse and rough game of association football took root, and soon other clubs slowly sprouted up. In Darlington the game of football which would be recognisable today also appeared. Darlington Football Club was formed in 1863 but played the rugby code, however, it was not too many years after this that the Feethams Cricket Ground witnessed both rugby and association games, although Darlington Association Football Club was not formed until 1883.

By this time, the game was spreading through the towns and villages of County Durham but, as far as the major conurbations are concerned, there is no doubt that the growth of the game took off around Cleveland before Tyneside or Wearside, as Middlesbrough faced the likes of South Bank and other pioneering local clubs such as Loftus and Eston.

So how did association football arrive in first Cleveland and then on Tyneside? There is no definitive answer to that question; however, there are three principle factors which are more than likely responsible for the game arriving in the north-east corner of the country. First was the migration north of the newly organised sport from the Yorkshire association stronghold of Sheffield.

The city of Sheffield was at the nucleus of football's emergence in the north of England. While most of the public schools and universities that originally favoured the game were situated in the deep south, football also found a breeding ground in the heartland of the steel city. A group of cricket enthusiasts and Collegiate School old boys formed Sheffield Football Club in 1857 and furthermore created their own code – the Sheffield Rules – widely used by embryo clubs in the North. This code rejected the use of the hands as well as hacking and tripping – they were firmly of the kicking and dribbling style of the game.

Apart from Sheffield FC, a group of other clubs were formed soon after, including Hallam FC, Attercliffe, Garrick, Heeley, Sheffield Albion and Thornhill United. By 1867 over 25 clubs were playing in the area. Quickly Sheffield Wednesday were formed, as were Doncaster Rovers. At the same time the word of association football was spreading north towards Cleveland, some 50-odd miles away.

The second factor was that as the association code found popularity in the North, the sporting youth took an interest in the now semi-organised game. Sportsmen who already played cricket and the rugby code naturally started to talk and chat about the association game at existing cricket and rugby clubs. No doubt after matches they would convene to the club-house or local inn and debate what was going on around the country. As we have seen, Middlesbrough FC was formed in this way. So too were many of the traditional football clubs of this country, Aston Villa, Preston North End and Derby County included. By far, cricket clubs were responsible for the creation of more football institutions than any other avenue of formation.

On Tyneside, local cricket clubs in Newcastle such as Stanley Cricket Club in Byker and Crown Cricket Club in Elswick soon began thinking about the association code. They eventually formed new footballing organisations which developed into the two clubs that would eventually takeover from the pathfinders and see Newcastle United rise supreme on Tyneside.

Thirdly, and probably the biggest influence, was from the old boys of the country's public-schools and universities. They spread the game during the middle part of the century and, while the great names in education were to be found many a mile from the

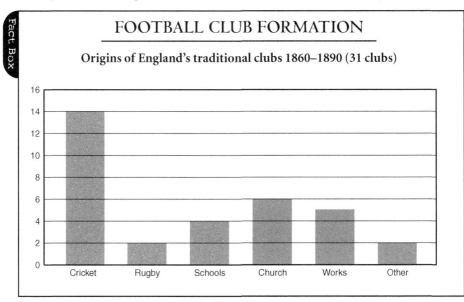

Fact Box

FOOTBALL CLUB FORMATION

Origins of England's traditional clubs 1860–1890 (31 clubs)

Charterhouse public school in London during 1862, one of several of the great schools of England where football developed.

North East at the likes of Eton and Harrow as well as Oxford and Cambridge, many of the region's young sons were sent south to gain the best possible education. The North East did have a handful of distinguished institutions but few, if any at all, saw the new game of association football as a sport for their curriculum, while sporting activity was very much restricted due to a lack of open playing fields.

The Royal Grammar School in Newcastle was one such prominent establishment. Formed in 1545, many famous names of the North East attended the school, including Cuthbert Collingwood, victor along with Lord Nelson of the Battle of Trafalgar. Yet the Royal Grammar School, as the region's leading education facility, had little time for the new sport. Based at Rye Hill at the time, the school only had a small patch of grass, and they played what was described as a 'primitive form of rugger called Lennary'. They also had the use of a two-acre field on Spital Field off Westgate Street for a period, but it appears that rugby was the chosen sport. Indeed, headmaster Samuel Logan gave a stern dictum that: 'No Association Football is to be played in this school in any form whatever.' By the time that association football first appeared on Tyneside in 1877, the Royal Grammar School was playing its home rugby games on the Town Moor. Ironically, as it turned out, the school moved to Eskdale Terrace in Jesmond during 1906 – where the pioneering men of football had played much of their football for the first decade.

Other scholarly institutions in the North did not appear to have much interest in the association code either. Both Durham University (founded 1832) and Newcastle University (founded 1834 as the School of Medicine and Surgery) were largely academic until much later.

It was left to those high-ranking scholarly pupils who were either sent south by the eminent families of the North East to learn and be moulded into young gentlemen, or those who found themselves in the region after their education, to be essentially responsible for starting it all as football migrated the 40-odd miles north from Cleveland to Tyneside within 12 months. It is found that many of Tyneside's footballing pioneers had links with the great colleges and universities of England: Oxford and Cambridge as well as Eton, Harrow, Lancing and Rossall, Charterhouse and Uppingham, Marlborough, Malvern and Repton schools.

The foundation of the association code with Tyne Association was closely linked with England's establishment. In *Hotbed of Soccer*, the important text on north-eastern football, published in 1960, Arthur Appleton wrote that the 'members of the Tyne club were sons of leading families in Newcastle and Gateshead who had learnt their game at public schools'. The respected *Football – A Weekly Record of the Game*, the first chronicle to be published on the new sport, contained a passage in 1882 that confirmed the club's links to the upper class of society. It was noted: 'The Tyne Club is almost entirely composed of old boys from the public schools.' And included in one of Tyne's line ups, it is noted, were 'three old Charterhouse boys'.

At the time Charterhouse School, formed in 1611, had recently moved from Central London to Godalming in Surrey and was – and still is – one of the country's foremost institutions. As we have seen, the school was one of the pioneer public schools that laid the foundation of the game. Over 100 years earlier, during the 1750s, Charterhouse boys were playing their version of football; the kicking, dribbling and passing camp rather than the handling and hacking faction of rugby. As such they were at the very forefront of the origins of the game. In *The Book of Football* published in 1905 it is noted: 'It is a matter of some difficulty to absolutely decide the best school at association football, but if the matter were put to public vote, pride of place would probably go to Charterhouse.'

Charterhouse was present as an observer at the meeting which founded the Football Association, and they have produced some of the earliest footballers of the highest pedigree, including several England internationals; William Cobbold, Gilbert Smith and Charles Wreford-Brown to name three eminent names of many. And in 1881 their Old Carthusians (Charterhouse old boys) won the FA Cup.

The young men who were involved in the early years of Tyneside's first football club certainly appear to have been from the bourgeoisie of the district. The three individuals quoted by *Football* were sent to the fee-paying Charterhouse by their parents and returned north with their experiences of public-school football – as well as an unequalled education – and became upwardly professional. They give a snapshot of the type of individuals who pioneered football on Tyneside. They became typical of the Empire builders of the Victorian era. One headed for North America, another became a solicitor and a third ended up in India.

Gilbert Ainslie hailed from Hawkshead in Lancashire from a noted family, his father for a time being Deputy Lieutenant for the county. When he left Charterhouse he spent some time in the North East before going to British Columbia and later settling in

Frank and Philip Messent were among Tyne Association's most prominent players. Frank is featured in this marvellous group of Charterhouse footballers in 1881; front row, far left, leaning on a chair. *(Charterhouse School archive)*

Eastbourne. After being with Tyne Association, Ainslie appeared also for the Bishop Auckland Church Institute side in the 1886 Durham Challenge Cup Final.

Brothers Frank and Philip Messant were both from Tynemouth. Frank, the eldest, was good enough to play for the Charterhouse First XI, a side that saw several prominent England footballers wear their shirt. Frank later became a solicitor in Newcastle. His younger brother Philip was afterwards a Fellow of Bombay University and chief engineer to the Bombay Port Trust. He acted as an umpire and referee in important local games. All three players were to be prominent for Tyne in those formative years.

Alfred J. Harrison and members of the Challoner family were also leading characters as the club was formed. Harrison had played in the very first association trial game in March 1877 that had led to the formation of Tyne and, on occasion, had raised his own team to provide the opposition for the embryonic association clubs. Indeed, when a proposed pre-season Tyne practice match in October 1878 (Committee versus Other Members) fell through because the club captain and one or two committee men did not turn up, it was Alfred Harrison and S.N. Challoner who organised two teams to give the members a much-needed game.

Although he was an early player, and indications are that he attended Uppingham public-school, Harrison became better known as an organiser and administrator. The son of a Sunderland-born civil engineer, he was actually born in Australia before settling down on Tyneside, living in what was then an upmarket area of Elswick, at Wentworth Place. He served on the Tyne committee, and he was the driving force behind the visit of the Scotch-Canadians team to Tyneside in January 1880, which did so much to promote the popularity of the game locally.

Harrison chaired the meeting held in the Turk's Head Hotel in Newcastle that resulted in the creation of a joint Northumberland & Durham FA, and he was elected as the Association's first honorary secretary. His term of office was brief, however, and Fred Knott of the Corbridge club soon took over the role.

But Harrison came to the fore again when Northumberland and Durham split to form separate associations in 1883. He became the Northumberland FA's first vice-president at a time when the president's position was unfilled and was also unanimously elected to represent the local association on the Northern Committee of the national Football Association. By 1884, the Bishop of Newcastle undertook the appointment but within a year had moved on to become patron of the association and Harrison became president, a position that he held for two years. He returned to take over the role again in 1890, but only for a year.

Members of the Challoner family were active sportsmen of the Elswick and Northern Rugby Clubs and also appear to have connections with the Tyne Rowing Club. A number of Challoners were enthusiastic sportsmen but, as far as association football is concerned, two members of the family deserve to be remembered. S.N. Challoner's early involvement has already been noted, but his enthusiasm was matched, and his playing achievements surpassed, by Thomas Davison Challoner who also played cricket. They were both early members of Tyne Association, and both went on to captain the team on occasion. Thomas Challoner, who lived on Dean Street in the centre of Newcastle, was good enough to be selected for the Newcastle & District team that faced the Scotch-Canadians in 1880, while he also served on the Tyne committee and became the club secretary. Thomas also captained a Tyne & District XI that faced the Edinburgh Association in Newcastle during December 1881 and was chosen to play on the left wing for a combined Northumberland & Durham side against the Sheffield New Association XI at Bramall Lane a couple of months afterwards. Later that year he served as Tyne's representative on the Northumberland & Durham Challenge Cup Committee and occasionally deputised as chairman of the meetings. In December 1882 he refereed a game between Newcastle Rangers and Queen's Park, the renowned Glasgow amateur team. But during that season, Challoner became less active as a player and, once the Northumberland and Durham Associations went their separate ways, his involvement in county and club administration ceased. Afterwards, he was a solicitor in Newcastle and became an early shareholder of Newcastle United. Members of the Challoner family also occasionally played for a new club which was soon to be established, Rangers. They became great rivals to Tyne as football broke new ground in the region.

Other early pioneers were Charles Cumberlege and Edward Simpson, as well as J.E. Evans and J.S. Watson, along with the Pattinsons, possibly a family of brothers. Cumberlege was born in India and another from a public-school background, attending

The Eton First XI of 1879 featuring pioneer footballer William Hitchcock, pictured in the back row, second from the right with the moustache. *(Eton College archive)*

Rossall on the Lancashire coast, a school noted for football and other sport. He was a keen cricketer, later serving on Northumberland Cricket Club's committee. A bank superintendant, he played for Surrey in 1872 and, when he moved north, for Northumberland as a right-handed batsman.

Cumberlege was typical of the many cricketers who tried the new game of association football, joining Tyne at the outset. Charles had three sons who all went on to play cricket at a good level, with one of his sons, Barry, appearing for Kent. Cumberlege senior was also involved in the founding of Newcastle Preparatory School in Jesmond during 1885, the institution being a supporter of the association code as a sport. Pupils used the adjacent fields – the pitch of Tyne FC – until the Royal Grammar School developed the site.

Tyne Association attracted many well-to-do enthusiasts for the game during their 10-year existence. One of the earliest players, who took part in that inaugural trial game at Elswick Rugby Club, is thought to be William Stuart Harris who attended Trinity College, Cambridge, and was a talented sportsman, appearing in the prestigious varsity football contest before moving to County Durham in the clergy.

William Lane Hitchcock, a Cambridge Blue from Pembroke College, was another prominent player. Hitchcock was the eldest of four brothers who all played football in those pioneer years. He attended Eton as well and was for a time a master at Fettes in Edinburgh. Thanks to the marvellous archives of both Eton and Pembroke College, much is known about Hitchcock. A Gloucestershire man from Bussage, his family moved to Whitburn for a period where his father was the reverend at a local church, and during this time he married a local girl. William played Eton's Wall Game, Field Game and Fives, so was a genuine pioneer of football. He was also a noted cricketer at Eton, a wicketkeeper, and

Tyne Association's Charles Hitchcock in a cricket pose with Marlborough school's cricket XI from 1879. *(Marlborough College archive)*

was described as having a character of 'cheerfulness and strong sense of duty'. Sadly Hitchcock died of consumption at an early age in 1886, being only 26 years old and a master at Eton, returning there after periods back in the North East.

His brothers Robert Aldous, Charles and George Edward all played in the region too, for both Tyne and Rangers, and all attended Cambridge University. Robert went to Marlborough College in Wiltshire, another of the early football enthusiasts, before attending Pembroke at Cambridge. He was later ordained in the clergy and lived in Suffolk, ending up as a rural dean. Charles was another pupil at Marlborough, who played cricket for the College First XI and was described as having 'painstaking and untiring energy'. He was later a graduate of Trinity College. Charles also followed a career in the church and afterwards lived in California, becoming president of the Military Academy at San Rafael. The youngest brother, George Edward, was an Eton pupil who took part in the school's various football games and went to Pembroke as well. From a religious family, he also entered the clergy with various appointments, eventually becoming a Canon at Gloucester Cathedral until his death in 1939.

Thomas Redmayne hailed from a Low Fell family and reinforces Tyne's many links to the public school and university fraternity. Thomas, who also later lived at Wentworth Place in Elswick, was the younger of two sons who graduated at Trinity College, Cambridge, and attended Repton School in Derbyshire. His family were associated with various manufacturing businesses on Tyneside. During spells back home from school and university, he appeared for Tyne and then entered the medical profession, becoming house physician and house surgeon at the London Hospital before moving to Sussex Hospital in Hastings.

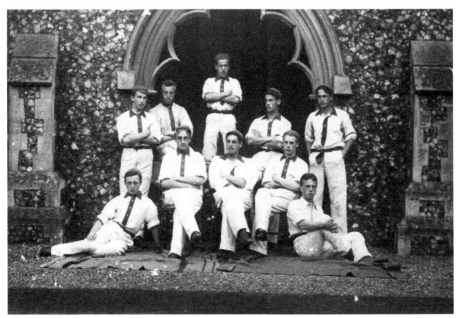

John Samborne was a noted player for Tyne, pictured in this team group of Lancing's cricket XI c.1879, sitting on a chair, far left. (*Lancing College archive*)

Another of Tyne's men was A.P. Arnold, a noted Durham University graduate who later studied at Newcastle College of Medicine. Also a rugby player of repute with Northern, he acted for a while as Tyne's secretary. John Stukley Palmer Samborne also starred for Tyne and for the county side too. He attended Lancing School in Sussex, another of the public schools that favoured the association code, noted in the school archives as 'a rough-and-tumble dribbling game in which the players followed the ball all over the field'. Although born in Timsbury Manor (near Bath) to a notable family, Samborne was for a period captain of Tyne and was a prominent sportsman, also being proficient at cricket. Leaving Lancing in 1880, he became a mining engineer and, although it is not confirmed, he may have been working in the North East for a period during his union with Tyne. John afterwards was a consulting engineer in London.

Tyne's declared objective of 'inducing other clubs in the area to play' was working; although they had to establish themselves first. They played regularly against various scratch teams and rugby clubs. For the first year of their existence they followed their policy of 'spreading the word' and usually won their matches, playing rugby sides such as Northumberland, the College of Physical Science, North Durham and Tynemouth. Indeed, when they faced North Durham in November 1877, Tyne had enough playing members to field a second XI (against North Durham Second XI).

Occasionally games were played in Newcastle that did not seem to involve Tyne but, in reality, they often did. As a result we find (as mentioned previously) the 1878–79 season starting with S.N. Challoner's team playing against A.J. Harrison's side. In fact, this was what would be referred today as a pre-season practice match, as both teams mainly comprised club members. It is interesting to note that this pre-season game was played at the beginning of October. At the time there was a rigid demarcation between cricket and football, with the latter strictly regarded as a winter sport. In any case, many of the footballers played for cricket teams as well.

Indeed, it is among the cricketers of the time that we first encounter a man who was to have a significant impact on football on Tyneside in the coming years. On 3 May 1878, Newcastle Cricket Club held its annual meeting at the Queen's Head Hotel on Pilgrim Street, Newcastle, William Coulson presiding. Coulson appeared as a regular player (although, apparently, not too successfully) with the cricket club in the summer of 1876 and, by 1878, was an active member of the committee. The significance of William Coulson is that he was eventually (in 1881) to create Stanley Football Club, which subsequently became East End and ultimately Newcastle United.

Back in the spring of 1878, the officers at the annual meeting of the Newcastle Cricket Club were able to report a fairly successful season for the previous year. The club played their home matches on a pitch between Warwick Place and Eskdale Terrace just next to Brandling Park which had been laid out during the 1870s. Brandling was named after a prominent local family, described as a 'desirable area'. The site is presently part of the Royal Grammar School campus.

It was reported at the time that the lease for the ground would probably be extended to cover the next four or five years. The extent of the lease was an important factor at the time as it was thought that the Northumberland Cricket Club would be deprived of their

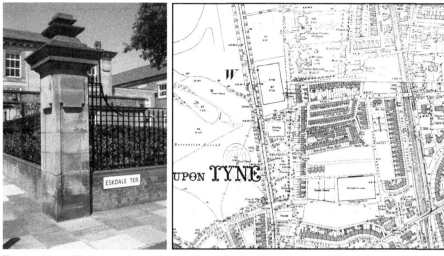

The location of Tyne Association's ground in Brandling Village, Jesmond, bottom right. The Royal Grammar School now stands on the site at Warwick Place and Eskdale Terrace. Close by was another pitch, north of the bowling green at Abbotsford Terrace.

prominent ground at Bath Road for development within the next year or two. Tyne played their home games on the Northumberland Cricket Ground and so needed to relocate, and their strong cricketing links were reinforced when they moved to Brandling in the summer of 1881.

Several of Tyne's main crusaders were based in Jesmond, a former farming and coal-mining area, but which was in the 19th century quickly becoming *the* residential suburb of Newcastle.

Many members of the Tyne football club also played cricket for the Northumberland club. In terms of cricketing prowess, Charles Cumberlege was pre-eminent. He was a more-than-useful batsman and was in a select Newcastle & District side that defeated a United South of England team that included the legendary W.G. Grace during July 1878. Admittedly, the local side played with 18 men, which was quite a bit of an advantage. The scorecard for the game shows that Jackson Ewbank, one of the Middlesbrough club's founders – yet another strong cricketing and football association – scored 33 before he was caught and bowled by the celebrated W.G. who, incidentally, took seven wickets for 90 runs in dismissing the local side for 251.

The Newcastle & District team won by an innings and 69 runs in a game that finished a day early. So, on the spare day, a special match was staged – XIV Gentlemen versus XIV Players. This time Cumberlege played in the same team as the eminent Grace brothers, William Gilbert and George Frederick. Indeed, the Tyne man opened the batting. Sadly he failed, collecting a duck. Ewbank, however, excelled again, opening the batting for the Players and this time scoring 41.

Apart from Cumberlege, a number of other Tyne players whiled away the summer playing for Northumberland too. We find S.G. Homfrey, R.L. Weeks, J.H. Berkeley and N.P. Pattinson playing for both sides. With so many cricketers among their membership, it is not surprising to find that Tyne also occasionally played the odd cricket game during the summer. In June 1878, for instance, they played against Northumberland Cricket Club on the Bath Road ground.

But Tyne were primarily a football team, and they continued to play their games against all and sundry – occasionally against various professions, although the opposition usually included some of the Tyne players. A game against Engineers in March 1878 was one of the rare occasions that Tyne lost (2–1); however, the Engineers' team included Alfred Harrison as captain with W. Blackborne and S.G. Homfrey in goal, all of whom could usually be found in the Tyne line up.

In fact, these teams were very much of a mix and match affair. Two players (L. Evans and A. Hurst) who appeared in that Engineers team had also appeared in the College of Physical Science side which had played Tyne a month earlier, while J. Bruce (who had captained the College side) and William Harris, who had also played for the College, turned out for Tyne against the Engineers. There were some consistencies, with the likes of Charles Cumberlege, S.N. Challoner, J.E. Evans and E. Liddell regularly playing for the Tyne side and not for the opposition; however, even in these cases there were occasional exceptions such as when Tyne played against a Bankers XI and the latter included Cumberlege and Evans as well as other Tyne players such as Edward Simpson and P.C. Fenwick. Usually either Challoner or Cumberlege was the Tyne captain, with the former often lining up both with and against his brothers.

As a consequence, too much significance should not be read into the fact that Tyne were usually (although not always) unbeaten against local opposition. Most players were merely local enthusiasts, mainly local professional businessmen, eager to play this comparatively new game of association football.

One contest that Tyne did not win was the first Tyne-Tees encounter (although, to be pedantic, it was a Tees-Tyne match), when the Newcastle club journeyed to Middlesbrough in January 1878 to play the local side on Albert Park. A reported crowd of 150 saw an even match that ended in a draw. A return encounter on Tyneside a month later also ended in a draw, 2–2, the game being played over four periods of 20 minutes each.

Tyne did occasionally lose. Significantly, they went down 2–1 against a Public Schools team in January 1878. As already explained, association football was initially a product of the public schools and experience was important. In this instance, however, the defeat probably had more to do with the fact that Tyne played throughout the game with only nine men. Significantly, the Public Schools team had started with nine, but two more had joined their ranks when the score was 1–1 and this had been enough to tip the balance in their favour. By a strange coincidence, another game against a Public Schools XI two years later ended in the same score with Tyne, once again, playing the entire match with nine men, a severe frost preventing some of their players from reaching the Northumberland Cricket Ground venue.

The Public Schools teams primarily consisted of undergraduates and students who had returned home to Tyneside from their universities and schools for the Christmas and New Year holidays. Consequently the games usually took place in January. The line

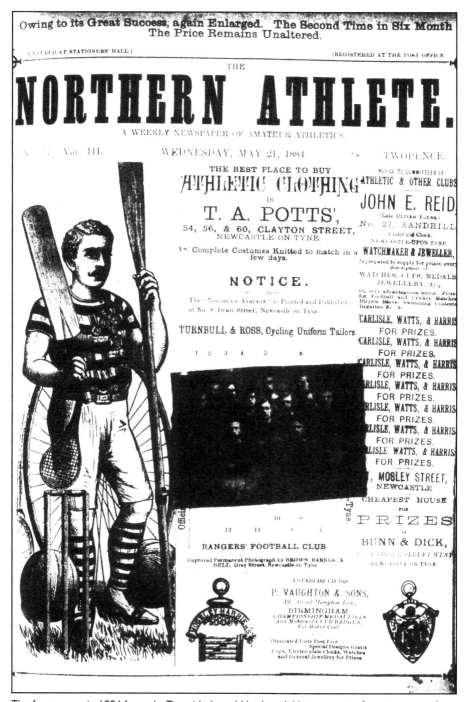

The front cover in 1884 from the Tyneside-based *Northern Athlete* magazine featuring not only an advert for football equipment, but also the only known illustration of Newcastle Rangers, unfortunately a substandard original image. *(Newcastle City Library)*

up included a number of sportsmen who were to become familiar to followers of the round-ball game in the years to come, with the surnames of Fenwick, Hitchcock, Hunter and Harrison liberally scattered throughout the side. Indeed, in the 1880 fixture, the Public Schools side included the four Hitchcock brothers and two Fenwicks as well as two Hunters. In fact, both sides included two Fenwicks – E. Fenwick (in goal) and P.C. Fenwick (forward) for Tyne and F. Fenwick (in goal) and T. Fenwick (forward) for the Public Schools. Coupled with the Challoners mentioned earlier, this adds credence to the belief that the games were very much family affairs and many of the pioneering men hailed from groups of relations and family friends.

Early in November 1878, the Newcastle Scottish Association held a meeting at the Neville Hotel in Newcastle with a view to forming a football club as rivals to Tyne. The meeting was held to elect officers and to launch the club in the public awareness. They started in a big way with Earl Percy and Sir William Armstrong accepting the posts of patron and president respectively, but the new club struggled from the outset and never developed. They lost 3–0 to a Tyne second team, Tyne A, in their first game and failed to attract sufficient playing members to survive. This was unfortunate because they seemed to have had progressive ideas, even expressing the intention of playing a game by electric light!

Such a game did actually take place, although it did not involve the Newcastle Scottish Association. A game referred to at the time as 'a football trial match' (under probably rugby rules) was played on the evening of 7 December on the Chester Road ground in Sunderland when Sunderland faced Northumberland (although most of the players who took part were members of the Sunderland club). It was intended to use four electric lights, two supplied by Mr Hutton of the Souter Point Lighthouse and two by Messrs Shuttleworth & Wake. Unfortunately, it was a stormy night with snow, and Mr Hutton deemed it inadvisable to use his lights. Nevertheless, the other two lights, driven by a traction engine, were brought into operation. Sadly, the experiment was not a huge success but some play did take place. Reportedly the light varied between 'very bright' and 'irregular', and the lights also went out completely on one or two occasions. It also seems that the game was not finished as it was reported that the experiment was eventually postponed 'until next year'. Nevertheless, this was the first time 'floodlit' football was used in the North East (although the term 'floodlit' was not utilised at the time and it would have been an exaggeration if it had been). The first recorded instance of a 'floodlit' contest nationally had been only a few weeks before when in October 1878, at Bramall Lane in Sheffield, lights were switched on for a similar trial match.

Around the same time, towards the end of 1878, the first sign of a real challenge to Tyne's local supremacy in the dribbling game was seen when another association club was formed in Newcastle. This new club, Rangers Association Football Club, had many initial problems. To begin with they were unable to obtain a field for their home matches and, additionally, the severe winter of 1878–79 prevented virtually any sport from being played in the region. During the first year of their existence, Rangers never even played a game. Indeed, when the club held their first general meeting at the Neville Hotel in Newcastle on a Saturday evening during October 1879, they were to formally report that 'no commencement was made last season'.

The annual gathering saw the election and appointment of officials for the season. Sir Henry Clavering, Bart, wrote to the club, formally accepting the office of honorary president, and the following officers were duly elected: F. Balfour (captain), W. Simms (vice-captain) and R. Stewart Bain (honorary secretary and treasurer – pro tem).

Balfour did not last long as captain, only playing in the first few games. Soon he was superseded by William Simms who, along with J.F. Ashbridge, Stewart Bain, G.M. Blake, John Lochhead and J. Wakinshaw, became the early stalwarts of the fledgling club. Simms was an influential figure for Rangers and a real pioneer of football in the district. So too were Ashbridge and Bain, who both were described as being 'founders' of the club.

Scot John Lochhead took over from Simms as captain. He first played the game in his native Glasgow for the Shaftesbury club alongside future Scottish international Andrew Holm. John headed for Tyneside in 1879 and soon joined Rangers, becoming a reliable full-back or half-back. Lochhead was also a regular for the county line up, being described as having 'cleverness and tact', and while he was an extremely tricky player it was noted that he 'never sacrifices effectiveness for showy play'.

James Philips soon came onto the scene as well, described in the early text *The Book of Football* as a crusader 'who laboured stupendously to give the game root on Tyneside'. A Rangers man from the outset, he later acted as an umpire and referee and became a leading administrator, secretary of the Northumberland FA, for a period up to September 1890 when he headed for the US, settling in Chicago. Rangers also found a player who was to become the district's foremost footballer in the next decade, Alec White, a school teacher from Heaton. But more of him later.

Brothers David and Robert Crawford were prominent on and off the field. Like several of the Rangers men, they would eventually move to the soon-to-be-formed Stanley (and later East End) camp. David Crawford would afterwards become a Newcastle United director and chairman in 1928. He was also Northumberland FA president for a period. John Douglas, a noted defender, was another who laboured to get football underway on Tyneside, as was Thomas Hoban, who would soon blossom into one of the region's top players like Alec White. William Muir was another who developed into one of Tyneside's stalwarts. With Tyne originally, he joined Rangers and later East End before emigrating to South Africa. As noted, the Challoners also played with Rangers on occasion.

Walter Dix was a resident of Byker and a fine sportsman, appearing for Rangers before becoming one of the earliest shareholders in Newcastle United. *(M. Dix collection)*

Many local sportsmen were attracted to the new Rangers club, including Norfolk-born Walter Dix, a one-time oarsman on the Tyne, who wanted to try the now flourishing game. A master engineer, he played a few games for the new club including a victory over Sunderland in November 1882 when he formed a left-wing partnership with Tommy Hoban. Later, as a resident and owner of an engineering business in the St Peter's area, he became a prominent Tyneside figure and one of the founder shareholders of East End – and, of course, Newcastle United. The shares stayed in the family for generations; his grandson, Malcolm Dix, was much later a fervent United supporter and aide to Sir John Hall as Newcastle United was regenerated in the 1990s.

The Rangers club was also able to announce that they had managed to obtain a home ground (on loan) for the 1879–80 season. Their pitch was on the Drill Field between Prince Consort Road and Alexandra Road, adjoining the North Durham Cricket Ground and Bowling Club in Gateshead. Eventually the cricket club took over the whole site, which today is still in existence near to Gateshead Civic Centre. But Rangers were none too successful in their first few games in Gateshead. They lost their first encounter with Tyne 4–0 during November 1879. Rangers' stay in Gateshead, however, was to be brief. They were to soon find a new home on the edge of the Town Moor at Leazes. Their new ground was to be called St James' Park.

It should be mentioned that conflicting reports of match results was not too unusual at this time. For most games each team nominated an umpire from their club membership and these gentlemen officiated during games. When one umpire disagreed about the validity of a goal and opinions were divided, it was often referred to as 'a disputed goal'. With no press match reporters, when secretaries sent their results in to the local newspaper for publication, they often reflected the scoreline that was most advantageous to their clubs. As a consequence there are often conflicting results recorded.

It was not too long after the introduction of competitive games that it was decided to introduce a third, neutral, official to whom the umpires could 'refer' on incidents of dispute. Then the 'referee' would decide. It would not be many years before the referee became pre-eminent and, eventually, the umpires were relegated to the sidelines and became linesmen.

Back in the 1879–80 season, Rangers occasionally struggled to field a team. They had to use four substitute players for a match at the newly formed Corbridge side (which they lost 1–0) at the end of January because some of their men did not turn up. But they persevered and gradually improved. A 3–1 reverse away to North Elswick (a rugby club) during December 1879 was avenged by a 2–1 win in a return fixture two months later.

There is little doubt that Tyneside football was still in its infancy and was a long way behind the rest of the country. When Rangers faced the Scottish side Athole (of Glasgow) on the Northumberland Cricket Ground in March 1880, the Tyneside team were thrashed 8–0. Against the Scots it was noted that 'the team placed in the field by the Rangers were unable to cope with the capital passing game shown by their more experienced and practised brethren of Glasgow'. Football was also largely a social affair. It is recorded that the Athole players were entertained to supper by the Rangers players after the game. A week later Rangers were able to trounce another new local side, North Eastern, 5–0.

While Rangers had kicked-off and did well locally, Tyne were undoubtedly the premier club in the district during these early days. They were just about on a par with Teesside neighbours Middlesbrough. In 1878–79 they played two further fixtures, home and away against the Boro, recording a narrow defeat (3–2) on Teesside, but a 1–1 draw in Newcastle. In the first four Tyne-Tees derby games, three of them ended in draws.

Many of the early games were played against rugby clubs under association rules. Occasionally, the compliment was returned. In March 1879, Tyne played Gosforth at rugby on the Northumberland Cricket field in Bath Road. Although some of the Tyne players had rugby backgrounds, they found it hard to revert back to the handling game and duly lost, by 'one goal, two tries and several touch downs'!

It should be remembered that both the tactics and style of football in Victorian England was far removed from the slick, fast and sophisticated game we have today. The tactics of soccer were still evolving. Although the *Laws of Football* had been issued by the Football Association, there was still debate between factions over how the game was played.

Team formation was also fundamentally different. There was no 4–3–3 or 4–4–2, no players 'in the hole', no defensive pivots or a twin centre-back system. Some teams played with 12 or more men, others with only nine. Times were variable; an hour and a half, or longer, or indeed shorter, especially if daylight faded. When Tyne faced Middlesbrough in those early Tyne-Tees derbies the two captains agreed the game should be 80 minutes long, played in four periods of 20 minutes each. In the Tyne versus

FOOTBALL MILESTONES

Fact Box

1846:	Cambridge Rules introduced.
1863:	The Football Association formed.
1863:	The FA's *Laws of Football* published.
1869:	Goal-kick introduced.
1870:	Eleven-a-side becomes standard.
1871:	Goalkeepers mentioned in the laws.
1872:	First FA Cup Final: Royal Engineers v The Wanderers.
1872:	First International; England v Scotland.
1872:	Corners introduced.
1874:	Umpires mentioned in the laws.
1875:	Cross-bar replaces tapes.
1878:	Referees use whistles.
1882:	Two-handed throw-in introduced.
1885:	Professionalism legalised by the FA.
1888:	The Football League formed.
1891:	Goal-nets first used.
1891:	Penalty-kick introduced.

Rangers fixture, Tyne played a 1–2–7 formation while Rangers adopted a 2–2–6 line up. Some teams, as we have seen, favoured the 'dribbling' style – notably in the south – or the 'passing' game – as in the north and Scotland. Tactics slowly developed into a 2–3–5 formation, and the 'passing' mode eventually won the day; although of course a combination of the two actually evolved. There was a goalkeeper, two full-backs – the defenders – three half-backs and five forwards. But this was largely not in place until after the pioneers had done their work to establish the game.

Balls were standardised in 1872, yet at first there were no field markings, no goal-nets and only a tape between the posts to act as a 'bar'. A standard marked-out pitch was not common until as late as 1892. Throw-ins were one-handed and heading almost unknown. Teams were kitted out in a variety of styles and colours. It was recorded in 1883 that Tyne played in 'orange-and-black-quartered' jerseys while Rangers wore 'dark blue with R.F.C. on the breast of the jersey'. Other early clubs in the north paraded in 'blue-and-white jerseys and hose' as well as 'black jerseys and blue band' or 'navy blue jersey, light blue sash, white knickers'. Tassled caps were the order of the day as well. The early games were also strictly amateur – to play for pleasure rather than for pay. But as the working class started to become involved, those Victorian ideals did not last long.

An important part of football's evolution during those embryonic years was the Football Association's introduction of the first competitive tournament, the FA Cup – which became, of course, for well over a century the greatest domestic competition in world football. In July 1871, at a meeting held in the offices of *The Sportsman* in London, a proposal by Football Association honorary secretary Charles Alcock, a local man (more of him later) was made 'that it is desirable that a Challenge Cup should be established in connection with the Association, for which all clubs belonging to the Association should be invited to compete'. The idea was met with favour and was finally approved three months later. The first FA Cup competition in season 1871–72 had 15 entries. Wanderers, a team formed by ex-public-school and university players, won the first Final. In that initial year of the FA Cup, or English Cup as it was known for some time, there were no clubs from the North East – instead there were several from the Home Counties, Donnington School from Lincolnshire and the Scottish entry, Queen's Park. The FA Cup did not arrive in the North East until eight years after its inaugural season.

While Tyne rarely lost association games against local opposition, in the 1879–80 season they decided to test their skill against the big boys of association football when they entered for the FA Cup, the first North East club to do so. Unfortunately they were drawn away to Blackburn Rovers in their first tie, soon to become football's strongest side with six FA Cup Final appearances in the next dozen or so years, winning the trophy five times.

Tyne travelled to Lancashire on 1 November and, before a crowd of 300, they lost 5–1 at Alexandra Meadows, the home of Rovers before their move to Ewood Park. Tyne's line up in a 1–2–7 formation for that historic FA Cup debut was: goal: Evans; back: Cumberlege; half-backs: Weeks, Gibson; right wing: Challoner (T.D.), Berkeley; centres: Bruce, Stanhope, Liddell; left wing: Thorp, Pattinson.

Blackburn's England centre-forward, 5ft 5in tall James Brown, to soon captain Rovers to three FA Cup triumphs, was a handful for the Tyne defence. He scored twice, and his pace and delicate touch proved too much to handle. Tyne were well beaten. But at least they had shown ambition, and in Charles Cumberlege and Thomas Challoner they had two players who did not look out of place against such august opponents as the Lancashire club. Bruce scored Tyne's only goal.

This ambition reached a new peak when Tyne invited a touring side, the Scotch-Canadians, to visit Newcastle in early January 1880. If there was any single game that acted as a catalyst in establishing the popularity of football on Tyneside, this match has as good a claim as any. It generated huge interest in the game of football. Major Francis Marindin (later Sir Francis), president of the Football Association, wrote to Alfred Harrison of the Tyne club complimenting them on arranging the contest. He urged the local pioneers to persevere and not to be disheartened, even if the strong Scottish side emerged triumphant.

This was thought very likely. The so-called 'Scotch-Canadians' were a side of Scots (almost all internationals) who were touring the country, playing a number of exhibition and challenge matches as they prepared for an intended high-profile tour of Canada and the US to promote the game on the other side of the Atlantic. Despite a great deal of

The Scotch-Canadians line up during their tour of England in 1880. Their visit to Tyneside was a catalyst for the game to prosper. *(Scottish Football Museum)*

publicity, the tour eventually collapsed and never took place.

The Scots fielded some of the finest early names in their history including 6ft 3in tall Dr John Smith, a great early amateur from north of the border who was capped at both association and rugby football. Left-back Tom Vallance of Glasgow Rangers skippered the side, one of the founder members of Gers and captain of the club for nine seasons. Several Queen's Park stars were on show too; Geordie Kerr, a master of close dribbling, full-back William Somers and Dave Davidson, nicknamed 'The Iron Horse'.

The Tyne men were realistic enough to know that they were nowhere near strong enough to face the experienced side from north of the border themselves. So a 'Tyne & District' side was chosen to represent the North East captained by Charles Cumberlege. This comprised a mixture of university men (Oxford & Cambridge) with north-east connections, Tyne players and three prominent Middlesbrough representatives, pioneers of the Teesside club. Jackson Ewbank, who had already played cricket alongside Tyne's men, was one of the individuals who founded the Boro side and actually scored their very first goal against Tees Wanderers in 1877. He was a fine player of the day, good enough to reach England trial matches, appearing for The North against The South. Many judges considered he was unlucky not to have won a cap.

Ralph Spencer starred for Tyne, pictured in 1880 at St John's College, Cambridge, as a regular with the universities football side. *(St John's College archive)*

Ewbank was joined by colleagues Charles Booth and Ossie Cochrane, later for a time Middlesbrough player-chairman. An Oxford graduate and a solicitor, he was another formidable sportsman of the era. Cochrane found a passion for the game at Uppingham School in Rutland where Thring had created those important early set of football rules. Ossie was also a school friend of Tyne's Alfred Harrison, so the early pioneers north and south of the region were allies.

Two other Oxbridge men appeared in that side – reinforcing the early links to the scholarly institutions – Tyne's William Hitchcock and Ralph Spencer, both of whom were at Cambridge University. Spencer hailed from Newburn, attended Harrow and played their early form of football at that historic school in London. Ralph was afterwards a prominent sportsman at St John's College, and their archive provides meticulous detail on his time there. He played football, rugby and cricket and was a regular player in all teams, noted as being a fast left-forward on the football pitch. Later Spencer ran the family steel business in Newcastle, Spencer & Sons Ltd. He resided at Netherwhitton Hall and died in 1926.

Played at the Bath Road cricket ground in Newcastle, the touring side won comfortably 5–0, and the Tyne & District XI lined up as follows: Evans (Tyne), Cumberlege (Tyne), Simpson (Tyne), Hitchcock (Pembroke College), Booth (Middlesbrough), Cochrane (Middlesbrough), Ewbank (Middlesbrough), Spencer (St John's College), Challoner T.D. (Tyne), Bruce (Tyne), Fawcus (Tynemouth).

The local press recorded that the game was a great advertisement for the sport: 'The extraordinary skill and smartness in using the legs, head and body without ever bringing the hands into requisition cannot fail to exhibit in the most attractive manner the best features of the Association game.' Crucially the game attracted a large crowd for the time of 1,300; although some reporters estimated the attendance as high as 2,000. In either case, it was by far and away the biggest crowd to witness an association football match on Tyneside so far. In their next game, the Scots trounced Blackburn Rovers 8–1; therefore, in its true perspective, the defeat in Newcastle was not too ignominious. This view is supported by results elsewhere in the country as the Scotch-Canadians continued their tour, sweeping all before them and defeating Darwen 7–3, Manchester Wanderers 8–1 and Nottingham Forest 2–0. A huge crowd of 6,000 was reported in the Lancashire town of Darwen. They played 13 games overall, winning 12, and although they never reached North America it was considered that the domestic tour was a significant success in promoting the game.

OLDEST CLUBS IN THE NORTH EAST

South Bank:	Cleveland	1868 *(unconfirmed)*
Middlesbrough:	Cleveland	1876
Tyne Association:	Tyneside	1877
Newcastle Rangers:	Tyneside	1878
Alnwick:	Northumberland	1879
North Eastern:	Tyneside	1879
Sunderland:	Wearside	1879
Corbridge:	Tynedale	1879
Burnopfield:	County Durham	1879
Haughton-le-Skerne:	County Durham	1879

Note: Several minor clubs were formed around Cleveland during the 1870s such as Loftus and Eston.

Tyne and Rangers were to dominate the first years of football on Tyneside and in the North East, north of Cleveland. Tyne took the lead, but within a few short years Rangers were being recognised 'as the premier club in the district', as recorded in the contemporary magazine *Football*. And while Tyne and Rangers can be considered as having led the way, other clubs can also be recognised as being pathfinders in the region.

While the Newcastle Scottish club did not advance, by the end of 1879 another Newcastle club had been formed. Mention has already been made of North Eastern Football Club. They were formed following a meeting of employees of the North Eastern Railway Company at their offices in late November 1879. Like so many other local association clubs, North Eastern was formed from a cricket club. Indeed, the committee of the latter gave permission for the football team to play on their cricket ground in Heaton. This was near the railway works close to Chillingham Road and opposite St Gabriel's Church.

At its formation, the football club had 11 honorary members plus 31 active members. Two of these, A. Hurst and W.G. Scotter, were appointed as joint secretaries and treasurers. Hurst, who was on the Northumberland & Durham FA committee, was based at the Engineer's Office at the Central Station and was a comparatively experienced player who had turned out regularly for Tyne until the formation of the new club. He was to make the odd guest appearance for Tyne thereafter but usually played for North Eastern – at least for the first few months of its existence. Scotter worked at the North Eastern Railway's Forth Goods Warehouse in Newcastle, and he was soon to take full responsibility as both secretary and treasurer.

Other notable characters were William Hume, the first captain; J.G. Russell; outside-left John Oliver, who became skipper as well as secretary; and James Oliver (perhaps a relation) on the right flank, a player with plenty of pace. William Hall was another good servant for several years.

The new club played its first game on the cricket field in Heaton just before Christmas when two scratch teams faced each other. Many of the members taking part were playing their first-ever game under association rules and the game ended as a draw, 3–3. With colours of red and white, North Eastern continued to be a noted local side without reaching the heights for over a decade, indeed outliving their more prestigious rivals Tyne and Rangers.

The game was now spreading from its Newcastle roots on Tyneside up the valley into Tynedale. A club was formed at Corbridge in the autumn of 1879 and they came to Newcastle to take on Tyne at the Northumberland Cricket Ground on the same day as the scratch game at Heaton. By now, Tyne were quite experienced and this showed as they emerged as comfortable 5–0 winners, despite apparently only having 10 men.

Followers of the association code seemed spoiled for choice that day because the North Elswick (rugby club) versus Rangers game mentioned was also played at Graingerville in North Elswick. Although Rangers lost 3–1, their team included a few players who were to establish themselves as the club grew from strength to strength over the next few years. Their goal, for instance, was scored by Stewart Bain who, with team member G.M. Blake, was to become a mainstay of the club. Interestingly, apart from

Tyne (who only had 10 men), the other three full teams playing that day fielded two full-backs and two half-backs, indicating that a 2–2–6 formation was the norm.

But the growth of the game was not restricted to Tyneside and Teesside in the region. Almost two years after football began in Newcastle it reached Wearside and, in 1879, was to see the birth of a club who, in the closing years of the Victorian era, were to become supreme in the North East and, indeed, in the whole of England. Sunderland first saw the light of day in October 1879 under the rather long title of Sunderland and District Teachers' Association Football Club. It was noted by one of the founding members, John Grayston, that at the time on Wearside 'the only football being played was Rugby football'.

The club was founded mainly thanks to the efforts of an Edinburgh schoolteacher, a past medical student of Glasgow University, James Allan, who had moved to Sunderland in 1877 to take up a teaching post at the Thomas Street Boys' School in Hendon. He had seen the growth and popularity of the game north of the border and as Grayston noted following Allan's holiday in Scotland, 'returned with a round football. He began to play with the ball, and our interest was soon aroused'.

Allan had actually played the game when in Glasgow, appearing for the Busby, East Kilbride and Oxford clubs as well as assisting the 3rd Lanark Rifle Volunteers FC, then a noted team in Scotland. He initiated a meeting that was held in the British Day School which was located on the corner of Norfolk Street and Borough Road near the centre of Sunderland. It was here that the club was formed, with Grayston elected secretary, Robert Singleton captain and Allan himself as vice-captain. James also turned out for both Tyne and Rangers, and he was described as 'one of the best left wing forwards in the district'. Once when in Rangers' colours he 'raised cheer after cheer by his determined play, dribbling nearly the whole length of the field time after time'.

Like most clubs in the area, Sunderland and District Teachers' AFC took hesitant steps to begin with. But these steps were forward, and gradually it began to grow. So much so that, within a year, the club had outgrown its teaching roots, and it was felt obliged to drop any reference to that profession from its name to make it more accessible to all enthusiasts. So, from October 1880, Sunderland Association Football Club played under its new name – and that is the way it has stayed ever since.

Other clubs, although less significant as history relates, were also sprouting up. A club was formed at Burnopfield above the Derwent Valley at the end of 1879. This side predominantly comprised pitmen, evidence that, in the North East at least, the game was slowly moving away from its public school roots and was to become the choice of the working classes. Like all inexperienced new clubs, they had mixed fortunes to begin with but they only succumbed 1–0 when they played Corbridge in January 1880. Burnopfield also lost by a single goal, 2–1, against the same opposition a couple of months later. They could, however, celebrate an occasional victory such as a 2–0 win over North Eastern in March 1880 before a crowd of 200. J. Bruce emerged as the key man in the development of the Burnopfield club, albeit briefly as he moved to join Tyne.

Further north, in the historic seat of the powerful Earls and Dukes of Northumberland, in Alnwick, another club was formed at about the same time. Early football, of course, had arrived in the form of the folk game in the town, and records from the 1880s show that a new club was formed shortly after an exhibition match was staged by Tyne Association in the Northumberland town during 1879. They played not far from Alnwick Station. As the train was the principle means of travel at the time, the location of grounds in relation to railway stations became of paramount importance. Some clubs were criticised for playing on pitches too far from the local station, although at Alnwick it was possible to take a horse-drawn bus to the ground.

In County Durham an association club was formed in Ferryhill. Further south still, Darlington Grammar School were taking up the game, although perhaps they bit off more than they could chew when they faced Middlesbrough in February 1880. The Teessiders overwhelmed the school side 11–0.

By then Middlesbrough had clearly developed further than Tyne. Two games in the same month saw the Teesside team record a double victory over their Tyneside counterparts. A 1–0 win over Tyne at the Northumberland Cricket Ground was followed, two weeks later, by a comfortable 4–1 victory at the Middlesbrough Cricket Club ground before 'a large concourse of spectators'. The Middlesbrough side of the time included perhaps the first star player in the North East, Jackson Ewbank, who had featured in that Scotch-Canadian exhibition. He was described as a 'sinuous' player who had a penchant for scoring goals.

Strangely, between the two defeats by Middlesbrough, Tyne recorded a creditable draw against Edinburgh University; although the result seems to have flattered the local side. Most of the play was in the Tyne half, and the Scots were clearly the more skilful players. But it is faithfully recorded that what the local players lacked in experience they made up for with enthusiasm and energy. It was against the run of play that Bruce gave Tyne the lead, which they held until half-time (the game was played over two periods of 40 minutes). Craig equalised for the Scots 10 minutes into the second half, but 1–1 remained the final score.

Tyne were praised for their preparations for the match, particularly for the arrangements

---

NEWTON FOOTBALL CLUB

v.

TYNE WASPS,

AT NEWTON, STOCKSFIELD,

SATURDAY, NOVEMBER 3RD, 1883.

KICK OFF AT 2·30 P.M.

FOOTBALL.

SATURDAY NEXT, AT 3 P.M.

TYNE

(HOLDERS OF NORTHUMBERLAND CUP)

v.

MIDDLESBROUGH.

(HOLDERS OF CLEVELAND CUP IN 1882 AND 1883.)

ON TYNE GROUND, NEAR WARWICK PLACE.

ADMISSION SIXPENCE.   LADIES FREE.

CLEVELAND

FOOTBALL ASSOCIATION.

MONDAY, NOVEMBER 5TH.

A Committee Meeting will be held on Monday, November 5th, in the King's Head, at 7 p.m., to select Team to play Northumberland at Newcastle.

Nominations to be sent to me by November 2nd, 1883.

JOHN REED, JUN.,
Honorary Secretary.

An advert for football in the local *Northern Athlete* magazine from 1883; a Tyne versus Tees derby with a difference. Ladies were admitted free of charge.

Fact Box

EARLY FOOTBALL LAWS

'Goal is when the ball is kicked through the flag-posts and under the string'. *Cambridge 1848.*

'Fair catch is a catch from any player providing the ball has not touched the ground or has not been thrown from touch and is entitled to a free-kick.' *Sheffield 1857.*

'Each player must provide himself with a red and dark blue flannel cap, one colour to be worn by each side.' *Sheffield 1857.*

'Kicks must be aimed only at the ball.' *Uppingham 1862.*

'Hands may be used only to stop a ball and place it on ground before the feet.' *Uppingham 1862.*

'No one wearing projecting nails, iron plates or gutta percha on the soles of his boots is allowed to play.' *Football Association 1863. (gutta percha is an inelastic latex)*

'The two sides shall change goals after each goal is won.' *Football Association 1863.*

'Neither tripping nor hacking shall be allowed, and no player shall use his hands to hold or push his adversary.' *Football Association 1863.*

'A player shall not be allowed to throw the ball or pass it to another with his hands.' *Football Association 1863.*

'If a player makes a fair catch, he shall be entitled to a free-kick, providing he claims it by making a mark with his heel at once.' *Football Association 1863.*

at the Bath Road ground. The pitch was roped off, and boards were put down for ladies 'of whom there were a large number present'. The formation of both teams was still 2–2–6. It is also interesting to note that Cumberlege was injured in the closing stages. In a later era (before the advent of substitutes), he would have continued on one of the wings, out of the way of any harm. In this particular game he went in goal instead – and kept the Scots down to only a single goal!

As has been evidenced through the formation of the North Eastern and Burnopfield clubs, football was now starting to become a pastime of the working class, from the giant railway works and many pit communities. As the game originated – as at the Tyne Association club – organised football was a sport for young gentlemen with rules created by men of social standing; however, football around the country began to expand from the public schools and grammar schools of the middle and upper classes back to its roots – to the working-class heartland as had been the case when 'mob football' was so prevalent. It was to take a few years for this change to take place, but when it did enthusiasm for the game became frenzied, and a new breed of both footballer and supporter arrived.

A typical breeding ground could be found in the urban sprawl of Elswick on Newcastle's western banks of the Tyne. As related, the area had already seen pioneers of the rugby game evolve under its banner, and the very first match under association rules took place at the Elswick Rugby Club. The community of Elswick grew enormously as the new industrial areas developed east and west of Newcastle's old centre; at Elswick, Benwell, Byker, Walker and Wallsend north of the river, and Felling and Hebburn as well as Gateshead on the south.

By the conclusion of the 1879–80 season and the beginning of the new 1880–81 campaign football was taking shape. It was recorded in *Football* that by then the game was 'firmly established' in the region. It was added: 'The present prospects of the Association game in this district are very bright. The Northumbrians are a thoroughly sport-loving people, and although at times sporting proclivities may be confined to shooting sparrows or watching dog-fights, still once shown something better, they soon take to it and patronise it thoroughly.'

The 'something better', of course, was football, and its first steps in the development process were complete with clubs established on Tyneside and in Northumberland, County Durham and Cleveland. Many more were to follow in the coming 12 months. In fact, there was to be a flood of new footballing clubs all over the region. Included were two sides from either side of the city of Newcastle – from the East End and West End – which were to have a huge bearing on how football would be shaped in the North East over the coming decade.

But before the association game thrived an important, indeed crucial, step needed to be taken. As it began to spread football was virtually unstructured and unorganised, and that caused untold problems. As more and more clubs sprouted up, there became an increasing need for organisation and authority to avoid the increasing chaos of ad-hoc fixtures and haphazard administration. Football in the North East needed a local governing body. Experience elsewhere had shown that the game could not prosper without some kind of order. Otherwise anarchy would prevail.

Chapter 3

THE HOTBED TAKES SHAPE

'It is but a few years ago that the pleasures of the game were confined to a select few. Now, however, all is changed.'
Football, 1882

The Football Association had been established, spreading and unifying the game for just over 16 years by the time its influence reached the North East of England. At the helm in London was a local man, Charles Alcock, born in Bishopwearmouth of Newcastle stock. The family had set up a shipbuilder's yard at Panns Bank on the Wear, but Alcock soon headed for London and was educated at Harrow, where he received a baptism of football. He helped form Forest Football Club – later becoming The Wanderers, one of the game's earliest and foremost clubs. Along with his elder brother John, the pair were both football and cricket enthusiasts and became involved in the formation of the Football Association. John was also present at the founding meeting in Holborn during 1863.

Charles soon became a prime mover in developing the game of football as the national sport, revered alongside such names as Lord Kinnaird, William McGregor and Charles Clegg. He was described as 'the doyen of the Association game' and noted as being 'connected with every movement on the chessboard of the game that has taken place'. Alcock dreamed up the idea of the FA Cup, and he was the first man to hoist the trophy as his club The Wanderers won the inaugural competition in 1872.

Charles Alcock hailed from Wearside and became one of football's most important figures before the turn of the century.

The Northumberland & Durham FA was formed during 1880 at the Turk's Head Hotel (left) on Grey Street, pictured just opposite Newcastle's Theatre Royal (right).

Apart from being a talented early player, appearing for and captaining England, he was also an astute administrator, appointed secretary of the Football Association as the game prospered and afterwards vice-president. He was also secretary of Surrey County Cricket Club. Charles was additionally a prolific writer on both sports, launching the first *Football Annual* in 1868 and the first periodical, *Football*, in 1882.

Part of Alcock's remit was to ensure that association football reached all corners of England – if not the rest of the world too. Other local and national associations throughout Great Britain were formed: Sheffield (1867), Derbyshire (1871), Scottish Association (1873), Birmingham & District (1875), Welsh Association (1876), Edinburgh (1877), Ayrshire (1877), Renfrewshire (1878) and Lancashire (1878). A Canadian Association was also set up in 1877.

Thus there were almost a dozen associations already in existence in Britain and the Empire when sides in Northumberland and Durham decided to set up their own body. No doubt due to the small number of clubs in the area, initially the two county regions of Northumberland and Durham decided upon a combined union.

A meeting was convened at the Turk's Head Hotel in Grey Street, Newcastle, on Friday 23 January 1880 for the express purpose of doing so. Alfred Harrison of the Tyne club occupied the chair, and there was a representative gathering of the leading association clubs in the region.

The new association was duly formed at the meeting, and provisional rules and bye-laws were discussed. Executive members were elected and the initial officers were declared. Harrison became honorary secretary, while his club colleague E.J. Simpson became honorary treasurer. The remaining committee comprised: J.E. Evans (Tyne), R. Stewart Bain (Rangers), Fred Knott (Corbridge), J. Bruce (Burnopfield) and A. Hurst

(North Eastern). Five vacancies on the committee were left over to be filled by election at a later meeting. It was recorded: 'The following clubs were in attendance: Tyne, Rangers, Corbridge, Burnopfield & North Eastern. These clubs decided to proceed with their intention to form an association to be called the Northumberland & Durham Football Association and so became the 12th association in Great Britain and the Colonies.'

The object of the association was to form a network of clubs and extend the 'dribbling code' further by playing games against the older established FA bodies and to offer a challenge cup for competition among the clubs that join. All teams playing the association rules game in the counties of Northumberland and Durham were eligible. They were encouraged to join, although it was not compulsory to do so. The clubs at that earliest time affiliated to the new association were: Tyne, Rangers, Corbridge, North Eastern, Sunderland, Haughton-le-Skerne, Burnopfield, Ferryhill and Darlington Grammar School.

The local morning newspaper, the *Daily Journal* published some of the new association's aims and a defence against possible intrusion into the established rugby game:

'As is pretty generally understood, the movement is not in the least directed against the Rugby Union Clubs, but as in other parts of the country clubs playing each code are able to prosper alongside each other, there seems to be no reason why the same state of affairs should not exist here. Take, for instance, Lancashire, a county which a few years ago was a hotbed of Rugby Union, which now room is found for a powerful association, and has this done the Rugby clubs any harm? If one is to take the team chosen to represent the north in the match to be played today against the south, as an example, we find that Lancashire was never more strongly represented, no less than eight of the team hailing from that county. Surely these facts prove that the games can live together. Such places as Sunderland, Shields, Durham, Darlington, Stockton and Hartlepool, ought to be able to support association clubs as well as those playing rugby. The association game, if properly played, is not a rough one, as the worst feature of the game (viz, charging) is not indulged in by good clubs, and it is to be hoped that young clubs about here will remember this, and try to play the game as it ought to be played, and make it a game of skill more than force'.

It was also added: 'In order to more firmly establish the rules, it was thought expedient to form as an association – a system which has been found to work very successfully in various parts of England and Scotland, more especially the latter – to embrace the counties of Northumberland & Durham.' Here we find a unity with the Scottish game which perhaps indicates an affiliation with the Queen's Park style of football, that of passing and moving rather than straight-forward running with the ball until a player lost it.

In the far south of the region clubs around Teesside were organising their own distinctive grouping. Middlesbrough, South Bank and other early Tees clubs formed the Cleveland Football Association a few months later. On 5 February 1881 a meeting at the Swatters Carr Hotel in Middlesbrough inaugurated the new association around Teesside and saw the whole North Eastern region come under the umbrella of the Football Association in London. It was a major step forward for local football. Alderman Dunning was voted into the chair, and it was he who proposed the formation of the association. This was seconded by Jackson Ewbank, Middlesbrough's skipper. He noted that there were then 20 clubs playing the association game in the district and expected that 12 to 16 of them would join the new grouping. The proposal was carried unanimously, and seven clubs were enrolled into the association that evening.

Apart from organisation, the region also needed real competitive action on the field. As the new 1880–81 season got underway it was noted that: 'The management of the Northumberland & Durham FA are to be congratulated on the success of their efforts to secure a challenge cup to be played for by the different teams during the forthcoming season, a success which is mainly due to the efforts of Mr Harrison of Newcastle who all along has taken the liveliest interest in the game.'

The Challenge Cup was to be competed for annually by the clubs belonging to the association, and the requisite funds for purchasing the Cup were raised by voluntary subscription. The new trophy was purchased for a sum of £50 from Messrs Cameron & Son of Kilmarnock. It was 2ft 6in tall, solid silver and finely engraved, displaying the coat-of-arms for both counties as well as a footballing scene.

In addition to the first XI competition, the association also arranged two other contests; a 'Second XI' trophy and a 'Junior Cup' for Under-17s. Both further broadened the interest of the game. The Cleveland Football Association was to follow with their own Challenge Cup and subsidiary competitions. Not surprisingly, Middlesbrough dominated the first years of its existence, winning everything in sight.

Although some of the Teesside clubs such as Middlesbrough and Redcar participated in the Sheffield Association Cup tournament in 1880 and Tyne, as already related, had sampled a brief taste of FA Cup action against Blackburn Rovers a year earlier, the North East generally had not yet 'enjoyed' competitive football. This all changed when the

---

NORTHUMBERLAND & DURHAM CHALLENGE CUP

Fact Box

Participating clubs (24) 1880–83

Northumberland:
Alnwick, Corbridge, Newcastle East End, Elswick Leather Works, Newcastle FA, North Eastern, Ovingham, Prudhoe Rovers, Rangers, Tyne Association.

County Durham:
Birtley, Bishop Middleham, Burnopfield, Chester-le-Street, Darlington Grammar School, Derwent Rovers, Ferryhill, Hamsterley Rangers, Hurworth, Haughton-le-Skerne, Sedgefield, Stanley Star, Sunderland, Whitburn.

Northumberland & Durham Challenge Cup got underway on 20 November 1880. In the first round, Tyne entertained Corbridge at the Northumberland Cricket Ground at Bath Road. It was noted that a 'considerable number' of spectators attended the game, among them a number of ladies who seemed to appreciate the new 'foot racks' which were provided for them. They were especially grateful as the pitch and sidelines were covered with two or three inches of snow. Tyne won easily 5–1, in the process Philip Messent scoring twice. Both he and R.C. Foster, who also grabbed two goals, were the stars of the game, and Corbridge 'keeper John Robson could do little to stop the Tyne onslaught.

On the other side of Newcastle town centre, Rangers took on North Eastern at their new ground of St James' Park – then no more than an enclosed field – in what was the first competitive game played there. Like Tyne, Rangers won comfortably 7–0, and their captain, William Simms, with four goals to his credit, was the best player on the field. North Eastern's full-back, Oliver, also came in for special praise in the match reports.

The local combined FA purchased a magnificent silver trophy as their Challenge Cup, later adopted by the Northumberland FA for their premier competition.

In the south of the region, Haughton-le-Skerne, a new club just outside Darlington, toppled Bishop Middleham also by seven goals; this after an earlier game had been abandoned when the ball burst with the home side one up! Sunderland received a bye, as did both Burnopfield and Ferryhill after their opponents, Chester-le-Street and Darlington Grammar School, both scratched.

In the second round, Sunderland moved into the semi-final by beating Burnopfield 2–0 in a replay at Rowlands Gill, while Haughton-le-Skerne took care of Ferryhill 2–1. In Newcastle the 'big-two' of Tyne and Rangers clashed, and following a 1–1 draw Rangers went through after a 2–0 victory. With only three clubs in the semi-final, Haughton-le-Skerne received a bye while the first Newcastle versus Sunderland 'derby' took place at St James' Park during February. Admission to the game was 3d (1p) by ticket, or 6d (2½p) at the gate. Sunderland were torn apart by a Rangers side on the top of their game. Goals from Mitchelson, skipper Simms and Lochhead gave the Tynesiders a 3–0 half-time lead, and another two strikes by Simms and Bain sent Rangers through to the region's first Final by a comprehensive 5–0 scoreline.

The following month, during March the inaugural Northumberland & Durham Challenge Cup Final was staged at the Northumberland Cricket Ground. The Final was postponed for three weeks because of bad weather but, eventually, before a reported crowd of 1,500, Rangers lifted the trophy in a closely contested game with their south Durham rivals Haughton-le-Skerne. The only goal of the game was scored by the Rangers captain William Simms who charged both goalkeeper Dodd and the ball over the line to score. These days it would have been a highly controversial winning goal. Back in 1881, and for many a year afterwards, charging the 'keeper was an accepted part of the game. The Mayor of Newcastle presented the winning team with '11 medals', and Rangers' first trophy-winning side was: Blake, Lochhead, White, Campbell, Hall, Hetherington, Bain, Simms, Herdman, Mitchelson, Wakinshaw.

The Final was one of the last matches to be played on the Bath Road arena, which was destined for redevelopment in the summer.

Rangers successfully defended their Cup success in the following season, 1881–82. Following a 1–1 draw, in the replayed Final against Corbridge on Tyne's ground at Warwick Place in Jesmond, they again lifted the trophy after a 2–0 win. Contemporary reports noted that feelings on both sides 'ran high and each team had a liberal number of partisans in the ground'. Simms opened the scoring for Rangers after 20 minutes, and full-back Lochhead wrapped up a second successive victory with a goal in the 78th minute.

Rangers' bid for a hat-trick of victories faltered when they were beaten 1–0 by Tyne in the 1882–83 tournament. That year saw 21 clubs in the competition, an increase of almost 100 per cent from the 11 sides in the opening season, albeit two teams scratched before a ball was kicked. It was left to their Newcastle rivals Tyne Association to ensure the trophy was kept in the city after a 2–0 victory over

---

NORTH EAST FOOTBALL DEVELOPMENT

Fact Box

Key dates 1

1868:	South Bank FC formed (Unconfirmed).
February 1876:	Middlesbrough FC formed.
March 1877:	First game on Tyneside at Elswick Rugby Club.
March 1877:	First Tyneside club formed, Tyne Association FC.
Late 1878:	Second club formed, Newcastle Rangers FC.
October 1879:	Sunderland FC formed.
January 1880:	Northumberland & Durham FA founded.
October 1880:	Rangers play the first game at St James' Park.
November 1880:	First competition, Northumberland & Durham Challenge Cup.

Sunderland at their home venue of Warwick Place in Jesmond at the end of March. The game was played in 'splendid weather', and there was 'a large assemblage of spectators'. The kick-off was delayed owing to the late arrival of the Sunderland team, and it did not start until 3.35pm, over half an hour behind schedule.

Sunderland adopted a new formation with three half-backs and a single centre-forward. Tyne, however, played in the now traditional style of two half-backs and two centres. Both teams reportedly showed great determination, Sunderland having the wind in their favour in the first-half while Tyne had the advantage in the second. They made the most of the elements in that second period with centres Thomas Redmayne and Gilbert Ainslie hitting the ball past Sunderland 'keeper Stewart. In fact the Wearsiders' custodian kept Tyne at bay a number of times, with the local press noting that the 'score would have been greatly augmented had it not been for the excellent defence by the Sunderland goalkeeper, who was frequently applauded'. Summarising, the weekly chronicle *Football* recorded that Sunderland had 'several fair players in their team', but added, 'the balance are not very smart, and the Tyne had not much difficulty in winning'. Included in the Wearsiders' ranks was James Allan, one of the Sunderland club's founders.

The Northumberland & Durham Challenge Cup was a rousing success. Competitive football helped enormously in stimulating the development of the game, both from a playing point of view and from stirring the interest of spectators.

Apart from the new knock-out tournaments, in addition it had been also decided that 'teams composed of picked men of the various clubs in the association will play against other association teams'. County representative fixtures arrived onto the scene, which further helped progression. Challenge contests against other associations were arranged, with county caps and badges being awarded to the individuals selected. It was noted that the 'colours of the association are maroon', although not long after it was also described that they played in 'dark green and white'.

The first inter-region county match took place during February 1881 when a Northumberland & Durham side faced the neighbouring Cleveland Football Association XI in Middlesbrough. It was not a good day for the new joint-county select XI – they lost 10–0! Cleveland included all the stars of the Middlesbrough club, including Cleveland's captain Ewbank, as well as Booth and Cochrane. The teams for that first county game were:

Cleveland: Howcroft (Redcar); Fidler (Redcar), Bastard (Middlesbrough), Cochrane (Middlesbrough), Booth (Middlesbrough), Cruse (Redcar), Ewbank (Middlesbrough), Harrison (Redcar), Kelleher (South Bank), Dales (Middlesbrough), Pickstock (Middlesbrough).

V

Northumberland & Durham: Dodds (Haughton-le-Skerne), Michael (Corbridge), Singleton (Sunderland), Roberts, Warne, Hetherington (all Rangers), Ainslie (Tyne), Simms (Rangers), Summerson (Haughton-le-Skerne), Allan (Sunderland), Messent P.J. (Tyne).

Further games were arranged by the local association, but the combined county side generally found it hard going. They managed to enjoy an occasional success, including a 2–1 victory in a return match with the Cleveland side in Newcastle, but most encounters ended in defeat, often heavy.

The local association also did much to ensure a sensible umpiring regime was in place and administered the inevitable disputes which occurred in days before neutral referees evolved. With both competing sides having umpires – in the 1882 Northumberland & Durham Cup Final, Rangers nominated T.D. Challoner while Corbridge appointed M.R. Maguire – the third official, a referee, was Philip Messent of the Tyne club. There was at times friction between opponents when decisions went the wrong way. As could be expected, arguments and fall-outs were not uncommon, and it was not unheard of for a brawl to also develop after debatable verdicts were reached.

When Tyne met Rangers during December 1880 in the Northumberland & Durham Cup second round, fierce debate ensued after Tyne were awarded the tie 1–0 through a highly controversial goal. One umpire decided the goal was void, the other admitting that he could not see what had happened, but the referee gave the goal. An appeal was submitted to the Northumberland & Durham FA Committee who eventually ruled that the match should be declared a draw and replayed.

With the Northumberland & Durham Football Association guiding the sport in the opening years of the 1880s, football prospered in the North East. It was recorded in the weekly regional news column of *Football* that there had been an 'extraordinary growth of our winter pastime'. It was added: 'One of the most satisfactory signs was the increased popularity of the sport with the sight-seeing public. It is but a very few years ago that the pleasures of the game were confined to a select few, principally past or present public school boys, and it was practically unknown to the general public. Now, however, all is changed.'

The national newspaper went on to note that there had been 'an enormous advancement in the game, clubs being formed on all sides, and the public interest, as shown by the increased attendances at matches, also largely awakened'. It was added that in the region the 'number of clubs playing was estimated at over 40, nearly all of which played two teams, and most of the older clubs had juniors also playing under their names'. In 1882 the *Daily Journal* recorded that in Northumberland and Durham 'there are now between 50 and 60 association clubs'. There was exceptional progress.

Even the local newspapers and periodicals by then began to give the sport increased coverage and importantly were beginning to separate the rugby and association forms of the game. The *Northern Athlete* was particularly pro-football and gave much coverage of the pioneers. In 1883 the Tyneside magazine reproduced the recently updated *Laws of the Game* and *Definitions of Terms* in full, asking for 'all those who take an interest in the game to read them up'. The editorial added that in understanding them, players, officials and spectators could 'avoid many disputes that would otherwise occur'.

By the summer of 1883, in terms of development, football was in a healthy position in both County Durham and in Northumberland, although costs of travelling around the two counties were causing concern. To ease that burden the early rounds of the Challenge Cup had been split between the two separate counties to reduce travelling expense. Such was the confidence of further advancement being made that there was a local debate on whether each county should have their own separate organisation to foster the game further and reduce financial outlays.

Instrumental in the split of the Northumberland & Durham FA was Aleck Peters, captain of one of the new clubs on Tyneside, Newcastle Football Association. He published an open letter in the *Daily Journal* proposing separate Cup competitions for each county and received substantial support. As a result of the discussions that followed, it was decided at a gathering at the Crown Hotel in Newcastle that the two parties would break-up at the end of the 1882–83 season. It was a separation without acrimony. Even the debt held by the association was split without squabbles, the official minutes noting: 'Mr Robinson reported that he had succeeded in getting all the accounts squared up, which showed a loss of about £4, to be divided between the two associations.'

The two organisations moved quickly to create their own bodies. At a meeting at the Alexandra Hotel on Clayton Street in Newcastle on 11 May the Northumberland Football Association was set up. The association's first president was the Lord Bishop of Newcastle. Peters was one of the main players in the Northumberland Football

NORTH EAST FOOTBALL DEVELOPMENT

Fact Box

Key dates 2

November 1881:	Stanley FC (Newcastle United) formed in St Peter's, Byker.
August 1882:	Newcastle West End founded.
October 1882:	Stanley FC change their name to Newcastle East End.
May 1883:	Northumberland FA formed.
May 1883:	Durham FA formed.
April 1889:	Northern League created.
May 1890:	Sunderland FC elected to the Football League.
February 1890:	Newcastle East End decide to become a Limited Company.
April 1892:	Sunderland FC win the Football League Championship.
May 1892:	Newcastle West End fold due to financial difficulties.
May 1892:	Newcastle East End move to St James' Park.
December 1892:	Newcastle East End choose a new name, Newcastle United.
September 1893:	Newcastle United and Ironopolis play their first fixtures in the Football League.

Association's beginnings and one of the men who signed the original charter. He was appointed the first secretary while Alfred Harrison of Tyne and George Hall of Rangers were also signatories and influential officials, the latter becoming the first treasurer. It was noted that 26 associate clubs were registered at formation, with some 40 playing the game, and it was urged that these existing members use their influence to start 'new clubs in the various towns and villages where the game is unknown'.

Two weeks after the Northumberland FA's creation, the neighbouring Durham Football Association was founded on 25 May 1883 at the Three Tuns in Durham. Sunderland's Robert Singleton became the county's treasurer and Whitburn's Alfred Grundy secretary who was instrumental in calling the clubs together. It is noted that nine clubs were represented at the meeting: Sunderland, Birtley, Burnopfield, Castle Eden, Derwent Rovers, Hamsterley Rangers, Milkwell Burn, Stanley Star and Whitburn.

The original Northumberland & Durham Challenge Cup competition was dissolved, and two new tournaments were unveiled for the 1883–84 season: the Northumberland Challenge Cup and Durham Challenge Cup. Sunderland were to lift the first Durham Senior Cup, as it was to be known, defeating Darlington 2–0 in a replay at Birtley. That was a controversial first Final, Sunderland having an earlier victory ruled as 'void' following a series of complaints from the Darlington team and which took two meetings of the Durham FA to resolve. On the Monkwearmouth Old Cricket Ground before almost 2,500 spectators, the referee, the Durham FA secretary Grundy, had disallowed a Sunderland goal and also been threatened by three of the Wearside players during the game, as well as by spectators! The support, as the official Sunderland history relates, was over-zealous, fans having 'intimidated both the referee and visiting players'.

A request was made for Major Marindin of the FA to act as referee for the replay to make sure of fair play; however, it seems he could not appear and another eminent FA official, John Lewis of Blackburn, took control. Sunderland lifted the trophy nevertheless – or would have done had Durham had one to give to the victorious skipper. Somewhat embarrassingly, the local association did not have enough funds at the time to purchase an actual Senior Cup to present after the victory.

There were 22 teams enrolled for the first Northumberland Challenge Cup, and there was no pristine trophy to compete for either. They were all after the existing Northumberland & Durham Challenge Cup after it was declared that the Northumberland FA had paid the sum of £15 for the handsome-looking silver prize and ensured they would not have an awkward moment when the match was concluded as had happened to their Durham counterparts.

The ongoing spread of football by 1883 had been noticeable. Those 22 sides in Northumberland were located throughout most of the county:

Newcastle: Tyne, Rangers, North Eastern, East End, Newcastle FA A, Newcastle FA B, Jesmond, Heaton Association, Elswick Leather Works, All Saints, St Cuthberts, Marlborough, West End.

Tyne Valley: Prudhoe Rovers, Mickley Rangers, Newton, Ovingham, Ovington.

South East Northumberland: Bedlington Burdon, Hastings Rovers.

Rest of Northumberland: Alnwick, Rothbury.

Not surprisingly, the region's two best sides, Tyne and Rangers, coasted to the Final and met in the Northumberland FA's first showpiece at Warwick Place in Jesmond during March 1884.

This game followed the Second Team Competition Final when Sleekburn Wanderers defeated Heaton 4–1. That contest had kicked off after 2 o'clock. The senior Final followed at 4 o'clock, by which time a 'numerous attendance of enthusiastic spectators' had gathered, no doubt attracted by what was fine weather. The teams had met twice earlier in the season with Tyne winning 2–1 and drawing 1–1 so they were regarded as fairly evenly matched sides. The contest was described at the time as an 'intriguing game'. Tyne had the advantage of an early goal, taking the lead in only the second minute through Frank Messent. But Rangers came back to level the scores by half-time when J.D. Brown equalised. Tyne had the benefit of the wind in the second half, however, and eventually emerged as comfortable winners 4–1, with Philip Messent putting them in front 2–1, before captain Samborne and Pattinson made sure of victory. The two teams were:

Tyne: Simpson, Samborne, Webb-Ware, Sumpter, Ker, Watson, Messent (P.G.), Ainslie, Phillipson, Pattinson, Messent (F.E.).
V
Rangers: McColl, Douglas, McKernan, Campbell, Crawford, Hetherington, Brown, Simms, Lochhead, Hoban, Hardy.

All of the Tyne men played well, with Simpson, Philip Messent and Pattinson coming in for special praise. A few of Rangers' players also stood out – McColl, McKernan, Douglas, Campbell and Lochhead – but this was not enough to prevent the 'orange-and-black' team from winning and becoming the first holders of the new competition.

In Tyne's line up was George Webb-Ware, an Australian who was a graduate of Pembroke Cambridge, the same college that three of the Hitchcock brothers attended. He also went to Malvern College and was an outstanding sportsman at the public school. Later, Webb-Ware became an engineer working on the railways.

Rangers included a young rising star in Tommy Hoban, who impressed many. He was to gain several honours at local level and become a hugely popular character on Tyneside in the following decade, notably for Newcastle East End. The *Northern Athlete* magazine described Tommy as 'a flashy left wing, but far too fond of gallery play'.

Both of the Northumberland and Durham tournaments were great successes and both became the region's premier competitions. The Challenge Cup – or Senior Cup

– in each county is still competed for now, over 125 years later. The Northumberland FA structured four main competitions as they went forward:

- The Northumberland Football Association Challenge Cup, later known as the 'Senior Cup'.
- The Northumberland Football Association Charity Shield, a competition by invitation to 'the four best clubs in the county' with games taking place in Newcastle.
- A 'Second Team Competition', on the same basis as the Senior Cup.
- The Northumberland Football Association Junior Challenge Cup, for teams with players under the age of 17 years old.

Much the same happened south of the River Tyne as the Durham FA organised a pyramid of competitions as well. The two associations also decided for a period to contest an inter-county championship challenge, in which the Northumberland Challenge Cup winners would play the Durham Challenge Cup winners. For a time this became a big draw in the region, attracting crowds up to 5,000 for the honour of being unofficial champions of the North East. The first of what was intended to be an annual fixture was staged during April 1886 when Morpeth Harriers met Bishop Auckland Church Institute at the Tyne ground. The County Durham team proved their superiority with a comfortable 3–0 victory.

Another early competition organised – although not strictly a Northumberland FA tournament – was part of the booming Temperance Festival, an immense summer gathering on Newcastle's Town Moor. During the era it was an extremely popular event held during Race Week and was very much Tyneside's very own party. In 1883 the *Northern Athlete* magazine noted the attendance in excess of 200,000, with 100,000

Both of the region's FAs soon awarded county caps for appearing in representative fixtures; pictured are two Northumberland caps that have survived over a century.

programmes printed, containing the name of every competitor. Part of the multi-sporting programme of events was an end-of-season football competition for both seniors and juniors, the Temperance Festival Cup. Some of the region's top clubs took part, although preliminary round matches were played well before the festival itself, and they were not full-scale games, being only 20 minutes each way. But the prizes were an attraction. In the senior competition of 1883, for instance, the finalists received the following:

1st – 11 goal medals, each engraved with the name of the winning team (value: £11 11s 0d).
2nd – 11 travelling bags (value £5 15s 6d).
3rd – 11 silver pencils (value £4 4s 0d).
4th – 11 football requisites (value £3 3s 0d).

Rangers won the Final that year, defeating North Tyne Swifts after Derwent Rovers retired from the tournament, however, 1883 was more memorable as it was the year that East End won their first-ever trophy, winning the junior competition by beating Marlborough 1–0 in the Final after disposing of Hebburn 2–1 in the semi-final.

The following year's Tyneside Summer Festival gave Sunderland a Cup Final victory over the team that was to become their arch-rivals in the century and more that lay ahead when, in the 1884 senior Final, they defeated East End, 2–1. The Newcastle club, however, could have had an excuse as they had just played 20 minutes extra-time (following a game of 30 minutes each way) against North Eastern in their semi-final, while Sunderland had cruised through their contest against Rosehill, 3–0.

Separate county teams were now established, and a friendly rivalry between Northumberland and Durham began. The Northumberland FA's first county trial fixture took place in September 1883 when four teams of Northumberland Colts played a double-header to allow the county's selectors the opportunity to pick the best players for what would be the first county match to take place in November. Further Colt trial games were arranged against club sides Tyne and Rangers before the final XI was chosen to face the Cleveland Association side. There were few surprises in the final choice, with the district's two top sides, Rangers and especially Tyne, dominating selection with nine of the 11 players between them. Northumberland was captained by John Lochhead, and the sides were:

Northumberland: Douglas (Rangers), Samborne (Tyne), Lochhead (Rangers), Leonard (Prudhoe Rovers), Watson (Tyne), Messent F.E. (Tyne), Pattinson (Tyne), Ainslie (Tyne), Potter (Newcastle FA), Messent P.G. (Tyne), Hoban (Rangers).
V
Cleveland: Dawkins (Middlesbrough), Alvey (Redcar), Grant (Guisborough), Blackburne (St John's), Agar (Redcar), Simpson (Redcar), Thompson (Stockton), Bulman (Redcar), Cornish (Redcar), Pickstock (Middlesbrough), Pringle (Middlesbrough).

The Northumberland County line up for the fixture against Lancashire at St James' Park in 1887. Although the players are not identified, in the side and included on the group are early stalwarts Hoban, Duns, Oldham, Barker and Raylstone, as well as four Shankhouse players (Thompson, Hedley, Ritson and Matthews).

Northumberland fell heavily against the Teessiders, as had occurred when the original combined Northumberland & Durham side kicked-off, this time 8–0. The more experienced and developed Cleveland players were too good, with Stockton's Thompson and Redcar's Cornish doing the damage, scoring six goals between them. Northumberland's cause was not helped when Ainslie had to leave early to catch a train with the score at 4–0! The situation was exacerbated when Samborne was forced to retire with a twisted ankle when six goals down.

The county's colours are not recorded for their early matches, but it is established that they played in maroon-and-blue stripes, even once in chocolate and blue, although they later settled on a 'black-and-white striped jersey' as their chosen attire. This was after it was announced in November 1883 that their colours would be red and white and a full set of jerseys were purchased; however, after some debate it was agreed that the colours were not suitable for the association and the strips were sold to new members Acomb Rangers.

The following month the first Northumberland versus Durham contest took place. That match was much closer, Durham winning 4–3 but only after controversy over one of their goals. There was some doubt in the second half as to whether Northumberland had actually kicked-off, but Durham took possession, broke away and scored. Despite Northumberland's protests, the referee awarded the goal.

But soon afterwards, Northumberland took another hammering when they faced a strong Renfrewshire County side in January 1884. They lost by 10 goals before a crowd approaching 1,000 at Tyne's ground in Jesmond – not a bad attendance considering the game was played in stormy conditions. The county were forced to field a weakened team and included five players who were making their first appearance at this level while the Scots were at full strength. Nevertheless, the local press enthused, 'The spectators witnessed the finest exhibition of association play it has ever been our privilege to witness since the Scotch-Canadians side'. But Northumberland, and local football generally, still had some way to go to catch up to other areas in the country.

These heavy defeats apart, however, and looking at a more local level, substantial progress had been made in the district. The profile and steady growth in popularity of the association game had been striking. By 1882 and 1883 attendances gradually improved from a few hundred to over 2,000 on occasion for the big matches. In the years that followed during the decade spectators were to flock to what were then very basic enclosures around the region. By the end of the 1880s it was not uncommon for prestige fixtures to attract gates of between 5,000 and 8,000.

Some of the largest attendances were recorded for high-profile exhibition games which in part were sanctioned and organised by the two local Football Association bodies. In January 1886 the recently formed amateur combination The Corinthians visited Tyneside as part of their 'Northern Tour', the first of several visits in the coming years during the New Year festivities. Steadfastly amateur in their principals, the

The Corinthians line up in 1885–86, featuring many of the stars to visit Tyneside including Andrew Amos, who later appeared for Gateshead. Back row standing, left to right: Jackson, McKisson, Rendall, Holm, Spilsbury, Smith, Amos, Tepper, Saunders. Front, sitting: Watson, Pawson, Cobbold, Pellatt (front), Holden-White, Lindley. *(A. Mitchell archive)*

Corinthians had been formed in 1882, their original constitution stating that that club could only field amateur players and play in no competitions whatsoever. They were the standard-bearers of the old ideals, described as 'for all that is fine in amateurism'. Most of their members had an ex-public school and university background, with occupations such as headmasters, solicitors, barristers and bankers. Several had been involved in the pioneering years of the game, yet many of those members at the time were the very best footballers in the country, most England internationals, and some had been capped for their country at cricket and rugby too. As a consequence their tours around England over the coming years – and into the later Edwardian era – proved to be a big draw. They were noted as being 'the greatest and most attractive team that football had then known'.

The Corinthians side that faced a Newcastle & District XI in January 1886 was packed full of famous names, the proverbial star-studded combination. No fewer than eight present or future England internationals were in their ranks including eminent names such as William Cobbold, the 'Prince of Dribblers' as he was known, and Dr Tinsley Lindley, Nottingham Forest's well-known centre-forward of the time. There was also George Brann, a formidable winger; Charles Holden-White, the side's first captain; and Fred Dewhurst, who became one of Preston North End's famed 'Invincibles'. Ralph Squire was another England player, as were two reverends: Francis Pawson and Andrew Amos, who had during the era been based in Bishop Auckland and had played for the local Church Institute side and for one of the new clubs on Tyneside, Gateshead Association.

What could be termed then as a substantial crowd of 3,000 saw that first visit and witnessed an exhibition display on Tyne's ground by the amateur combination as they cruised to an 8–2 victory. The local select XI, captained by Alec White, could do little to halt such a talented side, although the Newcastle & District XI led 2–1 at half-time having had the advantage of a strong wind. Two East End players, D. Scott and William Muir, scored the goals for the local side only for the Corinthians to play to their full capabilities in the second half and win comfortably.

It was much the same story for the following year's meeting. The Corinthians this time breezed to a 5–0 win, and again their line up brought many a famous name to Tyneside, nine internationals being in their side on this occasion. The game, staged at St James' Park, drew another crowd of 3,000, this time establishing record gate receipts of £62.

There was an improvement by the locals for their next challenge as the New Year of 1888 was celebrated – a sign that the region's football was improving. This time a Northumberland XI took to the field. The Corinthians still won but only 3–1 at the Jesmond Athletic Ground. The change of venue saw a lower attendance than in previous years, with around 2,000 turning up.

With similar games taking place in County Durham, the appearance of the Corinthians did much to promote football in the region. So did the visit of two of the country's emerging clubs to Tyneside, Nottingham Forest and Preston North End, who both played exhibition contests with the Newcastle & District side at the end of April 1886 at Tyne's home in Jesmond. Nottingham Forest were one of the oldest clubs in the country, and while they did not field their two best players, goalkeeper Sam Widdowson and striker Tinsley Lindley, who had already impressed for The Corinthians at the beginning of the year, they still fielded another three England players: Edwin Luntley, Thomas Danks and John Leighton. They were far too good for the local side, winning 5–1 in front of a crowd of 1,200 at Warwick Place.

The following day Preston North End arrived at the same venue in Jesmond, and one of the largest crowds on Tyneside up to that point turned up to see a club which was to soon complete the very first FA Cup and Football League double. A gate of 4,000 was thrilled to see a team which would become the best in the country in the coming years. Fred Dewhurst returned to Tyneside after Corinthians duty, and he was joined by John Goodall, one of the most illustrious names in the game. Full-backs Bob Holmes and Bob Howarth were to become prominent players for Preston and England too, while up front four notable Scots took the field: Jimmy Ross, nicknamed 'The Little Demon' and who scored eight times in Preston's 26–0 FA Cup thrashing of Hyde United in 1887, his elder brother Nick Ross, as well as Jack Gordon and George Drummond. All would have been regular Scottish international players had it not been for an Anglo-Scot controversy at the time which halted the international career of many notable players. While Preston, unsurprisingly, won, the scoreline of 3–1 gave the Tyneside side heart for the future. They were not totally outgunned by the illustrious line up from Lancashire. Afterwards the stars of Preston were 'entertained at Mr Murray's Duke of Northumberland' on Clayton Street in the city.

A major step forward took place nationally in 1888 when recognition among the leading English clubs that some sort of competitive programme of games was needed on a regular basis to halt the sometimes unorganised and unscheduled excess of friendlies. Championed by Scot, William McGregor, who said at the time: 'The lax and loose system which prevailed became intolerable.' This resulted in the formation of the Football League. Meetings were held during March of that year, and during April at the Royal Hotel in Manchester's Piccadilly a formula of home and away fixtures for points was agreed. This resulted in a League table and new Championship trophy for the best club with the most number of points, as well as a re-election system for the least successful.

When the first set of Football League fixtures was played on 8 September 1888, there were six Midland clubs and six Lancashire teams in the League of 12 sides: Aston Villa, Wolverhampton Wanderers, West Bromwich Albion, Derby County, Notts County, Stoke, Preston North End, Blackburn Rovers, Bolton Wanderers, Accrington, Everton and Burnley. The new format proved a tremendous success, with Preston becoming the first champions.

In the North East, fixtures were still restricted to friendlies and the local association knock-out tournaments, although the FA Cup competition by then had introduced a new Qualifying Competition which involved several of the region's clubs. The local governing body, however, also had to contend with an internal crisis when several clubs from north of Tyneside made a stand over how the organisation was run and formed a breakaway group, the Northern Association.

OLDEST CLUBS ON TYNESIDE

Tyne Association FC:	1877
Newcastle Rangers FC:	1878
North Eastern FC:	1879
Corbridge FC:	1879
Newcastle FA:	1880
Ovingham FC:	1880
Stanley FC (Newcastle East End/United):	1881
Ovington FC:	1881
Elswick Leather Works FC:	1881
Rendel FC:	1881

These militant teams were unhappy at the way the Tyneside clubs seemed to dominate the association, and their grievances built up. Morpeth Harriers seemed to be the biggest name to side with the rebels but, even then, the country clubs had little telling clout. But the breakaway became a reality when the comparatively powerful Shankhouse Black Watch club also fell out with the local FA.

The catalyst came when a controversial decision surrounded the Final of the association's Second Team competition at Blyth between East End Swifts and Shankhouse Second XI. There were only six minutes of the game remaining when the crowd 'encroached on the field of play'. The pitch invasion resulted in the match being abandoned. The Northumberland FA decreed that the last six minutes of the game would have to be played but that Shankhouse would have to come to Newcastle to play them. The venue chosen was probably a reflection on the consensus view that it had been the Shankhouse supporters who had 'encroached' as their team was trailing 1–0 at the time. Shankhouse denied that the miscreants had been their supporters and suggested that the full game should be replayed. When the Northumberland FA confirmed their decision, Shankhouse decided to throw in their lot with the rebels, who then felt strong enough to set up a rival body.

They had considerable support, with some 26 clubs backing them. East End and West End, however, retained their affiliation to the original association; although the St James' Park club held a meeting in September 1888 to consider withdrawing from the Northumberland FA and joining the rival body. In the end they decided to remain with the official association 'for the time being'.

Initially all went well for the new organisation. A patron financially supported them by guaranteeing expenditure up to £200 to buy trophies, medals and shields to allow them to set up their own competitions. This they did – for the senior teams and reserve XIs. They even staged a trial match to enable them to select a representative Northern Association team – North of the county v the South. The former included players from Amble, Spittal, Longhirst, Morpeth Harriers, Tweedside Wanderers, Broomhill and

Belford, while the latter predominately comprised Shankhouse players, although there were also representatives from Burradon, Bedlington, Seaton Burn and Weetslade. It seemed as if the association were trying to include as many teams as possible in their selection.

But their enterprise was doomed to failure – largely because the national Football Association (probably influenced by the Northumberland FA) refused to recognise them and therefore prevented them from playing against other associations. In effect, they had little long-term choice – either stagnate or return to the parent body. The schism did have some effect insofar as the Northumberland FA realised that feelings ran high among the dissenting clubs and that matters had to be resolved. Within a couple of years all of the clubs were back under the parent body's umbrella again.

In the same year as the Football League was in full swing another rival League competition was also formed, The Combination. But it was not a success and quickly disbanded while, a year later in 1889, the Football Alliance was established as another challenger, noted in some quarters as an 'unofficial second division' to the Football League. It fared little better, however, being only marginally more successful than The Combination. The Football Alliance lasted three years before giving way to the undoubted success of the Football League and the introduction of a second tier.

At this time another factor was at the top of everyone's agenda in the game, one which was to make a big impact on how the game developed. There was a sometimes bitter quarrel over the principle of payment for playing football. Up to 1885 the laws of the game outlawed payment apart from reimbursement of out-of-pocket expenses. Nevertheless, illegal cash handouts were rife in the sport, and most knew it. In July 1885, following much debate between the amateur and payment camps, professionalism was legalised in England and accepted under the Football Association's rules. And by the time the game had been captured by the industrial working class all over the country, the amateur ideals were destined for a much lower grade of football. The game moved rapidly from a 'gentleman's sport' to the 'people's game'.

On the other side of the Scottish border, however, payments were still controversially outlawed. And that meant, for some time to come, many a Scot headed across the Tweed towards Tyneside and Wearside to earn a 'legal' pound or two. Included in that number were some notable international stars who pulled on the shirts of local teams as they developed a step further.

Payment levels varied considerably at first. Some players were paid by the match or weekly, and most were part-time, with some having occupations linked to club officials at their place of business or their factory, for example. Top players received up to 7s 6d (37½p) a week with a 2s 6d (12½p) win bonus. By 1890 the ranked clubs on Tyneside – Newcastle East End and Newcastle West End – were paying their best men as much as 'ten shillings each win and 7s 6d a draw or loss'.

As a result of the rapid advance of the game and a new breed of clubs, and especially the introduction of professionalism, the pioneering organisations were left behind. Clubs like The Wanderers, Royal Engineers, Old Etonians and Old Carthusians who did much to lead the way were replaced by Blackburn Rovers, Aston Villa, West Bromwich Albion

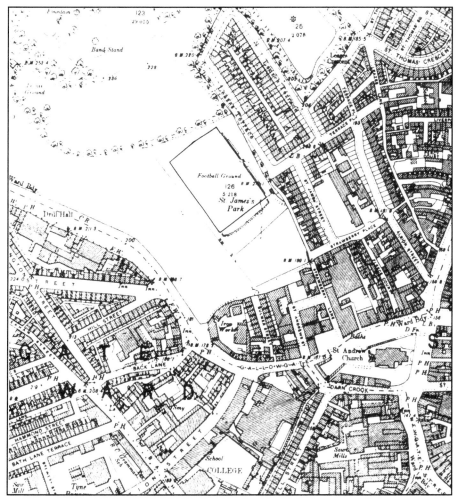

St James' Park was to become Tyneside's principle football venue, situated on the edge of the town centre and originally part of Castle Leazes.

and Preston North End, clubs which went on to dominate the early years of what was rapidly becoming a professional game.

On a different scale this also occurred on Tyneside, with both the Tyne and Rangers clubs overtaken by two sides who took on the mantle of professionalism, Newcastle East End and Newcastle West End. Elsewhere in the region, both Middlesbrough and Sunderland matured, especially so on Wearside where the Sunderland club was to rapidly join the likes of Preston and Aston Villa as one of the country's elite. The Boro stuck staunchly to their amateur values for some while.

Before all that occurred, the two trailblazing Newcastle clubs had forged a great rivalry, with Rangers eventually overtaking Tyne to become the stronger outfit. By this time Rangers had moved from their original home pitch in Gateshead to a new ground in the heart of Newcastle. They were planning to base themselves at Graingerville, off the West

The classical Leazes Terrace was the splendid backdrop of Victorian football at St James' Park. The present-day concrete and steel structure of Newcastle United's East Stand is built where the tree is pictured in the foreground.

Road, but then in September 1880 they had the opportunity of moving to a more favoured site on Castle Leazes close to Richard Grainger and Thomas Oliver's finely designed Leazes Terrace. They obtained a short-term lease on what could only be called a patch of grazing land. The local press recorded the event simply: 'A suitable field has this year been obtained in Newcastle.' Rangers called the ground St James' Park – after the nearby St James' Street – and it was quickly to become the most important venue on Tyneside and what is now the oldest football stadium in the North East, and one of the oldest remaining in the country, and it is still, of course, played on by Newcastle United today.

The Castle Leazes is an area of the city's vast Town Moor reserved in ancient times for grazing and haymaking. 'Leazes' derives from 'to gather the hay crop' – and was, and still is, owned and managed by the Freemen and the Corporation, leased out under very restricted uses from time to time. Importantly, the Freemen were generally supportive of recreational enclosures on the Town Moor, developments which were allowed by their charter. This included sport and football. It was noted in a guidebook of the time that Castle Leazes was a 'fine tract of pasture land and is much frequented by football clubs and cricketers and affords ample scope for the juvenile population for games and pastimes'.

The site of St James' Park is in close proximity to Newcastle's centre just outside the old town walls, on Barrack Road and Gallowgate leading into the Newgate area. The neighbourhood had been something of a 'genteel resort' around the strawberry fields close by, but, as the industrial growth of the town took place, much of the calm and tranquillity of the area vanished; although a peaceful spot could still be found in the

Victorian Leazes Park, sited to the north of the new football enclosure, while dwellings around Leazes Terrace and St Thomas' were decidedly up-market and stylish. But to the south it was a different matter. Breweries, tanneries and undertakers were now housed nearby the site, as were an abattoir, slate yards, lead works, livery stables, a smokery and a tripe proprietor. The Gallowgate wash-house and baths were a goal-kick away too.

St James' Park was also close to the site of the old execution gallows. In 1844, only 36 years before football was played on the site, the last hanging took place there when a certain Mark Sherwood of Blandford Street was led to the gallows in front of the elegant Leazes Terrace for the murder of his wife.

While football was more than likely played on Castle Leazes in an unorganised fashion before Rangers moved in, the first organised game took place on 16 October 1880 when the Rangers Captain's XI took on an Others side which contained 15 players! The *Daily Journal* recorded the event:

'Rangers club inaugurated their new ground close to Leazes Terrace on Saturday by a match between the 1st team against 15 of Others. After a very pleasant game of two hours it was found the Captain's team was victorious over his numerous but less experienced opponents to the extent of six goals to one. Some of the new members showed good form and with a little more expertise will prove valuable additions to the club. The new ground is very nicely situated and is close to the centre of town. It is 120 yards x 60 yards broad and is comparatively level.'

There was a touch of journalistic licence in the newspaper report, as the site actually had a pronounced fall of some 18ft from the north to south goal. Although subsequent ground improvements at St James' have levelled the pitch off significantly, part of the original slope can still be seen in the concrete and steel arena that is the modern St James' Park. Three weeks later, on 6 November, the first proper match took place when Rangers entertained Corbridge. The opposition had only 10 men but were still too good for the home side, Rangers losing 2–1 after 80 minutes of play. Rangers, though, found St James' Park to their liking in the 1880–81 season and scored plenty of goals in the process. Their headquarters was noted as 'Strawberry House, 78 St James' Park [sic, Street]'. Rangers remained at St James' Park until the end of the 1881–82 season when they moved to another pitch at Dalton Street in Byker.

Rangers tested themselves against better-quality opposition when they faced a Queen's Park XI in December 1882. Such was the prestige of the visit by Scotland's high-ranking club that it was noted that the majority of 'the association matches in the district have been put off to allow the players seeing the game'. Conditions were not good, with ice and frost widespread, but that did not deter 2,000 from turning up to watch the club who were termed 'Champions of Scotland'. Indeed, it was noted at the same time that 'curling and skating were being indulged in another part of the town'. There was doubt that the game should be played, but the two teams agreed to go ahead, and Rangers received a football lesson by the Glasgow side, who won at a canter 4–0 without fielding their first XI. It was noted that Rangers had a handicap, having to play with only 10 men throughout owing to one of their half-backs, Brown (the vice-captain), missing a train.

Despite being somewhat outclassed, Rangers did impress at times, a sign that their development as a football club was on course. One scribe at the contest wrote 'White at half and Lochhead at full-back were very good and their strong defensive play against such odds was much to be admired.' The Scottish correspondent in *Football* recorded 'The smart passing and sure tackling of the Queen's Park youngsters proved rather too much for the Newcastle club, who played pluckily to the last and are highly pleased with the exhibition they received of the dribbling game.' Alec White in fact was gaining much praise for his performances. In one match with Alnwick, a 6–0 victory, one of the goals came by way of a mesmerising run by the Rangers player. He dribbled nearly the length of the field past several Alnwick players to score.

Rangers' progress as a football club, however, came to an abrupt end less than two years later. Although at the club's Annual General Meeting during May 1884 Rangers were described as being in 'a healthy state', from contemporary records they do not appear to have played after October. There is no trace of any other matches in the local press. It is not noted why they ran into difficulties, but nine months later on 9 August 1885 secretary and treasurer F.W. Hardy formally advised the Northumberland FA of the winding up of the club. Financially they had the grand sum of one guinea in hand.

Rivals Tyne Association continued for a while longer, but not as the force they once were. Rangers had already surpassed them and professionalism, along with the tide of the new working-class clubs, overcame the public-school and amateur principles. The local newspaper noted that they had closed down in November 1886, yet remnants of the club kept going – they are recorded as having played West End in the Northumberland Challenge Cup as 1887 began. Soon afterwards Tyne were no more.

By the time both Tyne and Rangers had folded they had played a large part in the development of football on Tyneside and in the North East – at their peak being able to take on and challenge both Middlesbrough and Sunderland. They were undoubtedly the

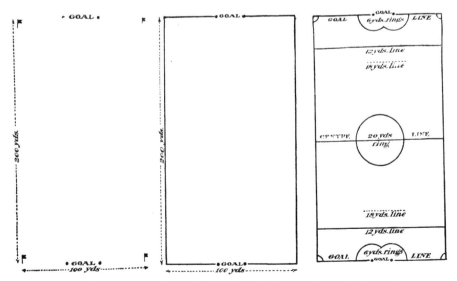

How the football field developed from 1869 (left) to 1883 (centre) and 1892 (right).

pathfinders and shaped the road for others to follow. Rangers were the first winners of the combined Northumberland & Durham Challenge Cup in 1881 and triumphed again in 1882. Tyne were winners of the last trophy in 1883 and of the first Northumberland Challenge Cup in 1884. Jointly they dominated the first four years of competitive football in the region.

With Tyne and Rangers destined to memory, football's development moved apace. With the success of the Football League on a national scale – albeit restricted to certain areas of the country to start with – there was soon talk of organising a local league in the North East. The vast majority of sides in the region were not yet developed enough to have a crack at the Football League or Football Alliance, although both Sunderland and a new breakaway club, Sunderland Albion, did have such aspirations and soon made bids to join football's elite. The mainstream, though, was content for the time being to remain in the local domain.

In March 1889, at a meeting at the Three Tuns Hotel in Durham, steps were taken to establish the region's first league competition by inviting 19 clubs from both Northumberland and County Durham for discussion. Charles Craven, the secretary of Darlington FC, was the driving force behind the concept, but only seven attended on the day – Morpeth Harriers, East End, West End, Sunderland, Sunderland Albion, Stockton and Middlesbrough. Subsequently, a second gathering took place on 2 April at the North Eastern Hotel in Darlington when, again, seven clubs attended, although not the same ones as had attended the earlier meeting. Morpeth Harriers had opted out due to the fact that most of the clubs would be in the south of the region and travelling would be prohibitive, and both of the Sunderland clubs refused to commit themselves. The second meeting saw East End, West End, Elswick Rangers, Darlington, Auckland Town, Stockton and Middlesbrough turn out and, despite the mediocre attendance, it was agreed that a Northern League would be formed. Eventually 10 clubs enrolled for the first Northern League season which included, by 1889, several sides that had become established and had taken over from the pathfinders, Tyne and Rangers. They were: Darlington St Augustine's, Stockton, Darlington, Middlesbrough, South Bank, Newcastle East End, Newcastle West End, Auckland Town, Birtley and Elswick Rangers. Most of the credit for the formation of the competition goes to Darlington's Charles Craven, a Derbyshire civil engineer who settled in the region, who became the first secretary. Middlesbrough's Albert Borrie was appointed the first chairman.

The Northern League saw its very first fixtures played on 7 September 1889, with three matches scheduled. Birtley defeated Elswick Rangers 4–1, but afterwards a protest was lodged by Elswick and the result was logged as a 'draw'. South Bank scored three without reply against Auckland Town, and on Tyneside Newcastle East End – becoming a new force then – beat Darlington 2–1 in front of a crowd recorded at between 1,500 and 3,000. It was noted in the account that the attendance 'proved that the game is becoming more and more popular every season'. The first champions were Darlington St Augustine's, but only by a whisker – on goal average, with Newcastle West End finishing on the same points. Just like the respective Northumberland and Durham Challenge Cup competitions, the Northern League was a success and had a significant influence on the development of the game in the region.

Other Leagues followed. In the same year, the short-lived North East Counties League was also formed, a rival to the Northern League. Their competition started for the 1889–90 campaign but was very much a second tier to the Northern League, Whitburn being the first champions. The 10 clubs that took part in that inaugural season were: Barnard Castle, Port Clarence, Bishop Auckland Church Institute, Rendel, Morpeth Harriers, Shankhouse Black Watch, West Hartlepool, Gateshead NER, Whitburn and Redcar.

Regional League football was on the map and prospered, giving the game competitive edge. Soon other competitions followed, with the Northern Alliance replacing the North East Counties tournament for the 1890–91 season. In that first campaign only seven clubs were represented: Gateshead NER, Elswick Rangers, Rendel, Bishop Auckland, Birtley, Sunderland A and Whitburn.

However, the Northern Alliance soon became the region's second-tier competition behind the Northern League, and membership quickly more than doubled. The Alliance's first secretary was Tom Watson, while Joseph Wardropper was an influential figure too. Both individuals were noteworthy characters on Tyneside in those early years. Watson, as we will see, became one of the most respected administrators at the very top of club football, while Wardropper was the flag-bearer of the Rendel club in Benwell. During the opening years of League action, Sunderland's second XI dominated proceedings, being crowned champions five times in the first six years. The Northern Alliance is still competed for today, well over a century later.

The football pyramid had started to evolve – and it is still a hugely successful system today. At the top, the FA Cup competition was the showpiece, now with regional qualifying stages. Each county association around England had their own Challenge Cup tournaments also, usually in two or three age groups. A league structure was headed by the Football League, with a Second Division from 1892. Local leagues prospered in each association, typically with an unofficial 'first tier', as in Northumberland and County

Fact Box

FIRST NORTHERN LEAGUE, 1889–90

	P	W	D	L	Pts
Darlington St Augustine's	18	12	2	4	26
Newcastle West End	18	12	2	4	26
Stockton	18	10	4	4	24
Newcastle East End	18	9	3	6	21
Darlington	18	7	6	5	20
Middlesbrough	18	8	3	7	19
South Bank	18	6	2	10	14
Auckland Town	18	4	4	10	12
Birtley	18	3	3	12	9
Elswick Rangers	18	2	5	11	9

The Three Tuns Hotel in Durham city, where the Northern League competition was initially discussed. The establishment is still a hotel today.

Durham in the shape of the Northern League, backed by lower-status Leagues such as the North East Counties League, Northern Alliance and Wearside League. More followed as the number of clubs increased. The Tyneside Football League, as well as the East Tyne League and West Tyne League catered for smaller clubs. Similar competitions were also created on both Wearside and Teesside. It was the shape of football to come.

The furthest outpost of the Football Association in Northumberland and County Durham had created a sound and stable infrastructure that allowed the game of football to thrive. There was now a rapidly growing interest in football – the hotbed had taken shape. While Tyne and Rangers had fallen by the wayside, during the 1880s football in the North East flourished, with a multitude of new teams being formed, including two clubs on either side of the community of Newcastle who were to take over the mantle of the pathfinders and develop the game to its next stage.

Chapter 4

STANLEY, ROSEWOOD & EAST END

'East End was bidding fair to improve considerably in public support, and displaying more enterprise than the Tyne or Rangers had ever attempted.'
The Book of Football, 1905

For many years there was a misconception that Newcastle United came about as a result of an amalgamation of two clubs – Newcastle East End and Newcastle West End. Indeed, for a time, some football record and history books promoted this fallacy – and fallacy is what it was, although perhaps an understandable one. The impression arose because, by the early 1890s, the two rivals had emerged as the pre-eminent clubs in the city. In 1892, East End moved their headquarters the two miles or so from Heaton across the city to St James' Park, which had hitherto been West End's home ground. The former Byker club seemed to subsume their West End rivals to a certain degree by not only taking over the lease to their ground but also adopting their reserve side, as well as co-opting a number of West End directors on to its board. So when, within a few months, the newly relocated club decided to change its name from East End to Newcastle United, it seemed as if both sides of the city had combined into one football club. In fact, they had – but it was because West End had ceased to exist and that East End had taken over. There was no formal merger.

The roots of both clubs go back to a decade earlier, and they had similar births. Both were formed from two cricket teams – one named Stanley from the Byker and St Peter's area in the east end of Newcastle, and the other West End which, as the name suggests, was located west of the town centre.

When the fledgling clubs were formed, Tyne and Rangers were still the principal sides in Newcastle. Both of the original pathfinders, however, were to fall by the wayside during the mid-1880s, and there were to be a number of contenders for supremacy, with East End and West End eventually emerging from this struggle for survival. East End became the stronger of the two in the end, evolving eventually into Newcastle United.

Tyne and Rangers, the first association teams on Tyneside, had arisen from rugby and cricket clubs. East End and West End were to develop from the summer game only. Both clubs were to see the light of day from two local cricket teams, although in East End's case it was from a club called Stanley, so named because they played on a field near Stanley

Street in the south end of Byker, in the area known as St Peter's, just over a mere cricket-ball slog from the Tyne.

So Byker is where Newcastle United originated and developed. It is therefore an important place in the club's annals. Byker has a long history, going back to Roman times when Hadrian's Wall, on its way from Segedunum (Wallsend) to Pons Aelius (Newcastle) topped the eminence of what eventually became known as Byker Hill. The name Byker is derived from Norse: *By* meaning a farmstead or small settlement, and *ker* relating to a marsh; thus Byker means a settlement by a marsh (or possibly marshy woodland).

Situated on a hill overlooking Newcastle, the ancient village was held by Nicholas de Byker. In 1340, it is recorded that John de Byker held the Manor and 'as much land as can be tilled in a year by one plough together with 100 acres of woodland'. Then, of course, Byker was an agricultural area separate from Newcastle. Gradually it developed from a small village surrounded by farms into the Township of Byker, which comprised Byker Village and the villages of St Peter's, Dents Hole, St Anthony's and Ouseburn. The narrow valley of the Ouseburn effectively cut Byker off from Newcastle, while the latter was so remote that it was by-passed by the worthy denizens of Byker who indulged in wool smuggling with Gateshead.

But Newcastle was casting eyes to the east and, in 1549, expanded its boundaries to take in the ballast shores of Byker. Coal-mining opened up in the 18th century while the community still retained its independence from Newcastle and by 1801 could boast a population of 3,254. This increased dramatically as the century advanced, but Byker itself was to undergo an even greater and more radical change.

By 1825, all of the collieries in the Byker area had closed, the pitmen moving north to the mining villages of Benton, Killingworth and Backworth (which were still operating pits). By this time the expanding industries of Byker were in glass, pottery and shipbuilding. Indeed, as early as 1808, Rowe's Shipyard in St Peter's was the largest on the Tyne.

Newcastle extended its boundaries to absorb Byker in 1835, and from that point onwards the former Township effectively became a suburb of Newcastle and came directly under the control of its big brother. Industrial development was inevitable, although it did not really come about until the advent of the railways. The Newcastle to North Shields railway opened in 1839, crossing a new Ouseburn Viaduct that bridged the Ouseburn valley. The line east of the viaduct more or less followed the boundary between Byker and the small village of Heaton. It was not long before a branch line was opened to give access to the south side of Byker with stations at Byker Platform, St Peter's and Walker (then another small village to the east). This Riverside line (opened in 1879) was the catalyst for change in south Byker, attracting heavy industry and its concomitant workforce.

By 1851, the population of Byker stood at 7,040. Within 10 years it was up to 13,000 and after a further 20 years to 30,500; although a significant part of the increase was due to an increase in the size of the civil parish. By the turn of the century, however, it was to grow further to 45,460, and by then Byker looked nothing like the village of 100 years before.

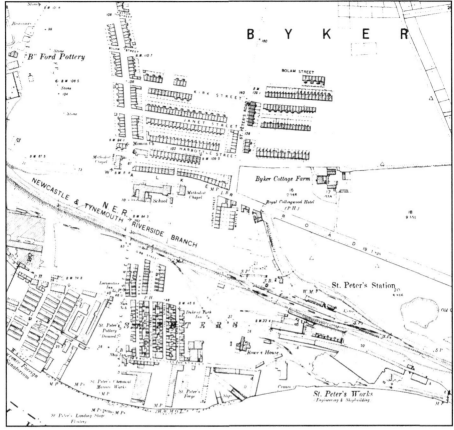

The St Peter's area alongside the Tyne during the 1880s. Newcastle United's origins are found around Stanley Street on Walker Road, opposite the school and chapel. Byker and Heaton lie to the north.

The closing decades of the 19th century saw the glass and pottery trade begin to decline to be replaced by heavy industry in the shape of shipyards and engineering works. Major employers included the Parsons site at the top of Byker. These were supported by ancillary industries, particularly for the shipbuilding sector in the shape of ships' chandlers, smiths, block and mast-makers as well as painters. This growth resulted in a steady development of residential areas to house the workforce. By the closing decades of the century the former sites of Byker Ropery, Lawson Main Pit, Byker Mill and the St Lawrence Chemical Works were all redeveloped for housing.

Away from the river front, however, much of Byker was still agricultural, with windmills dotting the landscape, but even that was changing. Byker Bridge opened as a toll bridge in 1878 and by 1885 R.J. Charleton in his book *Newcastle Town* was able to write: 'from the top of Byker Bank to Byker Hill we have one of the most remarkable illustrations of the recent growth of the area. A few years ago, the road (Shields Road) ran between open fields; now it runs through the middle of a new town'. Charleton called Byker 'that new suburb of Newcastle' and a 'new crowded town'. Another text published in 1889 recorded that 'Byker, which a few years ago consisted only of a few scattered houses, now forms in a measure a town of itself'. Byker had irretrievably changed.

The workers who grafted away in the engineering works, shipyards and other industries needed something to take their minds off the daily grind of the workday. Obviously some drank, hence the profusion of pubs in the area, and others gambled. But some wanted fresh air, and sporting recreation fulfilled their need. One of the chosen sports adopted was cricket. This had emerged as a favoured sporting and recreational pastime on Tyneside in the 1860s and grew steadily during the following decade as more and more men found that they had leisure time at weekends. As early as July 1870, a William Coulson played for Newcastle against Sunderland, scoring 10 runs out of the Tynesiders' total of 111, with Sunderland amassing a mere 45. The name William Coulson was to become a key one in the foundation of Stanley Football Club, although there is no definite evidence that the cricket player from 1870 was the same man; however, the indications are that he could have been.

As the 1870s progressed, a number of cricket teams sprouted up throughout the North East, many of them on Tyneside. Some cricket clubs branched out into other sports. In 1876 North Durham Cricket Club announced that they were forming a football club (albeit rugby), by which time they already had members playing quoits and lacrosse. But cricket was pre-eminent as a summer participation sport. In the same year, Tynemouth Cricket Club could claim to have 272 members, a clear reflection on the popularity of the game.

By the summer of 1877, cricket clubs existed in Gosforth, Wallsend, Benwell, Elswick, West Denton, Walbottle and Ryton, as well as one representing Newcastle itself and also the West End of the conurbation. The Town Moor was a popular venue for some of these teams.

By the following year, more clubs in and around the North East had emerged. It is recorded that the Newcastle Cricket Club then played their home games on a new field next to Abbotsford Terrace, at Brandling Village, and the Northumberland Rugby Club played some of their home matches at the same venue. Northumberland Cricket Club, of course, had their home ground in Bath Road near the centre of Newcastle.

By the summer of 1878, association football was taking its initial faltering steps on Tyneside in the guise of Tyne Association FC. At the same time William Coulson was serving on the committee of the Newcastle Cricket Club, and he presided over the annual meeting of the side at the Queen's Head Hotel on Pilgrim Street, Newcastle, during May. He was pleased to report that the club had won 10 of its 14 matches during the previous season, losing only three games.

However, a new cricket club was to arrive on the scene in the St Peters' area of South Byker, and this was called Stanley Cricket Club, as their home field was located near Stanley Street (which was, effectively, a section of Walker Road). Charleton's contemporary history of the city describes the birthplace of Newcastle United Football Club:

'St Peter's – a smoke-blackened district of narrow streets, with here and there detached dwellings, which have evidently known better days. A dusty, scrubby place it is, and it is hard to imagine it as, little more than two score years ago, being a pretty little village, with a sloping shore covered with bushes to the water's edge, with trim gardens and orchards, and houses inhabited by well-to-do and even wealthy people.'

It may have been 'dusty' and 'scrubby', but it was where the origins of the club now so passionately supported on Tyneside originated. Charleton notes St Peter's is really 'Sir Peter's key', a wharf so-called from having been leased by Newcastle Corporation to Sir Peter Riddell and corrupted over time to St Peter's.

In the early part of the 19th century the area was noted for its earthenware trade, but it was also somewhat notorious for the manure and fertilizer works close by which used mountains of animal carcasses; bones, blood and general refuse from slaughter-houses. The smell and vista was far from pleasant. At the eastern end of the village, shipbuilding was prevalent and booming as the century moved on; the T & W Smith, later Hawthorn Leslie, yard being prominent. Just across the river in Gateshead were the extensive Friars Goose Chemical Works, the Newcastle Chemical Company's Works and the Tyne Alkali Works.

Whether the location of Stanley's cricket field as well as the first football pitch was conducive to the enjoyment of fresh air is open to conjecture. One can just imagine the atmosphere on a pleasant sunny Saturday afternoon, playing cricket or football with a warm southerly breeze wafting the aroma over the playing field, especially if the tide was low on the Tyne which many regarded as an open sewer at the time and for many decades afterwards.

The environment of the area was to deteriorate further over the next decade or so with the closure of the local bottle factory and the expansion of the existing plants into the St Peter's Chemical and Manure Works as well as further development of the Tyne Manure and Chemical Works not so far away. Between these two stood the comparatively fragrant St Lawrence Foreign Cattle Sanatorium, with the excrement which undoubtedly resulted. The stench must have been overpowering, although by then, thankfully, the cricket club had folded and the resultant football club had moved away from the riverside.

Yet, in 1880, Stanley Cricket Club prospered and played games against other local teams such as St Anthony's, Royal Oak and Beaumont. A year later they were facing the likes of St Anthony's Royal Tyro, Gateshead Wanderers and – perhaps significantly for future years – Rosewood. These were merely friendly fixtures and were usually low scoring. The standard was not very high, possibly because the playing fields were precisely that – fields and not high-quality prepared wickets that are common even in village cricket today.

These cricket games were largely social gatherings and extended to activities off the field as well as on it. On 14 November 1881, the cricket club held its second annual concert in a packed Leighton Schoolroom at the Byker end of Heaton Road near its junction with Shields Road. Although there is no formal record of any discussions that took place that day, it is possible that the subject of the emerging game of association football was debated.

Less than two weeks later (on 24 November 1881), the annual meeting of the Stanley Cricket Club was held at the house of a Mr Allan in Shields Road, Byker. There has been some conjecture regarding who this Mr Allan was and why the meeting was held at his

THE GROWTH OF EAST END I

Timetable of Development

November 1881:	Stanley FC formed, playing at South Byker.
August 1882:	Stanley affiliated with Northumberland & Durham FA.
October 1882:	Stanley changes name to East End FC.
Late 1882:	Rosewood FC merge with East End.
January 1883:	First competitive game v Elswick Leather Works (N&D Challenge Cup).
June 1883:	First trophy success – Temperance Festival Junior Cup.
August 1883:	Home ground now behind Byker Vicarage.
November 1883:	First game v Sunderland (lost 0–3).
November 1883:	First game v West End (drew 1–1).
August 1884:	Move to Dalton Street, Byker.
January 1885:	First competitive victory v Elswick Leather Works (Northumberland Cup).
March 1885:	First senior trophy – Northumberland Cup (1–0 v Sleekburn Wanderers).
April 1885:	Win Northumberland Charity Shield (10–0 v Newcastle Association).

residence. Unfortunately no record exists detailing who attended the meeting. Census information for 1881 points to Thomas Allan who kept a confectioner's shop near to where St Mark's Church was to be later built near the top of the area known as Byker Hill. Thomas had been born in Heworth in 1844 and was therefore 37 years old at the time of the meeting. He had been a blacksmith in Headlam Street (near Shields Road) but had changed his trade to take over his wife's confectionery shop in Shields Road not long before the meeting.

It was reported that the cricket club was in a very prosperous state. The meeting also saw the election of the principal officers for the following season: William Coulson (captain), James Bell (vice-captain), William Findlay (secretary) and Joseph Simpson (treasurer). All of these gentlemen were to play key roles in the foundation of the football club that was to become, in 12 years hence, Newcastle United. There must have been discussion on expanding the club's sporting activities – and forming a football club.

Early Northumberland FA archives suggest that Stanley may have been founded in 1880 (or earlier), but some of the dates in these records were entered years after the actual events to which they refer and are somewhat suspect. Press reports in 1881 were adamant that the Stanley club did not formally come into existence until November that year and that the club's inaugural football match (against Elswick Leather Works 2nd XI) took place on 26 November 1881 – two days after the meeting at Allan's house. Without doubt it can be stated that Stanley Association Football Club (and therefore Newcastle United) was founded in November 1881.

The two sides for this historic first game lined up in tactical formation as follows:

STANLEY (2–2–6):
Goal: T.S. Phalp.
Backs: J. Hobson, J. Gardner.
Half-backs: A. Marr, J. Armstrong.
Forwards: J.P. Cook, R. Findlay, W. Coulson, W. Findlay, G. McKenzie, J. Dixon.
V
ELSWICK LEATHER WORKS 2ND XI (2–3–5):
Goal: J. Thompson.
Backs: C. Stratton, J. Whittaker.
Half-backs: P. Blaids, T. Thompson, W. Davison.
Forwards: M. Scott, W. Gibson, T. Mawse, T. Robinson, W. Sutherland.

It is interesting to note that three of the four principal officials from Stanley's cricket team also played in the inaugural football game, with William Coulson captaining the side in both sports. The exception, Joseph Simpson, was to appear later in the season. He sadly died at an early age, in May 1886, following a bathing accident at Tynemouth.

Other players from the cricket team also turned out for the football XI. In addition, the playing formation of the teams gives an indicative view of how association football was developing in the area. Stanley played in a 2–2–6 formation with two defenders – the full-backs – two half-backs and six forwards with twin centre-forwards, while Elswick adopted a more progressive (for the time) 2–3–5 style. Stanley recorded a handsome 5–0 win in their first game, and it is worth giving a report of that significant moment in Newcastle United's history. The *Tyneside Daily Echo*, writing in the style of the day, noted: 'The first half of the game was of a give and take description, but in the second the Stanley men with the wind in their favour made a rush with the ball to the opposite goal, when Coulson passed to Findlay, and during a scrimmage in front of goal it was put through the posts by McKenzie. The next goals were got very quickly by Dixon (2), Coulson and W. Findlay, thus winning a very pleasant game by five goals to nil.'

There were no headlines, no quotes from the individuals involved nor any action photographs (of course). But at least some details of the match were recorded for posterity, and the credit for scoring the club's first-ever goal can confidently be given to George McKenzie.

So the club that was to become Newcastle United began with a resounding victory, and the players who turned out for the South Byker team can be regarded as the founding fathers of the club. Interestingly, they were local men who were friends, workmates and associates. In an era when social class structures ruled supreme, they came from what may be termed a mainly working-class background, rather than being a product of the public schools and universities that had produced the earlier pioneers of the game on Tyneside.

Brief biographical details of the Stanley founding fathers, and the men who made Newcastle United, are worthy of inclusion, their place in history assured:

Thomas Shaw Phalp
Born in Byker in 1861, he also played cricket like many of the football pioneers. Although Thomas appeared in goal in this inaugural game, he was also to play in outfield positions later on. The 20-year-old worked as a clerk and lived in Heaton Terrace. Phalp later became associated with the Heaton Athletic Club, fulfilling the role of secretary. In 1898 he was working as a 'chemical cost clerk' at Lansdale's Company based in Warkworth Street, Byker.

John T. Hobson
He was another cricketer who also was to play in goal for Stanley in future games. Hobson had previously played for a Heaton cricket team, Woodbine, and was to return there in the following season to captain and play between the posts for their football team. Later Hobson appeared for North Eastern.

James Gardner
A defender who was later to join Heaton FC; he also briefly turned out for Rangers.

A. Marr
Operating in the half-back role, he was afterwards to play for Elswick Leather Works and also the Brunswick cricket team.

John Armstrong
The son of a Manchester ship-joiner, John Armstrong lived in Harbottle Street in Byker and worked as a joiner in the Tyne yards. He appeared in a number of positions for the football team, becoming East End skipper and also an original shareholder. Armstrong was a director of East End when the club became a limited company.

John P. Cook
Playing both football and cricket, he later had a spell as club secretary. Cook was a surveyor's clerk who resided in Heaton and operated in attack, often on the right flank.

Robert Findlay
Robert was a Scot and a brother of William (see overleaf). Both of the Findlays also played cricket and worked as clerks. Robert had previously played cricket for Rosewood.

William Armstrong Coulson
Stanley's first captain and regarded as the founder of the club. He also captained the cricket team and was a teacher whose brother also played on Tyneside. William was additionally to skipper East End in their first-ever competitive fixture during

January 1883 in the Northumberland & Durham FA Challenge Cup (co-incidentally against Elswick Leather Works first team); however, he was temporarily to sever his links with the club at the end of that season. Coulson afterwards made occasional appearances for the club, but they were limited.

William Findlay

Like his brother (as previous page) he was a Scot and worked as a clerk. William was the club's first secretary and took over from Coulson as club captain. He was to move to Newcastle West End and later became associated with the St Peter's and Science & Art clubs.

George McKenzie

As already recorded, George was the club's first goalscorer, but he only played for the side during their first season. He subsequently served Rangers, Heaton and St Silas, appearing in trials for the Northumberland county team when he was with Heaton.

Joseph (or John) Dixon

There were two football pioneers called J. Dixon associated with East End, and the player who played in Stanley's first fixture could have been either one of them. Joseph Dixon was a joiner from Byker Street who became an East End shareholder and one of the club's first directors. He was noted as residing in Ouseburn. John Dixon was a compositor from Addison Street in Heaton and also became an original shareholder in the East End club.

Initially, Stanley were only a small club as compared to the likes of Tyne and Rangers and did not display a very high standard of football. They usually played on Stanley's cricket field or on a pitch nearby which was close to the local Methodist Chapel – these days near where St Peter's Social Club is located on Raby Street, all on the fringe of the modern award-winning Byker Wall development.

They did not deem themselves important nor big enough to join the Northumberland & Durham FA and, in their first season (1881–82), they were content to pit themselves in friendly games against other minor clubs or the second string of the more senior sides. So Stanley faced the likes of the reserve or B teams of Elswick Leather Works, North Eastern, Newcastle FC and even Rangers, while also coming up against Derwent Rovers and Burnopfield. In the case of the latter, they faced their opponents' second team when they first met them, but they played their senior XI in a rematch.

Stanley did quite well in their inaugural season, winning more games than they lost. Records show that, of the 10 games played, they won six and drew one, although some of the results were questionable, with disputed goals claimed in some matches both by the South Byker club and their opponents. These usually arose because the umpires (one appointed by each team) could not agree whether a goal was valid or not. This was not an infrequent occurrence in the days before the regular use of referees.

A modern view of St Peter's Social Club near Raby Street, the vicinity where Stanley FC were formed and players first kicked a ball.

An insight into their style of play can be gained from a match report of an away contest against Elswick Leather Works 2nd XI in January 1882 when it was reported that 'Stanley lack the strength of Elswick but showed superiority in the dribbling and passing system'.

Certain players stood out as mainstays of the side in that first season, with most of the characters who appeared in the opening fixture becoming regulars. Gardner and Phalp were the exceptions, although they later turned out for the second team. Coulson appears to have managed to complete a full set of appearances with Hobson, Armstrong, Dixon and the Findlay brothers seemingly only missing one apiece.

The club also grew in terms of membership numbers as well. By January 1882, they were able to field two sides. The second team usually faced junior sides of other clubs such as Tyne Pilgrims, North Eastern, Rangers, Newcastle Association and a small outfit called Marlborough. By the end of the first season, Stanley FC had undoubtedly been a success. So successful, in fact, that it was time to grow further.

At the annual meeting of the Northumberland & Durham FA in August 1882, five new clubs were affiliated to the association: North Tyne Swifts (who were based in the village of Wall), Hurworth (on Teesside), Newton (Stocksfield), Prudhoe Rovers and Stanley of South Byker. By now there were 25 clubs affiliated to the local Football Association with in excess of 900 members between them. The game was undoubtedly thriving.

That growth saw another new organisation created in the east end of the city, also from a cricket club – Rosewood Juniors Football Club. Under their captain, R. Marr, and secretary, R. Murray, they were to become an integral part of the that that eventually became Newcastle United when they merged with East End. But that event was still a few months ahead.

Changes were already taking place insofar as Stanley FC was concerned. Association football had reached the town of Stanley in County Durham and, before the start of the 1882–83 season, one of the local clubs there, Stanley Star, applied (along with Whitburn, Birtley and Hamsterley Rangers) to join the Northumberland & Durham FA. Apparently, the local ruling body, anticipating potential confusion with two clubs called Stanley, suggested that the Byker club may wish to consider changing its name. It is possible that the members of the Tyneside outfit realised that they had to move away from the confines of an insignificant street name to gain wider recognition. The Sunderland club had done something similar when they had changed their name to broaden their horizons by dropping the profession 'Teachers' from their original name a year after formation. So the members of the Byker club agreed to a change, and it was announced in the local press early in October that at 'a meeting of Stanley A.F.C., held lately, it was resolved to change its name to East End'.

Why did they choose 'East End'? It is feasible the members had noted that another football club had recently been formed in the west end of the town and were called West End. Could the adoption of 'East End' have been influenced by this? It is a possibility. Whatever the reason, the football results for 7 October 1882 show: 'East End (late Stanley) 1 Hamsterley Rangers 0.' James Gardner scored the first goal under the East End title when he 'cleverly put through the posts'. The next stage in the evolution of Newcastle United was complete.

East End were content to spend their first season under their new name playing friendly games again. There is no record of the attendances at these games, although as the club was primarily socially based, crowds (a misnomer if ever there was one) were almost certainly very small, of a few hundred at best and usually much less. It was recognised, however, that East End was one of the growing clubs. A press report in October 1882 highlighted Stanley, St Cuthbert's and All Saints' as being some of the younger clubs in Newcastle who were all working their way upwards.

East End did not fare so well in their second season as Stanley had in their first. As already mentioned, they managed to win their first game under their new name, 1–0 at home to Hamsterley Rangers, but this was one of East End's few successes that season. Of their 10 recorded games (eight of them friendlies), they only won three and drew one.

Towards the end of 1882, Rosewood decided to throw in their lot with East End. They had recorded some useful results against other new clubs such as Heaton, West End, Newcastle Association and All Saints Second XI, all of whom they defeated, but it seems that they decided to join East End to help strengthen the Byker club. It was announced that, in future, they would go under the name of East End Second Team.

The 1882–83 season saw East End graduate from playing primarily against second teams to their opponents' senior teams. This meant that they were occasionally out of their depth. This was certainly the case when they suffered the biggest defeat so far in their short history when they faced the mighty Tyne in March. The 8–0 scoreline emphasised the gap in class between a well-established big club and a comparative newcomer whose players still had little real experience and a lot to learn.

This season also saw East End play its first competitive game. The club were becoming ambitious and decided to enter for the Northumberland & Durham Challenge Cup. In the first round during January they were drawn at home to Elswick Leather Works. A mere year earlier they had faced the Elswick club's second team in Stanley's very first fixture. The fact that they managed to give the Leather Works' first team a decent contest indicates how much the Byker team had improved. A press match report declared: 'During the first half each team scored one goal and in the second half Elswick scored another. The game throughout was played with great determination, Elswick making themselves the masters of the match.' The victors did not last much longer in the competition, however, being eliminated 5–0 by North Eastern in the next round.

The teams for East End's historic first competitive fixture were:

East End: Speight, Fenwick, Lightfoot, Gardner, Marr, Armstrong, Findlay (R.), Wilson, Findlay (W.), Coulson, Cook.

V

Elswick Leather Works: Brazendale, Johnson, Whitcomb, Cherry, Oman, Robertson, Robson, Harris, Lowery, Dobson, Bailiff.

It can be seen that some of the players from the early Stanley games were still active in the club but that there were a few new names as well. The mainstays of the 1882–83 season included Speight, Black, Armstrong, Cook and the Findlay brothers. James Gardner and William Coulson were still on the scene, but the club's founder was missing from the later games and William Findlay took over the captaincy. Most of the above regulars had played during the inaugural season, John Speight being the notable exception. He began the season with Rosewood but switched to East End long before the merger of the two clubs. Marr also played for both clubs, seemingly interchanging at will as he had played for Stanley the previous season as well. Others who turned out for Rosewood and graduated to East End's first team included R. Lightfoot and Charles

Hiscock, the latter appearing for East End's senior team, reserve team and junior team during that campaign. The Hiscock family produced footballers who were to become the stalwarts of East End during the next few years.

It was the East End junior team that was to win the first trophy for the club (and thus, effectively, Newcastle United's first silverware). This was in the summer Temperance Festival on the Town Moor in June 1883, a precursor of the modern day 'Hoppings'. East End entered teams in all of the football competitions. Their first XI went out in the first round (played prior to the festival) away to Bedlington Burdon, losing 2–0, but their junior team went all of the way to the Final. In the preliminary rounds (again, prior to the festival itself), they eliminated Rendel and Jesmond.

The Finals were played on the Town Moor on 28 June but were not full-scale games. Each match was played over two periods of 20 minutes. East End defeated Hebburn 2–1 in their semi-final and Marlborough 1–0 in the Final to lift a trophy valued at 90 shillings (£4.50) plus, as it was noted, photographs of the winning team! It was the first trophy of many for the club.

The standing of this football competition can be gauged by the fact that as much publicity in the press was given to other assorted events in the Temperance Festival as to the football. The counter-attractions of cricket and athletics are understandable. But kite flying? The festival also included military sports such as wrestling and bayonet v bayonet competitions! The children's sports featured leap-frog races, a standing skipping competition, three-legged races and 'Picking up stones set a yard apart and placing them in a basket'. Sadly it is not recorded how many of the estimated crowd of between 150,000 and 200,000 who congregated on the Town Moor preferred to watch children picking up stones to seeing East End's historic victory.

The club held its annual meeting at Mr Greenwell's Refreshment Rooms in Heaton Park at the end of April 1883 when the secretary's and treasurer's reports showed the club to be in a 'flourishing state'. The social nature of the East End club is indicated by the post-meeting proceedings when the members, who had turned out in force, sat down to a 'sumptuous supper provided by Mr Greenwell, to which they did ample justice'. This was followed by 'songs, recitations, readings, speeches, etc' to the great amusement of the company.

Another meeting was held in the Byker Cocoa Rooms during July when William Findlay was re-elected as club captain and John Cook as club secretary. In addition, William Coulson, the former captain and the man regarded by many of his contemporaries as the founder of the club, was presented with a gold scarf pin as a mark of esteem. His playing connection with East End was almost over. He was to temporarily disappear from the scene during the next season (1883–84), although he did turn out for a few games early in the New Year.

Early archives describe the club colours in 1883 as being 'navy-blue jersey and white knickerbockers'. No contemporary record exists to indicate the club's colours before this date. Afterwards other colours were chosen, occasionally chocolate-and-blue stripes and, more frequently by 1885, navy blue shirts with one orange stripe, blue hose (stockings) and white shorts.

There are also indications that East End no longer played at Stanley Street. There is no precise record as to when they moved, but before the start of the 1883–84 season it was reported that their home ground was located on a field 'behind the Byker Vicarage' not far away. It is possible that they may have moved some time before this, perhaps in 1882 when they had changed their name. The vicarage was St Michael's Vicarage in Byker Village, an area that has since been developed, demolished and redeveloped. Today, St Michael's Church still stands, high on a hill with a sweeping panorama down to the bridges over the Tyne, but sadly now it is in a semi-derelict state and no longer used as a place of worship. However, the 'Old Vicarage' is still in use, although it now consists of apartments. And 'behind the Vicarage'? There, within the environs of the renowned Byker Wall, can be found two football pitches. Admittedly they are miniature pitches for children, but they are football pitches nonetheless.

The new season saw East End grow in strength and reputation. Once again, most of the games were friendly matches, and they did reasonably well in the early part of the programme, which started during October in those days. One of their victories, a 1–0 triumph at Birtley, is particularly interesting because it illustrates the thorny issue of disputed goals at the time. The match was only played over two periods of 30 minutes and was a closely contested affair. A strong wind prevented good play, and the first half was goalless. The game was decided (if 'decided' is the appropriate word) by a controversial incident during the second period. East End claimed for a handling offence near their opponents' goal, and both sides stopped playing. Someone, however, shouted 'Play on', and an unnamed East End player fired the ball between the posts. At the time each team supplied their own umpires and there was no referee. The umpires failed to agree on whether the goal should have counted, so it was registered as a 'disputed goal', and this separated the teams at the end of the game.

Even as early as 1883, players were getting into trouble. East End Juniors defeated North Eastern Juniors, 3–1, in a local derby, but North Eastern's secretary was so appalled at East End's conduct during the match, that he submitted a formal complaint to the now separate Northumberland FA to the effect that the East Enders had resorted to violent conduct on the field of play. This was duly considered and the Northumberland Committee suspended the East End Juniors' captain until the end of the season.

Meanwhile, during November 1883 the first team suffered their first defeat of the season against, of all teams, Sunderland. This was the first-ever game against the club that was to become Newcastle United's arch-rivals. The two teams were:

East End: Broughton, Fenwick, Hiscock (M.), Wilson, Blackett (W.), Lightfoot, Findlay (R.), Armstrong, Findlay (W.), Speight, Cook.
V
Sunderland A: Stewart, Hall, Allan (W.), Elliott, Anderson, Atkinson, Allan (J.), Woodward, McMillan, McDonald, Brown.

According to contemporary match reports, this game was played at Heaton. It can be inferred that it was on North Eastern's ground, a well-established venue compared to

The cry from the crowd on Victorian Tyneside was 'Play Up East End!'

East End's home arena. The match was evenly contested in the first half when East End had both the ground slope and the wind in their favour. It was a different story after half-time, however, when play was almost entirely in the East End half. It was during this session that Sunderland scored three goals without reply to deservedly win the game.

A week later (on 10 November) East End welcomed the other club who were to become their staunch rivals, this time from within Newcastle. While East End were going from strength to strength, a rival club, West End, were similarly growing across the town. The teams for another historic local derby, which ended honours even at 1–1, were:

East End: Broughton, Fenwick, Hiscock (M.), Marr, Lightfoot, Bayles, Speight, Cook, Findlay (W.), Findlay (R.), Armstrong.

V

West End: Minnikin, Waggott (J.), Ormond, Henderson, Waggott (T.), Surtees, Mather (J.), Mather (W.), Tiffin, Fawcett, Longbottom.

There was a significant increase in the number of fixtures in that 1883–84 season, but the vast majority were still friendly games. An exception was when the club played in the Northumberland Challenge Cup. They were drawn at home to neighbours North Eastern, and the game took place at the beginning of December. East End acquitted themselves well but still went out by the odd goal in five. At the time, the press usually relied on club secretaries to submit match summaries, and it seems like it was the North Eastern secretary who reported this game because the visitors' goalscorers are faithfully recorded, with John Oliver striking twice and Pringle grabbing the other, but the scorers for East End were not documented.

East End registered their biggest victory so far early in February when they comprehensively defeated City Harriers 8–0. William Findlay, Edward Hiscock and John Speight were their best players, while the Harriers' full-backs were also apparently in good form – yet as they were the team's defenders, goodness knows what the rest of their side were like.

Hiscock, who was variously (and better) known as Ned, Neddy or Teddy, was now one of the club's best players, and he was chosen for a county trial game, playing on the left wing for a Newcastle & District side who beat a North Country XI 6–0 on the Tyne ground in Jesmond. He was once described in the press as 'amusing the spectators by his fine dodging'.

By the end of the season John Armstrong had taken over the captaincy from William Findlay, although the latter was still a regular in the team. It could be claimed that East End had made definite progress and had clearly established themselves as one of the better local sides. Many of the team had continued to play from the previous season with the likes of Broughton, Fenwick, Matthew Hiscock, Armstrong, Blackett, Speight, Cook and William Findlay all regulars.

Joseph Fenwick was a solid full-back from the earliest months of the club's existence. A coppersmith, he remained with East End until the 1886–87 season. William Blackett was the first and most prominent of four brothers to play for the side. A St Peter's family, afterwards Tom, Joseph and Frank all made appearances over a span of more than a decade. The youngest, full-back Joseph, later played for Wolves, Derby and Sunderland as well as Middlesbrough and Leicester Fosse up to and after the turn of the century. He also once played for an England XI against a Players Union XI. Defender R. Lightfoot, who had come to East End with Rosewood and had played a few games for the juniors and second team, also emerged as a fairly regular member of the first team.

But football was not quite over for the year yet. There was still the summer Temperance Festival competition, and East End were presented with the chance to avenge themselves for their defeat by West End when they were drawn together in a preliminary round that was played on the Town Moor during mid-June. By all accounts they were worthy winners, 2–0, and they progressed to the Finals which were staged as part of the main Temperance Festival on 25 June.

The various football contests were played on a strip of land at the north end of the Moor between the Grandstand and the Blue House. A crowd of approximately 120,000 attended the Festival but, as usual, there were a lot of other attractions apart from football. Events included Military Sports events, Good Templars' Sports, cricket, sport for the deaf and dumb, All Saints' Temperance Sports, as well as children's activities and football under both the association and rugby codes. The Salvation Army was also there for good measure.

Many hundreds of spectators watched the football ties and loudly applauded the teams who played in the semi-finals and Final. East End met North Eastern in their semi-final, and at the end of normal time (two periods of 30 minutes) the match remained goalless. So the teams played two periods of extra-time (10 minutes each way), and by the end of that time East End emerged winners by a 2–0 scoreline.

Sunderland defeated Rosehill 3–0 in the other semi-final so had a fairly easy time of it before the Final, where they proved too strong for East End, winning 3–1. Whether the fact that East End had taken part in a much harder-fought semi-final (plus extra-time) was a factor in this game is not known, but at least the Byker club had reached their first Final. No one either watching or taking part in the game could have imagined the rivalry that would develop between the two clubs representing Tyne and Wear in the century and more that lay ahead.

A change of grounds for East End in the close season heralded a dramatic rise in standing for the club and its emergence as one the major football teams, not only in Newcastle, but throughout the county of Northumberland. The East Enders had made an impression. It was later noted in *The Book of Football:* 'East End was bidding fair to improve considerably in public support, and displaying more enterprise than the Tyne or Rangers had ever attempted.'

They had outgrown the confines of their current location and, in the summer of 1884, decided to move to a better site near Dalton Street, not far away but regarded as a step forward. The pitch behind Byker Vicarage was to be eventually taken over by another local club, Cheviot FC, who had been founded a year earlier.

Rangers FC had also moved to Dalton Street from St James' Park two years earlier, but they were now on the decline, and this season would witness their demise. East End were to benefit from their passing, with a number of prominent Rangers players deciding to join the Byker team. Thomas Hoban switched ranks early, before the new season started. He was a skilful left-winger but was regarded as too showy by many critics. Nevertheless, he had already been capped for the county (appearing in the Northumberland FA's first-ever representative team against Cleveland during November 1883), and his signing was a major boost to East End's ambitions. Hoban was to be a good servant to East End in the years ahead and was soon to be joined by some of his former colleagues.

By the start of the 1884–85 season, Matthew Kerley Hiscock, the defender who had been a regular full-back last season, had taken over as secretary of the club. Born in St

Peter's, he was to fulfil similar defensive duties during the new campaign and was one of three members of the Hiscock clan who were to play for East End during the club's early years. Charles had briefly preceded him in the team and his cousin, Edward, had become a regular with Matthew last season. Teddy was soon to be capped for Northumberland, the first player to be so honoured while with East End. He was dubbed 'Cannonball' due to his powerful shooting. Ted was a riveter by trade in the shipyards.

East End made a superb start to the new 1884–85 season, apparently remaining unbeaten until the turn of the year; although all of these games were non-competitive contests. The most notable victory was a 9–0 win away to Hibernia – a minor team from Wallsend – in December when Teddy Hiscock and John Cook netted three apiece.

East End saw their first players honoured in representative fixtures at this time. Teddy Hiscock paved the way when he was chosen to play for Northumberland against Durham in November. Despite a 2–1 defeat, he retained his place in the county matches against Hallamshire and Lanarkshire that soon followed. Tommy Hoban also played in both of these games which, unfortunately, ended in heavy defeats for the North Eastern county. In fact, Northumberland were unable to record a victory in any of its games that season, losing all five played.

There was, evidently, a huge gap between the North East and other county associations, and this was to continue for a while. As the decade progressed, though, Northumberland, assisted by a fair number of East End players, were to improve significantly. So much so that by the end of the decade Northumberland won quite a few of its inter-county matches and found itself on a par with rival associations.

Possibly the most notable friendly fixture of the season was on New Year's Day when East End only managed a 1–1 draw at Rosehill. This game saw the East End debut of a player who was to be the finest of the early East End greats – Alexander Henry White. Alex (or Alec, as he was better known at the time) White was a Scotsman, born in Glamis, who had become a mainstay of the Newcastle Rangers team that had, along with Tyne Association, dominated the pioneer days of football on Tyneside. He had been a valuable member of the side that had lifted the Northumberland & Durham Challenge Cup in both 1881 and 1882.

A schoolteacher by profession, he was now, with the demise of Rangers and as a local resident, invited to join the East Enders. Alec readily agreed to do so, and it was a decision that neither he nor the club were to regret. White started off as a full-back with Rangers but later migrated to a centre-half role – what would be the midfield battleground of today's football – where he became an influential player with a penchant for scoring goals. He had emerged as a powerful defender, renowned for hefty clearances, often booting the sodden, leaden old leather case-ball from his own goalmouth comfortably into the oppositions' half of the field. This may be a common enough occurrence in modern times, but it was virtually unheard of in the 1880s.

Arthur Appleton in his classic history of North East football, *A Hotbed of Soccer*, refers to Alec as 'the outstanding figure in early East End history', and contemporary press reports referred to him as 'the life and soul of the team'. In the years to come White was to captain his club and county and also to be named as a non-travelling reserve for the

North versus South in a challenge match at the Kennington Oval in London during January 1886, no mean achievement in an era when the North East was regarded as a sporting backwater as far as football was concerned. That was one of three international trial matches in which selectors picked teams for the International Championship between the home countries during February to April. White was unlucky to be on the fringe, but his appearance in the wider squad was a huge boost for North East football and recognition that Alec was amongst the best around. He was the first Tyneside-based player to reach international consideration, although Charles Alcock had played for The North much earlier in 1870–71 under the 'Durham' title. By then, however, he was living in London. George Millar followed White two years later.

Greater honours were to follow for Alec, including selection for the Corinthians, effectively the England national amateur side (although he was, of course, a Scot). Even when East End's fortunes began to wane for a period and West End came to the fore, he continued to shine. The Northumberland team that played Ayrshire in 1887 contained six players from West End and four from Shankhouse. The odd man out was skipper Alec White.

When he eventually retired from playing, White maintained his involvement in the game, initially doing a spot of refereeing before gravitating into football administration, holding a variety of posts, most notably as treasurer of the Northumberland FA for 25

THE GROWTH OF EAST END 2

Timetable of Development

May 1886:   Win Northumberland Charity Shield (2–1 v Morpeth Harriers).

September 1886: Move to Chillingham Road in Heaton.

October 1886:   Inaugural game at Chillingham Road v Darlington St Augustine's.

September 1887: Cheviot FC merge with East End.

October 1887:   First FA Cup tie at South Bank (lost 2–3).

November 1887: Union Harriers FC merge with East End.

January 1888:   Record victory 19–0 v Point Pleasant (Northumberland Cup).

July 1888:   Tom Watson appointed secretary-manager.

October 1888:   First FA Cup victory (3–1 v Port Clarence).

April 1889:   Win Northumberland Cup (3–2 v Elswick Rangers) & Northumberland Charity Shield (walk-over).

May 1889:   Win N&D Inter-County Challenge Cup (1–0 v Sunderland Albion).

May 1889:   Tom Watson takes over at Sunderland.

June 1889:   East End turn fully professional.

years. He was deservedly given a long-service medal by the Football Association and eventually passed away, the 'Grand Old Man of North East football', in 1940. Alec White truly was the first of the greats as far as Newcastle United is concerned.

Back in 1885, when the Scot became first involved with the club, he was able to establish himself in the team before East End embarked on their Northumberland Challenge Cup campaign in late January. For the first time, the Byker club was able to progress beyond the first hurdle, defeating Elswick Leather Works 3–1 in the first round and receiving a bye in the second. An emphatic 8–1 win over Brunswick Athletic Villa followed and demonstrated that East End had become serious challengers for the trophy. Brunswick apparently escaped lightly because East End had three goals disallowed in this game, so it could have been much worse.

A semi-final showdown during March with the team that was to become their arch-rivals in the city, West End, now beckoned. The East Enders had home advantage but could only manage a 3–3 draw before 600 spectators (regarded as a 'large crowd' at the time), Alec White scoring two of the goals with John Armstrong grabbing the other. The replay was staged at a neutral venue, Tyne's ground in Brandling, probably because West End's home ground on the Town Moor was regarded as inappropriate. This time East End made no mistake, romping to a 5–0 victory, White striking two – one a magnificent solo effort – with Cook, Scott and Teddy Hiscock making up the nap hand.

A week later, East End faced Sleekburn Wanderers in the Final, once again on the Tyne ground. The game kicked-off at four o'clock and admission cost 6d (2½p); except for ladies, who were admitted free. Reduced admission was charged from half-time onwards for any late-comers.

Some 500 enthusiasts witnessed a close game and saw the Byker club lift its first-ever senior trophy, Charles Gorman scoring the only goal of the match in the second half. He also had another goal disallowed for offside. Sleekburn, however, had been handicapped during the contest after a knee injury sustained by half-back Jackie Atkinson. Nevertheless East End were, apparently, worthy winners.

It is interesting to note that the players who turned out for East End in the Final had played almost unchanged throughout the tournament: Speight, Fenwick, Matt Hiscock, Armstrong, White, William Blackett, Gorman, Scott, Cook, Hoban and Ted Hiscock. Hiscock missed one game in the Cup run, the match against Brunswick Villa Athletic when Parr stood in for him. The players who lifted the Cup were the mainstays of the team throughout the season, and most of them had been regulars from the previous campaign, Alec White, Tommy Hoban – who were both recruited from Rangers – and Charles Gorman being the exceptions.

Success saw East End participate in the Northumberland FA Charity Shield, and in the semi-final they faced Sleekburn once more. This time the Bedlington club were forced to field a weakened team and were disposed of easily, a 6–0 scoreline giving a clear indication of the one-sided nature of the game. Even so, that encounter seemed quite close compared to the Final of the competition when East End faced Newcastle Association. This team had nothing to do with Newcastle

United, although, co-incidentally, they did play in black and white – not stripes, but black jerseys and white shorts. Although they had beaten North Eastern in a replay to reach the Final, they were no match for the now mighty East End who thrashed them 10–0. Both Teddy Hiscock and Tommy Hoban scored hat-tricks with Gorman, White, Armstrong and Blackett weighing in with the other goals. Neither Matthew Hiscock nor D. Scott played in the Charity Shield games, R. Lightfoot and Charles Gray deputising. The latter was to take over as club secretary during the year.

A contemporary match report, describing the action in the script of the day, referred to East End's performance as displaying 'a fine combined game and every man in the team worked vigorously'. At the same time Newcastle were condemned for their 'utter lack of combination and a great want of sustained energy'. Alec White had already emerged as the star of the side, being described as a tireless performer and exceptional header of the ball. He was soon to succeed John Armstrong as captain of the club, but it was Armstrong who led East End to their first senior trophy victories in that 1884–85 campaign.

Unusually for the time, match reports in the Tyneside press again give an indication of the size of the gates for these games, with some 500 attending the semi-finals, which were both played at the same venue on the same day, paying 6d (2½p) a time to stand in the pouring rain. This crowd increased to 600 for the Final, which was played a week later on a scorching hot afternoon. It is safe to assume that these attendances were regarded as so exceptional at the time to be worth mentioning, certainly bigger than East End's normal home crowds.

One concluding major game was outstanding – a contest against the victor of the Durham Challenge Cup, Darlington, for what was termed the Northumberland & Durham Challenge Cup – the 'best of the best' in each county. This fixture would be a true measure of how far East End had progressed.

The local trophy holders met at Darlington's home ground, Feethams, late in April and, for the only time this season, East End met their match in a competitive tussle, going down 1–0 in a closely fought affair. The game was played in a gale, and the only goal was scored in the second half by one of the Quakers' forwards, Buckton. But the player of most interest in Darlington's team was their goalkeeper, Arthur Wharton from the Gold Coast. A talented black athlete, his career is related further elsewhere in the Pioneers story. Wharton had a fine game and kept the Geordies at bay, 'kicking and fisting out to keep his fortress intact'.

East End were disappointed in that solitary competitive failure but proud of their achievements nonetheless. At the annual meeting of the club held in the Grace Darling British Workman's club at the beginning of May of that year, the club president, J.T. Oliver, congratulated the members on a highly successful season, the Byker team having now displaced Tyne and Rangers as the district's premier club – although of course West End were to vigorously challenge for that title too and get the better of East End for a period. But season 1884–85 belonged to East End. The teams' match statistics make interesting reading, noting they now fielded four sides:

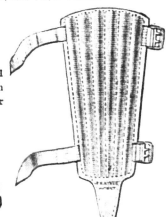
A contemporary advert for football goods: boots, shirts, balls and shin guards. Gamages also later published comprehensive yearbooks on the sport.

First team:	Played 14; won 11.
Second team:	Played 16; won 11.
Junior team:	Played 15; won 8 (drew 5).
Scratch team:	Played 8; won 5.

The club president was delighted to present the side with the magnificent Northumberland Challenge Cup and to award a silver medal to each player. The club were also pleased to announce that they were financially sound, their accounts showing a balance of £6.

East End entered two teams in Town Moor Temperance Festival during the summer – East End A and East End B. Both, however, were to be eliminated by Shankhouse Albion, the A team in a preliminary round and the B team in the semi-final.

There was to be change in club secretary before the new season commenced. It was reported that 'Mr Hiscock felt it necessary to resign as secretary', and he was replaced by Charles Gray, who lived in Shields Road, Byker. It was further announced that 'the clever and popular player' Alec White would be captain. Two new forwards were recruited for the programme's start. William Muir was a former Rangers player who joined East End from Heaton FC and Peter O'Brien was another local man. Both were to become first-team regulars.

East End's 1885–86 season followed a similar format to the previous campaign, with the club playing mainly friendly games until the turn of the year. There was one exception, however. They participated in the Benwell British Workman Temperance Festival in September and were eliminated in the first round, losing 3–0 to Elswick Ordnance Works. This seems to have been a rather strange tournament, with East End apparently having to give Elswick two goals start, although they evidently did not need it.

Otherwise there were mixed fortunes in the friendly matches. If East End did not win they usually drew, although they also suffered the occasional defeat. One of these was in Northumberland at Sleekburn Wanderers when the Byker club played with only 10 men in a game of 70 minutes and lost 3–2. This fixture is interesting as another insight into club attendances is recorded, with some 300 spectators attending the match. East End also fell by a single goal on home soil to Sunderland in another friendly encounter and played out a goalless draw with Berwick Rangers. There was also a draw, 1–1, with Tyne, the pioneering club now in decline.

There was one notable victory for East End, a 6–1 thrashing of West End on enemy territory during mid-November. Yet the West Enders were to recoup a little pride when they drew the return fixture 2–2 at Dalton Street on Boxing Day. Bearing in mind the rivalry which had already built up between the two clubs, this Christmas game demonstrated the extremes of sportsmanship on the part of each team. West End's second goal was controversial insofar as it may not have crossed the line before being cleared. The referee and the East End umpire disallowed the goal, but West End threatened to walk off the pitch such was their anger. However, East End captain Joseph Armstrong showed that it was the season of goodwill by agreeing to let the goal stand.

In early January, the Byker club exhibited its ambition when they invited the emerging Scottish club Dumbarton Athletic for a challenge contest, one of the first of many prestige challenge games both East End and West End organised on Tyneside. The Scots were one of the best teams north of the border at the time. They were a big attraction, and clearly too good for East End who lost 4–1.

By the time that the Northumberland Challenge Cup competition started at the turn of the year, East End were still trying to find a settled team. They received a little breathing space by being awarded a bye in the first round but had to face West End in the second. This was played on Tyne's ground in Jesmond, and East End's attempt to retain the trophy was short-lived because they were knocked out by their rivals 2–1.

The second team did somewhat better in the Northumberland Second XI Cup, reaching the Final. They had to travel to Shankhouse to play a local team, Cramlington Union Jacks, and fought out a 1–1 draw over the initial 90 minutes. Extra-time was played, and Cramlington managed to chalk up two more goals to clinch the trophy.

By now, East End regularly had players honoured at county and district level. Nevertheless, when it was decided which of the county's top four clubs would compete for the 1886 Charity Shield, they did not automatically gain selection. The County Cup joint holders, Shankhouse Black Watch and Morpeth Harriers, together with losing finalists, West End, were obvious choices, but the final place was contested by East End and Elswick Leather Works in what was essentially a play-off.

The game was played in a snow storm, but East End came back from a goal down to win comfortably 4–1, and they thus qualified to meet Shankhouse in the semi-final. That match ended in a 1–1 draw and resulted in an 'exceedingly rough' contest which blew up into a row between the two clubs over disputed handball decisions. Shankhouse were aggrieved at Hoban's equaliser in particular. Indeed, one Shankhouse player, Downey, appeared to storm off the field in protest! East End went through to the Final because Shankhouse were unable to return to Tyneside for the replay, maybe in protest, and scratched from the competition.

Morpeth Harriers had reached the Final by virtue of a victory over West End and faced East End in the Charity Shield Final in what was to be the last game played on Tyne's old home at Brandling in Jesmond. The area was to be developed, and the ground had to close.

The Final was a closely contested affair. Teddy Hiscock, criticised in the press in the weeks leading up to the tie for being too selfish, scored the only goal in the opening session with a solo effort. Although Wade scored for the Harriers in the second half, Scott grabbed a winner for the Byker side, securing the trophy for East End.

So the season ended with some success; although compared to the previous campaign it had been a little disappointing. The same nucleus of players had turned out regularly throughout the season: Hoban, Scott, White, Muir and O'Brien, as well as William Blackett, Lightfoot, Armstrong and Fenwick. Cook and Stephen Ryder also made occasional appearances as did two new goalkeepers, E. McClen and Alex McDougal. Former custodian John Speight and Charles Gorman were no longer to be found in the first XI, although the former did represent the club as an umpire. Teddy Hiscock had mainly been in the reserve side during that season, although he did still make the odd first-team appearance.

In the summer of 1886, both East End and West End decided to move grounds. The latter's decision to take over Rangers' old ground of St James' Park is covered elsewhere in this volume. Just as important at the time was East End's move further away from the river and from Byker into neighbouring Heaton, a more refined residential district than Byker. During the 1880s developers turned much of Heaton into a pleasant Victorian suburb.

They took over a ground previously tenanted by the Heaton Athletic Club next to North Eastern's old pitch on Chillingham Road near Heaton Junction. On the Byker-Heaton border and known also previously as the Heaton Bicycle Track or Heaton Athletics Field, a dedicated football ground was developed from North Eastern's old pitch. South of the established cricket area, just off Chillingham Road at the end of Hartford

East End moved the mile or so from Byker to Heaton in 1886, making a new home at the Heaton Junction Ground near Chillingham Road, formally the pitch of North Eastern FC next to their cricket ground.

Street and Spencer Street, East End were soon to improve the arena. They erected a fence, had a new flag-pole installed and removed the cycle track. To follow in the years to come was an elevated press box for reporters – a 'first' in the region – and a pavilion building constructed of timber in typical Victorian style, able to seat the club's members, guests and ladies. More than a century later, the site is now covered by terraced houses and industrial units and is still adjacent the railway – on the England-Scotland main line track.

At the time it was commonly agreed that the playing surface at Heaton was superior to that at St James' Park, which still had an enormous slope down towards the Gallowgate end of the site; however, the Chillingham Road ground was constantly criticised for its muddy approaches and, of course, West End's new ground had the great advantage of a central location. Therefore St James' Park came to succeed Tyne's ground as the main football arena in Newcastle.

East End provided the opposition for West End's first game at their new ground, and a massive crowd (for the day) of 2,000 turned up to see the now city adversaries go head-to-head. This was the biggest attendance ever assembled for a club game on Tyneside, and they saw an evenly contested match, the home team winning 3–2.

East End did not fare too well in their opening fixtures of the new season, only winning one of their opening four matches (all away from home), albeit by a comfortable 7–1 scoreline at the Drill Field, where Gateshead were the hapless victims. These generally poor results did not prevent White, Blackett, Scott and Muir from being chosen to play for Northumberland against Hallamshire at St James' Park in October. A 5–3 win gave the North East county its first success since March 1884.

A week later, on 23 October, the Chillingham Road ground was officially opened. Club president J.T. Oliver did the honours, and the selected opponents were Darlington St Augustine's. Everyone seemed satisfied with the resultant draw, although there was some criticism of the pitch because it was a few yards short of the required length and parts of the former cycle track could be seen under the grass. William Muir opened the scoring for East End at their new home after a 'clever pass' from O'Brien. Veitch equalised, and following the break the visitors took the lead before Tommy Hoban made it 2–2 just before the end of the contest.

This was well before the time of football managers. At East End, club secretary Charles Gray looked after the administration and Alec White captained the team on the field of play and would have largely decided upon tactics with other senior members of the side. There was soon to be a trainer engaged as well.

East End's squad of players was the best around, better than West End. No fewer than five East Enders were included in the Northumberland county team that defeated Durham 3–2 at Bedlington during November. White, William Blackett, Scott, William Muir and Hoban took part, and all of Northumberland's goals were scored by East Enders – through White, Scott and Hoban. The county were improving. East End's men also represented the Newcastle & District XI. The local side included the same five well-known East End players for the visit of the Corinthians compared to only two from West End (Duns and Aitken).

Despite the quality to select from, East End's season was not too successful; although a 1–1 draw away to Sunderland early in December was a more-than-decent result, as was the first defeat of the season inflicted on Rendel a week later in front of 400 spectators. The club was also strengthened when they signed a new goalkeeper, William Chard from Newcastle Association, before Christmas.

After the Festivities, East End embarked on their Northumberland Challenge Cup campaign and a tie at Brunswick in the first round. The latter were induced to play the tie at Chillingham Road for the sake of the gate and were systematically crushed 10–0. Both Teddy Hiscock and Tommy Hoban netted three apiece with Lord (2), White and O'Brien scoring the others. Again the pitch was criticised. The ground was low lying with little or no drainage and quickly became saturated in wet weather. The game was played with large, deep pools of water that made good football impossible. Perhaps there was a touch of humour in the summariser's press report that said Brunswick were 'out of their depth'.

Boundary FC were easily despatched 5–0 in the second round. A new signing, T. Marshall from Tyne, made his debut in this game and scored one of the goals, with a brace each from Hoban and Hiscock concluding the spree. Both were dangerous in attack and were frequently on the score sheet.

The next stage found East End at Berwick, and they attracted the largest crowd so far for a football match in the border town when they took on Berwick Rangers at the Pier Field. Another comfortable win saw the Newcastle club through to the semi-finals, though there was some controversy about the result. They were leading 4–2 and another goal was added as the referee blew the whistle for full-time. East End declared that they had won 5–2, but Berwick argued that it was only 4–2.

Shankhouse Black Watch, now a power in the region, awaited the East Enders in the semi-final, a game played at the neutral venue of St James' Park. There was a clash of colours for this game as East End's dark blue shirts were too similar to the black shirts of the pitmen, so the Heaton team turned out in the county colours of chocolate and blue. It did not bring them luck as Shankhouse won fairly comfortably 3–1 before a crowd of 3,000. The gate receipts of £45 were supplemented, as it was described, by 'those who cared to pay a little extra, and for the ladies, to enter the small enclosure reserved near the high ground'.

East End later showed that the club had a social conscience by playing a charity game against Shankhouse to support a distress fund in aid of the Shankhouse miners who were on strike. Most of the opposition were pitmen, and they had lifted the Northumberland Challenge Cup by beating West End. They found East End a different proposition, however, and the Newcastle team won comfortably 4–1. At the same time, East End informed the county Football Association that they did not want to participate in the local Charity Shield competition that year.

Once again, a nucleus of stalwarts from the previous campaign had generally made up East End's first team during the 1886–87 season: Lightfoot, William Muir, Hiscock, O'Brien, Hoban, White, Scott and William Blackett. Teddy Hiscock had comfortably been the top scorer. McClen had started the season in goal, but Chard soon became first choice after he was recruited. Other notable additions had been full-backs G. Goulden (ex-Heaton) and the former Tyne and North Eastern player J. Ferguson.

The summer interlude of 1887 brought some limited success to East End. Once again they entered a team for the Temperance Festival Junior Football Competition. Incidentally, this was the last year that football was allowed to be played on the Town Moor; winter football had already been prohibited. The official reason was that the holes dug to receive the goal posts were deemed to be a hazard to pedestrians and grazing cattle. At the end of June, East End's Under-17 team lifted the junior trophy for the second time by beating Red Rose 5–0 and St Silas 2–0 in the semi-final and Final respectively. So at least the club won some silverware.

East End were reinforced during the close-season when a minor club, Cheviot, came under their wing. Club founder William Coulson was appointed secretary, succeeding Charles Gray who had been heavily criticised for not informing the press of team line ups, while Charles Tinlin, a recruit from Cheviot, was appointed match secretary. Alec White continued as captain. A couple of months later a Byker junior club, Union Harriers, also joined East End. The club would now run five sides: a first XI, East End Swifts (the reserve XI), third and fourth teams, as well as East End Juniors.

Behind the scenes several individuals were driving the club forward, including Scottish-born brothers David and Robert Crawford. Both had arrived on the demise of Rangers and were pioneers of the game on Tyneside. They resided in Byker, and Bob trained the East End team for a period while both officiated at matches. The pair later became East End shareholders, with David becoming a prominent board member for many years.

On the playing side, the club signed two new full-backs. T. Campbell joined East End from Boundary and S. Stones, a former Guisborough defender, was also recruited. Other new signings included Michael Mulvey, an ex-Motherwell man who was very versatile, seemingly equally at home as a wing-half, centre-forward or winger. The Scot made

Previously with Newcastle Rangers, David Crawford – with his brother Robert – was a prominent figure at East End. He is pictured here as a Newcastle United director.

an impact and was referred to as the 'East End dodger'. Andrew Muir, William's younger brother who had arrived from Cheviot, also established himself in the senior XI alongside his brother, while T. Marshall also progressed from the second-team ranks.

Just as important as this strengthening of the playing staff was the managerial decision to enter for the FA Cup the following season, a competition in which the club were to gain so much distinction as Newcastle United in later years.

The early-season friendly games of 1887–88 produced no surprises and by the time the first round of the FA Cup arrived in October, several North East clubs were ready for the fray. Seven ties were played in the region, and among them was East End's fixture at South Bank on 15 October. On a miserable wet day which made the pitch somewhat slippery and treacherous, the Heaton team gave a good account of themselves after going behind before the break. The Tynesiders equalised but were eventually eliminated 3–2 after extra-time. East End's first FA Cup team was: Chard, Stones, Campbell, Marshall, White, Blackett (W), Hiscock (E), Hoban, Muir (W), Muir (A), Scott.

William Muir gets the credit for scoring the first goals for East End in this competition, but his brace was not enough on this occasion. They returned to Tyneside with 6s 9d (34p in modern money!) profit after expenses. But 15 October 1887 is notable in football history, not so much for Newcastle United's debut in the FA Cup but for another tie in that competition: Preston North End 26 Hyde United 0 – the highest score ever recorded in major English competitive football.

Back on the field of play, East End's performances began to decline. They were criticised for their overly physical approach in games which were meant to be what would be termed 'friendlies' today. There were also calls in the press for 'new blood in the team'. Alec White starred in virtually every game and was the only East End representative in the Northumberland team which defeated Ayrshire 4–0. He captained a side that included no fewer than six Shankhouse Black Watch players. The pitmen had emerged as the strongest club in the area and were to reach the last 32 of the FA Cup before bowing out to the mighty Aston Villa at St James' Park.

Scottish clubs and players were regarded as some of the best in football and were certainly vastly superior to the North East teams. This was proven over the Christmas and New Year holidays when a number of Scottish teams visited Tyneside to play both East End and West End. All returned over the border with victories under their belts. As far as East End were concerned, they faced the Scottish Cup semi-finalists Abercorn (from Paisley) on New Year's Eve and Partick Thistle a couple of days later, losing both games, 7–1 and 3–1 respectively. Alec White missed the first of those contests as he was chosen to guest for the illustrious Corinthians against Durham County. He also faced the Corinthians a few days later when a Newcastle & District team (which also include Hoban and Campbell) went down 3–1 in the last of the main holiday fixtures.

No sooner had the glut of holiday friendlies been concluded than the Northumberland Challenge Cup campaign began. East End received an easy tie in the first round during January 1888, a home game with minnows Point Pleasant, and one of the most amazing games in the history of Newcastle United beckoned. It was a monumental mismatch against the club from the riverside at Willington Quay; although

NORTHUMBERLAND ASSOCIATION CUP.

FIRST ROUND.

East End, 19 goals; Point Pleasant, nil.

Press headlines as East End ran up a 19–0 victory in 1888, Newcastle United's record scoreline.

there was little indication of the eventual outcome, with the game staying goalless for the first 20 minutes. Then the floodgates opened as Point Pleasant's overworked 'keeper Lamb was led to the proverbial slaughter! Scott notched the first goal, and this was quickly followed by two from Teddy Hiscock. Wakefield and White quickly followed, and Hiscock grabbed his third before half-time. The 6–0 lead at the turn-around was only a foretaste of what was to come. It was one-way traffic on Lamb's goal. Alec White, playing in a strange position for him (centre-forward), scored six further goals, Andrew Muir got five and Scott hit two more, giving East End a record 19–0 win. No other Newcastle United first-team combination has scored as many goals since. For the record, the team for that goal fest was as follows: Chard; Stones, Coxon, Blackett (W.), Wakefield, Armstrong, Scott, Muir (A.), White, Hiscock (E.), Hoban.

After that orgy of goals, however, East End's scoring flair deserted them. They crashed out of the Northumberland Cup in a home fixture against Elswick Rangers 3–1, and a week later they lost again 3–0 at home in a friendly against arch-rivals West End. Worse was to follow, as another seven days later they were thrashed 6–0 by Middlesbrough at Chillingham Road. Apart from the Point Pleasant result, they failed to record a single victory throughout December and January.

Doubts and anxiety were expressed, and soon an announcement was made that 'several prominent local footballists are going to try and resuscitate the East End team by the infusion of new blood in the club'.

Some of the gloom surrounding the club was lifted during mid-March at a semi-social event. The Northumberland County Challenge Cup Committee had, at long last, managed to purchase a Charity Shield, and as East End had won the trophy in 1885 and 1886 it was decided that it should be presented to them as the first holders. In presenting the silverware to Alec White, the treasurer of the Northumberland FA, George Hall, said how happy he was to do so as he regarded East End as the representatives of his old club, Newcastle Rangers, because White, Hoban and Muir were all previous members of Rangers. Alec went on to captain a Northumberland side that included teammate Campbell at the beginning of March 1888 and led the county to a 3–2 win over Cleveland at St James' Park.

At club level, however, all was not well. East End could comfortably manage to defeat minor teams, as evidenced by a 9–0 humiliation of Hebburn, but it was a different matter when they faced stronger opposition. A visit to Middlesbrough saw the hosts field a weakened team that included a number of reserves to make the match more even, but they still managed to win 3–1. The Tyneside team's performance was described as 'unscientific and lacking in combination and judgement'.

James Raylstone, the West End half-back, guested for East End during the Easter friendlies, and it soon became evident that this tough, uncompromising (some described him as 'dirty') player was on the verge of throwing in his lot with the Chillingham Road club. Raylstone, though, played for his parent team when East End faced West End in the semi-final of the local Charity Shield but was forced to go off injured at half-time. Even with 10 men, West End were too good for their rivals and won comfortably 2–0.

As the season ended, a faint gleam of success was felt in Heaton. East End Swifts (as the second team were now known) reached the Final of the Northumberland Second XI Cup and were tied to play Shankhouse A at Blyth. The Newcastle club were ahead 1–0 (or 2–0 as there was a disputed goal) when Shankhouse left the field of play following another controversial decision and a pitch invasion. They subsequently refused to return, leaving East End on the field with no opponents! They were declared the victors.

In May, East End arranged a visit by Preston North End. The local club, however, realised that they were totally inadequate to face such opponents and so formed a Newcastle & District side. This representative team included Alec White and Tommy Hoban and played well considering the opponents. The Football League was to start in the following season, and Preston were to go through the entire campaign undefeated, becoming the first League champions. So a 2–0 defeat at the hands of the illustrious Lancastrians was no disgrace.

Nevertheless, the season ended with rivals West End, winners of the Northumberland Challenge Cup and the Charity Shield, supreme in the county. East End could only sit back and wait for their star to gain the ascendancy again; and it would, eventually.

The year of 1888 saw a massive change in the administration of football, both locally and nationally. The biggest impact in England as a whole was the formation of the Football League, but the new set up had little immediate impact in the North East. One change that did affect local football, however, was the partial breakup of the Northumberland Football Association, as related previously. East End and West End, however, retained their affiliation with the old association.

Changes were also taking place at East End in the summer of 1888, when both the administrative and playing sides underwent drastic changes. Tom Watson, the secretary of West End, moved across the city to take over the administration at East End. He was, without doubt, the most progressive and influential football administrator that the North East produced in the Victorian era. Born in Heaton in 1859, he was living in Willington Quay when he first became involved in football, initially as a player on the local scene. But it was as an administrator, not as a player, that Tom found his true vocation. He soon took over as the secretary of the Rosehill club but was destined for bigger and better things, and it was not long before he took over the reins at West End, a much stronger and more enterprising club.

Watson was a cut above his contemporaries – forward-thinking and ambitious. So when East End enticed him across the city to take over as secretary-manager at Chillingham Road and turn their club around, as he had done at West End, he was quite happy to return to his roots in Heaton. In fact, he was not with East End long, merely a year, but he certainly made an impact. His real claim to fame arrived when he left Tyneside to take over at Sunderland and guide them into the Football League and, later, to revitalise Liverpool. But these moves lay years ahead.

Other changes took place at Chillingham Road apart from recruiting a new secretary. Charles Tinlin (who had been match secretary for the previous season) was appointed financial secretary, helping out Tom Watson, but the biggest upheaval at the time concerned the playing squad not the management. Alec White announced his retirement, somewhat prematurely as it turned out, and Tommy Hoban took over the captaincy. A number of new recruits were also brought in and a couple of them, wing-half Joseph Coupe from Blackburn Olympic, winners of the FA Cup in 1883, and centre-half James Raylstone from West End, immediately began to impress. Raylstone was soon in the headlines when in April 1889 it was reported that he 'narrowly escaped drowning' after falling into the water at South Dock in Sunderland. Unable to swim, a dock gateman and two river constables arrived to rescue him from his peril in the Wear.

Everything did not go according to East End's plan. In mid-September, after variable early results, Tommy Hoban suddenly announced his retirement. Scotsman Jock Smith, despite being a comparatively new recruit from Kilmarnock, took over the captaincy and his first game as skipper was at Middlesbrough where East End played at Boro's Linthorpe Road ground in front of around 2,000 spectators. East End lost, but only by the odd goal in five, which was not too bad a result in the circumstances. But the club management were not happy, and within a week they approached White and Hoban, asking them to come out of retirement and return to the team as there was a shortage of competent players. This they did and helped the club to a 5–0 victory at Hartlepool in the very next game, White scoring twice.

This 'shortage of competent players' was immediately addressed, and a huge influx of new recruits made their way to Chillingham Road. The Football Association had accepted a form of professionalism in July 1885, with strict provisions regarding residence, but all of the local players were ostensibly amateurs. Nevertheless, Scottish players were enticed over the border to the North East with promises of jobs. It was, apparently, common knowledge at the time that certain clubs were not averse to making under-the-table payments to some of their playing members – although these clubs were never named.

Many of East End's new recruits were men from the north. Bobby Creilly (Dunmore), James Millar, D. Henderson, W. Young (all Kilmarnock) and James Collins all came from over the border, joining Jock Smith (also Kilmarnock) and J.C. Irvine (Motherwell) who were already at the club. Some of these players stayed long enough to turn out for the club when East End changed its name to Newcastle United. Others came and left very quickly – Gilmartin and Smith (Rangers) and McGuiness (Clydebank) had brief stays indeed.

Bobby Creilly, right, featured on a Victorian card with Harry Jeffrey. Both were grand servants to Newcastle United's pioneers – wearing their colours of red and white.

Three players stood out. Collins was one of the best of all East End's early forwards, described as invariably giving 'splendid expositions of the game'. A county player for Northumberland who had two spells with East End, he later joined rivals West End but returned to the fold in time to become one of Newcastle United's stars as they entered the Football League. He resided in Byker and later totalled 52 senior outings for United. Sadly Collins died at an early age soon after playing for Chatham against New Brompton (Gillingham) in December 1899. He fell on a piece of flint and contracted tetanus, dying the following day. When on Tyneside he also played baseball – a sport which enjoyed some popularity for a fleeting period – appearing as a 'catcher' for the Brunswick club.

Half-back Bobby Creilly became a dependable player over the coming five years. Tough and uncompromising as well as a touch fiery and temperamental, he was a battler and looked the part too. Bobby was once suspended for using bad language on the pitch at officials while he also once stormed off the field due to his colleagues' lack of effort.

Creilly also later appeared for Newcastle United, on over 50 occasions, but afterwards he fell on hard times, later being described as in 'destitute circumstances'. He later was 'removed to Coxlodge Hospital', then a sanatorium in Newcastle.

Jock Smith hailed from Ayrshire and was only to have a short initial stay with East End before moving back to Kilmarnock, then quickly returning to the North East when he joined Sunderland. On Wearside the tricky forward proved a valuable asset in their emerging side before moving back to East End – but when they were Newcastle United, joining the club for a second time in 1894.

A few of the club's older players still held down places in the senior XI – such as White and Hoban. But most of the previous season's local first-team personnel now found

James Collins was one of many Scots to settle on Tyneside, he became a noted goalscorer.

Jock Smith turned out for East End, then Sunderland, and later for Newcastle United.

themselves playing in the second string (the Swifts) where they did very well, eventually winning the Northumberland FA Second Team Cup. Lightfoot captained sides that included former first-team regulars such as Chard, O'Brien, Tinlin, Scott, Andrew Muir, Caldwell and Teddy Hiscock. A few of these (Caldwell, Muir and Hiscock) also turned out for the first XI occasionally but not on a regular basis.

Not surprisingly, fortunes improved for the senior team, and this upturn coincided with the start of the FA Cup trail. East End received a home draw against Port Clarence in the first qualifying round and recorded their first-ever victory in the tournament with a 3–1 scoreline. Raylstone and Muir gave them a half-time lead and White added a third in the second half before the Teessiders managed to force a consolation goal. But the Newcastle outfit won comfortably enough.

The second qualifying round paired East End with Stockton. Surprisingly, although the Newcastle club received a home draw, the committees of both clubs endeavoured to have the fixture switched to Teesside. But they failed and the game went ahead at Chillingham Road. Tommy Hoban put East End ahead with a strong shot, and this was the only goal of the match until 10 minutes from time when Strachan equalised for the visitors from a cross. An all-out effort in the dying minutes saw the entire East End forward and half-back lines involved in a scrimmage around the Stockton goalmouth after a Collins ball into the danger area. In the fracas they succeeded in pushing the goalkeeper and ball over the line for the winner.

East End's Cup run came to an end at the next stage when they were tied with Sunderland, who were now well on their way to becoming the strongest team in the North East. In front of a 5,000 gate at the Newcastle Road ground on Wearside, the Tyneside players were not disgraced and gave a good account of themselves; although they succumbed to second-half goals by Davison and Jobling. So the first major encounter between the clubs that were to become the arch-rivals of north-east football ended in a victory for the Wearsiders.

The game that the sporting public of Newcastle really looked forward to more than any at the time – even more keenly than a Newcastle versus Sunderland clash – was the meeting of West End and East End. The battle cry of supporters crowding the touchline at Chillingham Road in the era was 'Play up East End!', and it was vigorously shouted at these early Tyne derbies.

The Christmas Day clash between West End and East End at St James' Park was eagerly awaited. On the weekend before Christmas, East End welcomed the glamorous Sunderland team to Chillingham Road, although as the Wearsiders arrived late, the match was played in two halves of 30 minutes each. Mack equalised Peacock's opener, and the resultant 1–1 draw satisfied both teams and ensured that both the players and officials enjoyed the social evening held at the Liberal Club in Byker after the match.

But the game that really counted was the contest on Christmas Day, and a large crowd of 5,000 crammed into St James' Park for the 11 o'clock kick-off. West End held the upper hand throughout the game, and their 2–0 half-time advantage was increased to 4–1 by the final whistle. Bragging rights lay with the West Enders – at least for the time being.

As was customary, East End welcomed clubs from outside the region to Tyneside for New Year holiday fixtures. But the days of total dominance by the visitors over the local opposition were at an end. Mossend Swifts were the first visitors, and they won their match against the dark blues; but Renton, Scottish Cup-holders and self-styled Champions of the World, received a bit of a surprise when the East Enders held them to a 2–2 draw before their biggest crowd of the season, some estimates reporting the crowd as large as 4,000. A day later, Airdrieonians completed a triumvirate of Scottish visitors to Chillingham Road but could also only manage a draw.

During the season more fresh talent arrived from the north. A new centre-forward signed for East End, P. Mack of Edinburgh Hibernians, and he made his debut against Elswick Rangers at the beginning of December, helping his team to a 2–0 win. By this time Raylstone had moved on to join Sunderland. A couple of important new signings followed in January when Alex McCurdie and Joe McKane were recruited from Clydebank in quick succession. Fellow Scot A. Sawers came from Clyde a month or so later. McKane in particular proved a noted acquisition. Another tough half-back, like fellow countryman Creilly, he was to become a mainstay of the side. The duo created a formidable partnership as East End moved forward apace. Joe went on to become an ever present in Newcastle United's first Football League campaign.

Interest on Tyneside was centred on the approaching East versus West return derby at Chillingham Road in early February. Before another 'big' crowd for the day, about 3,000 with gate receipts of £46, East End fought back from a half-time deficit to record a 2–1 victory. West End took an early lead through Hannah, but East End were unlucky to go in at the break a goal behind after Smith had struck a post. The home side attacked from the restart, and soon McKane set up Mack, who with 'a nice back kick dropped the ball through the posts' to equalise. Smith hit the winner 'darting thro' to score', although it was noted that West End's 'keeper Jardine made a bit of a mess of the effort.

The Byker and Heaton supporters were so pleased at the success of their heroes that they literally wined and dined them by providing a complimentary dinner for the team during the following week. Challenge and counter-challenge passed to and fro across the city as West End fretted at their defeat, but the two teams could not agree on another meeting to settle the rivalry for that season.

Soon it was time for East End to embark on the Northumberland Challenge Cup trail again, this season without West End as a contender as they had decided not to take part. In a bid to avoid a repetition of the 19–0 debacle against Point Pleasant of the previous season, the Northumberland FA seeded the Heaton side through to the third round where they encountered Ovingham. Some of the first-team players were ineligible, so a few of the older players who were now semi-retired or playing for the Swifts were drafted into the team. Playing in blue and white to avoid a colour clash, they were still far too good for Ovingham as they strolled to a 9–1 victory. Andrew Muir scored four of the goals.

A week later they met Ashington in the semi-final at Chillingham Road. The visitors protested against the state of the pitch which still had its problems, yet the game went ahead and East End recorded another comfortable victory, winning 5–0 in front of 1,000 supporters.

The Heaton team had already arranged to play Middlesbrough in a friendly match on the same day as that semi-final. So, undeterred, after a 15-minute break, they started their second match of the day! The friendly game was only of two halves of 30 minutes' duration, but eight of the players who had faced Ashington played against Middlesbrough and recorded a creditable 1–1 draw.

Early success in the 1888–89 season came the way of East End when their Swifts combination (their reserve XI) again reached the Northumberland Second Team Cup Final. They met the Science & Art School club and won the trophy after a 5–1 victory. Other successes were to follow.

The first team soon played their own Cup Final, facing Elswick Rangers in the Final of the Challenge Cup on the Jesmond Athletic Ground. A poor and boring game ended in a goalless draw in front of 3,000 spectators. The replay was staged at the same venue, with over 2,000 in the enclosure, and after much East End pressure a Hiscock goal gave the East Enders a half-time lead. Goals in the second period by Nugent and Baxter, however, gave Rangers victory – or so it seemed. After the game, East End discovered that one of Elswick's players, James Nugent (Jnr), had played in a match during the previous close-season contrary to regulations and was therefore ineligible; so they submitted a protest that was upheld by the Northumberland FA Committee. The match would have to be replayed.

The referee at Jesmond, John Douglas of Gateshead, had been heavily criticised in the press for his handling of the game so Fred Hardisty was brought up from Middlesbrough for the second replay. That took place at St James' Park and attracted a bumper gate of 5,000. East End built up a comfortable three-goal lead through Mack, Collins and Hiscock, but Rangers were resilient and fought back with goals from Nugent (Snr) and McKay. They could not grab the equaliser, however, and the game finished 3–2. It was now Elswick's turn to protest, and they claimed that one of the East End players had played in the close-season and was therefore ineligible; on top of which, they claimed, spectators had run onto the pitch. This time the Northumberland FA Committee overruled the protest, and so East End secured the Cup.

But the decision left a sour taste in the mouths of Rangers and, although they reached the Final of the Tyne Charity Shield, when they found that they would have to face East End again, they refused to play. So the dark blues from Heaton won another trophy, this time by virtue of a walkover.

Over the Easter holidays, East End embarked on their first tour out of the North East area when they travelled to Scotland. This was an indication of how far the club had progressed. Taking football to the Scots in 1889 was the equivalent of taking coals to Newcastle. Although they only won one of their matches against lesser Scottish clubs, they were pleased with their performances, facing Mossend Swifts (1–3), Glasgow Thistle (2–1) and Hurlford (1–4). Travelling with the officials and players by train were 25 of their supporters. The party did a spot of sight-seeing in the Edinburgh area, visiting St Giles Cathedral, the Forth Bridge and the Palace at Linlithgow.

On their return from Scotland, East End played hosts to the FA Cup holders and first-ever Football League champions Preston North End, who returned to Tyneside after remaining undefeated in competitive games that season, earning the sobriquet 'Proud Preston'. Perhaps not surprisingly, they proved too good for the local team, but East End gave a good account of themselves despite losing 4–1.

There was soon to be a departure not only from East End but also from England for one East End player. William Muir was no longer in the first team, and many of his friends were sorry when he decided to emigrate to South Africa.

Back on the field of play, Shankhouse had won the rival Northern Association Cup. So, when they met East End in the middle of May, the match was regarded as the Championship of Northumberland. James Collins scored the all-important goal in the first half (although some sources credit Jock Smith with the effort) to give the Newcastle team a 1–0 victory and earn each of the players a gold badge.

The most important game of the season was now approaching – a Northumberland & Durham Inter-County Championship clash with Sunderland Albion. East End kept in form by playing Wolverhampton Wanderers (lost 3–2), their own Swifts team (won 8–1) and a challenge match with the Cleveland Cup holders Darlington St Augustine's, which they won 2–0.

In late May, East End travelled to Hendon on Wearside to meet the Durham Cup holders for, arguably, the right to be called the best team in the North East. A very tight game resulted with only one goal being scored. That decisive strike came 10 minutes from time when a Mulvey shot was deflected by McFarlane past his goalkeeper to give the Tynesiders victory. This result was regarded at the time as East End's 'crowning success for the season'.

Albion were not happy with the result. Their supporters had been so confident of victory that one of them had ordered notepaper headed 'Durham and Inter-County Champions'. A challenge was issued to East End to meet them again. The re-match took place a week after the original fixture, this time at Chillingham Road where, in front of 2,000 spectators, East End confirmed their superiority with another 1–0 victory thanks to a John Barker goal. He was a guest player from West End, one of the most important footballers of the era. Barker was soon to switch camps permanently and join East End.

But East End had little time to bask in their glory during that summer of 1889. They were soon shocked when their shrewd secretary, Tom Watson, who had been such an influential factor in their rise to prominence, announced that he was leaving the club. He was not out of work long, soon taking over at the much richer Sunderland club. His capture by the Wearsiders is well recorded by John Grayston, one of Sunderland's founders. He wrote in his memoirs that he was asked to get the best man for the role, and Watson was that man: 'I found him eventually in a pub. I fitted him out in a new suit. He duly presented himself and got the job at £150 a year, and mighty grateful was he to get it.' Grayston added: 'He was a magnificent secretary. He could rule his team with kindness and firmness, and always made himself the chum of the rank and file, who looked upon him as his brother.' Sunderland also fixed him up with a side business venture – a tobacconist's shop opposite Monkwearmouth Station.

Watson was to take the Wearsiders into the Football League, help greatly to build the legendary 'Team of all the Talents' and take Sunderland to glory. Within three years he guided them to their first League Championship success and, in the next three years, won the title twice more, with one runners'-up spot for good measure. He is easily the most successful manager in Sunderland's history (although that was not his job title in an era before managers as we know them now). In 1896 Tom moved on to Merseyside for twice his salary and wove his magic with Liverpool as well, guiding them to two League Championship titles. He was arguably the greatest of the secretary-managers of the late

Victorian and Edwardian era. Watson was awarded the Football League's Long Service medal in 1910. When he died on Merseyside five years later, his coffin was carried by such renowned footballers as Ted Doig and Alex Raisbeck.

Watson was still with East End at an emotional and joyous evening in the Leighton Schoolroom on Heaton Road at the season's end. What was described as a multitude of Cups and medals were on view to celebrate East End's most successful season so far. They had won every local trophy that they had competed for and the first and second-team players were formally presented with their medals. Councillor Harry Walker also made a special presentation to Alec White who was retiring. A stopwatch, purchased by public subscription, bore the inscription: 'Presented to A.H. White by friends and members of the East End F.C. for services rendered to Club and County, 1889.'

Alec had played in four Northumberland Challenge Cup Finals (two with Rangers and two with East End), winning every time. He had won the Cup in his first season with East End and now, in his last full season, he had won it again. White had been East End's – and therefore Newcastle United's – first outstanding player, and with his retirement an era came to a close. The day of the amateur was drawing to an end. For the following 1889–90 season East End were to be a fully professional outfit, League games were to be played at Chillingham Road and the club developed into becoming a limited company. It really was the end of an era.

Chapter 5

RIVALS IN THE WEST

'West End seem determined to make themselves the "boss" club of the area.'
'Custos', *Daily Journal,* 1886

As East End grew from strength to strength in Byker and Heaton, another club was undergoing a similar development west of Newcastle's town centre. That club was West End, and its genesis was similar to that of East End, emanating from a cricket team made up of local friends and colleagues. The two clubs were to become fierce rivals as the years passed, and eventually it became a struggle for survival.

The suburbs to the west of Newcastle had similar backgrounds to those to the east. As in Byker and along the eastern riverside, during the 1870s and 1880s the villages of Elswick and Benwell on the western slopes of the Tyne were transformed as the industrial revolution took hold. Engineering, shipbuilding and especially armaments manufacture took over from the historic coal mining. It was this heavy industry that ensured the development of the sporting culture on Tyneside. Many of the early sportsmen worked in the factories and shipyards of Tyneside, whether it was on the slipways, Charles Parson's steam turbine works in the east of the town or Lord Armstrong's munitions factories to the west. The latter in Elswick saw an incredible growth and, by 1892, the Armstrong empire alone was one of the largest employers in the whole of the North.

But, in terms of population, Elswick and Benwell were dwarfed by the area west of Newcastle known as the Westgate Township. This densely populated area consisted of rows and rows of terraced houses around Arthur's Hill. In 1841, when Elswick still only had 2,384 residents, Westgate's population was already 10,063.

Newcastle cast its eyes on the neighbouring townships and villages. The Municipal Corporations Act of 1835 saw the town extend its boundaries to take in both Elswick and Westgate Townships, as well as Jesmond, Heaton and Byker. It was to take a few more years (until 1904) before the suburbs of Benwell, Fenham and Walker were to be incorporated, although to all intents and purposes they were already largely regarded as part of the town.

However, whether inside or outside the municipal boundaries, it all meant a vast working-class community and a huge catchment for the new sport of association football, and several clubs were formed in and around the new bustling suburbs to the west of Newcastle. One of these was a club that became known as West End Football Club.

In many ways, however, the name of the club was a bit of a misnomer. Although it had largely Elswick origins, initially it was an itinerant club, moving from one home ground to another as the members searched to find a settled location, and not all of the grounds used by the club were in the west end. They briefly used a pitch in Jesmond, which by no stretch of the imagination could be called the 'west end', being to the north of the city. Yet as 'West End FC' the club was formed and as West End it remained, for the time being at least. Eventually they were to settle at St James' Park, which is west of the town, although considerably nearer to the centre than, say, East End's home at Chillingham Road which was two miles away. But it was from the area around St James' Park, which included the environs of the Westgate district of Arthur's Hill and Stanhope Street, that West End FC gained most of their support in the late 1880s.

But that lay a few years ahead. In the beginning, West End, like East End in Byker, owed its origins to cricket. A West End Cricket Club existed as long ago as 1877, and they played their home matches on the Town Moor. They became well established and were by 1879 an apparently flourishing club, at least in terms of the social aspects of the game. In December that year they held their third annual evening party in the Masonic Hall on Maple Street in Newcastle and attracted some 80 ladies and gentlemen. Another gathering during the following December was once more a success. Yet, after playing cricket in the early summer of 1881, the club seems to have disbanded and disappears from the records.

Another West End cricket club soon emerged, however, having on the face of it no connection with the former one. The new club started out as the Crown Cricket Club, probably named after the area where it originated, Crown Street near to Elswick Park. Many of these small cricket and football clubs initially took their names from the streets where they began. Rendel and Boundary were two similar clubs as, indeed, was Stanley in South Byker.

A Crown Cricket Club was playing in 1878 (on the Town Moor), but whether there is a direct connection with the club that eventually became West End is open to conjecture. There seems to have been a hiatus until Crown CC appeared again in the summer of 1881. This club soon became established and, at a gathering of the members held during August of that year in Lockhart's Cocoa Rooms, a popular meeting place on Clayton Street in the town centre, it was announced that the club had decided to change its name to West End Juniors. It is probable that the 'Juniors' nomenclature was to reflect the potential standing of the club rather than the ages of its players. Crucially, the names of the club officers elected at the meeting were recorded:

Captain:	Thomas Waggott (re-elected).
Vice-captain:	John Bradley (re-elected).
Secretary:	Robert White.
Treasurer:	John Waggott (re-elected).

A number of players called Waggott, not all directly related, were to become key figures in the development of West End FC when it was eventually formed. In fact, in one game during the club's first season, no fewer than four Waggotts appeared in the team.

The cricket club continued playing as West End Juniors but a year later, in August 1882, it was decided to form a football club. Once again, the officers elected to run this embryonic team were documented:

Captain:	W. Scott.
Vice-captain:	John Waggott.
Secretary & treasurer:	William Tiffin.
Committee:	W. Mather, C. Wray & J. Blair.

William Tiffin was to become a particularly important figure in the development of West End and of association football generally in the North East. He is largely credited as being the driving force behind the early development of West End. As a left-sided

Bill Tiffin was the driving force behind West End. He later became a prominent member of the Football Association.

forward player he was a decent footballer, good enough to appear for the county side, but he became better known as a long-serving secretary of the Northumberland FA in the years ahead. Tiffin held the office for over 21 years (1889–1911) before being rewarded with the then unique accolade of Life Membership of the Northumberland FA.

As an administrator in the region Tiffin also sat on the Football Association Council and was described as having a 'cheerful and optimistic disposition', while the early text *Association Football And The Men Who Made It* noted Tiffin as giving 'ardent, energetic and tireless work' to the game. After serving West End as a player, secretary and other various positions, he joined East End on his own club's collapse, continuing to serve Newcastle United. He died in 1925.

Early records show that West End's colours were 'red-and-black jerseys and hose with white knickers' and rare team group photographs of the day show they were worn at varying times with a design of either hoops or quartered shirts. They played their home games on part of the Town Moor known as Newcastle Leazes not too far from where Newcastle United were eventually to make their home. The exact site is difficult to establish, but it was recorded in the great Colin Veitch's memoirs that his first club (Larkspur) played on the old pitch of West End, Veitch noting it as being located 'just below the path which now leads from the [Leazes] Park to Spital Tongues'. That would be off Richardson Road at the edge of Leazes Park.

West End did not fare too well in their early games in which they met other junior teams of a similar standing. They lost their first fixture, 2–0 away to Rosewood, on 7 October 1882. Unfortunately there is no record of their line up for this game. A further defeat a week later on the other side of the town in Heaton resulted in a single-goal reverse, but at least this time West End's team was recorded in tactical formation: goal: Fawcett; backs: Waggott (J.), Henderson; half-backs: Waggott (T.), Surtees; right wing: Waggott (H.), Lightfoot; centres: Mather (W.), Tiffin; left wing: Simms, Best.

It is interesting to note that both teams played in a 2–2–6 formation. In addition, the teams named indicate the itinerant nature of players as they moved from one club to another. The Heaton side included a number of players who had appeared in Stanley's first-ever game less than a year earlier – Thomas Phalp, John Hobson and Joseph Dixon. Perhaps this is not surprising given the geographic closeness of the two clubs from the east end of the town and the seemingly close relationship between them.

West End continued to have mixed results during that first season of 1882–83. They did not manage to win a game until early December (their fifth fixture) when they defeated Marlborough away, 1–0. Their biggest success of the campaign was a 4–0 victory at Leazes against St Cuthbert's in January.

As a minor team, they were allowed to enter the Northumberland & Durham Second XI Cup competition, but they were eliminated, 2–1 at Newcastle FA, in the first round. Another notable defeat came in their last game of the season when they went down 3–0 away to East End's second team; however, it would not be too long before West End would be on an equal standing with the club that became their arch-rivals.

Several players pulled on West End's red-and-black colours in its inaugural season, including R. Lightfoot who also briefly played for East End's first, second and junior teams during the season, as well as for Stanley's reserve side last year. He was not a regular at West End, but quite a few players were: Bill Tiffin, Henry Waggott, John Waggott, Edward Surtees, T. Fawcett, A. Best, W. Mather and Thomas Minnikin, a Scottish goalkeeper who also played outfield and was a decent swimmer in the district. It can be seen that some of the club officials were also regular players.

During that summer of 1883, West End also entered for the Temperance Festival Junior Football Competition but went out at the first hurdle, losing 1–0 at Hebburn. Yet, despite a non-too-successful first season in which, as far as can be ascertained due to the lack of comprehensive match reports, they only won three out of 13 games, the club seemed to grow and were able to field a second team during 1883–84 when results, and performances, for the senior XI significantly improved.

The club's second annual meeting was held, once again, in Lockhart's Cocoa Rooms during July and saw the election of new officers for the forthcoming season. W. Mather became the club captain with Thomas Waggott the vice-captain. Bill Tiffin continued as treasurer but A. Best Jnr took over the role of secretary. The club committee comprised E. Surtees, T. Fawcett, Charles Ormond, Edward Waggott and Minnikin. Tom Minnikin also acted as captain to the second team, for which he was also secretary.

An early 4–0 reverse south of the Tyne against Birtley second XI was to prove a false alarm, and soon West End enjoyed winning ways as they went from strength to strength. That early defeat was easily their worst of the year. Indeed, with one notable exception (which is covered later), they only conceded more than one goal on a single occasion for the rest of the season, in a 5–3 victory on a trip to face All Saints during March. Even then, one of the Saints' goals was disputed.

It was early in the 1883–84 season that the first West End players received official recognition from the county association, albeit in a small way. During September, the Northumberland FA held a series of trial matches in an attempt to select a representative county side. Two West End men, Bill Tiffin and John Waggott, were selected to play in these games, referred to as 'Colts matches'. John actually progressed to a final trial, but neither made the county team. It was a sign, though, that West End were improving.

At club level, victories became the order of the day, at least in the friendly games (called 'ordinary' fixtures at the time). Some of these wins were by more than comfortable margins, such as 4–0 at Jarrow in October and also by the same score on home soil to Hebburn during November. Another four-goal success soon followed, this time 5–1 against Rendel on their Leazes pitch. It got even better: a 7–0 triumph against Drysdale just before Christmas was followed by a massive 10–0 thrashing of Brunswick on New Year's Day. It was looking too easy. Then came the rude awakening.

As explained in an earlier chapter, the Northumberland and Durham Football Associations went their own ways during 1883 and split into separate associations. West End naturally became affiliated with the Northumberland FA. Both of the new associations launched their own Challenge Cup competitions, with West End deciding to enter the Northumberland tournament. They were fortunate to receive a bye through the first round, but their luck ran out when the West Enders had to face the still mighty Tyne Association in the second tie. West End now learned the harsh realities of football

Newcastle Central Station around 1880, the hub for travelling around the Victorian North East.

life. It was one thing chalking up massive victories against local minnows, but it was another matter facing a much bigger club with more experienced players. Against Tyne, they were simply outclassed, and a three-goal half-time deficit was increased to 7–0 by the final whistle.

The teams for that historic fixture, West End's first senior competitive game, were as follows:

Tyne: Morrison, Gould, Webb-Ware, Watson, Harrison, Messent (F.), Pattinson, Phillipson, Redmayne, Messent (P.), Ainslie.

V

West End: Minnikin, Waggott (T.), Lowe, Waggott (J.), Surtees, Henderson, Mather (W.), Mather (J.), Tiffin, Fawcett, Best.

It can be seen that a number of the West Enders who had played in the club's very early fixture were still representing the club. Yet they had definitely improved during the season, and the best example of that was when they faced East End in a home fixture during March. The previous season they had lost 3–0 against East End's second team; now they defeated their first-choice XI, either 2–0 or 3–0, different reports giving different scorelines. Club captain W. Mather scored two of the goals, although one of them was disputed.

Many of the players who had turned out for West End during its inaugural campaign had still been mainstays for the club during the season just ended. Only Henry Waggott no longer appeared for the first team, although he turned out regularly for the second XI. Others came into greater prominence, including Thomas Waggott (who had made a handful of appearances in 1882–83) and newcomers Charles Ormond and J. Mather. Another player to turn out as a guest was William Findlay, who had started the season as the East End captain.

The Mathers were prominent pioneers for West End, but little is known about them, not even their Christian names. The local match summaries added confusion by using, and likely mixing up, differing initials; however, it is probable the two players were W. Mather and J. Mather. They both originally played for the Elswick Ordnance Works team at both cricket and football before joining up with West End. It is also likely that J.A. Mather is the same individual who helped form Elswick Rugby Club and played in that first game of football on Tyneside in 1877.

West End entered a combination for the Summer Temperance Festival, but their interest was short-lived once more as they were defeated 2–0 by East End in a preliminary round and never reached the Finals.

They developed well during the following 1884–85 season, however, losing only one fixture before the turn of the year, and that by a solitary goal at home to Rangers. They even defeated Tyne 3–2 in Jesmond just before Christmas. Newcastle's former 'big two' of Tyne and Rangers were now on the wane, but victories against the pair were still feathers in the cap.

Defeats for West End were few and far between so hopes were high, once again, when they entered for the Northumberland Challenge Cup. As in the previous season, the Leazes club received a bye through the first stage, and their luck held this time with the draw for the second round. They had to play North Tyne Swifts, hardly a major team, and the tie took place on the Jesmond club's pitch at Moor Edge on the North Road, possibly because West End's ground was not good enough. West End were not stretched as they chalked up a 6–1 triumph.

The next round was a tougher proposition – against Newcastle Association; this time the tie was to be staged on Tyne's ground in Jesmond. West End won again, but

Supporter collector cards were all the rage throughout England at the time; 'Play Up West End!'

only 2–1, and Newcastle's officials were far from happy. They submitted a protest to the Northumberland FA against the referee, but it was rejected and West End went on to the semi-final, where they had to meet East End, once again on Tyne's ground.

A substantial crowd for the time of 1,500 turned up to witness an epic struggle as West End battled back from a 3–1 half-time deficit to force a draw. The replay was staged a week later and this time the Byker club proved far too strong and won comfortably, 5–0, before a crowd of 600. So the Cup campaign ended in failure for West End, but there had undoubtedly been progress.

They had also entered their second team for the Northumberland FA's Second XI competition, and this also saw controversy. West End faced Backworth Hotspur (once again at the Jesmond ground) and went 2–1 ahead. The Backworth players, however, were furious that West End's second goal was allowed and stormed off the pitch in disgust. They protested to the Northumberland FA, who this time upheld the objection and ordered that the game should be replayed – at Backworth. Hotspur made the most of their home advantage and won 4–2.

Nevertheless, the season was regarded as a success. West End had fielded three teams, and a summary of their results was presented to the club's annual meeting at the beginning of May:

First team:	P25	W20	D3	L2
Second team:	P18	W13	D3	L2
Junior team:	P13	W4	D4	L5

The nucleus of enthusiasts who had played in the club's first two seasons were still active players, with Tiffin, John Waggott, Best, Minnikin, Fawcett, Surtees and W. Mather all stalwarts from the first season and Ormond and Tom Waggott from the second. Newcomers who had been regulars in the season just ended had been Edward (Ned) Waggott and Joseph Welford.

Ned Waggott, the younger brother of Tom, was a particularly interesting character. When he was only eight years old, Ned had suffered the traumatic experience of losing his father in tragic circumstance. In 1875, when he was only 35, Ned's father, William, had been badly injured in an accident on the coal staithes on the River Tyne. He was carried to his home nearby in Herbert Street (just off Scotswood Road), where it was decided that his injuries were so bad that an operation would have to be carried out immediately. His leg was amputated on the kitchen table but, sadly, he died.

Ned, though, was made of stern stuff and, when he was 13 years old, he was indentured as a fitter with the engineering firm of Donkin & Nichol who were based in St Andrew's Street off Gallowgate, and he served his apprenticeship with them, soon starting to play the association game of football. He eventually joined Armstrong, Whitworth & Co in 1888 and was to work for them for over 50 years, gradually working his way up to manage the Shell Department. During World War One, armament production was essential to the survival of the nation, and it was imperative that it was maximized. Ned was so highly thought-of that he was given an illustrated address, a gold

Ned Waggott en route to the Town Moor Temperance Festival; a cabinet photograph of family, friends and dogs! Ned is the tallest of the three men at the rear. *(D. Waggott collection)*

watch and chain, as well as a signet ring from the company in 1916 and was awarded the MBE in January 1918. He continued working for the rest of his life, right until the end of World War Two. Ned was then 78 years old, and he told Mr Jamieson, the chairman of Vickers, that he would not rest until Germany was beaten. They surrendered in May 1945 and Ned died a month later, his objective achieved.

A number of Waggotts played for West End in the 1880s, and they may have been distantly related. The four most prevalent were John, Thomas, Edward and Henry. As explained, Tom and Ned were brothers, with the former (aged 19 in early 1885) the elder by two years. Similarly, John and Henry were also different brothers, with John (aged 20) also two years older than Henry. They lived in Jefferson Street, which was near Stanhope Street.

A couple of players who had not been regulars in 1883–84 but who had made a few appearances in the following season were J. Mather and W. Moat. One regular player from last season who did not make any appearances in 1884–85 was James Henderson. Otherwise, there was a remarkable continuity in the staff. This was soon to change.

West End entered a team for the Temperance Festival in the summer and reached the semi-final, defeating Shankhouse Blues and Rendel in the preliminary rounds to reach the Finals on the Town Moor at the beginning of July. But here they failed, losing 5–4 against Bedlington Burdon in the semi-final in a game of two periods of 30 minutes and then losing 3–1 against an East End B team in the third-place play-off.

A change of grounds was soon to be forced on West End. During that same summer of 1885, clubs were barred from playing on the Town Moor and, as the Leazes was part of the Moor, they had to re-locate, as did their neighbours Newcastle Association. Both clubs arrived at the same solution to their problem. They decided to share the former ground of the recently defunct Jesmond FC, adjacent to the North Road. Precise directions were given in the press regarding the location of the ground – 'the first field north of Brandling Park', which was off Abbotsford Terrace, a short walk from Tyne's headquarters at Warwick Place. That field is still used now as a football pitch over 124 years later.

By this time John Barker Jnr had taken over as secretary. The club took part in a pre-season tournament – the Benwell British Workmen Temperance Festival – during September. Billy Tiffin captained the team on this occasion, although they were not full matches, merely seven-a-side, with a number of games being played on the same day. Nevertheless, it was estimated that 1,000 spectators watched West End defeat North Eastern 3–0 in their first round only to lose 2–1 to Elswick Ordnance Works at the next hurdle. Shankhouse Black Watch won the tournament.

Once the new 1885–86 season started in earnest, West End once again had an encouraging first few games. Admittedly there were defeats, none worse than a 6–1 reverse against East End on Tyne's ground in mid-November. But this was a rare West End defeat, and offset against this were a number of comfortable triumphs such as a 4–0 (or 5–0 with a disputed goal) home success against Newcastle FA and a treble of 6–0 victories against Tyne, Ovingham and the Elswick Ordnance Works. Too much should not be read into the defeat of Tyne. The pioneer club was now in decline and, in this particular game, which was played over two 30-minute periods, they only had 10 men.

West End were still trying to find a settled team by the time the first round of the Northumberland Challenge Cup arrived in January. A home tie against minnows Cathedral seemed as if it was going to be a formality, but it was not even that because their opponents only turned up with nine men and refused to play. So West End received a bye into the next round, where much sterner opponents awaited them – East End.

There had been a 2–2 draw with East End in Heaton on Boxing Day, so the West Enders were by no means overawed despite the early season thrashing. Once again, the game was played on Tyne's ground in Jesmond and W. Mather gave the West End supporters a dream start when he scored within two minutes. This lead was soon increased when J. Mather scored, but East End pulled a goal back by charging goalkeeper Telford and the ball over the line to make it an exciting finale. But there was no further score and West End progressed into the next round.

A week later they faced Rendel, winning 3–2. Then West End opposed Backworth Hotspur in the semi-final on Tyne's ground in front of a poor crowd of 300. On a snow-covered pitch, goals by Welford and J. Mather were enough to guide the West Enders into the Final where they met much stronger opposition in the shape of Shankhouse Black Watch. This was, once again, played at Tyne's arena, and a crowd of over 2,000 saw a classic game; although the pitmen from south-east Northumberland proved to have the edge and were too strong for the townsmen. Goals by James Welford and Billy Tiffin made a contest of it, but two from the Shankhouse centre-forward, Matthews, and one from winger Hedley were just enough to win the game.

In spite of the Cup Final reverse it had been a satisfactory season for West End, and they had undoubtedly developed into one of the better teams in the region. Perhaps this is best illustrated in two contests on Wearside with the powerful Sunderland outfit. West End may have lost both games, but in those fixtures during February and March they fell on each occasion by just one goal.

West End were invited to take part in the Tyne Charity Shield competition at the end of the season, but their interest did not last long as they were eliminated by Morpeth Harriers, suffering a 2–0 defeat in their semi-final.

Some of the earlier enthusiasts still provided the backbone of the team during the 1885–86 season, but the side was slowly changing. Still frequently appearing were club captain John Waggott, vice-captain Joseph Welford, Ned Waggott, Billy Tiffin and W. Mather, while J. Mather had now become a regular after only making occasional appearances in the previous year. Edward Surtees also played in a few games without being classed as a regular, similar to the previous season. Newcomers who had made an impression were James Taylor, ex-Jesmond defender R. McDougall and John Barker. The last named had been captain of the Drysdale club and was to become a stalwart of West End in the years ahead. Another notable recruit, although he only played in the last few games of the season, was James (or John) Angus who came down from Scotland and had also played rugby with Northern. His appearance was a foretaste of what was to come in the next few years.

At the club's annual meeting, held at the club's headquarters (the premises of Mrs Hall on North Road, Newcastle) in early May 1886, the usual election of officers for next season was carried out. These included prominent local personalities Joseph Cowen MP and J.W. Pease JP as club patrons, as well as Dr W. I'Anson as club president, and Messrs Robinson, Stanger and Maughan as vice-presidents. The first-team captain was named as J. Mather, with James Taylor elected as vice-captain.

Thomas Waggott was to be the second-team skipper and W. Kennon the juniors' captain. John Waggott became honorary treasurer and William Tiffin the financial assistant secretary.

But the most important appointment was that of new honorary secretary, Thomas Watson, who was to have an enormous influence on West End. When he took over the club was described as having 'neither a sou in the bank nor an enclosed ground to play on'. That changed rapidly. Soon *Custos* (the nom de plume of the football columnist writing for the *Daily Journal*) commented that 'West End seem determined to make themselves the "boss" club of the area and I am sure the plucky West Enders will deserve every bit of success they get'. Watson's efforts would see the club emerge as the best on Tyneside for a period. Both he and Billy Tiffin were appointed as club representatives to the Northumberland FA.

The meeting heard of the club's playing record during the 1885–86 season:

First team:	P22	W13	D2	L7
Junior team:	P14	W6	D3	L5

The club had also fielded a second team, but it was announced that due to the bad weather so few fixtures had been completed that no record had been kept of the scores!

An influential figure behind the scenes for West End was William Nesham, who later became Newcastle United chairman.

At the same meeting, two momentous decisions were made. Possibly influenced by Tom Watson, it was decided that the club would enter for the English FA Cup the following season, and it was also decided to relocate to another new ground. At the time it was merely stated that 'three gentlemen interested in the club are negotiating for the lease of a field, which will be one of the best in the district'. The field turned out to be the old Rangers pitch between Gallowgate and the Leazes. West End also decided to retain the old name for the ground – St James' Park.

Although not revealed at the time, clues to the identity of these 'three gentlemen' were given a few months later by the Sheriff of Newcastle, Thomas Bell, at the opening of the new ground. He specifically praised the efforts of the club president Dr I'Anson, a prominent supporter of West End's cause, as well as Mr Robinson and Mr Stanger (vice-presidents) for the manner in which they had worked so hard to secure the ground. In addition, another West End enthusiast and keen local sportsman, William Nesham, who held the lease of the 5.25 acres site from the Freemen, was deeply involved. Both Nesham and I'Anson had been brought up in the game of cricket locally and no doubt knew each other well.

The original lease for the ground was only for four years. Nevertheless, a number of men were employed in levelling the pitch and enclosing the field behind a substantial paling, 8ft high. The cost of these improvements was estimated at £200, and it gave the club a sort of identity from the rest of Castle Leazes. It was the start of a long development path of the ground, which would also be commonly known as 'Gallowgate' due to its proximity to the old thoroughfare into the town.

A number of prominent new signings were made by West End before the 1886–87 season started. The foremost newcomer was Scottish international outside-left Ralph Aitken, who had been capped against England while playing for Dumbarton the previous season. The other key arrival was Robert Oldham, the Elswick Leather Works goalkeeper, who was acknowledged as the best Tyneside custodian and who had made a couple of appearances for West End two years earlier. So far, West End had not really fielded a regular specialist goalkeeper. Different players were tried out but were to be found as often in an outfield position as between the posts. This all changed with the recruitment of Oldham.

West End obviously had ambition and, when they inflicted the first home defeat for two years on Morpeth Harriers in the opening game of the season, it appeared that the signings had been successful.

As mentioned, Thomas Bell, the Sheriff of Newcastle, formally opened St James' Park on 2 October 1886 with a short speech before the kick-off. The visitors were East End, and the biggest crowd ever assembled for an 'ordinary' club match in Newcastle, 2,000, witnessed a closely fought and sporting game. For the record, the teams for this match were as follows:

West End: Oldham, Taylor, Chalmers, Waggott (E.), Mather (J.), Campbell, Tiffin, Angus, Mather (W.), Aitken, Barker.
V
East End: McClen, Heron, Goulden, Lightfoot, White, Blackett (W.), Scott, O'Brien, Hoban, Muir (W.), Hiscock (E.).

The honour of scoring the first goal almost fell to Billy Tiffin, but his effort was disallowed for offside. It was left to Ralph Aitken to register the opening goal with a high shot; indeed he may have scored the first two but, as was not uncommon at the time, there are conflicting reports regarding the identity of goalscorers. It is more probable that W. Mather scored West End's second goal, with Aitken grabbing a third before half-time. Peter O'Brien and William Muir notched a couple of second-half

THE GROWTH OF WEST END I

Timetable of Development

August 1881:	Crown Cricket Club changes name to West End Juniors CC.
August 1882:	West End FC formed from West End Juniors CC.
October 1882:	First game v Rosewood (lost 2–0).
December 1882:	First victory v Marlborough (won 1–0).
February 1883:	First competitive game v Newcastle FA, lost 2–1 (N&D Second XI Cup).
September 1885:	West End move from Leazes to Moor Edge, Jesmond.
April 1886:	First senior Cup Final – Northumberland Cup (lost 3–2 v Shankhouse BW).
May 1886:	Tom Watson appointed secretary & West End move to St James' Park.

goals for East End to result in a nail-biting finish when only a brilliant save by Oldham prevented a last-minute equaliser. Tommy Watson, West End's secretary-manager, must have been happy with both the result and the attendance.

On the other hand, according to another published match report, John Barker scored a hat-trick, giving West End a 3–0 lead, with Ned Hiscock scoring both goals for East End. The same report praised Alec White for 'completely bottling up the clever little international Aitken'. Ralph could hardly have been 'completely bottled up' if he had scored two goals. What is indisputable, however, is the final score: West End 3 East End 2.

The press at the time published a contemporary view of West End's new home: 'The ground is situated at the bottom end of Leazes Park and is called St James' Park. It is very large and, with improvements that are yet to take place, will make it one of the best, if not the best, grounds in the north.'

Reports indicate that the club continued to play in red and black that season. One of their players, James Duns, a full-back, received county recognition when he was included in the Northumberland team that defeated Hallamshire 5–3 during mid-October, reflecting the growing regard in which the West End players were now held.

Early results generally went well for them, and attendances of between 500 and 600 for 'ordinary' matches were reasonable. A solitary defeat, 4–0 away to Bishop Auckland Church Institute, was more than compensated for by a 10–1 win at home to Gateshead during October when they scored eight times in the first half and took it easy after the break. But excitement was mounting around Gallowgate with the approach of the first round of the FA Cup in October 1886 which had paired West End with Sunderland.

Controversy surrounded the tie, which was played at the Wearsiders' Newcastle Road ground before 4,500 spectators when the teams lined up as follows:

Sunderland: Kirkley, Elliott, Oliver, McMillan, Smart, Dale, Rooney, Erskine, Smith, Lord, Davison.

V

West End: Oldham, Duns, Waggott (J.), Campbell, Mather (J.), Chalmers, Dobson, Welford, Angus, Aitken, Barker.

Lord (Sunderland) and Campbell (West End) notched first-half goals, and the score remained level until the end of normal time. The referee decided to play extra-time, but West End objected as it was already getting dark. In fact they originally left the field but were persuaded to return. Two minutes from the end of the extra period, in the gathering gloom, John Lord grabbed the winner to give the Wearsiders victory – or so they thought. West End immediately submitted a protest to the Football Association who sustained the objection and ordered a replay at St James' Park.

That took place a fortnight later before a 4,000 crowd recording gate receipts of £44. West End made changes to their team, with James Taylor and Billy Tiffin coming into their line up in place of Welford and Barker, but Sunderland remained unchanged. Another closely fought encounter ensued on a wet pitch during which 'Dowk' Oliver, the Sunderland full-back, suffered a broken collarbone. Only one goal divided the teams at the final whistle, and it was West End who progressed to the next round, with Angus heading the all-important winner from an Aitken corner 10 minutes from time. Now it was Sunderland's turn to protest. They based their objections on three grounds:

1) In scoring the winner the ball did not touch any player in its flight from the corner flag to between the posts.
2) The Football Association Committee had no right to order a replay.
3) The West End team was partly comprised of professionals who were not qualified by residence to play for the club.

All three protests were rejected, and West End marched on to meet Gainsborough Trinity in the second round of the competition.

This time the visitors from Lincolnshire proved to be too strong for the Tynesiders. West End made a contest of it in the first half, but they still found themselves two goals down at the interval, despite Aitken and Dobson finding the net. Two further strikes by Trinity in the second half made the score an emphatic 6–2, and West End could have no qualms about their defeat.

At least West End were still on good terms with Sunderland, despite the protests and objections that had surrounded their Cup tie. When the Wearsiders decided to hold a benefit match for the injured Oliver the Gallowgate club were only too willing to travel to Newcastle Road to provide the opposition. An excellent attendance of between 5,000 and 6,000 raised almost £30 for the full-back. The 1–0 victory for Sunderland was of comparatively little importance.

At the beginning of December, the club held a meeting at the Lord Hill public house on Pitt Street, just across Barrack Road from St James' Park. The pub, under the ownership of supporter John Black, was to become an important venue for the club in the next few years when the players used to change there before and after games. Black

John Black was a keen supporter of West End's cause, afterwards becoming a Newcastle United director like Nesham.

lived close by in Buckingham Street and later became a Newcastle United director.

The primary reason for the meeting seems to have been to vote for a replacement for J. Mather who had resigned as captain. Two candidates were proposed: James Duns and Ralph Aitken. Duns, the former Alnwick player, was elected by a small majority, but Aitken was voted into a vacancy on the club committee.

There was still discord at certain games. A home fixture against Bishop Auckland Church Institute was reduced to 15 minutes each way because the visitors were late in arriving. By this time, many of the spectators had given up and returned home. Nevertheless, the match went on, but it did not even last the full 30 minutes because West End scored a controversial goal near the end that the visitors claimed was offside. The referee, however, allowed the goal to stand, so the Church Institute players walked off and refused to complete the game.

A number of strong teams visited St James' early in the new year of 1887, such as Dumbarton Athletic (who won 3–1) and Albion Rovers (1–1). An interesting feature of the second game was the appearance of a number of Dumbarton players as guests in the West End side. They had obviously stayed behind for a few days after the Dumbarton match. But the most welcome visitors were the famous Corinthians who, with several internationals in their side, comfortably defeated a Newcastle & District XI 5–0. Ralph Aitken and James Duns played for the local team.

Aitken was to leave Tyneside not long afterwards to return to Dumbarton. He had accepted a position on the West End committee just over a month earlier, obviously intending to stay on Tyneside. But he was more than likely approached when the Scots were at St James' and persuaded to return to Dunbartonshire. His move was primarily for monetary considerations as he had been offered a better-paid job on Clydeside than the 39s 0d (£1 95p) a week he was earning on Tyneside. His departure was not universally lamented in Newcastle. While acknowledging his undoubted ability, *Custos* commented: 'I don't think that his absence will be much of a loss to the West End club. Either he was demoralising their team or their team was demoralising him, so in either case he is better away.'

The first round of the Northumberland Challenge Cup saw West End comfortably defeat a fading Tyne 6–0, Scotsman James Raylstone scoring three of the goals. A similar scoreline disposed of Prudhoe Rovers in the second round, but a trip to Benwell to face Rendel in the next stage seemed a trickier tie; however, two goals by

Billy Tiffin in the first three minutes gave his team a dream start, and the final 3–1 score was comfortable enough.

The semi-final against Morpeth Harriers at the neutral venue of Chillingham Road was even more comfortable, a 5–0 result giving a clear indication of West End's superiority. Following a goalless first half, West End took advantage of a strong wind. Angus grabbed the first two goals, then Barker secured the tie at 3–0. McDonald and Raylstone completed the second-half superiority.

The Final, played at the same venue, was a different matter. Here West End encountered mighty Shankhouse Black Watch who had eliminated East End in the other semi-final. The miners' outfit proved far too strong for the Gallowgate side and won 5–1, with Billy Swinburne scoring West End's consolation goal. The attendance of 4,000 was a clear demonstration of the growing popularity of the sport, and this figure did not include another 1,000 who scaled the fencing to get in without paying.

The end-of-season Tyne Charity Shield contest led to some controversy as far as West End were concerned. East End had advised the Northumberland FA that they did not want to participate in the competition, but West End blotted their copybook by initially agreeing to do so but then refusing to meet Elswick Rangers in a preliminary round. The governing body were not pleased and immediately announced that it was barring West End from the following year's tournaments, and it was only thanks to the eloquence of the club's secretary-manager, Tom Watson, that the association revoked their decision.

Half a dozen players could be regarded as the mainstays of the club at that time: Taylor, Angus, Barker, Chalmers, Oldham and Duns. They received good support from other committed players in Raylstone, Campbell, Tiffin, Swinburne, A. McDonald, John Waggott, J. McDonald and, of course, Ralph Aitken until he returned to Scotland. Many of the pioneers of the club were still active and turned out when the need arose. These included J. Mather (who had been particularly effective until he had surrendered the captaincy), W. Mather, Joseph Welford and Ned Waggott. But the old school were now gradually being replaced.

James Taylor played over 100 games for West End and developed into a celebrated player. A full-back in the main, he remained with the club to its demise and represented both the Northumberland and Newcastle & District teams. James Angus was another respected footballer on Tyneside able to grab plenty of goals up front. It should be noted there remains uncertainty over Angus as there were three Scottish players named J. Angus

West End's James Taylor sketched wearing his Northumberland county cap.

to play the game at the same time; Jack, James and John. Jack played for Sunderland Albion as a goalkeeper, and it appears two also turned out for Everton, including Jack. It looks like West End's player was either James or John.

The club seemed to be following a policy of importing players, many of them Scots like Angus, who were justifiably regarded as the foremost exponents of the dribbling game. Although the Football Association had accepted a form of professionalism two years earlier in July 1885, with strict provisions regarding residence, and the Northumberland FA had agreed to it in principle, the local body had still decreed that the game under their jurisdiction should remain amateur at present. Nevertheless, Scottish players such as Aitken were enticed over the border to the North East with promises of jobs. It was also, apparently, common knowledge at the time that some clubs were not averse to making under-the-table payments to certain players. Although these clubs were never named, the influx of stars at West End suggests that the St James' Park club may have been one of them.

The club's annual meeting was held in St Andrew's Hall on Percy Street, Newcastle, early in June 1887 and the honorary secretary, Tom Watson, read the financial report which was published – a valuable early indication of football finances of a pioneering club. He was obviously pleased to report that the club was in a healthy position, having made a profit of £45 16s 4d (£45 82p) the previous season. The Income and Expenditure Account makes interesting reading:

INCOME				EXPENDITURE			
	£	s	d		£	s	d
Subscriptions	21	8	6	Entrance Fees	4	0	0
Match Receipts	175	6	7	Match Expenses	124	1	10
Use of Ground	13	8	0	Rent	33	5	0
Sundries	6	2	0	Sundries	9	1	11
				Balance (Profit)	45	16	4
Total	**£216**	**5s**	**1d**	**Total**	**£216**	**5s**	**1d**

However, all was not well with the committee and with certain individuals who ran and backed the club. Several retiring members refused to stand for re-election, and a long and heated discussion ensued, with Tom Watson threatening to resign as secretary at one point. As tempers became frayed, a decision was made for the meeting to be adjourned for a week when a committee would then be selected. Emotions were calmed and a crisis was averted.

For the start of the 1887–88 campaign West End could boast a strong squad of players. The club held their pre-season gathering in the Primitive Methodist Chapel on Derby Street, near Barrack Road and St James' Park, during August and it was noted that White Rose FC had amalgamated with the West Enders and would go under the name of West End Swifts. White Rose had won the Temperance Festival Second Team Competition by defeating Shankhouse 3–0 at St James' Park in July. However, within a year they broke away from West End again.

Leaders of the club's five sides were elected for the new season:

First-team captain:	J.D. Wardale;	**vice-captain:**	W. Swinburne.
Reserve-team captain:	J.A. Waggott;	**vice-captain:**	R. Davison.
Swifts captain:	J. Fitzgerald;	**vice-captain:**	T. Miller.
Second-team captain:	H. Seers;	**vice-captain:**	T. Stanger.
Junior-team captain:	J. Robinson Jnr;	**vice-captain:**	W. Creighton.

New skipper Wardale was a recent signing from Gateshead FC and also played for Durham University. Seers was also a new recruit. He had come to West End with White Rose where he had been captain of their A team.

It was also announced that season tickets would be made available to the public at a price of 4s 0d (20p). These would allow the public admission to all games except two which would be chosen by the committee during the season.

In fact, the new season had a bad start when a prestigious game at home to the Scottish Cup holders Hibernians belatedly fell through. The Edinburgh club sent a telegram that was received on the morning of the match, saying that they could not come as they had a Scottish Cup tie to play. Notices were put up informing the public that the Hibs game was off, but many supporters turned up anyway. Most left, but about 2,000 entered the enclosure to watch West End play a scratch game which was of an 'uninteresting character'. Ralph Aitken had travelled from Scotland to play for this one match as a 'guest', as had Renton's fellow international Bob Kelso. He was to become another prominent West End signing in the not-too-distant future.

A week later, West End made their first long-distance away trip to Edinburgh to play St Bernard's. A 4–2 defeat at the Powderhall stadium was not too bad considering the perceived superiority of Scottish football. The difference compared to previous years, of course, was that many Scots were now south of the border and playing for English teams.

Wardale did not last long as captain, resigning the position and leaving the club to rejoin Gateshead after only one game. Vice-captain William Swinburne took over the role and led the team for the rest of

A local newspaper drawing of West End's skipper William Swinburne in 1888.

145

the season apart from a month when he was injured. Swinburne was also a well-known rugby player, being captain of the Northern club on occasion.

West End soon had more problems. After appearing in the first game, goalkeeper Robert Oldham announced that he would not be able to play this season owing to business commitments. A replacement was eventually found early in October when the former Dumbarton custodian, Thomas Fyffe, joined the club. His first outing was in a home fixture against Sunderland, a match which West End not only lost, 3–2, but in which they also had their centre-half Raylstone criticised for dirty play and making gestures to the crowd.

The FA Cup again gave West End a touch of success – at least it did in the first round. They had an easy 5–1 victory at St James' Park against Redcar, a game in which the robust Raylstone again indulged in foul behaviour that was 'far from flattering to his club'. He received his due punishment when West End travelled to play a friendly with Gainsborough Trinity during mid-November. Raylstone arrived to find a telegram informing him that he was suspended on account of his foul play in the Cup tie against Redcar. West End had to play with 10 men and held their own, with the score standing at 1–1 until Trinity scored the winner five minutes from time following a blatant handball. The West End players were furious and walked off the pitch, only for Gainsborough to accept that the last goal was not valid and declare the result a draw, over-ruling the referee in the process.

Interest in the FA Cup came to an end in the second round during November when West End were tied to meet their old rivals from the previous season again – Sunderland. The Wearsiders had already beaten West End at St James' Park in a friendly encounter a month earlier, but they found a determined Newcastle team when it came to the FA Cup. Some 8,000 spectators filled the Newcastle Road ground on Wearside, and most of them were shocked when McColl gave the Tyne visitors a half-time lead. Sunderland equalised through Stewart in the second half to take the tie into extra-time when two further goals by Halliday and Stewart for the Wearsiders steered them through to the next round.

After the Cup tie, West End remained unbeaten for six successive games, although four of them were draws. In one of these, a home fixture against Elswick Rangers, the match was never finished as passions among spectators surrounding the pitch boiled over. The catalyst for a pitch invasion was a heated conflict between George McKay, the Rangers wing-half, and John Barker, West End's acting captain. Prolonged arguments ensued before the spectators crowded onto the pitch a quarter of an hour from time and the game was abandoned. Another factor may have been that there had been heavy betting on the result and many spectators had vested interests. As in pre-football days, gambling was very much part of sporting culture in the North East.

The club received a major shock just before Christmas of 1887 when Tom Watson tendered his resignation as secretary. He was to eventually take over at rivals East End, and his position at St James' Park was to be filled by John Haig, who had formerly played for both the Tyne and Jesmond clubs.

There was never better evidence of the strength of the Scottish game at the time than the fixtures at St James' Park over Christmas and New Year. Four Scottish teams visited

West End, and they all went away with victories. Scottish Cup holders Hibernians thrashed the local side 6–0, Cambuslang won 4–0, Dumbarton Athletic 5–2 and Motherwell 2–0. On the other side of Newcastle, Abercorn from Paisley (Scottish Cup semi-finalists last season), and Partick Thistle were doing just as well against East End at Chillingham Road with 7–1 and 3–1 victories respectively. But the crowds flocked to see the experts in the dribbling code from north of the border with respectable attendances of 2,000 at St James' Park for both the Dumbarton and Motherwell games.

Soon it was time to play competitive matches against local teams again; the Northumberland Challenge Cup ties began, and in 1888 it was to be a competition in which West End were to taste ultimate success.

Lady Luck smiled on them in the first round, giving the Red and Blacks a bye. But perhaps West End did not need any fortune as an away tie against Berwick Rangers in the next round saw them rack up a 5–0 success. Another insight into local football finances can be gauged with this fixture. The normal admittance charge at Berwick was 3d (1p) and, after paying the referee's fee of £1 0s 0d, printing costs of 7s 6d (37p), teas to the value of 9s 9d (49p) and gatemen's fees of 2s 0d (10p), a grand total of 5s 9d (29p) profit was left to be shared out between the two teams (2s 10½d each, 14p). Rangers were later to note that each club's share of the gate was 7s 10½d (39p), so perhaps there was some additional income apart from what was noted in the press. What is known is that spectators could see inside the ground from outside the fence, and approximately 3,000 saw the contest without paying!

It was around this time that West End announced that they were going to make all of their 'native' players professionals. At the time a 'native' player was one who had lived long enough in the area to qualify to play in Cup matches in accordance with the recently introduced Football Association rules on professionalism.

A week after the Berwick tie, West End chalked up a 3–0 victory over rivals East End at Chillingham Road; although this was in an 'ordinary' fixture. Nevertheless, confidence was undoubtedly high when they met North Eastern in the third round of the Northumberland Cup at St James' Park during February. The confidence was not unfounded as the game became a travesty, West End turning a 6–0 half-time lead into a club record 15–0 victory by the final whistle. Nicholson (4), Angus (4) and Raylstone (3) did most of the damage. It was noted that West End 'bombarded the North Eastern goal' and that even goalkeeper Thomas Fyffe joined in the forward-line towards the final whistle!

The semi-final, played during late February in a heavy snowfall at the neutral venue of Chillingham Road, provided much stiffer opposition in the shape of Elswick Rangers. The pitch was covered in four inches of snow at kick-off time but still went ahead, and West End found themselves trailing to a Nugent goal at half-time. Tom Nicholson equalised matters in the second half to earn the St James' Park side a replay, a result that they must have been happy with considering that they had played most of the game with 10 men, half-back Joseph Smart being carried off injured in the opening exchanges.

The replay took place two weeks later at the same venue in front of a crowd variously reported as approximately 3,000 or 4,000. This time they made no mistake and disposed of the Elswick side 3–0, with McDonald scoring twice in the first half and John Barker weighing in with the third early in the second period. With that fine victory West End reached the Northumberland Challenge Cup Final for the third successive year.

They had fallen foul of Shankhouse Black Watch in the two previous Finals, and the colliery team provided the opposition on this occasion yet again. Once more, East End's neutral ground at Chillingham Road was the venue and West End relied mainly on the side that had started the first game against Elswick Rangers in the semi-final, the only change being forced upon them was the absence of Smart, who was still injured. Into his place for the semi-final replay and Final, they brought in a reserve defender, Harry Jeffrey, for his first-team debut. Harry was to stay in the limelight in the years ahead to eventually become a regular player with Newcastle United when they were elected into the Football League.

The teams for that Northumberland Challenge Cup Final during March 1888 lined up as follows:

West End: Fyffe, Taylor, McDermid, Raylstone, Swinburne, Jeffrey, Barker, McColl, Nicholson, McDonald (J.), Angus.
V
Shankhouse Black Watch: Wood, Todd, Bryden, Reilly, Turpin, Ritson, Metcalf, Thompson, Matthews, Hendy, Hedley.

West End, who had been lauded on Tyneside as having done more in recent years to promote the popularity of the association game, now received their due reward. After having tasted the bitter tang of failure in the previous two years, now they could taste the

An early team group of West End with the Northumberland Challenge Cup in 1888. Unfortunately the players are not identified on this rare photograph.

sweet flavour of success as they romped to a 6–3 victory before a massive crowd of between 6,000 and 7,000. The spectators had to witness a strange beginning to the game, however, as the referee George Millar, the Birtley favourite, did not turn up in time for the kick-off, and one of the umpires, Mr W. Scott, had to officiate for the first 15 minutes.

These were well before the days when players had numbers on their shirts, and newspaper match reports differ in identifying the goalscorers. There was no doubt about who opened the scoring, McColl after 14 minutes, but thereafter elements of uncertainty about the identity of some of the West End players crept into match reports. The consensus of opinion was that Tom Nicholson probably hit a hat-trick, with Matthews and Angus scoring the others in addition to McColl's opener. On the other hand, Barker may have scored one of Nicholson's goals. All reports agree that West End held a virtually unassailable 4–0 lead at half-time and that Shankhouse bravely fought back in the second half with goals by Matthews, Metcalf and Hendy. All reports also agree that West End deservedly won the trophy.

Both clubs must have been delighted with the attendance for the Northumberland Cup Final and also with their share of gate receipts. In total, these amounted to a substantial £70 2s 6d (£70 12½p), although it was ruefully announced that this sum included five 'bad sixpences'.

The players and officials from both clubs retired to the Northumberland Restaurant on Clayton Street in the city after the match 'where an excellent knife and fork tea was partaken of, the meal being presided over by David Crawford, the President of the Northumberland FA'. The Cup was filled with champagne and passed around 'and the evening was spent in a harmonious manner'. The social side of football was clearly still alive and well in 1888.

West End were not finished yet for this season. They participated in the Tyne Charity Shield and, after disposing of East End 2–0 in the semi-final, they went on to complete a double over Shankhouse in the Final with a 3–0 win. Brady, Angus and Nicholson scored the goals.

There was one last major hurdle to overcome, and that was in a Tyne-Wear derby. Sunderland had won the Durham Challenge Cup and the winners of the two local trophies were to contest the Northumberland & Durham Challenge Cup in an Inter-County Cup-holders match at the end of April. The Wearsiders were certainly a club on the rise, and their visit to St James' Park attracted between 5,000 and 6,000 to the Gallowgate enclosure. Most of the spectators wanted to see a West End triumph, but they were to be disappointed as goals from Sam Stewart and Bob Gloag gave the visitors a half-time lead, which they held until the final whistle despite much West End pressure. It was reported that Sunderland's goalkeeper Bill Kirkley, with a string of saves, had won the trophy for the Wearsiders.

So Sunderland proved that they were the top team in the North East in 1888 and, two years later, they were to show the way for the rest of the region by joining the Football League. But West End could gain some consolation from the fact that they were undoubtedly king-pins on Tyneside and they could look down on their rival across the city in Heaton. Their policy of bringing in imports was paying dividends – for now.

The club's annual meeting took place late in May when West End were able to announce that their success in the local Cup competitions, and increased gate receipts had seen them end the season £21 15s 11d (£21 79p) in the black. The results of the various teams were summarised:

First team:	P38	W20	D7	L11
Swifts team:	P26	W22	D2	L2
Second team:	P19	W10	D6	L3
Junior team:	P17	W9	D4	L4

With 250 club members and a substantial balance in the bank, everything in the St James' Park garden seemed rosy; or at least it did for the time being.

There was still a nucleus of those leading players from the previous campaign who turned out in most games: James Taylor, James (or John) Angus and John Barker formed the core of the side. Others who had made a few appearances last term now emerged as regulars: hard man James Raylstone, J. McDonald and, particularly, William Swinburne, who had successfully adopted the mantle of captaincy after Wardale had returned to Gateshead not long after being voted as West End skipper. A few from the previous season had departed after limited appearances in a West End shirt: goalkeeper Oldham (after only one game), Chalmers and James Duns.

Bob McDermid appeared for West End and East End, and also for Sunderland and Sunderland Albion.

They were replaced by newcomers Thomas Fyffe (the Dumbarton-born goalkeeper who replaced Oldham between the posts), free-scoring Tom Nicholson (who hailed from Manchester), D. McColl (another Scot who had formerly played for Renton), ex-Sunderland half-back Joseph Smart and Bob McDermid (another former Renton player) who was destined to become a much-travelled defender and later appeared for Newcastle United in senior football. At full-back McDermid actually served all four of Tyne and Wear's leading clubs of the time: West End and East End, as well as Sunderland and Sunderland Albion. The Scot became a regular for Newcastle United in Football League action between 1894 and 1897 and afterwards became a publican in South Shields.

John Barker, like his colleague James Taylor, developed from a local background into a dependable footballer and one of the most prominent players in the region. Although born in the South, John settled at an early age on Tyneside and served West End for nearly seven years and afterwards East End too, appearing for Newcastle United in the 1892–93 season. Apart from being a star player, Barker was also influential behind the scenes as a committee member and for a period as secretary. Almost 6,000 watched his benefit match against East End, evidence of his popularity. John was also a noted cyclist, appearing for the Clarion club. Like McDermid, he became a publican on Tyneside.

John Barker was a prominent player for West End, who later also joined rivals East End.

Occasionally the club's pioneer players, who had mostly played for the second team that season, helped out the senior side when required. Ned and John Waggott, as well as Billy Tiffin, fell into this category. There was also the occasional guest; Alec White, from East End, appeared once. But the most famous guest was Scottish international Walter Arnott of Queen's Park who was in the middle of a 10-year international career which would earn him 14 caps in an era when they were awarded only for Home International appearances.

The new 1888–89 season was, as already described, a momentous one for association football in England, as the Football League was formed that year. There were substantial changes taking place at St James' Park as well. Tom Watson, the secretary-manager who had done so much to propel West End to local supremacy, had left the club and travelled across the city to Heaton taking over at East End. Gritty defender James Raylstone made the same move. Other first-team regulars also departed. McDermid joined Sunderland, Angus moved to Everton and goalkeeper Thomas Fyffe to Bootle Athletic, also on Merseyside.

But the policy that had been pursued during Watson's term of office at St James' Park whereby reliance had been placed on Scottish imports continued. More Scots arrived at Gallowgate, among them former Renton star and Scottish international Bob Kelso, fellow countryman D. McKechnie and new goalkeeper William Jardine. It was amusingly stated in the press about McKechnie that he 'will be seen to better advantage when he has reduced the rotundity of his corporation'. He did not stay long, moving to Wearside.

The state of the St James' Park pitch seemed to leave a lot to be desired as the season commenced at the beginning of September. The press reported that the grass had not

Fact Box

THE GROWTH OF WEST END 2

Timetable of Development

October 1886:	First game at St James' Park v East End (won 3–2).
October 1886:	First FA Cup tie v Sunderland (lost 2–1, but game replayed after protest).
November 1886:	Win FA Cup replay v Sunderland (1–0).
March 1887:	Northumberland Cup finalist again v Shankhouse BW (lost 5–1).
August 1887:	White Rose FC merge with West End.
August 1887:	Season tickets made available – 4s 0d (20p).
December 1887:	Tom Watson resigns as secretary, succeeded by John Haig.
January 1888:	West End decide to make all qualifying players professionals.
March 1888:	Win Northumberland Cup v Shankhouse BW (6–3) & Tyne Charity Shield v Shankhouse BW (3–0).
August 1888:	White Rose FC split from West End.
May 1889:	West End become a professional club.

been cut during the summer, the *Daily Journal* suggesting 'possibly not for years'. It was described as a 'boundless prairie'.

West End began the season with a flurry of home fixtures, among them some memorable victories including a 7–0 win over Notts District and 8–0 success against Kelvinside Athletic of Glasgow. These were supplemented with a 4–1 win against Shankhouse and a 2–0 victory over Middlesbrough. All of these games saw crowds around the 2,000 to 3,000 mark.

The first qualifying round of the FA Cup gave West End an easy 7–2 success on Tyneside against Bishop Auckland Church Institute, Tom Nicholson scoring a hat-trick. But the next round was to bring controversy. They were drawn at home to Sunderland Albion and a high-scoring game saw the Wearside team win 5–3. Incredibly, no fewer than 16 Scots took part in this Cup-tie, five of them West Enders. The team line ups illustrated the influx of players from north of the Cheviots at the time, something that was to continue for decades to follow on Tyne and Wear.

However, the Sunderland tie was not over yet. West End submitted a protest on the grounds that one of the Albion players, Bob Gloag, had not been on their books for a month and therefore, in accordance to the Football Association rules at the time, had been ineligible to play in the FA Cup. The protest was sustained, and the FA instructed that the game would have to be replayed, again at St James' Park.

A very good crowd for the time of 4,000 (an extra 1,000 above the original tie), turned up for the replay and they saw a closely contested match; although, perhaps strangely, Gloag still took part – bizarrely he was one of the umpires! Tom Nicholson gave West End a dream start early on, but Sam Stewart equalised before half-time. Despite the best efforts of both sides, the second half remained goalless, and the tie went into extra-time. It was then that a goal by half-back James Richardson settled it for Albion and West End's FA Cup interest was over for another year.

After elimination from the premier competition, results generally went well and included a notable 3–2 win away to Middlesbrough (when an estimated 600 Tyneside supporters accompanied their team to Teesside) and huge wins at home to Rendel (6–0) and in south Durham at Bishop Auckland Church Institute (9–0). But the result that must have given the West End supporters the most satisfaction was a comfortable 4–1 home win over arch-rivals East End on Christmas Day before an exceptional crowd of 5,000 despite (or perhaps because of) a morning 11 o'clock kick-off. Kennedy and Barker gave the home side a first-half lead, which was increased by McColl after the interval. Blackett's goal for East End to reduce the deficit turned out to be merely a consolation, with another Barker effort completing the scoring.

West versus East derbies attracted big crowds on Tyneside but, for most other fixtures, attendances were normally just around the 2,000 level and, with the undoubted success of the Football League further south, it could have been that the local supporters wanted something more than friendly games to whet their appetites. Even the visits of Sheffield Wednesday just before the New Year and West Bromwich Albion in February failed to attract the crowds in appreciable numbers.

West End rarely journeyed away from the North East for games; perhaps they were not a big attraction elsewhere. But when they did occasionally travel, as to Bootle in mid-January 1889, they probably wished that they had not bothered. A 12–1 defeat chastened them; although the fact that they were down to nine players in the second half and actually finished the match with only seven men on the field played a big part! In addition, the fact that the players had to trek most of the night by train to get to their destination on Merseyside may have had something to do with their performance.

West End's star character at this time was the Scottish international half-back or full-back Bob Kelso. Capped both before and after his time in England, he was only at West End for this one season, but the Scot was an immensely popular player with the Tyneside supporting public during his time there. It was reported that, during West End's trip to Bootle via Liverpool, he had been approached by Everton, but he stayed on to see out his season on Tyneside.

Acutely aware of the need to attract crowds and cognisant of the lack of drawing power of most local teams, West End decided to withdraw from the Northumberland Challenge Cup for the 1888–89 season. There was also an element of a lack of confidence in the Northumberland FA Committee, and this also influenced their decision. But the reaction of local teams was immediate. Some accused West End of not being good enough to defend the trophy that they had lifted the previous season, implying that they were afraid of local opposition. But the St James' Park committee were not concerned with such minor criticisms and, in January 1889, showed that their ambitions rose above petty accusations by passing a vote to adopt professionalism and to sign any players, professional or amateur, which they deemed necessary to confirm their supremacy on Tyneside.

Whether they were supreme or not was soon put to the test when they played their return fixture with East End at Chillingham Road early in February. No precise attendance figures for games were recorded at the time, although the press estimated that the crowd was around 3,000 with gate receipts of £46. These were significantly down on the corresponding figures at St James' Park on Christmas Day. Perhaps the fact that the game at Gallowgate had been played on a public holiday may have been a decisive factor.

But a bigger crowd was all that West End had to boast about after the return fixture. Despite Hannah giving them a first-half lead, East End took the honours and the bragging rights with second-half goals by Mack and Smith. The West Enders were fuming at their defeat, and challenge and counter-challenge for a rematch flew to and fro across the city but, for one reason or another, a replay never materialised.

West End continued with their policy of inviting the top teams from around the country to St James' Park and occasionally the Tyneside players found themselves out of their depth. What they did not need when they played such visitors were goals scored against them by the match officials. This happened in a 2–0 defeat against West Bromwich Albion when the opener went in off one of the umpires!

Scottish clubs were always welcome, and one highlight was a visit by Celtic when 4,000 saw a seven-goal thriller with the Glasgow team just squeezing home. There were also plenty of goals when the FA Cup finalists Wolverhampton Wanderers came to Gallowgate in April but, unfortunately, not many of them from West End. A 9–2 home defeat vividly illustrated the gap between the local teams and the elite from elsewhere.

While West End were being mauled by the Wolves, their rivals across the city were doing considerably better. They invited the League and Cup double winners Preston North End as their prestige opponents. Although the Chillingham Road side lost 4–1, they had acquitted themselves well. On top of that, they won the Northumberland Challenge Cup, the Tyne Charity Shield, the 'Championship of Northumberland' (a challenge between the Northumberland FA Cup holders and the Northern Association Cup holders) and the Northumberland & Durham Challenge Cup (defeating Sunderland Albion). West End could only look on in envy and with considerable internal criticism. East End were now top-dogs locally.

There had been a hard core of eight players who had carried the hopes of the supporters in that disappointing 1888–89 programme: Jardine, Taylor, Kelso, Swinburne, Barker, McColl, McDonald and Jeffrey. The only newcomers in the squad were goalkeeper William Jardine and Bob Kelso. The rest had played in the previous season, although Harry Jeffrey had emerged from being a supporting player to becoming a regular. A tough Geordie full-back, Harry was described when at his peak as being a 'stylish and scientific exponent of the game'. He led Northumberland on occasion and was at times a temperamental and controversial figure, often being in trouble on and off the field. Jeffrey later appeared for Newcastle United, taking part in the club's very first Football League contest.

Others who had played a number of games during the campaign but who could not really be classed as regulars were McKechnie (who had left to join Sunderland early in the season), Nicholson, Watts, N. Hannah, Kennedy and Downes. Once again, the occasional veteran turned out to help the team when required such as Bill Tiffin and Ned Waggott. There was also the occasional guest appearance again, notably former player Bob McDermid, then with Sunderland, who played once.

The outstanding footballer of the side had undoubtedly been Bob Kelso. He had been undeniably popular but was only to spend one season on Tyneside before going on to join Preston North End and earn conspicuous success.

West End's annual meeting at the end of the season was something of a heated affair. Their acting secretary, J.J. Watkins, openly criticised the club committee for withdrawing from local competitions and for their policy of inviting star teams to Tyneside with concomitant heavy

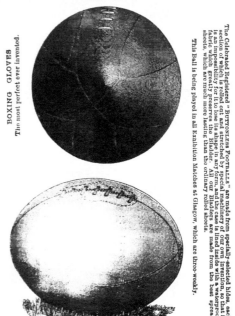

As this Victorian advert notes, the celebrated 'Buttonless Footballs' were used for both codes of the game.

guarantees which had resulted in financial losses to the club. Extracts from his annual report give a fascinating insight into the running of the club: 'I regret that through various causes I cannot congratulate you on a successful season as that of 1887 and 1888, neither can I congratulate you on the winning of the "pot" and shield which for a season adorned the sideboard of our worthy president. At the same time I feel sure that we could again have carried off both trophies had we not withdrawn from the competition. Your committee have had a very uphill fight; the great loss on gates where we had heavy guarantees to pay, the result of bringing crack teams to the town, often being sufficient to dampen the ardour of the most enthusiastic devotee of the game.'

William Tiffin, the financial secretary, confirmed the monetary situation. In terms of gate receipts and guarantees, the former more than accounted for the latter: £514 compared to £354. But when ancillary costs were included, the club lost money. Refreshments came to £78, train fares just over £50 and other expenditure to a significant £232. Miscellaneous sources of income such as club subscriptions (£65) and share of gates and guarantees received (£70) were not enough to cover the losses.

The meeting also learnt that club membership now stood at over 260 members and also heard details of the season's playing record:

First team:	P38	W19	D6	L13	F114	A76
Reserve team:	P19	W11	D2	L6	F45	A20
Second team:	P16	W12	D3	L1	F50	A9

At the meeting, significant decisions were made. William Nesham became chairman with Bill Tiffin, so long a stalwart of the club, taking over the role of match secretary at an annual salary of £20. A club council of 30 members was formed to run the organisation with a committee of nine to act with executive powers. Nesham was elected as chairman of the council and the committee, with G.T. Graham as treasurer and J.J. Eddy as financial secretary. Dr W. I'Anson continued as club president. Nesham, sometimes referred to as Neasham (although official club documents record Nesham), was a wealthy Tyneside dignitary, a merchant who resided in Leazes Terrace which overlooked St James' Park. In his early years he was a respected local cricketer, having played for the Northumberland Cricket Club where he was later a vice-president. On West End's downfall he joined the East End camp, becoming Newcastle United chairman from 1895 to 1901. William was later also president of the Northumberland Football Association.

From a playing point of view, it was proposed that the first XI the following season should consist entirely of professional footballers and that the club would only field two sides. The senior team, however, would be playing competitive League football for the very first time – in the shape of the newly formed Northern League.

Within a few months, the club would become a limited company like their rivals across the city. A sea change was about to take place in football in the North East and the next few years would see a battle for survival between West End and East End. In the end, one would flourish and one would go to the wall. Only time would tell which it would be.

Chapter 6

IN THE CITY

'I fancy we shall see them make a name for themselves amongst our local clubs. They play a strong and determined game.'
'Mercutio' (on Elswick Rangers) *Daily Leader*, 1886

Apart from the pathfinder clubs of Tyne Association and Newcastle Rangers and their local successors, East End and West End, several other clubs in Newcastle helped to popularise football during the 1880s.

By the start of the decade the boundary of the region's capital had spread well beyond the old Town Walls. It was written at the time that 'the increase in buildings has gone on like rapidity' and that 'it seems of late three towns had clustered round the old one – Gosforth on the north, Byker or Heaton on the east, and Elswick or Benwell on the west'.

While the vast industrial growth had seen new working-class neighbourhoods emerge in those areas, there were still outlying areas – now very much part of the vast Tyneside conurbation – of village communities then separated by green countryside and not yet swallowed up by the urban sprawl. Over the coming decades, though, that was to quickly change.

Gosforth, although expanding, was still more of a leafy residential suburb than an industrial landscape of chimneys and factories. Fenham was also slowly developing but remained largely rural until it bordered the Benwell area. Denton was still a district outside the city with fields either side of Denton Bank on the route westwards. Kenton, north-west of the Town Moor, was much the same, with pastoral fields between outlying lodges and fine houses.

In mediaeval days, most of the villages surrounding Newcastle were based on coalmining. In the 14th century much of the land west of the town was owned by Tynemouth Priory. It is recorded as long ago as 1330 that the prior of Tynemouth let a colliery, called Heygrove at 'Elstewyke', for £5 a year and another in the East-field nearby at six merks a year. 'Elstewyke' was, of course, Elswick.

Then Elswick was a village outside Newcastle which, although initially rural in nature, owed its existence to the mining industry. Nevertheless, it must have been a relatively pleasant spot overlooking the Tyne. Elswick Hall was located on its banks with extensive grounds less than a mile from the old Town Walls at Westgate. Tyneside developer Richard Grainger had purchased the large estate and planned a wholesale redevelopment project before heavy commerce took over. He said at the time: 'I will not stop until I have made Elswick Hall the centre of town.' However, his finances collapsed and the grandiose plan never happened.

Armstrong's vast Elswick Works during the 1880s; Lord Armstrong is featured in the inset.

Gradually, during the 19th century, Elswick changed. It became one of the focal points of the heavy engineering industry which ensured Newcastle's prosperity during the industrial revolution. Livestock sheds and tanneries sprouted up by the riverside but these eventually gave way to thriving engineering, shipbuilding and armament works. Coal-mining was still important and Elswick retained its local pit, the Elswick Colliery. But it was rapidly surrounded by heavy engineering factories, producing shipbuilding, engines, hydraulic machinery and armaments, notably under the banner of the Elswick Ordnance and Engineering Works. Established in 1847 on a comparatively small site, by 1887 the plant occupied over 70 acres and was still growing. Owned by William Armstrong (later Lord Armstrong), its expansion was noted in the *Jubilee Chronicle* booklet at the time as having 'no parallel in this country'. By 1892, the Armstrong empire employed some 13,000 men and women.

With this industrial surge came a proliferation of workers and an influx of Scots and Irish. Elswick's population grew from 3,539 in 1851 to 27,801 some 20 years later, and it kept growing. Housing had to be built to accommodate this new workforce, and it soon spread into the neighbouring village of Benwell.

The two old communities were transformed into industrial centres. They would soon become something of a football breeding ground, with no fewer than four clubs developing the sport among the recently built terraced rows of workers' houses and flats. All four were to be important in the widening of the game on Tyneside.

There were other significant employers in the area apart from Armstrong's. There was a long-established Elswick Gas Works, as well as Elswick Leadworks near the Redheugh Ferry. Slaughter and tannery works next to the enormous railway sidings and the 'Cattle Dock' provided another large complex of activity. The site serviced the whole region to the borders in the north, as well as County Durham and even parts of Cumberland.

Many of the young men employed in this compact district turned to sport in their spare time. As already related, rugby was linked to the Elswick community when the first club was formed, the Elswick Rugby Club, and so too was cricket where clubs like Gloucester, Crown, Benwell Athletic and Benwell Hill were all established.

Football followed when workers at one of the biggest factories – the Elswick Leather Works – formed a team in February 1881. The local press reported the arrival: 'The workmen employed at the Elswick Leather Works the other night formed a club which is to be called the Elswick Leather Works Football Club.' The company was a well-established business in the area, founded in 1850 with a factory originally in Shumac Street before moving to a new purpose-built site alongside the Tyne at Railway Terrace in 1863. Run by brothers John and Edward Richardson, it was noted that they dealt in a huge range of skins, 'sheep, goat, calf, seal, colt and pigskin', though it was added that 'more exotic pelts of lizards, snakes, alligators were also handled'! The company was prominent on Tyneside for many decades, until 1970.

Elswick Leather Works' first captain was W. Pumphrey (soon succeeded by James Johnston) with Joseph Dobson acting as their secretary. They played their football on a field on the Town Moor – the location of many of the community's early clubs. Indeed, the earliest years of football saw several other locations on the Moor, such as the Castle Leazes, used for playing the game. Other sports like cricket, rugby and bowling also took advantage of the wide open communal spaces of the Moor. The exact sites of what were basic areas of rough grass are difficult, almost impossible, to establish; however, clues indicate a favoured spot was near Chimney Mills on Claremont Road. The old windmill, opened in 1782, has partly survived, close to a favourite watering-hole, the North Terrace public house. As we have seen, West End played for a period nearby, south of Spital Tongues on the Leazes. Minor clubs kicked a ball here too and also played on the neighbouring Nuns Moor, as well as a setting close to the 'Blue House' at the junction of Grandstand Road and the Great North Road.

For the most part, both the Freemen and town corporation of the day supported sporting activity on the open spaces of the Moor. But in September 1885 there was a controversial moment when the town clerk of the council issued a notice 'prohibiting the putting of posts on the Town Moor or the Leazes'. By this time, some 20 clubs played on the Moor, and it was decided to put the ban to the test. The Brunswick club played West End in defiance of this ban, and the secretary of Brunswick FC was confronted by a certain policeman, Constable Scott, who had been sent to the Moor to record details of any footballing offenders. The Brunswick secretary had his name taken, although the game went ahead.

Public support was behind the clubs, and the Northumberland Football Association decided at a meeting held at the Crown & Thistle Hotel during mid-September to test the validly of this edict in the local Magistrates Court, although action was initially deferred pending the submission of a direct appeal to the corporation and the Freemen. Meanwhile, other sports that did not require the

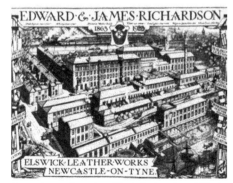

An advert for the Elswick Leather Works showing the extent of the complex alongside the Tyne.

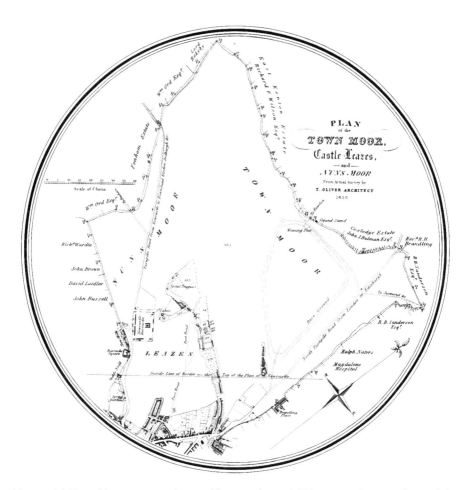

Newcastle's Town Moor comprised a sizeable area of over 1,100 acres and was made up of the Moor itself as well as Castle Leazes and Nuns Moor. The racecourse is marked on Oliver's 1830 plan, reproduced in one of publisher Frank Graham's valuable books.

sinking of posts, such as bowling, continued to be played. It appears, however, that football was only allowed if specific permission was granted – such as at St James' Park (which was part of the Moor) – or in laid-out recreation grounds like Bull Park (later the Exhibition Park).

The new Elswick Leather Works club was well thought of from the outset and the weekly *Football* chronicle commented: 'They practice a good deal and are forming into a very good team.' They were also described as a 'most enthusiastic band of players'. Being together in the factory and on the football field meant everyone knew each other well. They were soon to move from the Town Moor, well before the ban was implemented, settling at a location nearer to their factory. By 1883, they were playing in New Benwell and used to change in the Crown Hotel opposite the Elswick Road tram terminus. Their colours were described as 'royal blue jerseys and hose, white knickers'.

Originally most of their players were employees of the works, but soon they brought in other capable men. Notable personalities of the club included Matt Scott, the former Newcastle FA skipper. He was a prominent footballer before moving to a new club in the same neighbourhood, Elswick Rangers. So too were James and William Scott, thought to be brothers. They also were to join the rival club after serving the Leather Works XI. John Eden and Joseph Welford were regulars too, Welford also giving good service to both West End and Gateshead NER. William Davidson was another fine player.

The Leather Works team entered in the very first Northumberland Challenge Cup competition in 1883–84 and reached the quarter-final before pulling out of the tournament when they were due to face Newcastle Rangers. While the Elswick club never lifted a senior tournament, their junior XI won the Northumberland FA Junior Cup on three occasions in a row during the 1880s decade; in 1884, 1885 and 1886. It has to be said, however, that there were occasionally a few doubts over the age of some of their players. After the 1886 Final it was reported that 'Elswick had one or two players who might not be under 17 in the side, who were men rather than juniors'.

Elswick Leather Works are also, of course, closely tied to Newcastle United's origins – being the opponents for Stanley Football Club's first-ever game on 26 November 1881 when their second XI met Newcastle United's pioneers in South Byker.

Apart from the Elswick Leather Works club, another factory side developed out of Armstrong's extensive armaments plant alongside the Tyne. Founded in 1884 as the Elswick Ordnance Works Football Club, they also ran a cricket team in the area. Prominent were brothers W. Mather and J.A. Mather, later both closely associated with West End. They initially wore white jerseys and shorts with black hose (stockings), but within a year they had switched to black-and-white shirts. They also played their home games on the Town Moor.

While the factory clubs of Elswick Leather Works and the Ordnance Works were the first sides to be formed in the area, it was Elswick Rangers that became the strongest of the three Elswick clubs. Established in 1886, they recruited many of the better players of their rivals, especially from the Leather Works team. Indirectly, the rise of Rangers led to both the works clubs folding in the later years of the 1880s decade. The Leather Works club struggled in the summer of 1887 when they failed to find a pitch for the new season.

From the outset, it was predicted that Elswick Rangers would become a force to be reckoned with. *Mercutio*, writing in the Tyneside-based newspaper the *Daily Leader*, was not alone when he commented 'Being under influential and distinguished patronage, and in connection with such a large industrial concern (Elswick Works), a bright future should be open to the organisation under energetic management.' He added 'I fancy we shall see them make a name for themselves amongst our local clubs. They play a strong and determined game.' He was right. They developed quickly with James Duke as their first secretary. They played at the top end of Elswick at Graingerville, on a pitch at Mill Lane near Bentinck Road, an upmarket suburb with several conspicuous large villas. There was very little in terms of facilities on the ground, however, and occasionally teams changed at the Belgrove Hotel at the top of Mill Lane. The site of the pitch is now occupied by allotments and the Mill Lane Youth Club.

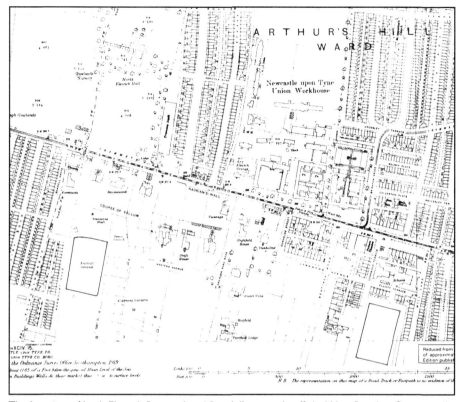

The location of both Elswick Rangers' and Rendel's grounds off the West Road in Graingerville; Mill Lane right, Normount Road left.

Within a year of its formation, the Elswick Rangers club were challenging in the country's primary competition, the FA Cup. With the tournament being expanded in the middle years of the 1880s to allow more entries and more local preliminary contests, many of the region's early clubs played for the famous silver trophy, although, of course, without much hope of winning it. A new 'Qualifying Competition' was introduced in 1888–89, with the games staged between October and December. The winners took part in the 'Competition Proper' from February onwards – much like the format we now have over a century later.

Elswick Rangers entered the action in 1887–88 when they met Bishop Auckland Church Institute in round one during early October. On the same day giant clubs of the future also took part: Everton, Nottingham Forest and Aston Villa.

Following a thrilling 3–3 draw, Rangers went through after a 2–0 victory and faced another club from the south of County Durham, this time a strong Darlington line up. Another marvellous game resulted as the Elswick club narrowly lost 4–3 in front of a 2,000–3,000 crowd at Feethams during November. In fact Rangers had been somewhat unlucky, being ahead 3–1 at half-time through McDonald, Nugent and McCallum. The scores were level at full-time, but Elswick conceded what was the winner in extra-time, Darlington's Hutchinson scoring the goal.

The match proved a touch unsavoury, with the Tyneside press emphasising the unsportsmanlike behaviour of the Darlington spectators, who were unstinting in their praise of the home team but never uttered a good word for the visitors, who were treated very shabbily indeed. The crowd became so excited that the home players became animated and lost all control. Darlington, spurred on by the partisan crowd, disregarded the scientific game and went for the man and not the ball.

The following season Rangers again competed in the FA Cup along with several other clubs in the North East. They defeated Ashington 4–0 and then, in the second round, were tied with Sunderland, a club by then almost good enough to be eyeing Football League status. A 5,000 crowd at the Newcastle Road ground – not far from where the Stadium of Light now stands – witnessed a compelling match, with Rangers holding the much more experienced and stronger Sunderland side at 3–3 by half-time. In the end the Wearsiders won 5–3, with Ayrshire-born John Breconridge registering a hat-trick.

Rangers went quickly out of the FA Cup in 1889–90 to Gateshead NER (1–0) and also in the following year's tournament when Newcastle West End won 5–2 in an entertaining contest at Graingerville. A gate of 1,200 saw Rangers match their more illustrious opponents, and it was 1–1 at the break, Robert Calderwood scoring for West End and R. McLucas equalising off the post for the home side. Calderwood was a Scottish international forward, which emphasised the difference in ability between the two sides. Yet it was the Elswick club who went ahead after the interval when Stewart converted a pass from Jefferson. That only signalled a West End revival, however, and, much like when Rangers faced Sunderland, by full-time they had been soundly beaten. In rapid succession West End equalised then went ahead to secure the tie, scoring four times. Calderwood added his second, then skipper Dempsey, another capable Scot from the noted Cowlairs club in Glasgow like Calderwood, scored another. A double from Roger Patten gave the West Enders victory.

Elswick Rangers were founder members of the Northern League, the region's first League competition, during the 1889–90 season. In fact they played one of the opening fixtures – against Birtley – but lost 4–1, although they successfully lodged a protest to have the game ruled as a 'draw'.

The Tyneside club battled against the odds that season. They were perhaps out of their depth against undoubtedly stronger and bigger clubs like Middlesbrough and Newcastle's East End and West End pairing. However, Rangers did compete against the best in the North East – with the exception of the Sunderland club – and played in front of some big crowds. They were Middlesbrough's first League opponents during September at the Linthorpe Road ground on Teesside, and almost 4,000 saw Boro win 3–2. Rangers' danger-man James Nugent scored twice. Once again, the Elswick club submitted a protest over Middlesbrough playing an unregistered player, and the result was officially declared a 'draw'.

Rangers had a somewhat torrid time in the Northern League and finished rock bottom of the table after suffering several heavy defeats: 8–0 against Stockton and 8–1 in a Tyneside derby with West End. Consequently, confidence and enthusiasm waned. By the end of the season in March the Elswick camp had just about thrown in the proverbial towel. They even turned up late for a League fixture with Auckland Town with only four men! It is recorded in *Northern Goalfields*, the official history of the Northern League: 'The visitors were compelled to field a patchwork team made up from local volunteers.' Elswick's goalkeeper – no doubt one of the volunteers – did not even take his coat off. Not surprisingly Auckland Town won easily, 10–2.

Elswick officials had by then gained a reputation for being quick to spot anything unfair, even trifling, and to lodge protests to the local governing body. Indeed, in that Northern League season of 18 matches, they submitted no fewer than 10 protests in 11 games! The Northern League competition was a step too far for Elswick Rangers. They resigned at the end of that first season, joining the unofficial next tier, the Northern Alliance.

Apart from James Nugent, a top-notch striker who played for both the county XI and Newcastle & District side, Rangers fielded several other notable footballers. Alf Perkins and Willie Knox – who appeared for Partick Thistle – were also prominent for the club, as was Jack Beattie at full-back who played for the county team as well. So too was goalkeeper Matt Scott, having moved from the Leather Works side. He was later to appear for both East End and for Sunderland in senior action during the 1893–94 season. Scott was reserve to the legendary Ted Doig on Wearside, and afterwards he rejoined East End – when they were Newcastle United – and played for the club's A side. Matt also appeared for the county XI.

James Scott and William Scott, thought to be relations to Matt, also pulled on Elswick's colours, as did another set of brothers, Andrew and William Muir, both of whom were to join East End in due course. Like Matt Scott, another Rangers goalkeeper was Joseph Ryder, who went on to serve Newcastle United. From a noted footballing family at the time, Joe was Northumberland's custodian and played for the future Magpies in Football League action during 1893–94. His brother Isaac Ryder also appeared for Newcastle United.

Apart from competing in the FA Cup and Northern League, Elswick Rangers were also prominent in the Northumberland Challenge Cup, reaching the semi-final in 1887–88. On the way they faced what was, on paper, a tough meeting with East End

IN THE CITY: PRINCIPAL CLUB LOCATIONS

West End
Elswick Leather Works, Elswick Ordnance Works, Elswick Rangers, Rendel.

East End
North Eastern, Stanley/East End, Heaton Association.

City & Jesmond
Tyne, Rangers, Newcastle Association, West End, Science & Art, Jesmond.

during January. In a second-round clash Rangers travelled to Heaton and before a 'numerous' attendance played well and progressed to the next stage with a 3–1 victory. On a wet, slippery pitch due to overnight rain East End did not play to form, and Baxter put the Elswick side ahead with an excellent shot. Tommy Hoban equalised after fine play by Scot Michael Mulvey but, before half-time, the enterprising James Nugent regained the lead for Elswick. In the second period Baxter scored his second, a long shot which crashed against the post before hitting East End 'keeper Chard and crossing the line.

Rangers actually defeated East End not once but twice that season – and therefore can claim to have beaten Newcastle United as well, later inflicting a 4–1 defeat. They were also to repeat that achievement in future years, illustrating their prowess at the time.

In the 1888 semi-final they met the other half of Newcastle's footballing stronghold, West End, on a snowy February day at Chillingham Road in Heaton. Indeed, the conditions were so bad, with around 3in to 4in of snow on the pitch, that the game almost did not take place. Referee Wilson called both captains together to decide if the match should proceed or not. They went ahead but, with a snow storm developing, perhaps the two skippers had both wished they had not.

Both sides struggled with the conditions, especially West End who lost half-back Smart very early in the game with an ankle injury and had to operate with 10 men thereafter. An incident surrounding the opening goal gives a fascinating insight into the limitations imposed on referees at the time. A West End player clearly seemed to handle the ball, and all of the players stopped playing. The referee did not blow his whistle, however, and William Scott, who had possession on the Rangers' right wing, quickly realised the situation and raced off up the field with Nugent in support. Scott slipped a pass through to his teammate, and Nugent shot past Fyffe in the West End goal who, expecting a free-kick to be given for the handling offence, made no attempt to save. John Haig, the secretary of West End, claimed after the match that the referee, Dr Wilson of Birtley, admitted that he saw the offence but, as neither umpire had indicated a foul, he was powerless to take action and had no option but to award the goal.

The Lord Hill men (as West End were called at the time because they operated out of the Lord Hill public house in Pitt Street near St James' Park) considered making a protest after the game but decided not to do so. The game ended 1–1 with the consensus of opinion attributing the equaliser to Nicholson, although one report claimed that Angus scored the goal. The draw meant that both sides would have to try again, this time in more favourable conditions.

The replay was held once more in Heaton during March, and this time the weather was spring-like, bright and sunny. Around 3,000 to 4,000 lined up behind the ropes at Chillingham Road and saw a contest largely dominated by the West Enders. They went ahead through two McDonald goals in the first half, with Barker adding a second after the break. The 3–0 result was a fair reflection of the play.

Rangers went one better in the following season of 1888–89, reaching the Final of the competition. In the semi-final they defeated neighbours Rendel but not until a protest nullified a single-goal defeat. They claimed that some of the Rendel players had played in the close season, an activity that was strictly prohibited at the time. The Northumberland FA Challenge Cup Committee duly heard the protest and sustained it, ordering a replay. In fact the committee heard protests from both of the defeated semi-finalists, Ashington complaining that the pitch for their game against East End had been unfit for play. But as their objection was not made until after they had lost the game, the committee rejected it.

Protests were the order of the day. Elswick duly defeated Rendel 3–1 in the replay, only for Rendel to decide to lodge a protest; however, they changed their minds and withdrew it before any committee meeting.

The Final was held during March at the Jesmond Athletic Club ground. Elswick Rangers faced East End again for the prize of the Northumberland FA's prestige trophy. A reported crowd of 3,000 behaved in what was described as an 'enthusiastic manner, and in perfect order'. The game was a close and tight affair, with stalemate resulting at 0–0 at the close. It was also a bit of a robust contest and referee John Douglas, the Newcastle Rangers and Gateshead favourite, had to reprimand several players for fouling.

Two weeks later the replay went ahead at the same venue and another good crowd, variously reported as 2,000, 3,000 or 'fully 4,000' turned out. The players continued where they had left off with a full-blooded and well-matched encounter taking place. East End exerted the early pressure, and they opened the scoring when Hiscock found the target. They could have gone further ahead but for Rangers' last line of defence Matt Scott being in fine form, holding firm. That good defence paid off as Nugent made it 1–1 with a stinging shot that struck a post and went over the line. Before the final whistle Baxter converted a free-kick to give Rangers a 2–1 advantage and victory. But before the end matters got a bit rough on the field as tempers became frayed and scuffles involving players and spectators resulted in a brief suspension of play near the end.

The trophy was presented to Rangers by David Crawford, President of the Northumberland FA; however, matters were far from over. East End were furious and quickly lodged a protest, claiming that one of the Elswick players, Nugent Jnr, had been ineligible to play having already appeared previously for another club. The Northumberland FA Committee decided unanimously that Elswick Rangers were in default and the Final was ordered to be replayed, the Elswick officials having to return the trophy.

The third contest was held at St James' Park during April, and around 5,000 went along to the Leazes ground, attracted by what had become an intriguing battle between the two clubs on and off the field. East End soon took an early lead following a half-fisted clearance by goalkeeper Scott that was headed home by Mack. Then James Collins made it 2–0 with a 'swift shot' before the interval. In the second half Rangers were given an advantage when East End's Young retired hurt, yet it was the Heaton club who scored again – a pass from Smith to Edward Hiscock who converted the chance. But Elswick battled on, and James Nugent pulled a goal back before a McKay shot went past Scottish goalkeeper Henderson to make it 3–2 with five minutes to go.

Despite vigorous attempts by the Rangers men to equalise, East End held on to win the trophy. But now it was Rangers' turn to protest – complaining that the East Enders had fielded an illegible player and also that 'spectators had interfered with play'. Another meeting of the Northumberland FA had to consider the complaint, but the committee decided to dismiss the objection. East End were thus crowned Challenge Cup victors. That was not the end of the bitterness between the two clubs, however. Rangers and East End were due to meet again at the beginning of May in the Northumberland FA Charity Shield but Alex Murray, the secretary of the Rangers team, advised the parties that they would not face their rivals again. The Elswick camp was noticeably aggrieved at the outcome.

While the Northumberland Cup was taken from their grasp, Rangers did win some silverware during those years. They lifted the Temperance Festival trophy in the summer of 1887 after disposing of East End 3–2 in the semi-final and then getting the better of a west-end derby with Benwell neighbours Rendel. A large attendance of over 5,000 saw that encounter, Rangers winning 2–0 on the Town Moor. They also had strength in depth, being three times winners of the Northumberland FA Junior Cup at this time.

It can be appreciated that Elswick Rangers were a powerful force during the later years of the 1880s. They could challenge and defeat both East End and West End, as well as Rendel, another emerging side from their own district. The Tyneside area commanded a rivalry between local clubs that aroused much passion. Crowds were decent for those Newcastle derby matches, and spectators were vociferous in their support. Apart from getting behind their respective clubs, they also had to grumble at the dubious decisions of officials.

Even back in 1886 umpires and referees were under the microscope. In one such hot-blooded derby between Elswick Rangers and West End (won 5–1 by Rangers) it was noted in the local press that supporters were 'astonished' that 'the referee did not order Duns, a West End player, off the field'. Rangers' McGirrell was dribbling the ball towards goal and 'would infallibly have scored had not Duns come behind and collared him *a la Rugby*'. Fans showed their anger at the official – and to Duns – in the now-accustomed way as found on any football ground in the country!

The neighbouring community of Benwell had been even more rural in aspect than Elswick before industrial expansion transformed the area. Like Elswick, Benwell also had its own colliery, at Delaval, but industry was low-key. That was to all change with Elswick's sprawl spreading into much of Benwell; however, towards the western edge of the community towards Denton it largely remained as it was with Benwell Tower, located on the old site of the Prior's summer residence, and Benwell Hall, a former mansion of the Shaftoe family, prominent landmarks.

Formed from a local cricket club, Rendel Association Football Club was established in 1881 and was named after Rendel Street, which itself was titled after one of the men who made the community prosperous, George Wightwick Rendel, a former manager of the Elswick Ordnance Company and designer of the first naval cruiser built at Mitchell's Walker Yard. Rendel also became Civil Lord of the Admiralty. The street was one of the many new terraces that ran up from Scotswood Road and the giant Elswick Works.

The club initially played on what was described as a 'field west of Elswick Cemetery' and then later found a pitch also in the Elswick-Benwell area, off the main West Road

Benwell Village as the 19th century drew to a close. Benwell Tower is just visible in the background on the right.

arterial route near Grainger Park Road at Normount Road. It was almost on the course of the old Roman Vallum and only a short walk from Elswick Rangers' pitch at Mill Lane. They played in 'blue-and-black jerseys with a red stripe on the arms, white knickers with blue-and-black hose'.

Rendel soon developed – much like Elswick Rangers – into one of Tyneside's prominent clubs, maybe not as strong as East End or West End, but a side which earned respect nevertheless. They reached the Northumberland Challenge Cup Final in 1890, meeting West End, and almost lifted the trophy. Rendel first defeated West End's great foes East End in the semi-final after two close games. During February they played out a 1–1 draw at Heaton in 'wretched weather' as rain fell incessantly causing something of a quagmire. The replay, staged in the following month, was an entertaining match, Rendel fighting back after first Michael Mulvey put the East Enders ahead and then, just on half-time, Miller increased the lead (although one report credited Gibbon with the goal). Two goals down, Rendel had the advantage of the wind in the second half and made it tell. Cameron scored twice to equalise the scores (although, once again, a contradictory report credited Herdman with the first goal), and after that it was the Benwell side that controlled the match. They ran off 4–2 winners, thanks to an own-goal by Miller and a final strike from Jefferson.

It was noted in the press that the Rendel side was made up 'entirely of players who were purely amateurs and were all from Northumberland, with no Scotch men'! That was something of a gibe to the now fully professional East and West End clubs who had brought in many a Scottish player from over the border for handsome reward.

The Final against West End was played in Jesmond at the end of March. Admission for the game was 6d (2½p) and 1 shilling (5p) in the stand. There was a good crowd of 4,300, with gate receipts totalling £89, and those supporters saw a classic Final with West End, playing in white rather than their normal colours of red and black, coming back from a three-goal deficit at the break as Rendel appeared to have the trophy secured. It was regarded as a Northumbrians (Rendel) versus Scots (West End) contest, such was the make-up of the two teams.

Rendel raced to a 3–0 lead with goals by Wood, Herdman and Smith, West End 'keeper Dave Whitton having rather a testing time between the posts during the early onslaught. It could have been worse too as Jefferson also struck the woodwork. Amazingly, though, West End turned the tide in the second period and forced a replay after a thrilling 3–3 draw, with goals by Barker and McDonald and a scrimmaged effort in between.

Three weeks later the replay took place, again at Jesmond. Rendel, as it turned out, had already had their chance of lifting the trophy in the first fixture. West End thrashed the Benwell club 5–0 in front of a 4,500 attendance (receipts £90), with goals by Nicholson, McColl and a hat-trick by Mackay, although, yet again, some reports attribute some of the goals to others. Following the tie the two sides dined together, as was the custom, at the Alexandra Hotel on Clayton Street.

Rendel went on to reach four successive Finals between 1890 and 1893. They lost in the 1891 and the 1892 Finals, on both occasions after close contests. Firstly they faced Shankhouse Black Watch, and it took three meetings to decide the destiny of the Cup. It must have been galling, after two draws, 0–0 and 2–2, to see the trophy slip from their

Rendel FC became a noted combination; a rare group photo from 1891 or 1892.

grasp again and presented to their opponents after a 1–0 Shankhouse victory. The following year saw West End – fielding their second XI – win 2–1.

Then, in 1893, Shankhouse again lifted the trophy at the expense of Rendel, who refused to turn up for the replay following a 1–1 draw at St James' Park. They objected not only to the choice of the Blyth ground for the return match, but also to the date of the game and even to the referee! They informed the Northumberland FA that they would not put in an appearance. Shankhouse did so and, after consideration, the local governing body awarded them the trophy, charged Rendel the expenses of the match and suspended them until the end of the season. The final element of the punishment was not all that severe, however, as the season was almost over.

The pitmen were to prove to be something of a nemesis to Rendel, as they defeated them in the Final again, two years later, 3–0 at St James' Park. So the Benwell club suffered the despair of reaching five Finals in six years without winning the trophy.

Prominent for Rendel were members of the Wardropper family, brothers Joseph and James, appearing for the club for nearly 10 years while other relations, T. Wardropper and W. Wardropper, also pulled on their colours. The elder of the brothers was Joseph. He was the leader of the family and of Rendel, being captain of the club and at times also skipper of the Northumberland county side. He acted as club secretary for a period and

Rendel's Joseph Wardropper sporting his Northumberland cap, a prominent figure on Tyneside.

lived in Brunel Terrace near Elswick Park and later Clara Street in South Benwell. Sporting a splendid moustache in the style of the day, Joe also played for West End briefly as they battled for survival but was a Rendel die-hard for almost a decade. A keen cricketer too, he worked at the Elswick Works and was the son of a Russian engine fitter. Joe later became a referee and moved to Barrow on the west coast, employed at one of the local shipyards. His son Fred appeared for Darwen and Barrow after World War One.

Sam Wood hailed from Greencroft near Annfield Plain and was a favourite of the crowd in the 1880s, appearing for a number of clubs including West End and East End. He played alongside Joe Wardropper on many occasions and they created a formidable duo. Wood was once described as 'a dashing forward with good shooting power'. He also appeared for Middlesbrough after his spell in Benwell and was a county player at both football and cricket.

Robert Forster served Rendel for almost a decade like Joe Wardropper. He later was also a West End player and was Rendel's regular goalkeeper, appearing also for the county representative side. Rendel also signed R. Danks, the brother of famous England international forward Thomas Danks who had found headlines at Nottingham Forest and played in exhibition matches on Tyneside for his club and for the Corinthians. Danks Jnr was one of three Forest men who arrived on Tyneside to join West End at the start of the 1889–90 season. Unusually, Danks was deaf and dumb, but he moved on to Rendel and proved a decent recruit.

It seems hard to imagine now, but the team from Benwell followed their neighbours Elswick Rangers and entered the FA Cup as the 1890s decade opened. In the 1890–91 tournament Rendel appeared in the first qualifying round alongside such names as Sheffield United and Ardwick, now billionaire club Manchester City.

Rendel faced a trip to Bishop Auckland, seat of the Bishops of Durham, to play Auckland Town – later to become more famous as the amateur champions Bishop Auckland. The Bishops were too good for Rendel, however, the Tyneside club losing 3–0 at the Flatts Farm ground. The following season, after receiving a bye in round one, Rendel faced a repeat contest away to Auckland Town who won again, this time 4–2.

In 1892–93 the Benwell club had a quick route to the second round once more, receiving another bye. Rendel then played a second tier Tyne versus Wear derby when they were drawn with Southwick. Following a 2–1 victory, remarkably Rendel were, for the third time in three years, tied with Auckland Town, this time on Tyneside. But the outcome was the same as Rendel fell again, 3–1.

For the fourth year in succession, the club participated in the FA Cup for the 1893–94 season when they met Shankhouse Black Watch in the opening tie. With the exception of Tyneside's East End and the Wear's Sunderland, Rendel and Shankhouse at this time were regarded as two of the strongest clubs in the region, Shankhouse being winners of the Northumberland Challenge Cup on six occasions by the end of the 19th century. A good crowd turned up at Rendel's home, off the West Road, and saw a most convincing 5–1 victory, a clear indication of the growing strength of the Benwell club.

The second round saw Rendel paired with Leadgate Park, and they were firm favourites to progress. The short 12-mile journey to the Durham hills gave their small band of supporters cheer, winning 2–0. Early in December Willington Athletic, from further down the Tyne, faced Rendel, but the Benwell club were somewhat surprisingly dumped out of the FA Cup following a 3–1 defeat.

Rendel were founder members of the ill-fated North East Counties League in 1889 and, following the competition's demise, joined the Northern Alliance from the start a year later. Rendel's own Joseph Wardropper was an energetic figure in making the competition a success. He was chairman of the new League and was determined, alongside Tom Watson, to ensure the region began to develop some kind of unofficial tiered and structured system of league competition below the Football League and Northern League.

Both Elswick Rangers and Rendel, of all the clubs in Newcastle that followed Tyne and Rangers, were best equipped to compete with East End and West End. They were by far the strongest of the rest. By the opening years of the 1890s, however, both East End and West End had become focused upon a bigger dream of becoming not just a local force but a nationally recognised one, with the East Enders developing all the way as Newcastle United.

A gap quickly resulted. In the 1890–91 season East End Reserves thrashed Elswick Rangers first team 9–1 and 10–2. Rendel fared little better, being walloped 6–1 and 8–1 by the Heaton club. Both Rangers and Rendel would soon be playing at a lower level of football as East End/Newcastle United entered national competition in the shape of the Football League.

In August 1882, on the east side of the city only a mile from where Stanley FC was taking its first faltering steps, another club, Heaton Athletic Association, was also formed. Linked to a cricket club that had been established a year earlier, the leading figures were skipper John Hobson and secretary Thomas Liddell, although the latter was soon replaced by T.H. Wright. The club's treasurer was James Gledson who had featured in Stanley's first season of existence. He later served North Eastern and Gateshead NER. Liddell and Gledson both played football for the club alongside their administrative duties. John Speight, Dan Lord (who succeeded Wright as club secretary in 1884) and James Gardner appeared notably for Heaton too, and all three featured for Newcastle United's pioneers, as did Hobson. On the committee was Thomas Phalp, another Stanley man. Indeed, Heaton Association had many close links to Stanley and thereafter East End, due no doubt to the proximity of the clubs around the Heaton and Byker areas. Heaton was the more fashionable and affluent suburb compared to the working-class Byker.

Other prominent players included later captain James Henry and George McKenzie, who also turned out for the Rangers club. Sam Wood, who later gained prominence with Rendel, pulled on their shirt for a period too. Heaton's colours were 'blue-and-black jersey and hose and white knickerbockers' while the club shared the Heaton Junction Ground, next door to North Eastern's home on the cricket field.

Heaton Association had a degree of success, becoming winners of the Northumberland & Durham FA's Second Team competition in 1883 and also playing in the first Northumberland Challenge Cup tournament during the following year, although they lost 6–0 to Newcastle Rangers in the first round. They were always second best to their neighbours East End, being beaten 9–0 by them in February 1886. The strength of East End in the Heaton and Byker suburbs ensured that Heaton Association never developed, and they folded during that same year.

Trafalgar Football Club was formed later in the pioneering era, during 1887, and like many sides they also had a sister cricket club. They initially played their games at 'Leazes', not far from St James' Park. When East End moved to the Gallowgate site in 1892 and vacated the Heaton Junction Ground, within 12 months Trafalgar had moved in. They also jumped into East End's boots so to speak when the latter were renamed Newcastle United – Trafalgar becoming the 'new' East End in 1895!

Based in the Heaton area, Trafalgar also had many links to the East End club, and several East End players also appeared for Trafalgar. They became members of the new Tyneside Football League which was formed to cater for the profusion of lesser clubs. Trafalgar were the first winners in 1891–92 then joined the Northern Alliance. Several

James Lockey made a name for himself with Trafalgar and later joined Newcastle United.

Jack Patten was a fine player and afterwards became a noted administrator in north-east football.

outstanding players pulled on Trafalgar's shirts, including three men to later appear in Newcastle United's first XI. Full-back James Lockey was a true Tynesider, in his younger days playing for the St Thomas' and Caxton clubs before joining Trafalgar. A Northumberland county player, he eventually joined Newcastle United in 1895 and turned out for the Magpies in First Division action. Goalkeeper W. Lowery was another Trafalgar youngster who did well at Gateshead NER before going on to sign for United and become a member of their Football League set-up at St James' Park.

Jack Patten was developed by Trafalgar too, and he became a prominent name in north-east football for many years. At outside-right he was Trafalgar's captain and secretary for a period and went on to have spells at both West End and East End. Jack was at the time described as a 'typically blunt Geordie' and went onto play for Newcastle United in Football League action against Ardwick (Manchester City) in 1893. After retiring, Patten concentrated on the administration side of the game in the region. He acted for United behind the scenes but was better known as a long-serving member of the Northumberland FA – having 24 years as a councillor (1903–27), two as vice-president (1927–29) and 18 as secretary (1929–47).

On the northern fringe of the city, Jesmond Football Club also entered the action for a few short years. In 1890 the smart neighbourhood was described as 'the Kensington of our northern metropolis'. It was a pleasant suburb where 'artists never tire of depicting its delightful scenery'. Jesmond FC were established in June 1883 and played on 'the first field north of Brandling Park'. They sported colours of maroon and white. From their inception they fielded two teams, with W. Telford the captain of the first team and T. Marshall skipper of the second. Their secretary was John S. Haig, later associated with West End. They participated in both the senior and juniors competitions during the Summer Temperance Festival of 1883 and also entered for the Northumberland Challenge Cup for 1883–84, although they were eliminated in the first round, losing 4–0 to Newcastle B. They gained revenge during the following season, eliminating Newcastle B in the first round but bowing out to Brunswick in the second. Sadly, Jesmond were soon to fade from the scene and within a year or so folded altogether.

In the centre of Newcastle was found one of the oldest clubs, Newcastle Football Association, commonly referred to as Newcastle FA or Newcastle Association to avoid confusion. As we have seen, this was Aleck Peters' club, formed in 1880. Following what could only be called these days as a kick-about on the Town Moor on the 23 October, a meeting was held at the nearby North Terrace Hotel – still a regular haunt of Newcastle United supporters. The *Daily Journal* noted: 'A very successful game under association rules was played on New Town Moor with the object of forming a club.' The enthusiasts decided to create a football team, and Newcastle FA came into being. William Scott was appointed captain, with M. Charlton elected secretary and, at the inaugural meeting, it was unanimously decided to join the Northumberland & Durham FA. Within a couple of years, Andrew Robinson had taken over the mantle of secretary, but he was soon to give way to the Peters brothers.

Although Aleck initially shared the secretary's duties with his brother, W. Peters, it was the former who became the keystone of the club. He was described in a *Northern Athlete* biography of the day as 'worthy of a place amongst the best known athletes of the district, not because he shines forth prominently as an exponent of any branch of sport, but as a thorough hard worker in the interests of cricket and football'.

Born in Gloucestershire in 1857, Peters left that county in 1860 and went to Edinburgh where he was educated, and he soon developed a love of athletics, winning several hundred-yards handicaps and mile walking races. Aleck came to reside in Newcastle and, for several seasons, went in for swimming, winning many races. In 1878, in conjunction with John Geddes, he formed the Trinity Association Cricket Club, accepting the post of honorary secretary, and he soon took in the development of the association game too. It is believed that he gained his first impression of the science of the new sport from the visit of the Scotch-Canadians team to the city. As a football player he was noted as being 'very energetic and, though not brilliant, he is a useful, hard working member of his team, playing usually at back but being capable of taking up his position as a half back, centre forward or in goal'. Later Peters was also secretary and vice-president of the Northumberland FA before he sailed to a new life in Australia, where he played a big part in developing football around Perth.

In 1881 Newcastle FA amalgamated with Trinity Association – an offshoot of the cricket side – and were quickly playing the likes of Sunderland. During December 1881 Newcastle actually defeated the Wearsiders 1–0. They fielded several good players, including goalkeeper and later West End star Robert Oldham. He was from Elswick and also played for the Leather Works team and reached county recognition. He was also a noted runner for the Newcastle Harriers Athletic Club. Tyne pathfinder

Brandling Park in Jesmond. At the far end of the park, with a view to Abbotsford Terrace and the Orphanage (top middle), could be found a football pitch used by several of Tyneside's pioneer clubs. The Warwick Place ground of Tyne Association was to the bottom right.

George McQuillen also had a spell with Newcastle FA, while William Scott was a regular stalwart.

Newcastle FA's colours were originally noted as 'navy blue jersey and hose, navy-blue-and-red striped cap' but these soon gave way, rather appropriately, to black and white; although in this instance it was 'black shirts and hose with white knickers'. In 1885 they had changed their colours again to 'cardinal-and-light-blue quartered jerseys'.

They initially played on the Town Moor near North Terrace but soon switched to a location just off the Great North Road on 'the second field from Brandling Park' opposite the Orphanage. The area was a football hot-spot. Already Tyne had found a home in Brandling, while a pitch was located adjoining at Abbotsford Terrace. There was another field further north again, at the Blue House near Grandstand Road, where Moor Edge Farm stood. The contemporary press often referred to Moor Edge when describing a club's venue in the vicinity.

Led by Peters, who was a forthright character on and off the field, Newcastle FA were an ambitious club. They sent out not just one side in senior action but two for some competitions: Newcastle A and Newcastle B. Both featured in the Northumberland Challenge Cup for the 1883–84 season, with the A side being eliminated by Tyne 5–0 early on, while the B team defeated Jesmond 4–0, Ovington 6–2 and North Eastern 4–3 before losing heavily in the semi-final, to Tyne again, 6–0. It would have been novel had the A and B sides met in the later stages if not the Final itself.

The club had enterprise and invited Preston North End to Tyneside during April 1883 for an exhibition game on Tyne's ground in Jesmond. Although founded only two years before, Preston were catching the eye on the national scene, importing many celebrated Scots. The Deepdale club sent a strong line up and were certainly further advanced in football schooling than the Tyne clubs. They included figures who became household

William Milne was one of several footballers to develop from the Science & Art club. His father later became Newcastle United chairman.

names in the coming decade as Preston were crowned double holders as winners of the FA Cup and Football League in 1889. Included was Fred Dewhurst, to be first capped by England in the 1885–86 season and who at centre-forward or inside-forward was a test for any defender. He was to return to Tyneside as a member of the Corinthian line up.

Preston won easily 6–1 in front of a crowd of around 500. Dull and threatening weather severely affected the attendance which was well below the organisers' hopes and expectations. Both sides fielded a guest player: Gilbert Ainslie (Tyne) turned out for Newcastle and Joe Beverley (Blackburn Rovers) was drafted into the Preston team. Normally a full-back, Joe scored four goals and was another celebrated player, capped by England in the following years. The visitors' passing game baffled the Newcastle defence, and it was thanks to Mills between the posts that the score was kept to respectable proportions in the second half.

Newcastle FA's ambitions of matching the best never came close to fruition. Indeed, by 1885 they were some way behind the district's emerging top sides, West End and East End; in fact, in the Tyne Charity Shield Final they were mauled 10–0 by the East Enders. In 1887 Newcastle FA merged with the smaller club Brunswick Athletic (formed in 1883) who had played on the Town Moor 'near the Blue House'. However, a year later they appear to have folded.

The college side of Science & Art Football Club was also a well-known name for a period as football developed. Created in 1883 in the heart of the city by the masters and pupils, they played football with much credit for many years. Based at the college site on Bath Lane in which a complex of schools had been originally opened in 1871, the football club was formed out of a new School of Science & Art which quickly earned a high reputation – for both education and sport. Later it became Rutherford College, named after its founder Dr John Hunter Rutherford in the early years of the 1890s, and who still played football into the modern era as Rutherford AFC.

Science & Art were amateurs, and although they initially played on the Town Moor they soon switched to a field near to the Orphanage in Brandling Village, near the old site of West End's pitch, just north of Brandling Park. Playing in colours of 'black jerseys and hose, and white knickers', they were winners of the Northumberland FA Junior Cup in five successive years (1889–93), taking over the mantle of Elswick Leather Works in the competition. Science & Art also won the Northumberland FA Minor Cup in 1890.

They had a reputation for developing young talent, and their players moved on around the district's clubs. A handful also went on to appear for Newcastle United in Football League action including, just before the turn of the century, the celebrated Colin Veitch. Tom Bartlett was given the nickname of 'Knocker' after his celebrated foraging and bustling play. He was a popular character on Tyneside, a Northumberland XI player and good enough to join Newcastle United in 1893 and to make his League debut against Notts County later that year. He went on to strike a marvellous hat-trick for the Magpies in a 5–1 victory over Lincoln City.

Jack Carr at left-half was the son of a local councillor, and after impressing for Science & Art, like Bartlett, he was given a chance by United, joining the St James' Park staff in 1894. His Christmas Day debut for the Magpies the following year resulted in a 6–0 victory over Crewe. Another Science & Art junior with a notable family background was William Milne, who became a top all-round sportsman on Tyneside, being a fine cricketer as well as footballer. He played for Northumberland in both sports and was signed by Newcastle United in 1894. Milne appeared at outside-right on six occasions over two spells, returning to St James' Park after a period with Sunderland. His father, George Taylor Milne, was a well-known local figure, a West End supporter originally who later became a United director and chairman of the club from 1911 to 1913. He was also president of the Northumberland FA from 1902 to 1917.

In addition to the principal clubs around Newcastle, there were many other minor sides created during these years as football prospered. Boundary FC were formed around 1884 and were named after Boundary Street in Elswick where they originated. They also ran a cricket club, but their footballing progress was cut short in October 1887 when they ran into difficulties, not being able 'to raise a team'. Several other sides were named after terraces in the area, Malvern, Gloucester and Maple included.

Marlborough FC were in existence in 1882, noted at the time as 'another newly formed local side'. Richard Hedley was a fine player in the early years of the 1890s decade for Marlborough. An outside-right with a dribbling style, he later appeared for Newcastle United, playing a handful of matches for the club before he was controversially involved in a players' strike when several amateur reserves demanded payment for their services. He ended up being dismissed along with several of his colleagues.

A year after Marlborough were formed, Cathedral FC was established. They played in maroon-and-white colours on a pitch at Bath Road, where a field still existed for a while after the Northumberland Cricket Ground had been developed.

Another club, St Mary & St James (also known as SS Mary & James), played the game at the top of St Thomas' Street on the Leazes (on the site of where the Royal Victoria Infirmary now stands). They were formed in 1884 and pulled on unusual colours of 'chocolate jersey and green sash' to underline the vast range of strips worn by the North East's Victorian footballers. They were named after the historic chapel of St James and the 12th-century hospital of St Mary Magdalene, both originally situated in the same area.

Newcastle Wednesday, formed in 1886, were based at St James' Park alongside West End. They often loaned players to the West End club and actually outlived them – playing football on Tyneside until the 1920s.

From left to right: Tom Bartlett, Jack Carr and Richard Hedley all appeared for local Tyneside clubs and later pulled on the jersey of Newcastle United in senior action.

There were such clubs dotted all over the city. Examples of these smaller clubs could be found in Heaton, where Heaton Rovers, Heaton North End, Heaton Templars and Heaton Wanderers played football. Wanderers were the first winners of the Northumberland FA Minor Cup in 1888–89. Victoria Wednesday were located in that neighbourhood too.

All Saints FC (officially known as All Saints Cricket and Athletic Club) were founded in 1882 in the city centre, close to the All Saints Church on Pilgrim Street. They played on the old cricket field at the back of Ellison Place, like Cathedral, and wore black, cardinal and sky-blue jerseys with dark knickers. Under the driving guidance of C.T.W. Trigg and supported by other members of the Trigg family, they became the first winners of the Northumberland FA's Junior Cup in 1883.

The Guild of St John FC hailed from St Anthony's in Walker and had been formed in 1884. St Cuthberts were in action during the early weeks of 1883 and were originally, like Science & Art, from the complex of schools on Bath Lane.

By the end of the 1890s decade football had certainly taken hold in Newcastle and its outlying districts. The same was to be seen in the Tyne Valley and all points north and south. The association code had taken root and was here to stay.

Chapter 7

ALONG THE TYNE

'He had never known such a place as Corbridge for football.'
Local resident, *Hexham Courant,* 1882.

The Tyne Valley in Victorian Britain was much as it is now; urbanised and industrial from Newcastle eastwards to the coast, yet charming and peaceful to the west and the Pennines. In both of these contrasting landscapes football found a home. Perhaps surprisingly, some of the district's earliest clubs were based in the outlying towns and villages of the rural Tyne valley, notably in Corbridge, Ovingham and Ovington. Corbridge Football Club was a founder member of the Northumberland & Durham FA in 1880, while Ovingham and Ovington quickly joined the fold as well.

Why football found a stronghold in Corbridge so early in the game's development in the region is not determined. Back in 1880, the village had a meagre population of less than 2,000, yet they not only had a football club, but also a cricket side and a rowing club. Football and cricket also thrived in both Ovingham and Ovington, only seven miles along the Tyne valley from Corbridge. They were even smaller communities with populations of less than 500 each. All three sides, however, were prominent in those youthful footballing days as Tyne and Rangers led the way.

Corbridge was originally an important Roman settlement on the junction of strategic Roman roads: the Stanegate (to Carlisle and the west) and Dere Street (south to York and north to present day Scotland). Before Newcastle upon Tyne rose to prominence it was the most important crossing point on the Tyne. Afterwards it became an Anglo-Saxon Royal Burgh and now is a delightful and busy commuter centre for Newcastle. It was in the Victorian era, as it remains today, one of the most picturesque spots in Northumberland.

Corbridge Association Football Club was formed in October 1879 when a meeting was called in the village, with a certain Bernard Powell presiding over a gathering. A club was formed, and their earliest games were played at Eastfield, on land owned by local landowner John Walker of Eastfield House, Corbridge. Eastfield is located just off the present A69 near Howden Dene. Many of Corbridge's early players came from the local business and land-owning community which could afford to fund the new club.

Edward Docker, a resident of Riding Mill, was the first captain, but the driving force behind the club was Fred Knott. Much of Corbridge's enthusiasm for the association game rests with Knott who led the club from its first steps. He was on the Northumberland & Durham FA committee from its outset and later became secretary of the governing organisation. Fred also played for his side during the earliest months alongside his brother William.

The Post Office at Corbridge, located opposite the Angel Inn, showing a Victorian horse brake of the type which would have ferried many a pioneer footballer from the railway station. The buildings all still stand, and the Eastfield pitch was close by. *(Newcastle City Library)*

The Knott family were blacksmiths who had a business on the outskirts of the village on land leased from the Duke of Northumberland since the 1850s. The family operated there until around 1970. Fred, however, was a solicitor's clerk who worked initially in Elswick and later in Gateshead. He was deeply involved in football organisation for many years in the region and a regular referee at matches all over the district. Knott was also secretary of the association football competition at the Tyneside Summer Temperance Festival in 1883.

The club's first recorded game was against Tyne Association's second XI on 1 November 1879 (a 1–0 defeat), and the local Tyneside press soon after described the club as one of only three association teams in the district alongside Tyne and Newcastle Rangers. They played various friendly games during the first year of their existence against both Tyne & Rangers elevens and also against scratch teams like the Planets from Newcastle (13-a-side, as the visitors brought too many players to Corbridge). Corbridge also played Burnopfield and North Eastern, recording a 7–0 triumph against the railwaymen at Heaton in March 1880.

The club held its annual meeting at the beginning of September 1880, Charles Michael presiding, when a 'fair number' of members were present. John Straker of Stagshaw House, Corbridge, was unanimously re-elected as club president. Charles Michael's brother, Arthur Wellington Michael, also played for the club and became a Northumberland & Durham trialist. He was appointed as Corbridge vice-captain for the 1880–81 season. Both brothers were clerks who had been born in Newcastle and then resided in Corbridge. Fred Knott was elected secretary and treasurer.

Corbridge were one of the early successful teams in the region. A claim to fame could be that they were the first visitors to win a game at St James' Park. This was during November 1880 when they defeated Rangers 2–1. Technically, however, they were not the first combination to win at St James' as a Rangers practice game (Captain's XI v Others XV) had taken place before this.

Corbridge were involved in spreading the word about the association game, taking part in exhibition matches at Ovingham (which led directly to the formation of Ovingham FC) during September 1880 and at Chester-le-Street the following month, which also led to the founding of Chester-le-Street FC. The latter encounter saw a 12–0 win over North Eastern recorded. They had to play with three substitutes who knew little about the game.

Outside-right J.W. Marshall was a good footballer, appearing in the early Northumberland & Durham combined representative side when with Corbridge. Another well-known man connected with the club in its early days was Nicholas Richley. He was initially a tailor-draper who was a member – as were several of their players – and skipper of the Corbridge Cricket Club, and he became captain of the football club for the 1880–81 season. He was a rather tragic figure. Richley changed his profession and took over as licensee of the Golden Lion Inn in Corbridge. Unfortunately he went bankrupt and moved to Hexham and became in itinerant publican. Sadly Richley met an untimely end when out ferreting with friends in 1903. He was climbing a fence with his gun when he stumbled and shot himself.

One of the original clubs that met at the Turk's Head Hotel in Newcastle to form the local association, Corbridge took part in Northumberland's new governing body's first Challenge Cup tournament. Unluckily for them, they faced Tyne Association at the Northumberland Cricket Ground in the first round and fell by 5–1.

In the following season, 1881–82, they reached the Final of the competition. On the way to meeting Newcastle Rangers in the county's showpiece fixture during March, Corbridge defeated Ovingham, Ferryhill and then Alnwick 3–2 in the semi-final, following a contentious match over a disputed Alnwick goal that saw the local football rulers decide in favour of the Tynedale club. The Alnwick umpire produced a copy of the rules to show the referee, to illustrate that the match official was wrong in disallowing an Alnwick goal. The referee then produced a copy of his rule book to show what constituted a foul. Alnwick's second goal was scored after the referee called time, but Corbridge agreed to let the goal stand provided the score was not changed from a 3–2 victory. At the end of the match, the referee said that the score was 3–1, but Alnwick claimed that it should have been a draw. The Cup Committee ruled in Corbridge's favour.

The Final was played on Tyne's ground in Jesmond when Corbridge faced an emerging Rangers team and held their own in a close match that ended 1–1. One of the side's twin strikers, centre-forward T. Forster, had given Corbridge a first-minute lead, but Crawford equalised after 35 minutes. The two clubs turned up at the same venue in Newcastle at the beginning of April and tried again. Richley up front was prominent for the Tyne valley side, but Rangers were impressive, lifting the trophy after a comfortable 2–0 victory.

This reverse seemed to dispirit many of the Corbridge players who seemed to lose interest. They were unable to raise a team for a trip to Newcastle FA during November

1882 and scratched from the Northumberland & Durham Challenge Cup that year after being drawn against North Eastern in the first round. The club seemed to have lapsed then, if not folded altogether.

Fred Knott was instrumental in assisting setting up the new Northumberland Football Association in 1883. There are reports of him also trying to resuscitate the Corbridge club in October of that year, and he partially succeeded as the club played a few matches against Wall and Hexham Wanderers, but it appears that they only ever played spasmodic games against minor or junior clubs at this time. In 1885 they played on a pitch at Hall Bank in Corbridge and their colours were recorded as 'red and black'. But it remained a struggle to keep the club going.

Fred presided over a meeting held in the Angel Inn in Corbridge during October 1886 to, once again, try to resurrect the club. Many of the early enthusiasts still lived in the locality, and he succeeded in generating enthusiasm again. Landowner John Green donated fields near the railway station and that became their home ground. This location is still used for football today. Tynedale Rugby Club play there now as do the modern Corbridge United Junior FC.

Corbridge was rekindled enough to appear again in the Northumberland Challenge Cup during the 1887–88 season. They received a bye in the first round but went out to North Eastern in the second; however, they were soon to disappear from sight and by 1890 had died off again.

At their peak Corbridge also ran a second XI team and were a significant influence on developing the game along the Tyne Valley. A local resident in 1882 commented in the *Hexham Courant*: 'He had never known such a place as Corbridge for football. He had witnessed many a closely contested game in the street between youngsters who used anything as a football from an old boot to a tin can. He thought the newly formed junior club with strong wiry youths would be a good one'. At the time a Corbridge Juniors FC had been just established in the village.

The villages of Ovingham and Ovington, settlements nestling on the slope of the river valley only a mile apart, have their origins back in Anglo-Saxon and Norman times. These days, like Corbridge, they are pleasant retreats from the hustle and bustle of Newcastle. Ovingham was described in 1889 as a 'pretty village of great antiquity'. Like Corbridge, cricket had an influence on the origins of football in both communities.

The village of Ovingham had an active cricket team before it had an association football club. Indeed, it was thanks to the members of the cricket club that football got off the ground in the village at all. Quite a few of the cricketers became members of the football club. The cricket club loaned the use of their field to the football enthusiasts to allow Corbridge to play Tyne in an exhibition match during September 1880. Corbridge won 2–0, although one goal was disputed. It was such a success, however, that a meeting was convened after the match and a decision was made to form a football club. Three days after that exhibition game, a meeting was held to form a committee and settle the rules. Officers were elected and 30 members were enrolled, with Thomas Cook acting as secretary. A vote of thanks was passed at this inaugural meeting to Fred Knott of Corbridge for arranging the exhibition match.

Within a week, Ovingham chose their colours – Cambridge blue and black – and they decided to join the local Football Association. Their first recorded game was a home encounter against neighbours Corbridge second XI during mid-October (a 2–1 defeat), but two weeks later they recorded their first victory, a 3–1 success against Blaydon Rugby Union Club. Thereafter Ovingham played a mixture of second XIs and first teams with mixed results. A visit to Sunderland in late November saw them lose 4–0 against the Wearsiders' seniors.

The first annual meeting of the club took place at the start of August 1881 when the secretary's report showed the club to be in a 'most flourishing condition'. The captain was noted as B. Wright, with J. Dodson as vice-captain. W.C. Turner was treasurer and Thomas Cook remained as secretary, although by 1884 Turner had taken over the secretary's role. From team line ups, the captain and vice-captain were full-backs, while Turner and Cook played as centre-forwards, often together.

No precise date is known when Ovington Football Club was formed, but they were playing as early as December 1881 when Ovington Wanderers lost 5–0 at Ovingham. The Ovington team was occasionally (but not always) referred to as Wanderers in the early years.

Ovington had a second XI themselves, although at times they struggled to raise a team, and they also fielded a junior side. In March 1882 Ovington School beat Ovingham School 6–1, so the game was clearly spreading to schoolboy level too.

Both Ovingham and Ovington were competitors in the early Northumberland & Durham FA Challenge Cup and then became rivals in the later Northumberland Challenge Cup, although they never progressed to the concluding stages. The furthest either side reached was the quarter-final in 1882–83 when Ovingham were taken apart by Tyne, 6–0. There was even a local derby contest with a difference in the 1884–85 tournament when Ovingham played Ovington. A hard-fought game was expected, and George Hall, the respected treasurer of the Northumberland FA, was appointed as referee. Those who predicted a close encounter were not disappointed,

ALONG THE TYNE: PRINCIPAL CLUB LOCATIONS

Fact Box

Tyne Valley; West
Corbridge, Ovingham, Ovington, Prudhoe Rovers, Wylam, Newton, Mickley Rangers.

Industrial East
Rosehill/Willington Athletic.

Industrial South
Gateshead Association, Gateshead NER, Birtley, Hebburn Argyle, Hebburn, Jarrow.

with the 'Hams winning by the only goal of the match; although a great deal of credit for their victory went to their goalkeeper Elliott.

By 1884, Ovingham were playing at the 'west end of village' and their colours were noted as 'royal blue-and-black jerseys and hose, white knickers'. Ovington found a pitch in their village also and pulled on shirts of 'black and amber'.

Getting to outlying places like Ovingham and Ovington could be a bit of a problem in those Victorian days. It was not quite as easy as a quick drive in a car or bus along the A69 as now. Train was the only real link, and while there was not a direct route to Ovingham and Ovington the Newcastle to Carlisle line did run along the valley; however, a stop-off at either Corbridge, Prudhoe or Wylam and then a walk or charabanc drive to the village was not the ideal preparation for a football match. There could be some tortuous journeys in those days, such as Shankhouse in the Northumberland coalfield to Bishop Middleham in County Durham; although the local associations did attempt to keep distances to a minimum when making draws for competitions. That did not always work, however, and some players did not fancy lengthy travelling on a cold winter's morning.

It was not uncommon for visiting teams to turn up at such locations with a reduced compliment or being somewhat weary. In 1882, during a week of damp and wet weather, the Rangers club had problems travelling along the Tyne valley. It was noted: 'Three of the Rangers team did not turn up, which left only eight men to go out of town to play Ovingham.' A few years later in the 1888–89 season East End endured travelling difficulties for a Challenge Cup fixture. It was recorded that the 'visitors had arrived 40 minutes late and this made it an uncomfortable wait for the spectators in the cold wind'!

The local *Daily Leader* newspaper describes the Sunderland team's journey (with several supporters) for a match at Shankhouse in 1887 by explaining how they left the Royal Hotel on Wearside just after lunch and travelled in a pair of four-in-hand well-horsed brakes 'by way of South Shields and by ferry to North Shields and then through Seaton Delaval to Shankhouse where they arrived, after a very pleasant ride, shortly after 4.00pm'. That was a trip of two and a half hours! After the contest, the return was just as weary. 'After partaking of tea at the headquarters of the Shankhouse club, the Sunderland men left at about eight o'clock and arrived at Sunderland at a quarter past 10, being frequently cheered as they entered the town'.

As the 1880s progressed, Ovingham and Ovington, as well as neighbouring Corbridge, were noticeably being left behind as the newer and bigger Newcastle clubs dominated the local football scene. In February 1889 East End inflicted a 9–1 defeat on Ovingham in the Northumberland Challenge Cup. As they fell by the wayside, all three clubs were eventually consigned to a small place in football's history.

Close by, several other footballing teams followed and were formed in an area along the Tyne valley that was to become a rich breeding ground for many a notable footballer of the future. The proximity of several small collieries more than likely prompted the workforce to start playing football.

The fortress village of Prudhoe, with an historic past linked to the Umfreville and Percy families, was at the time situated over a toll bridge from Ovingham. A brickworks and coal-pit probably spurned a football club, Prudhoe Rovers, in 1882. In February that year, Ovingham FC played an exhibition game in the village against Newton, winning 3–0. The game led directly to the formation of Prudhoe Rovers. Prudhoe can boast that they once defeated Newcastle United (when they were East End) 4–1 back in March 1884. Rovers played in the unusual colours of 'blue-and-salmon hoops', and they appeared in the earlier years of competition in the region.

Wylam, famous as railway engineer George Stephenson's birthplace, was a small parish nearby with another modest colliery. Led by secretary G. Raisbeck of Castle Hill Hall, the local lads formed a club there in 1883 with shirts of 'blue jerseys and white sash'.

Another neighbouring village with a pit-wheel was Mickley where again a club was established a year earlier. Ovingham played another exhibition match against Ovington at Mickley Square during January 1882 (winning 8–1) on a field loaned by Joseph Humble of Eltringham House, and it was soon noted that 'a new club has been formed'. Eltringham is located on the south banks of the Tyne half a mile from Mickley Square. There was a ferry across the river at Eltringham to Ovingham and Ovington. Mickley went on to play in the Northern Alliance from the second year of the Championship in 1891–92 and won the Northumberland FA Minor Cup in 1891.

Both the Prudhoe and Mickley clubs took part in the first Northumberland Challenge Cup tournament in the 1883–84 season. Indeed, they met each other in the opening round, Prudhoe winning 5–1. Mickley can even boast they took part in the FA Cup qualifying competition during the 1892–93 season, gaining a bye in round one then facing Bishop Auckland at the next stage. However, they lost by seven goals to a much stronger Bishops side.

On the higher slopes of the Tyne Valley, above Ovingham and Ovington, the village of Newton also created a football club. Remarkably maybe, looking back now, this tiny community of a population of around 150 possessed a pioneer line up which also encompassed the Stocksfield area (indeed, their ground was a field 'within five minutes walk of Stocksfield Station'). Their secretary was W. Lisle and they were one of the original clubs to take part in the inaugural Northumberland Challenge Cup in 1883–84. They faced Ovingham over three matches, two drawn games and then a convincing 4–1 victory for Newton. They then met Bedlington Burdon in round two and recorded another eye-catching win, this time by 5–0, which sent them through to meet Tyne, the eventual winners of the trophy. In Jesmond the minnows of Newton only narrowly lost by the odd goal in three.

North Tyne Swifts were based in the village of Wall – another tiny village, this time located almost on the Roman Wall – and they were to eliminate Newton from the Northumberland Challenge Cup of 1884–85 before going out to Newcastle West End, losing 6–1.

There were other minor clubs in this area of 20 miles along the Tyne valley between Newcastle and Hexham. Not long after the earliest clubs were formed, the principle market town of Hexham possessed two clubs; Hexham Excelsior and Hexham Star. The Excelsior team went on to lift the Northumberland FA Minor Cup in 1894.

Teams were also established in villages even further west, at Haydon Bridge and Haltwhistle, while a club was also playing the game at Greenhead near the Northumberland-Cumberland border. Due to the proliferation of new sides being formed, the Northumberland FA eventually established the West Tyne League in 1892.

Closer to Newcastle, both Lemington Rangers and Walbottle were formed. Lemington were the bigger club, although by no means were they a major influence on the development of the game. Guided by secretary J. Weatherley of West View, Lemington-on-Tyne, they first appeared in 1883 and sported colours of 'black-and-blue jerseys and hose with white-and-blue knickers'. They progressed sufficiently to enter for the Northumberland Challenge Cup in 1886–87 but encountered the emerging Elswick Rangers in the first round and were quickly eliminated. They never ventured into such senior company again.

To the east of Newcastle the industrial heartland was a powerhouse of activity – shipbuilding and marine engineering was in full flow with major employers like Hawthorn, Leslie & Company, Swan & Hunter as well as Wigham Richardson and Palmer & Company, all to be at the forefront of the shipbuilding world. The landscape was in direct contrast to the rural west Tyne valley. Here factories, chimneys and cranes dominated the panorama.

On the north banks of the Tyne, down river from Newcastle East End's heartland of St Peter's where Newcastle United was conceived, were to be found a line of industrial centres: St Anthony's, Walker and Wallsend to Rosehill, Howdon and Willington Quay. Today they are virtually rolled into one and are part of a giant, sprawling conurbation stretching some nine miles from Newcastle to Tynemouth. In the 1880s they were gradually merging together to serve the shipbuilding and engineering yards on the riverside.

Rosehill supported both a cricket and football club. The association code team was established in October 1883 with a pitch just off Rosehill Road near the Willington Rope Works, described as being within 'two minutes walk from Howdon Station'. Rosehill sported wonderful shirts in an era that saw many unusual mixes of colours and inventive sashes and bands; cardinal and navy blue jerseys and a hosed band, with navy blue shorts.

The club reached the semi-final of the Northumberland Challenge Cup in the 1884–85 season, losing to Sleekburn Wanderers, and one of their earliest stalwarts was Tom Watson. A Heaton man, as already mentioned, he became one of football's finest club administrators, much later leading both Sunderland and Liverpool to an array of top honours. Watson developed his enthusiasm and love for the new sport as a player with Rosehill in 1881, living close by in Willington. He was by no means outstanding on the field of play, although he did skipper the Rosehill second XI. Tom also played cricket for the club, and he soon became secretary and their guiding influence until he was persuaded to move across Newcastle to join the up-and-coming West End in the summer of 1886. Afterwards he switched to East End.

Rosehill changed its name around 1888, utilising the larger community of Willington as the club's title to become Willington Athletic. They continued to develop and became a strong local combination in later years, lifting the Northumberland Challenge Cup in

Rosehill as the century drew to a close. The football pitch was to be found at the top right of the picture beyond the terraces.

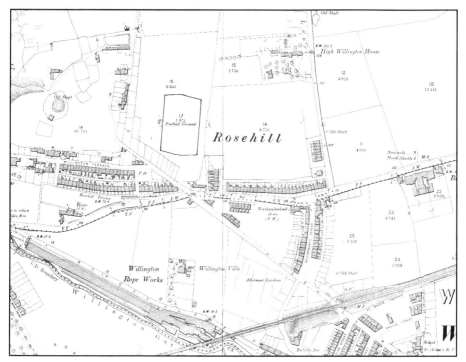

The location of Rosehill and Willington's ground.

Tom Watson began a celebrated career with Rosehill but became famous for leading both Sunderland and Liverpool to Football League titles.

1896–97 while Willington Athletic also developed into a noted non-League side after the turn of the century with an FA Cup giant-killing pedigree. That association in the competition began much earlier, first taking part in the famous tournament in seasons 1891–92 and 1892–93 when they were knocked out by Shankhouse on both occasions.

In the following campaign Willington gained their first FA Cup scalp with a 1–0 victory at Rosehill over Darlington, then in the Northern League and a substantial step up in level from their own status. They defeated Blyth following a replay, then faced a tough contest with Rendel during December 1893. With home advantage in Benwell, Rendel were favourites, but Willington recorded a fine 3–1 victory. At the next hurdle – now one step away from the competition proper – they had another difficult encounter when tied with Middlesbrough, still amateurs and then in the Northern League, eventual champions that season. Not surprisingly the Geordies lost 4–1 to the Boro, a side that went on to lift the FA Amateur Cup the following year with star players like centre-forward Joseph Gettins and future England men Tom Morren and Phil Bach in the line up.

Rosehill and Willington produced several fine players at that time, some of whom went on to become prominent elsewhere. Included in that number was right-back James Lockey who joined the club after spells at St Thomas', Caxton and Trafalgar. He afterwards joined Newcastle United and appeared in Football League action, indeed taking part in the crucial Test Matches of 1898 which decided United's promotion to the top echelon of football for the very first time. Lockey was a brass finisher by trade in the Tyne shipyards.

Willington Athletic twice won the Northumberland Charity Shield and Northumberland Challenge Bowl at the beginning of the 1890s and were early members of the Northern Alliance. But they had grandiose plans, perhaps beyond their station. After the turn of the century in 1903 they even attempted to join the Football League, their chairman of the time noting that there was no reason why the club could not 'provide one of the finest League teams in existence'. However, at the Football League's annual meeting at the Tavistock Hotel in Covent Garden they stood little chance, only receiving one vote – thought to be from Middlesbrough. (It should be noted that Willington Athletic are often confused with County Durham's Willington FC, near Spennymoor, who were founded much later in 1911.)

A neighbouring outfit to Willington Athletic were Point Pleasant Football Club, situated between Wallsend and Rosehill and, as has been mentioned, once demolished by all of 19–0 by East End in a Northumberland Challenge Cup tie during 1887–88. They were a minor side, but one which has now gone down in history as the club Newcastle United created their record competitive victory against in first-team action. There was also another small club a few hundred yards down river, Howdon Rangers, who even competed in the FA Cup in 1893–94. They lost that early qualifying match 2–1 to Tow Law Town.

Towards the mouth of the Tyne, where rugby had a stronghold with the Percy Park and Rockcliffe clubs, association teams were being formed, but all were of a lesser standing until Whitley Bay and North Shields Athletic were set up much later, in 1896 and 1897, both becoming something of a local force after the turn of the century. There were also Wallsend Park Villa and Hibernia, another side from Wallsend, who were both playing the game well before the arrival of the North Shields club. During the early years of the 1890s the East Tyne League was formed for that level of football to compliment the competition west of Newcastle.

Situated across the river from Willington and Rosehill on the south bank of the Tyne, Hebburn and Jarrow both supported football clubs too. Hebburn Juniors, founded early in 1883, played on a field adjoining the Hebburn railway station under the captaincy of James Allan, with Antony Martyn of Thistle Street in Hebburn acting as secretary. They donned black-and-white colours and faced Newcastle West End just before Christmas 1883, drawing 1–1 at home, but were well beaten, home and away, when they met West End again in the following year. They were to drop the nomenclature of 'Juniors' following a meeting in the town's Reading Room during August 1883 and were afterwards known as simply Hebburn AFC.

By this time Jarrow FC were also playing football, and they faced both East End and West End away from home in the latter half of 1883, losing both times. They played a memorable game against Sunderland in October 1883 when, despite playing for the first 25 minutes with only 10 men, they led the Wearsiders until just before the interval when Sunderland claimed that they had equalised. Jarrow insisted that it was not a goal as the ball had passed over the string that bridged the top of the posts. There were no umpires for this game, so the effort was regarded as a 'disputed goal'. It was of little consequence, however, because Sunderland scored eight undisputed goals without reply after the interval.

But both Hebburn AFC and Jarrow were to be eclipsed by another club in the area, Hebburn Argyle. They had been founded earlier, in 1882 as St Aloysius Juniors, and were nicknamed 'The Irish Highlanders', being created by a group of young catholic parishioners. They were guided by the Revd Toner who became the new club's chairman.

Playing on the same field near the railway and close to the local church on Argyle Street in the town (another engineering and ship-building community), it was appropriate to rename the club Hebburn Argyle, and in 1888 they moved to a better-enclosed ground. Two of the original founders of the side, T. Richardson and J. Mitchell, were instrumental in their rise while, on the pitch, Paddy Inglis was a mainstay, described as occupying 'almost every position on the field'. Born at Bill Quay nearby, Inglis was normally a half-back and was captain of the team by the time they had fully established themselves at the beginning of the 1890s.

Yet there was still quite a class-gap between Hebburn and the bigger local sides. However, they became a strong side at their own level, competing in the FA Cup for the first time in 1893–94 (a 4–1 defeat at Blyth), the year they joined the Northern Alliance. Hebburn went on to reach the Durham Challenge Cup Final in 1895 and lifted the Alliance title in 1897, in the process stopping a fourth consecutive victory by the Sunderland A side by a whisker, only on goal average.

Lastly, to the town of Gateshead, always in the shadow of Newcastle in terms of commerce, prestige and history, as well as, ultimately in this context, football. Its bigger neighbour directly across the Tyne even tried more than once to annexe the town, but Gateshead always thwarted such attempts – except once in 1553 when it was annexed to Newcastle by an Act of Parliament following the temporary dissolution of the bishopric of Durham. But within a year the bishopric was restored, and Gateshead reverted to County Durham.

One of Hebburn Argyle's early star players, Paddy Inglis. (P. Brennan, www.donmouth.co.uk)

On the site of the ancient route north, for a long time Gateshead was in control of the Prince Bishops of Durham who for centuries ruled much of the land between the Tyne and Tees. The principal footballing clubs to represent the town in those early years were Gateshead Association, Gateshead NER and Birtley on Gateshead's southern boundary. All were established largely as a result of the huge industrial growth along Tyneside's riverside.

As late as the early decades of the 19th century Gateshead was still a small town by comparison to its widely spread borders now. Census statistics show that the population grew from 19,945 in 1801 to 131,432 by 1881 (when football first appeared) and to 195,743 in 1901. Although now a thriving community,

Dr Johnson's infamous view that Gateshead was 'a dirty lane out of Newcastle' was in part a true picture at the time.

Large industrial works were scattered throughout the town; chemical and brickworks, large engineering factories of John Abbot & Co and Hawks, Crawshay & Sons, as well as the giant railway plants of the North Eastern Railway Company and Black, Hawthorn & Company. There were coal-pits dotted in and around the town too; at Redheugh – where much later Gateshead's Football League club played their football – and at Oakwellgate. Amidst all this industrial activity, football found a perfect breeding foundation: a working-class community who wanted to express themselves in sport.

The oldest of the trio of footballing teams was Birtley Football Club. From a village on the outskirts of the town on the old Great North Road and now part of the Tyne-Wear metropolitan area, its population at the time was only around 3,500. Although the place-name derivation is 'bright meadow', Birtley was anything but that in the later years of the 19th century. Iron works and collieries surrounded the village, and one of those pit-heads now features Antony Gormley's famous Tyneside landmark *Angel of the North*.

The year Birtley FC was formed is debatable, as various sources note their birth as either 1881 or 1882. It has been established, though, that they were playing in 1882 and during their early days played at a pitch described as 'in Wrekenton', a village close by and now part of Gateshead.

Birtley participated in the Northumberland & Durham Challenge Cup during the 1882–83 season, eliminating Hamsterley and Derwent Rovers (the latter following a dispute) before succumbing to the growing Sunderland outfit. The club reached the Durham Challenge Cup Final in 1886 and faced Bishop Auckland Church Institute at Feethams in Darlington. A crowd of 1,500 saw the Bishops win 3–1. Robert Wilson was one of the club's earliest devotees, but without doubt full-back George Millar became their most famous player. From South Shields, he was captain of the side and a regular for the Durham County XI and good enough to appear in North versus South trial matches – one step away from full international recognition.

Millar first played in the representative game of 1888 at The Oval and then at Sunderland's Newcastle Road ground the following year. He played alongside such huge footballing names as John Devey and Dennis Hodgetts, who both became Aston Villa legends in the following years. An amateur of the old school and a Corinthian player, Millar had also spells with Middlesbrough and Ironopolis as well as Sunderland. A solid and resolute defender, George also played for the Sunderland Albion club in the Football Alliance. He won the Cleveland Association Cup twice when at Boro and was described as 'a very powerful man and a sterling player'.

In the 1888–89 season Birtley entered the FA Cup qualifying competition and were tied in their opening game with Darlington during October. Following 90 minutes of stalemate, Birtley won the contest in extra-time 2–0 and progressed to face Morpeth Harriers in a second-round Cup tie that proved highly controversial. On the Howard Terrace ground in Morpeth, Birtley were second best to Harriers and were three goals down by the break. Brown did pull a goal back, but the visitors lost 3–1. However, like many clubs of the era, Birtley lodged a protest to the Football Association and a replay was ordered.

The Tyneside club objected on the grounds that the crossbar was 4in below the regulation height and the field was 'rigged' (ridged) instead of being level. They claimed that 'the goal uprights were placed in the furrow with the rig [sic] coming directly under the middle of the crossbar, thus causing the deficiency'.

Morpeth were not happy and sent a legal-type document to the umpires and referee, soliciting their signatures to affirm that, in their opinion, the ground was up to the average standard on which Cup ties are normally played. The match officials were, umpires M. Hall (Morpeth) and R.K. Wilson (Birtley), along with referee Mr Reed of Middlesbrough.

Nevertheless, the Football Association ordered that the tie should be replayed at Birtley. This took place during November before 'the largest gathering ever seen on the Birtley football ground'. The match was reportedly noted as being 'fearfully rough' following on from the first contest, which had been no 'friendly' encounter in itself. Two of Morpeth's players had been injured, one of whom had not recovered by the time of the replay. Harriers played what was described as 'a dirty game', particularly in the second half after Morpeth's full-back Bates had been knocked out with a blow to the chin in the first 45 minutes and had had to go off, although he returned for the second period.

After the break, Harriers roughed up the lightweight Birtley forwards, most of whom were badly injured; although they lasted until the final whistle. Bolam sustained a broken rib, Standley 'had a foot lamed' and McAvoy was also hurt, with Shaw, Kennedy and Millar injured too; however, Birtley battled through the tackles and the decisive goal of the replayed tie was scored by them on 75 minutes when Shaw grabbed what turned out to be the winning strike.

In round three later during November, a Tyne-Wear derby with a difference took place; Birtley versus Sunderland Albion. The Wearsiders were a strong and ambitious club, recently formed after a difference of opinion in the original Sunderland club's ranks. Travelling to Birtley's home soil, Albion won 5–2 after all was level on 90 minutes at 2–2. The referee, Charles Glover of Darlington, declared that extra-time had to be played; however, both teams objected as it was getting dark. Nevertheless, he insisted. In the descending gloom, the heavy ground told on the Birtley players, and they were almost out on their feet in the additional period. By the time Kilpatrick had scored Sunderland's fifth goal the light was 'very bad', but the tie was concluded with Albion well in control. Birtley made a protest due to the bad light, however, and this was initially accepted by the authorities and a replay ordered. It was then Albion's turn to lodge an appeal. That was dismissed, but Birtley then refused to play! Sunderland progressed to the FA Cup competition proper, where they faced Grimsby Town, losing 3–0.

In that same season Birtley were also defeated by Albion in the Final of the Durham Challenge Cup, losing 3–0 at Feethams before a crowd of 6,000, but not until a controversial first meeting had been abandoned. Albion were comfortably ahead 2–0 at Bishop Auckland's Kingsway ground when crowd unrest spilled onto the pitch after Birtley had thought they had pulled a goal back, only for it to be disallowed. The Birtley crowd behind the goal were enraged, and a free-for-all ensued on the pitch – with players and fans in the middle of the hubbub. Sunderland's skipper was struck on the head and suffered a nasty wound. Officials ushered the players from the field, and when the pandemonium calmed down – some 45 minutes later – they returned with Albion down to 10 men. Order was not restored, though, as another invasion caused the match to be abandoned. Birtley's followers at the time earned a reputation of being over-exuberant. More trouble was to follow.

That was not the end of Birtley's FA Cup exploits. In 1889–90 they defeated Bishop Auckland 3–1 in the opening round at Birtley and then faced Newcastle West End on home soil during October. Birtley got off to a bad start when star full-back George Millar scored an own-goal as he attempted to head a shot clear. Before the break they were 2–0 behind when Alex Brady recorded West End's second goal. After the interval the contest became heated, with McDonald (West End) and Kennedy (Birtley) coming to blows on the field. Incensed spectators ran over the ropes onto the pitch as well, and what was described as 'a scene of turmoil and disorder' resulted. Police had to restore order, and both players were sent off. Birtley did pull a goal back, scoring from a scrimmage and variously attributed to Knox or Minns, but could not force an equaliser.

The following season saw a terrific FA Cup contest with Shankhouse Black Watch which resulted in a Football Association-ordered replay. Birtley travelled to Shankhouse in October, and an enthralling Cup tie resulted. Birtley played with a strong wind in their favour in the opening half and were soon two goals up. But once Shankhouse had the elements in their favour after the interval it was a different matter, and a 3–1 deficit soon became a 5–3 lead; although a late Birtley goal led to a nail-biting finish. Shankhouse won 5–4, but Birtley made a protest and earned a replay, held two weeks later, again in south Northumberland. The miners of Shankhouse made no mistake this time, winning again, this time by 5–1.

Birtley FC were founder members of the Northern League and took part in one of the opening fixtures during September 1889 against Elswick Rangers. They thought that they had recorded a good 4–1 victory, but Rangers belatedly lodged one of their many protests that season. Following a brace of goals from Knox and McAvoy, Birtley's officials and players were content that they had picked up their first two points in League competition, but Rangers claimed Birtley had played an unregistered player.

For weeks the result stood and was reflected in the published League tables; however, in what was a long-running dispute, some two months later it was reported that the protest had been successful. The Northern League Committee had agreed with the Elswick club, deciding that 'the match should be counted as a draw, with the scores still standing'! Birtley's two points were reduced to one, although both teams' goal averages were unaltered.

Birtley did not have a good time in the Northern League. They were beaten 7–0 by Darlington (forward Tom Devey grabbing four goals), 5–0 by St Augustine's and 5–1 by Middlesbrough. They finished second-bottom of the League, on the same number of points as Elswick Rangers – a paltry nine – after winning only three games all season. They switched to the Northern Alliance for the 1890–91 season as a founder member but struggled to raise a team for the start of that campaign and scratched from the competition without kicking a ball. After some restructuring of the club, they later did eventually play in the Northern Alliance, but they continued to struggle in League competition.

Gateshead Association Football Club were formed out of the demise of Newcastle Rangers in December 1884. They were originally known as the 'Casuals' but dispensed with that title quickly, being referred to instead as Gateshead Association. Several Rangers players moved to the new club including William Simms, their first captain, John Douglas, the secretary, and James Frazer. There were also several other noted ex-Rangers men in the new club's ranks: Hetherington, Wardale, Innes, Rule and Tommy Morpeth. Some of these players were to eventually play for Newcastle West End. Indeed, J.D. Wardale briefly captained them at the start of the 1887–88 season before returning to Gateshead.

Playing in colours of 'white and blue', Gateshead's home ground was on the early pitch of Rangers at the Alexandra Road Drill Field, but afterwards, in the summer of 1887, they moved to another field nearby in Bensham and then, for the 1888–89 season, to a ground in the Teams area of Gateshead.

Apart from the array of former Rangers men, Gateshead fielded several other outstanding names of Tyneside's early football scene. Tyne's A.P. Arnold played for a period with Gateshead, as did forward William Boswell who was, like Arnold, a Durham

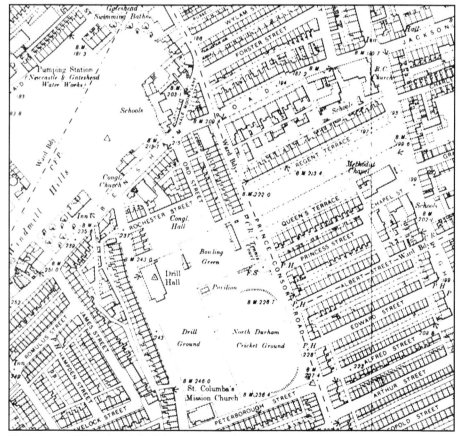

The location of Gateshead's Drill Ground arena, the venue of much of the town's sporting activity: football, cricket and bowling.

University man and Durham county player. He also had a spell with West End and rivals Gateshead NER. Prominent for several seasons was Scot George McQuillen, another ex-Tyne player who later skippered the side.

Gateshead could also call upon one of the most prominent names in football, albeit for a brief period, the Revd Andrew Amos who played for England against Scotland in 1885 and faced Wales in 1886. He had appeared on Tyneside before with the Corinthians when they had visited Newcastle. Although born in Southwark in London, he settled in the North East for a period and was another pioneer of the game who attended Charterhouse School, as did Tyne's Ainslie and brothers Philip and Frank Messent. Amos was

The Drill Ground cricket and football pitch can still be viewed today, next to the original bowling green which retains its 1865 plaque. Gateshead Civic Centre is now situated opposite.

England's Andrew Amos played for Bishop Auckland Church Institute and Gateshead. Pictured at Cambridge University in 1886 with several stars who played international football. Back row, left to right: Amos, Squire, Marchant, Lindley. Front: Saunders, Strother, Spilsbury, Cobbold, Walters, Blenkiron, Pike.

a regular with the Old Carthusians, a major force in the FA Cup during the Victorian era. After attending Cambridge, Andrew was based at Bishop Auckland as he worked towards entering the clergy. He played for the Church Institute side in 1887–88 and then for Gateshead during the 1888–89 season. Noted for feeding the attack from half-back, like many Corinthian amateurs he also played cricket and rugby, also appearing in the North East for North Durham Cricket Club and Durham Rugby FC. Amos moved back to London in 1889 and later became Rector of Rotherhithe.

Gateshead Association entered the FA Cup for the first time in season 1887–88 but were unlucky to be drawn against Darlington, one of the stronger clubs in the region. The Quakers travelled to Bensham and won at a canter 3–0 in front of a healthy crowd of 2,500. The club rarely made headlines after that and struggled somewhat. By the end of the 1880s they had begun to decline, and in September 1890 it was announced that the club had folded.

The giant North East Railway Company works in Gateshead was situated on the notable Rabbit Banks Road between the High Level Bridge and later built King Edward Bridge, which carried the London to Edinburgh rail link. Overlooking the Tyne, this was the site where, decades earlier, Geordies had flocked to watch the aquatic sculling races. The engineering company was formed in 1852 and became the source of another football club in Gateshead. It was the town's biggest employer, building and repairing locomotives and carriages as well as everything connected with that huge industrial sector.

Workers of the company decided to create an association club during 1889, and Gateshead NER quickly overtook their rivals on the south bank of the Tyne; Birtley and Gateshead Association. Many of the local players also joined the NER ranks. They initially played on a field off Park Lane close to one of the NER works buildings and near to the old Park Lane House estate.

The works team soon began to compete in the FA Cup. Highlights included a 7–2 hammering of Ashington and a 10–4 success at Whitburn. That tie on Wearside during October 1891 was a memorable one. Allison gave the home side the lead from the penalty spot and Whitburn led at the break. Wilson equalised for the works outfit in the 55th minute, and the match up to that point was a close affair with little sign of the goal deluge to unfold. Whitburn then powered 2–1 ahead, then 3–1 and 4–1 with Allison completing a hat-trick. It looked a sure bet the Wearsiders would cruise into the next round. But in the closing period of the match the Geordies made an improbable come-back to level the game at 4–4 and force extra-time.

Gateshead were now in the ascendancy and rattled in three more goals in only three minutes – making it six in a short space of time. That gave them an amazing 7–4 advantage. In the closing period Whitburn were reduced to 10 men, and NER grabbed another three goals to reach 10 for the day.

There was also a notable Tyne versus Wear derby in 1892–93 when NER met Wearsiders Southwick in round one, and although they lost 3–2, as often happened in those Victorian footballing years, a protest was lodged and a replay ordered. Southwick must have been aggrieved as to the outcome, as they played with an edge to their game, inflicting a heavy 5–0 defeat on the Gateshead lads. The works side also lost heavily to another Wearside club – Sunderland Albion – losing 8–2 in the first round of the 1890–91 competition. Some 1,500 spectators were attracted to NER's ground, and they were encouraged when Monaghan equalised an early Miller goal. But after that the railwaymen were outclassed. Press reports described two of Albion's goals as 'flukey', but the defeat was comprehensive, with Hannah scoring a hat-trick for the visitors.

Gateshead NER joined the short-lived 10-club North East Counties League as a founder member and afterwards participated in the Northern Alliance. They were runners-up to Sunderland A in the first title race.

With clubs in the rural countryside, around various pit communities and in the heavy engineering centres of the urban riverside slopes, football had taken a firm grip along the 30-odd mile stretch of the River Tyne from west to east. It was also to take a hold from the very north to extreme south of the region – from the Scottish border to the mouth of the River Tees.

Chapter 8

FROM TWEED TO TEES

'William McGregor reckoned that Sunderland had a "talented man in every position"; the so-called "Team of All Talents" was born.'

The Official History (Sunderland AFC)

Throughout the 1880s the spread of football was far reaching. Having been scarcely known, never mind played, as the 1870s came to a close, the new sport rapidly took hold in the new decade. Progress was slow at first, then it gained momentum to an extent that football quickly replaced many of the traditional activities in the North East. The football express was on its way.

By the beginning of the 1890s almost every corner of the North East saw the game played. The oldest club outside Tyneside in Northumberland was Alnwick, formed in 1879. Arguably the county's most attractive town, historic Alnwick overlooks the valley of the River Aln and is dominated by its huge and inspiring castle belonging to the Dukes of the county – now often used as a film set. The mediaeval folk football was of course played in the town, and a Shrovetide contest still takes place. It is recorded that the founders of the Alnwick United Services Club had links to the annual Shrove Tuesday festival game.

The sport under Football Association rules was first played in Alnwick in 1879, the Northumberland FA's archive recording that 'the Tyne club sent a team to show the natives how it should be played'. A club was formed as Alnwick United Services, later renamed Alnwick United Juniors at the turn of the century. The original Alnwick club adopted red-and-black jerseys and cap as their colours.

Alnwick FC was one of the earliest clubs in the region, founded in 1879.

A glorious view of Alnwick Castle and the Pastures between the river and the fortress, where the traditional folk game of football was played.

There was also an early football club called St Michael's Guild Athletic Club formed in the town, reportedly during May 1883. They played on a field behind the vicarage at Gotten Row, Alnwick, and played in 'buff-and-blue jerseys and stockings and white knee breeches'. Their secretary at their formation was Robert H. Taylor. A year later, the same R.H. Taylor was joint secretary of a club described in the Northumberland FA's register of clubs published in the *Northern Athlete*, as 'Alnwick (founded in 1879)'. They played on the Waggonways, half a mile from Alnwick Station, and their colours were described as 'maroon jerseys and hose and white knickers'. A year later (in 1885), the club had moved to the Recreation Ground (a mile from the station) and Charles Briggs had taken over as secretary. At the turn of the century, the club moved to the 'other' St James' Park, land leased from the Duke of Northumberland, and this was to become their permanent home. Only a handful of other clubs in the whole of the region are older.

Alnwick appeared in the Northumberland & Durham Challenge Cup from the second season of action in 1881–82 and reached the semi-final that year after eliminating Elswick Leather Works and Sedgefield, the latter tie played on Tyne's ground in Newcastle probably because of the distance and transportation difficulties between the two clubs. Alnwick controversially lost to Corbridge in the semi-final when there was a difference of opinion regarding the rules of the game between the Alnwick umpire and the referee. Alnwick appealed to the Northumberland FA but to no avail.

Alnwick also participated in the early years of the Northumberland Challenge Cup competition but with limited success. In 1883–84 they defeated Hastings Rovers 4–0 in the first round but came up against Newcastle Rangers in the second and were summarily despatched 6–0. In the next two seasons they fell at the first hurdle, going out to Sleekburn Wanderers and Morpeth Harriers.

Later during the 1880s another team, Alnwick Working Men FC, started to compete in local football too. It was the Working Men club who had the most success in the early seasons of the County Cup. During the 1888–89 competition they reached as far as the third round, albeit with a bye through the first. They comfortably disposed of Berwick Rangers 6–3 at the next stage and did reasonably well against mighty Elswick Rangers in the third round before succumbing 2–0.

James Duns was a prominent player for Alnwick, a defender of note who graduated to the county side and later moved to West End for a period before returning to the town. A cabinet-maker by trade, Duns was also good enough to play for the Newcastle & District XI and was also captain of both Alnwick and West End.

Alnwick reached two Northumberland Minor Cup Finals in the opening years of the 1890s but lost on both occasions; in 1890 against Science & Art and three years later against Newcastle North Eastern. As the Victorian era moved to the Edwardian one, the original Alnwick club changed names back and forward, eventually settling on Alnwick Town. The same team still exists, playing in the Alliance Premier Division and, until recently, competed regularly in the Northumberland Challenge Cup, over 125 years after first doing so.

Further into the Northumberland hills and moors lies the small and pleasant town of Rothbury on the River Coquet, where Lord Armstrong built his impressive residence at Cragside with the financial rewards from his Tyneside industrial enterprise. Like Alnwick, Rothbury has old traditions of shrove football dating back to mediaeval times. A football club was formed in 1881 and, when the Northumberland FA was created, they took part in the first Challenge Cup tournament of 1883–84. In fact, they participated in the first three years of the competition (1883–86) but went out at the first hurdle on each occasion. By the mid-1880s their 'costume', as playing kit was often referred to, was

Berwick Rangers around 1890 at the Pier Field. Prominent members Bob Rhind and Colin Campbell are featured, sitting third and fourth from the left.

described as being 'navy blue-and-white striped jersey and hose, white knickers'. They played on the 'Brewery field' in Rothbury.

The most northerly town in England is Berwick upon Tweed, a strategic border stronghold that has changed hands between English and Scottish rule over a dozen times. Even now many people consider Berwick to be a Scottish town and, of course, these days their football team plays in the Scottish League. But Berwick is English and has been so for the past 500 years. The community is split down the middle in terms of its patriotic allegiance, although many are neutral 'Berwickers', while football support is divided largely between Rangers and Celtic on one hand, and Newcastle and Sunderland on the other.

A Victorian card featuring Berwick Rangers and their star Bob Rhind.

Berwick Rangers, although playing in the Scottish League since 1951, came initially under the auspices of the Northumberland FA. Their origins owe much to the pioneer footballers of Tyneside when a group of railway clerks from Newcastle played an exhibition game against a Scottish XI from the Tynefield club of Dunbar. Berwick were formed soon afterwards, towards the end of 1881.

Although originally playing in 'white jerseys, hose and knickers', the club switched to black and orange in 1885 and have more or less retained their colours – now black and gold – ever since. Berwick's first games were fixtures against Alnwick, their inaugural home match being played on Soldiers' Flat in Berwick. Their leading figure during those formation years was Peter Cowe, who, along with his brother James, gave Berwick their first regular ground at Bull Stob Close. In 1886 they moved to a pitch at Pier Field, by all accounts a fairly exposed site on the coastline, before moving again in 1890 to Shielfield in Tweedmouth. This became their home for over a century and where Berwick would play and defeat – as unique English members of Scottish football – some of the best sides north of the border, including famously in the Scottish Cup, Glasgow Rangers.

Prominent among their early players was J. Colin Campbell and their first captain Willie Bald. Later Bob Rhind was a 'robust and untiring' skipper, the heart of the club for several seasons. They also competed in the Northumberland Challenge Cup in the 1880s – but only with limited success. They lost in the first round to Shankhouse Black Watch in 1885–86 but made a bit of an impact in the tournament during the following season. They disposed of Seaside Rovers and SS Mary & James in the early stages but came up

Henry Murton's outfitters in the centre of Newcastle, as featured on this 1887 advert, provided football kit for all of the North East pioneers, including Morpeth Harriers and Shankhouse Black Watch.

against Newcastle East End in the third round and found the future Newcastle United team too strong for them, going down 5–2. It was similar story during the following season when, after defeating Border Hibs, Berwick encountered the other well-established Newcastle club West End in the next round. The 5–0 defeat reflected the difference between the two clubs.

Berwick did better when they switched their attention to the Northumberland Minor Cup and managed to lift the trophy in 1892 when they defeated Godfrey FC 6–2 in the Final at Alnwick. By then there were other sides playing in the borders area of Northumberland: Tweedside Wanderers, Border Hibs and Seaside Rovers as well as Spittal Rovers and Royal Oaks, a team made up of North Sea fishermen.

For many years, Morpeth has been an important market town and today is a major commuter centre for Newcastle. As we have seen, football was played nearby as early as the 13th century, so it could be said the game was bred into the local population. During April 1883 it was reported in the *Football* weekly newspaper that enthusiasts in the area had created a football club after witnessing an exhibition game. The new side was known as Morpeth Harriers, and their colours were noted as 'black jerseys, gold band, white knickers'. They played originally on a pitch known as 'Mr Almond's field', off Howard Terrace, then on the northern outskirts of the town near to the parish church of St James the Great.

After establishing the club during the 1880s, Morpeth Harriers were one of the few sides to attend the historic meeting which decided upon the start of the Northern League in 1889. They were keen to take part in the competition but, after consideration, decided to opt out due to the heavy travelling commitment between mid-Northumberland and the south of County Durham, as well as the strong competition they would have to face. Instead they joined the North East Counties League, which still resulted in journeys south to Barnard Castle and to Teesside but was at a more suitable football level.

Morpeth developed into a notable side, with James Jobling at the forefront of affairs as a player and club secretary. He had replaced an earlier secretary, J. Mavin, within a couple of years of inception. They became strong and at times feared opponents in the Northumberland Challenge Cup during the middle to late years of the decade, during which time they reached the semi-final on three occasions – and in addition they actually won the trophy under unique circumstances, without ever playing in the Final.

The Cup competition of 1885–86 became famous for the remarkable semi-final meeting between Harriers and Shankhouse Black Watch. Morpeth reached that stage by eliminating Alnwick, Rosehill and Ashington Rising Sun before facing their neighbours Shankhouse, an equally powerful team from a pit community in the Northumberland coalfield near Cramlington. The two evenly matched sides went on to play out a five-game marathon – which never reached a proper or telling conclusion.

The first of the semi-final meetings was held at neutral Bedlington before a 3,000 attendance and ended all square. The next was another draw fought in snow while the third encounter ended in stalemate too, this after a waterlogged pitch forced a hasty search for another field, players and officials carrying goal-posts and tape, which then acted as a bar, to another pitch away from the water.

A fourth meeting was staged in Newcastle and ended in controversy after the two teams were heading for another draw at 2–2. Just before the end a supporter blew a whistle and caused a furore. Some of the Morpeth players stopped playing, thinking the referee had blown to halt the proceedings, but Shankhouse did not and planted the ball between the posts to give them a 3–2 lead. That is how the game finished, but afterwards there were howls of protests and the Football Association adjudicated, with secretary Charles Alcock deciding that there must be a replay – and yet another game, the fifth meeting.

Morpeth Harriers developed into a strong outfit, and football was popular in the town.

A further close battle took place, and yet again deadlock was the outcome. As extra-time was played the referee even decided he had seen enough, leaving to catch a train with another official stepping in. The teams decided to play on…and on. Apparently some four hours after the kick-off there was still nothing between the two teams when eventually darkness forced a halt to the long-running contest. After around 10 and a half hours of football the teams could not be separated.

After that fifth game the two sets of officials met and decided to throw a coin to see which club would go through to the Final. They also agreed in a gentlemanly fashion that whoever won the toss would represent both clubs in the Final and, if successful, that the silverware would be held jointly. Shankhouse won and went on to meet Newcastle West End and duly lifted the Cup. Harriers consequently shared the trophy with their semi-final opponents, being 'joint-winners' of the competition.

The following 1886–87 season, Morpeth again reached the semi-final, but there was no long, drawn-out sequence of games this time as they lost heavily 5–0 to West End. They got to that stage of the tournament for the third time in a row in 1887–88; however, they again lost, on this occasion to Shankhouse, an intense and friendly rivalry between the two clubs forming at that time.

That season was a notable one for the club as Morpeth faced the might of Sunderland in the FA Cup qualifying stage. A year earlier, during October 1886, the two clubs had met on Wearside for the very first time in an absorbing match. Played in front of a 'capital gate' at the Newcastle Road ground, Sunderland got a bit of a shock as Morpeth took the contest to their stronger and more experienced opponents. Jobling gave Harriers a surprise early lead and Manners added a second just before the break. Sunderland had to step up a notch in the second half, and this they did – Davison and Erskine levelling the game at 2–2. Harriers then faded, and Lord added another. A total collapse followed with Sunderland finally scoring no fewer than seven goals in the second period, outside-right Billy Erskine completing a hat-trick.

Morpeth were out for a spot of revenge when the two sides met again in the 1887–88 FA Cup tie. On Wearside another memorable encounter took place, but it was one surrounded in controversy. Sunderland won another goal feast 4–2; however, a replay was ordered after a dispute arose between the two clubs. Morpeth complained that Sunderland's full-back Peter Ford, described as a 'young and promising' lad, had not been registered in time to play, and therefore Sunderland had fielded an ineligible player. The governing body agreed, and a rematch was ordered to be played at Morpeth.

With around 800 Wearside supporters making the trip over the Tyne, the Northumbrians had a great start and went ahead through Waterston. Harriers were 2–0 up within five minutes when Crackett added a second. But by half-time Sunderland had pulled a goal back and in the second period again showed their superior quality. Scot George Monaghan did the damage. He scored twice as the Wearsiders eventually won 3–2 with Stewart grabbing the winner. But Sunderland did not have a good FA Cup campaign that year, being the subject of another FA inquiry. After beating both West End and Middlesbrough they were disqualified for fielding three players who had received illegal payments – including Monaghan.

Another contentious Morpeth FA Cup match was a meeting with Birtley in the following 1888–89 season. Having disposed of Whitburn 5–0, they thought they had recorded a convincing 3–1 triumph over their rivals from north Durham; however, in the manner of the time, Birtley protested due to an infringement and a replay was ordered. Harriers were knocked out by a single goal.

In the neighbouring Northumberland coalfield around Morpeth, football quickly became popular with the working miners. Clubs sprang up in almost every colliery and town. In an area from Newcastle to Morpeth, then north and east to the coast at Amble, pits were studded across the landscape.

After 1850 the expansion of the local railway network and a demand for more and more coal saw the North East coalfield in both Northumberland and Durham as a whole rapidly grow. In south-east Northumberland this expansion was prominent north of the old Tyne valley pits. Collieries became larger, and settlements developed as new mines opened up. Mining communities could be found around Cramlington, Plessey and Seghill, around the Blyth coast and at Ashington, Pegswood and Newbiggin. In the vicinity of Bedlington and Barrington the pits expanded and shafts could be found at Bebside, Choppington and Netherton. To the north at Amble, Radcliffe, Broomhill and Shilbottle there was also the unmistakable sight of the pit-wheel and slag-heap.

The most prominent football club by far to be formed out of this extensive working-class heartland was Morpeth's great rivals in that notable Challenge Cup semi-final; the wonderfully named Shankhouse Black Watch. Back in the 1880s the population of the Cramlington and Shankhouse area struggled to reach 10,000. Now, the district is one vast new-town, designed and built to serve Newcastle's burgeoning hinterland, and it is hard to find the original Shankhouse village. But it is there, just off the important A189 spine route to Ashington.

The football club was formed by members of the Shankhouse Primitive Methodist Chapel bible class in 1884, and it was reported that enthusiasts had to walk to Newcastle to buy their first football. Two characters called Ord and Simms were noted as the prime movers of the committee at the outset along with club secretary J. Wood. It is thought that the Black Watch title was adopted as a tribute to the famous Royal Highland Regiment. There was also an East Cramlington team which used the same tag of Black Watch for a period, as did others on Tyneside, Wearside and Teesside, but Shankhouse were the most famous.

The new club amalgamated with another village team, Shankhouse Albion, in 1885 while there was yet another side too, Shankhouse Blues, who were also formed in 1884. To make matters a touch more confusing Shankhouse Black Watch appear to have dropped the Black Watch label around 1888. Their colours were 'black shirts with red sash, black hose' and they played at a pitch known as 'Shankhouse Row Field', also sometimes referred to as 'Stickley Farm', a ground shared with the Blues.

Shankhouse Black Watch were to become three-time finalists in the Northumberland Challenge Cup and twice winners during their early years. They went on to even more success locally. In a decade between 1885 and 1895 they reached no fewer than seven Finals. During the 1885–86 competition they reached their first Final by knocking out

Berwick Rangers, Sleekburn Wanderers and Elswick Leather Works. Then came that absorbing series of games with Morpeth Harriers and, as already related, with a toss of a coin Shankhouse went through to the Final.

On the Tyne ground in Jesmond during April, before a crowd of over 2,000, they met West End and a terrific match was played out. Shankhouse opened the scoring when Hedley converted, but West End equalised before half-time, before two goals from William Matthews turned the result. His match-winning double gave Black Watch a 3–2 victory by the end. But, of course, true to their word, they shared the trophy with Morpeth Harriers.

Shankhouse retained the trophy – and won it outright this time – in the 1886–87 tournament after defeating Weetslade, the two Elswick clubs – Rangers and Leather Works – then East End, before meeting West End again in the Final. This time they won comfortably 5–1. An estimated 5,000 spectators gathered for this Final held at the Heaton Junction pitch during March, and quickly Black Watch took a grip on the contest. They went 3–0 ahead, and by then there was little doubt of the outcome. William Matthews and J. Metcalf hit two goals apiece, with Willie Thompson striking the other.

The miners' club had the opportunity of recording the first hat-trick of Northumberland Cup victories when they met West End for a third time in succession in the 1888 Final; however, in front of another huge gate, estimated at approaching 6,000 or 7,000, at the same Chillingham Road ground in Heaton, they lost 6–3 after an intriguing end-to-end match. The West Enders were determined to exact revenge and

Shankhouse Black Watch were a feared XI, pictured here with the Northumberland Challenge Cup trophy. They reached seven Finals between 1885 and 1895.

opened up a 4–0 advantage by the break. But Shankhouse managed to make a game of it in the second period with goals by Matthews, Metcalf and Hendy, although they had little hope of totally making up the deficit.

Shankhouse also lifted the trophy in 1890–91, defeating East End in the semifinal before meeting Rendel. Two draws resulted, 0–0 and 2–2, before the pitmen emerged victorious by a 1–0 scoreline at St James' Park. Harry Reay won the contest for Shankhouse by scoring the only goal of the decisive game. He later became a

Shankhouse winger Harry Reay, who went on to appear for Newcastle and Everton.

prominent player and moved to East End and to Everton and was one of several of the Shankhouse players to have a go at top-class football. An outside-right of some ability, it was noted that he thrilled local crowds, and by the time he joined East End shortly after his trophy-winning goal, he was one of the most popular personalities of those Victorian years. A reporter for the *Northerner & Athlete* magazine wrote that he was 'simply irresistible'! Harry played for East End in Northern League and FA Cup football before heading to Everton were he made a handful of Football League outings.

By the opening years of the 1890s the Northumberland Challenge Cup had been somewhat devalued as a competition, and both East End and West End decided their focus was on bigger fish – in the shape of the Northern League and the objective of Football League membership. Both clubs played their reserve or A sides in the competition – and Newcastle United still do so today.

Shankhouse became Cup victors again in 1892–93, once more at the expense of Rendel who refused to turn up for the replayed Final at Blyth. The Shankhouse team appeared, kicked-off, immediately scored a goal and claimed the trophy. The Northumberland FA Challenge Cup Committee considered the matter and duly awarded them the Cup. Shankhouse recorded a treble of victories by also securing the trophy in 1894 and 1895.

Shankhouse's rise to prominence led to FA Cup adventures and to some headlining ties, none more so than in the 1887–88 season when they met the mighty Aston Villa as holders of England's flagship trophy. Black Watch's run to that prestigious tie in the later stages of the tournament was one of the highlights of the pioneering era in the North East. They had defeated Scarborough (5–3) and Darlington (2–0) before being given a dream tie with Villa in round four of the competition.

The visit of Aston Villa, then the most famous combination in the country, as the Northumberland FA archive recorded, produced 'a great wave of enthusiasm' that 'swept through the county'. Shankhouse were offered the opportunity to switch the game to Villa Park for the sum of £50, but the Shankhouse officials wanted the tie played in the North East in true FA Cup traditions.

Aston Villa with the old FA Cup trophy in 1887–88, the season they met Shankhouse at St James' Park. Back row standing, left to right: Coulton, Warner, Dawson, Simmonds, Allen. Front row: Davies, Yates, Brown, Hunter (with ball), Vaughton, Burton, Hodgetts.

Such was the fascination surrounding the fixture that the match was indeed switched from Shankhouse, but only 10 miles to St James' Park in Newcastle. Many sides, including East End and West End, cancelled their fixtures for the day to allow supporters and players to watch the spectacle. Events did not go exactly to plan, however, on and off the field. It was noted that 'arrangements for admission at the ground were primitive' and that the staff could not cope with 'the crush that ensued and dozens got through the gate without paying'.

On a lovely December day a good attendance, reported at between 5,000 and 7,000 (depending on how many gained free entry), packed into St James' Park. It was described as the largest crowd seen at a football match in the district, all there to see 'a display of skill and artistry accomplished in goal-getting'. Despite the 'free entries', gate receipts still reached £120 – a huge sum in those days. Villa fielded a strong line up including many of their stars – England internationals Albert Allen and Denny Hodgetts up front, as well as captain Archie Hunter who was one of the most celebrated players of the time. It was arguably the biggest fixture played on Tyneside up to that point in football's development. The two sides were:

Shankhouse: Wood, Todd, Brydon, Reilly, Turpin, Ritson, Metcalf, Thompson, Matthews, Hamilton, Hedley.
V
Aston Villa: Warner, Coulton, Cox, Burton, Simmonds, Yates, Brown, Green, Hunter, Allen, Hodgetts.

While local supporters were hoping for an upset, it was no real surprise that Shankhouse were truly overwhelmed by the Villa side that raced into a 4–0 half-time lead. They eventually won 9–0, with two goals each coming from Allen and Hunter, as well as braces from Albert Brown and Thomas Green. Denny Hodgetts was on the score sheet too in what was simply a rout. By the time Brown had registered the ninth goal it was noted that the Shankhouse players were 'exhausted'.

The following year Shankhouse fell early in the FA Cup, losing heavily again 8–2 to Sunderland Albion. They did not progress far in 1889–90 either, when they lost 4–0 to East End, and both the 1890–91 and 1891–92 campaigns saw them lose on each occasion to East End once more – a hat-trick of defeats at the hands of the Heaton club.

Shankhouse reached the FA Cup first-round proper in 1892–93, this time facing another of early football's leading names – the oldest professional club, Notts County. Having beaten Blyth (3–2) and Willington Athletic (4–0), Tow Law proved a problem tie in the third qualifying round. At Tow Law's old Church Lane ground, Shankhouse actually lost 4–3 after extra-time, but they protested to the Football Association over the state of the pitch – it being too short – and were awarded the tie! A 2–1 victory over Bishop Auckland Town saw the Northumberland side progress into the later stages alongside the biggest clubs in the country for the second time in five years – no mean feat for a local team, then perhaps equivalent to a non-League side reaching the third-round stage these days.

Shankhouse then faced a 170-mile trip to Nottingham's Trent Bridge ground, a venue now more associated with international Test cricket. It was long journey and certainly not a customary trip for North East clubs, few having played out of the area until then. In front of a 5,000 crowd against the Football League side, albeit a team relegated from the First Division that season, they lost 4–0, with Scottish international Tom McInnes scoring twice. Star player James Oswald, another eminent Scottish forward capped by his country, also grabbed two goals (although some reports note that Oswald recorded a hat-trick). Notts County, despite their League troubles, were a decent side, and they lifted the FA Cup in the following season.

Willie Thompson was a star up front for Shankhouse. He joined East End and became a centre-forward hero for Newcastle United.

Shankhouse fielded many fine local players and, like Harry Reay, a few went to the very top. Striker Willie Thompson was, alongside Reay, the most well known and outstripped them all in terms of achievement. From North Seaton, he was a dashing goal-getter at centre-forward, not too big, but swift and possessing a telling shot. Willie also sported a magnificent moustache in the style of the day and was a county player before making the switch to the big-time with Newcastle East End in May 1892. He went on to become Newcastle United's first centre-forward hero, scoring almost 50 goals for the club in senior action. Thompson is on record as having scored United's very first Football League hat-trick, against Arsenal in September 1893.

Left-half Tom Rendell and inside-right Bobby Willis both played for Newcastle United too. Willis especially was a well-known footballer, a Northumberland county player who fired home a goal on his debut for United against Small Heath (Birmingham) in 1893. Shankhouse had a nucleus of notable names; goalkeeper J. Wood along with W. Todd, J. Hudson, R. Reilly, as well as W. Hedley and C. Ritson. All played in both Northumberland Cup wins of 1886 and 1887. So did brothers G. and William Matthews.

Many of the Shankhouse team regularly represented Northumberland at county level. In October 1887 six of their players were in the line up to face Ayrshire: Wood, Ritson, Matthews (W), Hedley, Hamilton and Thompson. Matt Gibson was a later star, appearing in the FA Cup tie with Notts County and many of their successful XIs in the years before the turn of the century. He later emigrated to the US and died in Illinois.

Shankhouse were at the forefront of establishing the Northern Alliance, joining the new League from the outset. They lifted the title in 1893, and during the decade before the turn of the century the club was recognised as one of the most powerful sides in the North East aside from the top clubs – Middlesbrough and Ironopolis, Sunderland and Sunderland Albion, as well as Newcastle's West End and East End. Shankhouse were described by one of the founders of Sunderland, John Grayston, as a 'redoubtable opponent'. Sunderland played them often during those early days, and Grayston recalled that he 'experienced some rough times' against the Black Watch.

Shankhouse played on for many decades, indeed they defied the ravages of history and survived for a century, although the latter-day Shankhouse team is not the same club. Their influence encouraged many local sides around the Cramlington area to play the game.

Several other clubs were also created in the south-east Northumberland coalfield area. Ashington, now such a famous town for its much later footballing heritage, thrived as a mining community in the 19th century. Centred on the local pit, Ashington Rising Star were founded in 1883, playing in colours of black jerseys with star, and black knickers. The current Ashington club was formed out of Rising Star. They played at the Recreation Ground, situated next to the pit-head, a common add-on in mining communities to the workplace.

Rising Star first entered for the Northumberland Challenge Cup during the 1885–86 season and enjoyed a modicum of success, defeating North Seaton Rovers and North Eastern before bowing out to a much bigger club, Morpeth Harriers, in the third round. They continued to compete in the tournament for the rest of the 1880s, with some, although never complete, success. They reached the third round again in 1888, knocking out Blyth and Weetslade before coming up against mighty Shankhouse Black Watch. Then, in the following year, they actually reached the semi-final – strangely without beating anyone! They received byes through the first two stages before being drawn against West End. Amid controversy, the St James' Park club sensationally withdrew from the competition, leaving Ashington to face the other Newcastle giants, East End. The future Newcastle United proved far too strong for the Colliers, winning comfortably 5–0 before going on to lift the trophy.

Ashington were ambitious from the outset and, despite their minor status, entered for the FA Cup as early as 1888. They eventually joined the Northern Alliance in 1892, although they were soon to switch to the East Northumberland League.

The great Jackie Milburn's grandfather, also called Jack Milburn, played at full-back for the Colliers around the end of the decade and was capped for the county when Northumberland made their first visit to Carlisle to play Cumberland in November 1890, winning 6–2. He also appeared against East End in that semi-final of the Northumberland Challenge Cup in 1889.

On the River Blyth, Bedlington was a town that flourished due to the coalfield like its neighbour Ashington. Bedlington Burdon originated in 1882 and were one of the oldest of all the coalfield clubs, taking part in the first Northumberland Challenge Cup in 1883–84. Their colours were described as 'navy blue-and-white jerseys and hose, and white knickers'. The football ground and a running track was found near to Bedlington Colliery.

Burdon had the distinction of defeating Newcastle East End (and therefore Newcastle United) in a Cup tie during their early years. Admittedly, it was not a full-scale game, but victory over the Byker club in the Tyneside Summer Festival tournament of 1883 was still a notable success. Later, another club in the town was also formed, Bedlington West End.

Next door to Bedlington a rival team, Sleekburn Wanderers, was created in 1882 as well. They possessed a pitch adjoining the railway station at Bedlington and played in 'black-and-yellow jerseys and white knickers'. The Wanderers reached the Northumberland Cup Final in 1885 following victories over Alnwick, Bedlington Burdon, Ovingham and Rosehill. They met East End at Tyne's ground in Jesmond and only lost to a single goal scored by Charles Gorman.

The Barrington Union Jack and Cramlington Union Jack clubs were both seen in action during the middle of the 1880s as were Weetslade FC, located near to Killingworth. On the outskirts of Morpeth, Longhirst Excelsior (formed 1884) played in the Northumberland Cup for the first time in 1885–86, as did North Seaton Rovers (formed 1884) and Backworth Hotspur. By this year, some 30 clubs entered for the county Challenge Cup. Cambois FC joined the fray the following season.

Hastings Rovers were another local club. Founded in 1883 and based in New Hartley, they joined the Northumberland FA soon after their formation and entered for the County Cup for the 1883–84 campaign but were eliminated by Alnwick in the first round.

TWEED TO TEES: PRINCIPAL CLUB LOCATIONS

Northumberland
Berwick Rangers, Rothbury, Alnwick, Morpeth Harriers.

Northumberland Coalfield
Bedlington Burdon, Ashington Rising Star, Sleekburn Wanderers, Blyth, Shankhouse Black Watch.

County Durham
Burnopfield, Hamsterley Rangers, Chester-le-Street, Ferryhill, Stanley, Stanley Nops, Tow Law, Crook.
Bishop Auckland Church Institute, Auckland Town.

Wearside
Sunderland, Sunderland Albion, Whitburn.

Cleveland & Darlington
Middlesbrough, Ironopolis, South Bank, Stockton, West Hartlepool, Redcar.
St Augustine's, Darlington, Haughton-le-Skerne.

On the coast, Amble FC were playing the game in 1883–84, and the first club to appear in the port of Blyth was Blyth Waterloo Rangers, established in 1885. By the summer of the following year they appear to have decided to use the straight-forward title of Blyth FC. They entered the FA Cup for the 1892–93 season – a competition these days romantically linked to the town in true Cup tradition. It should be noted, however, that Blyth Spartans were a later club, formed in 1899. Newsham Rovers were formed on the outskirts of Blyth during the 1880s too.

Football developed just as profusely in other areas south of the River Tyne; in County Durham, on Wearside and around Darlington and Teesside. As in Northumberland's south east, many of the clubs originated in the pit towns and villages of the Durham coalfield where the workforce was readily attracted to the new sport.

Burnopfield, between Gateshead and Consett, was one of the earliest clubs. Like many, they were created from the local colliery. They participated in the first Northumberland & Durham Challenge Cup tournament during 1880–81 and were one of the nine original clubs that set up the Durham Football Association in 1883. Sometimes referred to as Burnopfield Wanderers in the contemporary press, they opposed Newcastle United's pioneer club, Stanley FC, as early as 1881–82. Indeed, they fielded a second XI in that season too. In the summer of 1883, however, Burnopfield changed their name to Hobson Wanderers FC, apparently because they operated from the local Hobson Hotel. Derwent Rovers, founded in 1880, hailed from the same community.

The industrial town of Stanley, located on a hill between Chester-le-Street and Consett, was at the time surrounded by coal-pits which gave the town its wealth. Two clubs developed in those fledgling years. Stanley Star appeared in Northumberland & Durham's knock-out competition in 1882–83, although they were sent packing in the opening stage, losing by all of 10–1 to Sunderland. The club were also present at the formation of the Durham FA. Stanley Nops were in existence at the same time. They later became Stanley United once they amalgamated with the Stanley Albion club in 1890.

That fixture with Sunderland proved a controversial meeting and gives an intriguing insight into the problems that plagued the early pioneers of football in the North East. The tie was scheduled for 9 December, and Sunderland travelled to Stanley only to find that the field was covered in deep snow and unfit to play. The two clubs agreed to re-arrange the tie and meet again on 23 December; however, Stanley afterwards wrote to the Wearside club to advise them that they could not raise a team on that day and asked for the game to be cancelled. Sunderland refused and turned up at the appointed time. The referee was also there, but there were no Stanley Star players! They did not turn up, and the official accordingly awarded the tie to the Wearsiders, only for the home side to protest to the Northumberland & Durham FA. The basis of their appeal was Rule 13 of the competition which stated that ties had to be completed by an appointed date, in this case by 20 January. After consideration, the Challenge Cup Committee ruled that the tie had to be played, but the venue should be moved to Sunderland and that Stanley should bear the costs of the referee. The game was duly played on the deadline day of 20 January, with Sunderland showing no mercy by scoring those 10 goals.

Tow Law FC were initially founded in November 1881 and were relatively active during their early years, playing friendly matches against neighbouring sides. They faded from the scene for a while but were reformed around 1890 and became founder members of the Auckland District League in 1892, the same year that they joined the FA Cup fray. They were awarded a tie against Ashington when the game ended 3–3 and the Northumbrians had 'refused extra-time'! The following year, the Lawyers won the Durham Amateur Cup, defeating Leadgate Park in the Final, and they joined the Northern League in 1894, finishing a creditable third in their first season. But their greatest success around that time was in 1896 when they won the Durham Challenge Cup, defeating Darlington in the semi-final and the powerful Sunderland A team 1–0 in the Final.

Another team was to be found nearby in Tantobie, playing the game in 1883 and taking part in the Durham Challenge Cup competition. Neighbouring Tanfield Lea Rangers also took to the field during this decade.

Located near to Chopwell in the Derwent valley, Hamsterley Rangers were in action on the field during 1882, becoming Newcastle East End's first opponents after they changed their name from Stanley FC. Although an original member when the Durham FA was formed a year later, the Hamsterley club appear to have faded from the footballing scene soon after. Also in the vicinity was another side, Milkwell Burn FC, established again from the local pit workforce around the same time.

The town of Chester-le-Street was formally the Roman fort of Concangis, and it has seen a form of football played on its streets as a mob contest. As far as the association game is concerned, Chester-le-Street FC came into being following an exhibition match between Corbridge and North Eastern in the town during October 1880. Within days a meeting was held in the club house of the Chester-le-Street & District Athletic & Cricket Club when it was resolved to form a football club. The venue of the meeting was rather appropriate as Chester-le-Street is now internationally known in a sporting context as being the headquarters of the Durham County Cricket Club at the Riverside arena. The new football club adopted blue and white as their colours.

Seven miles south of Durham City on the Great North Road, Ferryhill FC was another team to play during the very earliest days of the game in the North East. Founded in early 1880 and guided by secretary J. Mann and captain John Hodgson, they were also an outfit with a characteristic Durham mining background. They joined the Northumberland & Durham FA that summer.

Further south, between Ferryhill and Sedgefield, a football side representing Bishop Middleham was formed early in 1880 too. They played in red, white and blue. All three clubs took part in the draw for the very first Northumberland & Durham FA Challenge Cup in 1880–81; although Chester-le-Street did not kick a ball, opting out before the first match.

Enthusiasts from the town of Crook were playing football during the later years of the 1880s. The club was founded in 1889 and quickly progressed, joining the Northern League in 1896 and going on to win the FA Amateur Cup in 1901, defeating Kings Lynn 3–0 in a replayed Final.

Spennymoor claim to be one of the very earliest clubs in the region, perhaps even dating back to 1877. But the first recorded seeds of the game in Spennymoor were witnessed in 1887–88 when Spennymoor St Paul took to the field.

Clubs were being formed all over County Durham. Even the Durham County Asylum regularly fielded a side in the early 1880s. Presumably this was a team of employees, not inmates!

There were important pioneer clubs also in and around Darlington in the south of the county. Darlington Rugby Football Club had been formed as early as 1863, one of the earliest (if not the earliest) clubs in the North East. Darlington Grammar School were the first association football club in the town, certainly playing during the opening months of 1880 when they travelled to Middlesbrough and were walloped 11–0 for their pains. They joined the Northumberland & Durham FA in 1880 and entered for the combined counties' first Challenge Cup in 1880–81; however, they scratched from the tournament before a ball was kicked.

There were other amateur clubs in the district and, during July 1883, enthusiasts met at the Grammar School and decided to form one club to represent the town. That meeting saw Darlington Football Club created. Darlington were based at the Feethams ground, in existence as a cricket venue since the 1860s. They took part in the first Durham Challenge Cup Final in 1884 – losing to Sunderland after a replay. Darlington lifted the trophy the following year and were regular finalists in the opening decade of competition, appearing in seven of the 10 played. They were second only to Sunderland as County Durham's top club.

The Quakers' prime mover was Charles Craven, the team's secretary and influential member of the Durham FA. He later became an FA Council member and was largely responsible in setting up the Northern League. Darlington fielded plenty of notable players, many regular Durham county men, but one of the most unusual was goalkeeper Arthur Wharton, one of the first black players in this country. He played for the county too and for the Newcastle & District XI in the 1885–86 season.

Although, like the rest of the players, Wharton was an amateur at the time, he was to go on to become the first-ever black professional footballer in the world. Born in Jamestown, Gold Coast (now Accra, Ghana) in 1865 of a mixed African and Scottish family, he moved to England in 1882 to train as a Methodist missionary. He was a supreme athlete and soon abandoned his missionary vocation to concentrate on sport. Arthur was a keen cyclist

Goalkeeper Arthur Wharton served Darlington and had a remarkable life-story.

and an accomplished cricketer as well as an eye-catching athlete. He is credited with setting a world record of 10 seconds for a 100 yard sprint in an Amateur Athletic Association Championship meeting in 1886, but by this time he had made a name for himself as a footballer.

Joining Darlington in the year that they won the Durham Challenge Cup in 1885 and had defeated East End in the Northumberland & Durham Challenge Cup, Wharton soon attracted the attention of bigger clubs, and Preston North End persuaded him to go to Deepdale and play for them. Although Preston had become a professional club at the first opportunity in 1885, Arthur joined them as an amateur and played in the side that reached the semi-final of the FA Cup two years later.

He left Deepdale in 1888 to concentrate on his running but returned to football in 1889, joining Rotherham Town as a professional. There was one last connection with North East football as far as Wharton was concerned. In 1894 he moved to Sheffield

United where he played largely as an understudy to the legendary William 'Fatty' Foulke, but he did manage to make one First Division appearance for the Blades, against Sunderland. He thus became the first black player to play in top-flight football in England.

Unfortunately his life story has a sad ending. After his sporting career was over, he slowly descended into poverty and became an alcoholic, dying penniless in 1930 at the age of 65. He was buried in an unmarked grave in Edlington, an almost forgotten man; but not quite. A campaign by the anti-racism group Football Unites – Racism Divides, achieved a tangible success when, in recognition of Arthur's achievements, it resulted in his grave being given a headstone in 1997. Better was to follow. In 2003 Arthur Wharton was inducted into English football's Hall of Fame in recognition of his impact on the game in the land of its birth. So perhaps his story did have a happy ending after all.

The St Augustine's club were also from Darlington and started playing around 1883. They were centred on a team from the St Augustine's Roman Catholic Church in the town and were, not surprisingly, known as 'the Saints'. They played on a ground known as the North Lodge at North Road and later at Chestnut Grove. By the end of the 1880s St Augustine's had developed into a forceful side. They were the Northern League's first champions in 1889–90 and had a policy then of having, as *Northern Goalfields* pointed out, 'imported several highly paid Scottish professionals'. But that did not work, as they failed to win a game the following year. Their approach was futile and, it was recorded, they had paid 'the price of playing second and third rate Scottish professors'.

The oldest club in the Darlington area, though, was to be found a mile from the town. On the outskirts of Darlington was situated the village of Haughton-le-Skerne, now part of the urban area, but back in Victorian County Durham it was a separate community on the River Skerne. The villagers were keen footballers and formed a team during the 1879–80 season. They played in amber and navy blue and were represented at the meeting which created the Northumberland & Durham FA with John Glover the leader of the club on and off the field.

John Glover was a pioneer of Haughton-le-Skerne and Darlington. He is pictured in later years as a Durham FA representative.

Haughton-le-Skerne reached the very first Final of the Northumberland & Durham Challenge Cup in 1881, beating Bishop Middleham 7–0 in the opening round then Ferryhill 2–1. They were fortunate to gain a bye in the semi-final and then travelled to Newcastle to meet Rangers in the region's inaugural Cup Final. Haughton only lost by a single goal. In those early seasons Haughton-le-Skerne fielded several good players, both Brown and skipper Glover being selected for the county XI. John Glover later joined Darlington's ranks and was involved at the very heart of the new Durham FA. He was elected secretary and afterwards became a member of the FA Council, a respected figure in the game. He also went on to be a noted umpire and referee at many games in the region.

The history of football in the town of Bishop Auckland is intertwined between three clubs: Bishop Auckland Church Institute, Auckland Town and Bishop Auckland, the present-day side. The Church Institute team, established by Oxford and Cambridge students studying theology at Auckland Castle, was the original club and began playing the sport during 1882, appearing in the Oxford-Cambridge colours of light-and-dark-blue halves. The Church Institute side found a pitch at Flatts Farm, later moving to a site at South Church Lane late in 1887. A year earlier they had won the Durham Challenge Cup by beating Birtley 3–1 at Feethams and had received a heroes' welcome on returning to the town with the trophy.

Several distinguished names of both the church and of football played for the club including Andrew Amos, who, as we have seen, played for England as well as Gateshead Association. There were also three future bishops associated with the club during those early days; the Revd Edward F. Every (later Bishop of the Falkland Islands), Revd George Rodney Eden (Bishop of Wakefield) and Revd John Reginald Harmer (Bishop of Rochester).

Auckland Town were formed as a result of a controversial moment in the Church Institute club's earliest years when, during March 1887, they were investigated by the Durham Football Association after certain players had acted in what was described as 'in a manner calculated to bring disgrace on the name of the Durham FA' – not what was expected from a club with a staunch religious background. Details of the players' misdemeanours are vague, but it appears local bye-laws and club rules had been infringed. Six players were ultimately suspended, and a split in the ranks followed as a result. The outcome was that a new club came into being, Auckland Town. They also played at the Flatts Farm pitch until a new ground was found at Kingsway in 1892.

The Church Institute team never really recovered from the 1887 debacle, and they faded, eventually folding in 1892. The players and officials left at the closure combined with Auckland Town's staff and Bishop Auckland FC was formed. They went on, of course, to become a celebrated amateur combination, first winning the FA Amateur Cup in 1895–96.

Not far away at Barnard Castle in the far south-west corner of the county, a club was playing the likes of Middlesbrough as early as 1877. They were one of the earliest teams and were the first club to defeat Middlesbrough, but they never developed a powerbase and declined.

To the coast at the mouth of the River Tees, clubs came under the authority of the Cleveland Football Association which was formed early in 1881. While some were located in North Yorkshire, they are in football terms classed as North East sides. Middlesbrough, created in 1876, reigned supreme to start with, the club of course being the oldest next to South Bank which was possibly an even older club.

Middlesbrough played in colours of white shirts to begin with, although at one stage they came up with a novel addition to the collar, cuffs and centre trim of blue with white dots. They developed a strong team which contained some of the best early players in the region, notably Ossie Cochrane, Charles Booth and Jackson Ewbank, all of whom took part in that significant match against the Scotch-Canadians on Tyneside. Booth and Ewbank – along with Fred Thompson and Fred Hardisty – are recognised in official Boro annals as the club's founders, all having a well educated middle-class background.

Other favourites at Middlesbrough were Billy Pickstock and Albert Borrie. The bald-headed Pickstock apparently never took his cap off when he played, except to 'doff it' politely! He played in five successive Cleveland Cup-winning teams for Boro, as did Borrie who was a solicitor-footballer. Born in Gateshead and a formidable goal-getter in those years, Albert later served the club as secretary and was a leading figure in the formation of the Northern League.

The club retained their amateur status for a long time – with only a short spell experiencing the professional game from 1889 to 1892 – until they decided to dump their ideology and throw in their lot with the rest in 1899. Yet Boro twice lifted the FA Amateur Cup in 1895 and 1898 before turning professional.

Middlesbrough Ironopolis in 1892. Back row, left to right: Stevenson, McNair, Elliott, Chalmers, Langley, Millar, Boldison (secretary). Front row: Hill, Hughes, Coupor, McReddie, Seymour. George Millar was a notable North East pioneer footballer, also appearing for Birtley.

Middlesbrough's first and brief taste of professionalism resulted in a rift within the club. In 1889 a row erupted over the ideals of amateurism, and a new club was formed in the aftermath. Director and ex-player Alf Mattison led a revolt and the Ironopolis Football Company was formed during December of that year, and they followed a professional path. Known as the Nops or the Washers, they soon overtook the original club and even reached Football League status in 1893, at the same time as Newcastle East End. Middlesbrough FC were given the rather unflattering sobriquet of the Scabs!

Ironopolis sported colours of 'maroon and green' stripes or halves and later switched to 'red-and-white shirts, white shorts'. They played at the Paradise Ground – which was far from 'paradise', named after a local Paradise Mission – close to Middlesbrough's home on Linthorpe Road. They joined the Northern League on its inception and recorded a treble of Championship victories in the opening four seasons of competition.

Included in their ranks at that time was skipper Willie Chalmers from Glasgow. He was a goalkeeper of note who appeared for Rangers and Clyde as well as for Scotland in 1885–86. He was to be succeeded in goal during Ironopolis' Northern League days by Charlie Watts, a Teesside-born 'keeper who eventually joined Newcastle United and made over 100 competitive appearances for the Magpies. William McReddie was another Scot who established himself in the Ironopolis side. He was described as an exciting forward who also played for the Middlesbrough Pioneers baseball team. John Stevenson hailed from north of the border too, one of the many Scots to flock to the Tyne, Wear and Tees at that time. At right-half he learned his football with Kilbirnie and Third Lanark and was a highly rated player.

Around the Cleveland area there were other significant clubs. South Bank were (and are) regarded by many as the oldest side, and it is claimed that they were formed in 1868. In 1885 they merged with two other clubs in the town, South Bank Erimus and South Bank Excelsior, and became a stronger outfit. A year later another club, South Bank Black Watch, were incorporated into the club which became known throughout the region as the Bankers. F. Beadle was captain of the enlarged club, with Frank Rowland the secretary-treasurer, although he was also a noted centre-forward, once hitting a hat-trick against Whitby.

They played at a local cricket field and in 1886 moved to the Paradise Field, a site which was much later developed as part of British Steel's giant Cleveland Works. South Bank moved once more before the turn of the century, to a new ground at Normanby Road in 1889. They provided the opposition for Newcastle East End's – and Newcastle United's – first FA Cup tie in season 1887–88, and they won 3–2 in extra-time on home soil. The winning strike came from Jones, who 'ran away with it and made a victorious assault upon the enemy fortress'!

The Bankers reached the semi-final of the FA Amateur Cup in 1895 when they almost made it an all-Teesside affair but unfortunately lost in a replay to the Old Carthusians. The team of former public-school men went on to meet Middlesbrough in the Final at Headingly in Leeds, and it was the Boro who brought the country's foremost amateur trophy back to Teesside. The Bankers had to wait until 1913 before lifting the 'pot' themselves.

Cleveland was a stronghold of amateurism, with Stockton FC also shunning the professional game, although they did have a spell as a professional outfit. Sadly they found it little more than a way of losing money and soon had to revert back to their amateur status. Established in 1882 with colours of black shirts with three red hoops, then, soon after, red-and-black-quartered jerseys, they became known as the Ancients. They played initially on a cricket field site at Flatt's Farm, now part of Preston Park.

Stockton, after trying the professional game and even fielding a Scottish international in James Hutton, went on to become one of the country's leading amateur sides. They did well in the FA Amateur Cup, runners-up in 1897 at a time of Northern dominance and winners two years later. North East clubs were in the Final for nine of the first 10 years of the competition, recording seven victories. Both South Bank and Stockton were founder members of the Northern League in 1889.

In the rugby stronghold of Hartlepool the first association club to be established was in early 1881 when West Hartlepool Amateur FC were formed. Although founder members of the Durham FA, they had a precarious early existence due to the popularity of the oval ball game. Nevertheless, they did become established and eventually became one of the foremost amateur clubs in the country, winning the FA Amateur Cup in 1905 by defeating Clapton in the Final at Shepherd's Bush. But they were soon superseded in the town by a new professional club, Hartlepool United, when they came on the scene in 1908.

At the very estuary of the Tees, Redcar started kicking a ball around during the late 1870s and played evenly contested games with Middlesbrough at the turn of the decade. Indeed, a Sheffield Association Cup tie between the two clubs in October 1880 attracted a crowd of 1,000 to the cricket ground on Linthorpe Road. There was keen rivalry between the two clubs, and when they met in the Final of the Cleveland Challenge Cup during March 1882 no fewer than 1,500 turned up to watch the encounter, including 'the gentry of the district'. That game finished 3–3, and it was not surprising that an even bigger crowd, 2,000, came out for the replay three weeks later when Boro lifted the trophy after a 2–1 win. By the 1885–86 season, Redcar were participating the FA Cup.

Port Clarence at Haverton Hill were also in action at an early stage. Both Redcar and Port Clarence competed in the original North East Counties League in 1889–90 alongside West Hartlepool.

Loftus, near Redcar, were another old established club, playing as early as 1878, as were Eston. North Ormesby and Linthorpe were also early clubs in the district. There is no doubt that the association game blossomed on Teesside before it did on either Tyneside or Wearside. By 1888 it was recorded that the Cleveland Football Association had 24 senior and six junior clubs in membership.

As we have seen, Sunderland AFC became a formidable club and the most ambitious of all the North East sides over the first 15 years of the game's development in the region. Following their formation in 1879 they went from strength to strength; although, as is normal, with more than a few hiccups along the way. Sunderland's early colours were not the now famous red and white, but 'blue shirts and blue knickerbockers'. In December 1884 they started to wear new colours of red-and-white halved tops, while in September

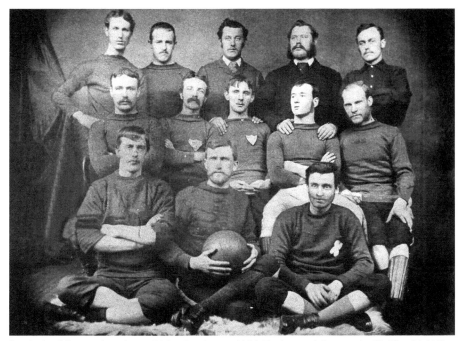

Sunderland featured in their all-blue kit during 1884. Back row, left to right: Kirkley, McMillan, Lumsden, Singleton, Murdoch. Middle: McDonald, Allan (J), Hall, Grayston, Allan (W). Front: Leslie, Wade, Innes. *(P. Days, Sunderland AFC historian)*

1887 they first pulled on a red-and-white-striped shirt. They played initially, and somewhat appropriately, at the Blue House ground in Hendon, then at Newcastle Road.

The Wearside club rapidly gained prominence, and within a decade they were not only the top North East side, but also respected on a national level too. Several distinguished names were to play for Sunderland in those formative years. Goalkeeper Bill Kirkley (also often referred to as Kirtley) was a stalwart. Nicknamed 'Stonewall', he was to remain with the club until the 1930s, while John 'Dowk' Oliver was also prominent as Sunderland was being developed. Jimmy Hunter was another noted early footballer. He arrived from Scotland and was perhaps the catalyst for an invasion from north of the border to head for Wearside. There was a never-ending trail of Scots, many of whom were also looking for employment in the shipyards. Included were more than a few of the greats of Sunderland's coming mastery. Bob Gloag was one of those to settle on Wearside, and he became an instant hit with supporters. More were to follow.

As noted, they did have a few ups and downs and, like on Teesside, the amateur versus professional debate was a major point of friction. Following an intense row over actually paying players to play against Middlesbrough, there was an acrimonious split in the Sunderland camp. As a result, in March 1888 the Sunderland Albion club were formed when the original founder John Allan defected and established a rival organisation.

Although Albion were very determined and go-getting in attitude – no doubt because of the leadership of Allan – they had a short-lived existence. During their brief life-span they encountered a running and bitter battle with their foes and 'mother club' on

Sunderland Albion in 1889, great rivals to their Wearside neighbours. Back row players only, left to right: McDermid, Angus, McFarlane. Middle: Hannah, White, McNichol, Stewart, Brand. Front: Smith, Weir, Kinnaird. *(P. Days, Sunderland AFC historian)*

Wearside. The new outfit played in white shirts with royal blue shorts and used Sunderland's old ground at the Blue House Field, a short walk from the North Sea coast. It took a while for Albion to sort themselves out. Indeed, when they played their first game during May 1888 against Shankhouse Black Watch they could not raise a team and had to 'loan' no fewer than five players from Elswick Rangers, including prominent goal-getter James Nugent. They won 3–0.

However, soon Albion attracted many top names including West Bromwich Albion's England goalkeeper Bob Roberts, a giant of a man at 6ft 4in tall. There were plenty of Scots: Peter McCracken, John Rae, Jimmy Weir and Jake Stewart, as well as Cutty Smith of Renton. Jimmy Hannah and James Gillespie were regulars too – and both Scots as well – but they soon became noted players in their Wearside rivals' colours. Also to play for Albion was Bob McDermid, who appeared for both Tyne clubs, West End and East End.

Just as on Tyneside, clubs were also formed around Wearside but were fewer in number and, Sunderland and Albion apart, mainly of lesser quality. There were no sides of the standing of Rendel or Elswick Rangers, although there was one exception, Whitburn FC, who were formed in 1882 by a local schoolmaster in the village, Alfred Grundy. They were one of the founding clubs of the Durham FA a year later when he was the driving force at its start. Grundy was a prominent figure in the district, President of the Durham FA for 18 years and also a keen supporter of cricket in the county.

Other clubs were created by the start of the 1890s around Wearside including Southwick, Boldon Star, Monkwearmouth and Ryhope. There were several from within the town of Sunderland too: West End, Swifts, Celtic, Black Watch and Olympic.

At Castle Eden near Peterlee, a club was formed known as Castle Eden Red Star, an original member of the Durham FA as well. To cater for a growing number of smaller clubs, the Sunderland Alliance and Sunderland Combination were formed. The more prominent Wearside League was set up in 1892.

Both of Sunderland's top sides were the first in the region to join the English senior Leagues – the Football League and Football Alliance – doing so some three years ahead of Newcastle East End. At the Football League's Annual General Meeting in 1889, both Sunderland and Sunderland Albion attempted to gain election to the new national competition, but neither got very far. Each club was given all of five minutes to stake its claim. Sunderland claimed just two votes and Albion none.

The Albion club were not content with that disappointment and switched their attention to the rival Football Alliance and found a place for the inaugural season of 1889–90. They did well too, finishing in third place behind champions Sheffield Wednesday, then finishing as runners-up to Stoke the following year. But after that, Albion returned to the Northern League due to the expense of travelling south and having to give financial guarantees to visiting clubs heading north for matches on Wearside.

Sunderland once more made a bid to join the Football League elite, as did Albion, at the AGM gathering at the Douglas Hotel in Manchester during May 1890. Albion fared

From left to right: John Campbell and John Harvie were grand servants to Sunderland, and they later also appeared for Newcastle United.

no better, but this time Sunderland were successful, replacing the bottom club Stoke who were to move to the Alliance. It was recorded in the official Football League history *League Football* that Sunderland 'had to promise to pay any additional travelling expenses that clubs would incur through their membership'.

That heralded the beginning of a great era for Sunderland AFC, and the club became one of the finest in the country. Indeed, they became the very best for a period. After they had demolished Aston Villa (either by 7–2 in 1890 or 6–1 in 1892, records differ) the eminent William McGregor, director of Villa and founder of the Football League, was hugely impressed. Sunderland's centenary publication *The Official History* notes: 'William McGregor reckoned that Sunderland had a "talented man in every position"; the so-called "Team of All Talents" was born.'

More Scots had landed on Wearside to form the nucleus of the line up, many to play for their country, including John Auld, generally recognised as the first skipper of the side to be known in history as the 'Team of all the Talents'. He was eventually replaced by the great Hugh Wilson, who was joined by an array of Scottish geniuses like John Harvie and Johnny Campbell, two fabulous forwards, both to later join Newcastle United, as did Auld. There was Jimmy Millar, another exquisite forward, as well as David Hannah and goalkeeper Ted Doig. Jimmy Hannah and James Gillespie switched from Albion, and both had spells with West End in Newcastle. While the influence of the side was very much Caledonian, there was the odd Englishman – Geordie full-back Tom Porteous being a notable inclusion. He also played for his country.

Sunderland's first Football League outing was in September 1890 at Newcastle Road when they faced Burnley. The visitors took the points after what was something of a rough contest in a 3–2 victory before a crowd of between 5,000 and 8,000. Sunderland's first Football League side was: Kirkley, Porteous, Oliver, Wilson, Auld, Gibson, Spence, Millar, Campbell, Scott, Hannah (D).

The North East had their first club at the top table, some 13 years after Middlesbrough and Tyne Association first kicked a ball in March 1877. While rivals Sunderland Albion faded, the original Sunderland club – embracing professionalism – became Football League champions in 1891–92 and 1892–93 with that celebrated 'Team of all the Talents'.

When Sunderland Albion were wound up in August 1892, *Athletic News* summed up the footballing battle on Wearside: 'The conclusion is irresistibly forced upon one that there is not room for two expensive professional teams in Sunderland, and it is quite in accordance with the Darwinian theory of the survival of the fittest that the Albion, being the weaker of the two, should go to the wall.'

At the same time on Tyneside the rivalry between East End and West End was to take a similar 'Darwinian' route. The result was Newcastle United. They had some way to go to catch up their Wearside rivals but were to soon lay the foundations of their own emergence as one of England's top sides.

Chapter 9

A TASTE OF THE BIG-TIME

'The pastime of football in this district has risen in popularity by leaps and bounds.'
'Captain', *Daily Chronicle*, 1888

By the later years of the 1880s, football's development in the country as a whole was in full swing and moving apace. The FA Cup and new Football League had taken hold, while locally around the regions – as in the North East – clubs were being formed in almost every community, be it in the town and city or in the countryside. Boys and young adults played the association code with enthusiasm. Football was now quickly becoming the 'people's game' and would soon be the 'national game'.

During the decade after 1883 the amateur pioneers were largely overtaken by a select group of new and rapidly emerging clubs around the country. By far the most successful were the Lancashire pair of Blackburn Rovers and Preston North End. Rovers were winners of the FA Cup on five occasions, while Preston reached two Finals, winning once, and also lifted the Football League Championship twice and were runners-up three times. They also achieved the very first League and Cup double. In addition Blackburn Olympic, a rival club in the Lancashire mill town, won the Cup as well, while another Lancashire club, Everton, also emerged as a club of renown.

West Bromwich Albion led the Midlands' challenge; they reached four FA Cup Finals and stood aside with Wolves and Aston Villa, who, afterwards, along with Sunderland, were to become dominant in the years up to the turn of the century lifting eight Championship titles between them. Sunderland showed the potential for a future hotbed of the game in the North East.

In Scotland the early years of football were dominated by Queen's Park. The Scottish FA Cup began in the 1873–74 season and, during the first 20 years of competition, Queen's lifted the trophy on no fewer than 10 occasions. Not only that, but the renowned Scottish amateurs also took part in two Finals south of the border. Three other West of Scotland clubs, Dumbarton, Renton and Vale of Leven, were also forces to be reckoned with, all tasting success in the Scottish Cup. Dumbarton were also the first winners of the Scottish League, lifting the title twice in the early 1890s. But then Celtic began to tot-up their vast accumulation of honours, as did their great rivals to be, Rangers.

The new Football League competition had been a success and Sunderland's entry had boosted the game in the North East. Their title victories of 1892, 1893 and 1895 were to put the region on the football map. On Tyneside there must have been more than a few looks of envy towards Wearside. At the time of Sunderland's admission into the big-time, both East End and West End may well have had aspirations to join their neighbours, but they were still some way behind their rivals. Football on Tyneside remained very much a local affair with the odd FA Cup foray on the national scene.

By 1890 a growing number of the sport's enthusiasts on Tyneside had started to gain an appetite for a higher grade of football fare. Since the mid-years of the 1880s a procession of England and Scotland's top sides had arrived on Tyneside to play in prestige friendlies or exhibition contests against East End and West End, now that both clubs were strong enough to at least challenge the best in the country, if not beat them. Previously a Newcastle & District team was put together which faced the likes of Preston, Nottingham Forest and the famous Corinthians, while Newcastle Rangers had faced Queen's Park.

In these years virtually all the principal clubs on both sides of the border travelled to Tyneside to entertain the Geordies. West Bromwich Albion, Preston and Wolves arrived, so did Sheffield Wednesday, Blackburn Rovers and Everton. Aston Villa, together with Nottingham Forest and Notts County, headed north, while the Corinthians' tours often included Tyneside. From Scotland, the Newcastle public saw visits from Dumbarton and Renton, and the notable combinations of Hibs and Vale of Leven, as well as the Old Firm of Rangers and Celtic. When Hibs and Renton arrived on Tyneside, the self-declared 'Champions of the World' were even on show! All these teams brought with them many of the country's finest players who helped educate both the local clubs and supporters on Tyneside.

In addition, with East End and West End both taking a professional path as the decade drew to a close, a number of top-class footballers found a home on Tyneside for short periods, prominently with the West End club. Put together, this gave officials, players and supporters a taste of the big-time. East End and West End learned much from this period, and it whetted their appetite for bigger things. They both wanted to join Sunderland at the highest level.

Among the biggest attractions to Tyneside were the holders and finalists of both the FA Cup and Scottish Cup and later the Football League, Alliance and Scottish League champions. A succession of top-drawer names from both sides of the border arrived in the North East. First on show were Dumbarton Athletic who made a trio of visits to Tyneside between 1886 and 1888. They came from a corner of Scotland north of Glasgow where football had found something of a hot-bed with three formidable sides – Renton, Vale of Leven and, Athletics' rivals and the much stronger side, Dumbarton FC. The two Dumbarton clubs were to later amalgamate and lift the very first two Scottish League Championship titles.

Athletic first lined up against East End at Tyne's ground in Jesmond at New Year 1886 – for what were to become regular big-draw holiday attractions. Dumbarton contained in their team several established names and international players to be, including goalkeeper John McLeod, half-back Geordie Dewar, a somewhat ungainly but wonderful footballer, and outside-right Alexander Latta, who would become a star and title-winner with Everton. There is no record of the crowd, but attendances were generally good for

EAST END & WEST END: VERSUS TOP OPPOSITION (TO 1892)					Fact Box
East End:	P15	W3	D3	L9	Win ratio 20%
West End:	P21	W4	D1	L16	Win ratio 19%
Total:	**P36**	**W7**	**D4**	**L25**	**Win ratio 19%**

these exhibition matches, much bigger than normal fixtures – at times on par with matches against the Sunderland clubs or when East End faced West End. Dumbarton were too good for East End, winning comfortably 4–1. The Scots also played a game two days later against Sleekburn Wanderers at Bedlington, winning again, this time 4–2. The crowd was recorded for that fixture, with around 400 in attendance; however, gates would increase dramatically over the coming five years.

The following year it was West End's turn to test their progress against one of Scotland's best. At St James' Park Dumbarton again triumphed, 3–1. Twelve months on, the West Enders had another go over the Christmas and Hogmanay programme in front of a 2,000 crowd. But they fell once more, 5–2. The St Bernard's club of Edinburgh also travelled to Tyneside at this time, twice facing West End in Easter fixtures. The Tyne club did a bit better, winning one of the matches, both of which resulted in 3–1 scorelines.

During the season in which Aston Villa arrived on Tyneside to face Shankhouse in that notable FA Cup tie and showed the region how football should be played by racking up nine goals (1887–88), the other Midland giant, West Bromwich Albion, also took to the field in the district. The Albion had an even more distinguished combination then, reaching the FA Cup Final three times in succession and winning in 1888. Indeed, when they arrived on Tyneside at the beginning of April they had just lifted the trophy 10 days before by defeating Preston 2–1 at The Oval in London. And the following month they played a headlining so-called 'Championship of the World' fixture at Hampden Park against the Scottish Cup holders Renton. They lost that encounter 4–1, which incidentally was refereed by future Newcastle United secretary and doyen Frank Watt. When Albion arrived at St James' Park to face West End they had few peers, and interest was considerable.

A huge crowd of 4,000 to 6,000 congregated at the Gallowgate arena to see such famous England players as Billy Bassett, brilliant at outside-right, and captain Charlie Perry, a polished and commanding half-back. There was also George Woodhall – who had scored the FA Cup Final winner – and Jem Bayliss, a formidable striker, two more England men of the era. Giant 'keeper Bob Roberts was on the field too, another international who soon joined Sunderland Albion.

The match started evenly, with East End star Alec White guesting for the St James' Park club. Albion's Wilson and Nicholson of West End each scored to level the contest 1–1 at the break; however, after the crossover the visitors' class showed as they stormed ahead. Albion hit the West Enders for four more goals and won 5–1.

West End also faced Scottish Cup holders Hibernian that season, who had declared themselves the first 'Association Football Champions of the World' after beating Preston at Easter Road. West End fared no better. In fact they were on the wrong side of a 6–0 hammering on a snow-covered pitch. Scottish international Jim McGhee was prominent for the Edinburgh club, a grand servant to Hibs as captain. He was a hugely popular figure. West End could not handle his forward thrusts, while Hibs were described as 'an excellent team with clever manoeuvres'.

The 1888–89 season saw no fewer than six top clubs visit Tyneside for prestige challenge matches against East End and West End. It was a benchmark for both clubs – a marker of how their football development was advancing compared to the rest of the country. Results in this eight-match test showed both clubs had some way still to go. Only two draws were logged, the visitors recording victories in all the other contests; however, the local sides were facing the best in the country, and some of the matches were closely fought affairs. Progress was definitely being made.

West End started what must have been a mouth-watering programme of friendlies for both players and supporters with the visit of Sheffield Wednesday just before New Year, a club destined to become the new Football Alliance champions in the following season. But really the visit of the Yorkshire club was just a taster for what was to follow. A crowd of 2,000 were pleased that West End matched their visitors for most of the 90 minutes, only losing by a single goal scored after a corner by Tom Cawley, a noted striker for the early Tykes.

Hailed as 'Champions of the World', Renton visited Newcastle in 1888. Back row, players only, left to right: Kelso, Hannah, Lindsay, McCall (A.), McKechnie. Front row: McCallum, Campbell (H.), Kelly, Campbell (J.), McCall (J.), McNee. Bob Kelso, John Campbell and John McNee all played for Tyneside clubs. *(A. Mitchell archive)*

East End's holiday attraction hailed from north of the border – and there were few clubs more respected than Renton, the Scottish Cup holders who had defeated West Bromwich Albion in that 'Championship of the World' clash seven months earlier. From a mere village near Dumbarton, the Renton club had developed into one of the most powerful sides in Scotland, fielding many of that country's finest players – some of whom came to wear the colours of Tyneside clubs and for Newcastle United over the coming years. Two members of the team that saw off Albion, John McNee and Johnny Campbell, later played for the Magpies in Football League action.

Three Scottish internationals appeared in Renton's dark-blue shirts against East End: goalkeeper John Lindsay, right-back Andrew Hannah – a formidable tackler who won honours with Everton – and Harry Campbell, a neat and tidy inside-forward who also did well in England and was an FA Cup winner with Blackburn Rovers. In addition, David Hannah (no relation to Andrew) was in the line up too, along with Johnny Campbell. Both were influential forwards who no doubt would have been capped by their country as well had they not moved south, back to the North East, joining Sunderland at the end of the season. Both would lift title medals on Wearside.

A crowd of 4,000 pushed their way into the Heaton ground to see the stars of Renton, and they were delighted to roar their own favourites to a creditable 2–2 draw. Although East End piled on lots of early pressure, with Mulvey going close, it was Renton who opened the scoring following a gaffe by 'keeper Henderson; the East End custodian 'tried to kick out but he slipped and fell', allowing the ball to roll into the goal! In the second period Collins equalised (although at least one report credited Mack with the goal) and then East End sent the crowd into raptures after a move that saw White send Smith on a penetrating run which ended with a neat pass to Mulvey who gave the home side the lead. The game was an open one, and Renton levelled the score following a neat dribble and shot by Campbell. Yet, East End almost clinched victory when Jock Smith hit the woodwork following an exciting run and shot.

Renton's neighbours and pioneers of the Scottish game, Vale of Leven, also visited Tyneside at this time, facing West End in a New Year's Day attraction. The Alexandria club had reached the Scottish Cup Final six times, lifting the trophy on three successive occasions (1877–79). Once, however, they had failed to turn up for the Final! They were to reach it again in 1890. A gate of 2,000 saw an entertaining 3–3 draw on a near quagmire of a pitch at St James' Park.

During February and March of 1889, West End brought both West Bromwich Albion and Glasgow Celtic to Tyneside, both clubs having reached their respective Cup Finals. Albion's second visit to St James' Park saw poor weather keep the attendance down to 2,000, and the crowd were frustrated to see the visitors' opening goal actually scored by umpire George Phillips! In a goalmouth scramble the ball was driven towards the posts and ended up going past West End 'keeper Billy Jardine off the unfortunate official's leg. The Midland club made it 2–0 soon afterwards, and that is how the score remained, despite West End's second-half siege of the Albion goal. It was noted that they had no fewer than 41 shots, but England goalkeeper Bob Roberts stopped everything fired at him in style.

The following month Celtic arrived on Tyneside for their very first visit a month after appearing in the Scottish Cup Final where they had finished as runners-up to Third Lanark. The Glaswegians were just beginning to develop into one of the clubs – along with Rangers – to take over from Queen's Park, Renton and Vale of Leven as Scotland's finest. Indeed, the 1888–89 season was to be Celtic's first-ever campaign, and their side included several prominent names of the club and of Scotland. Half-back James Kelly and outside-right Neilly McCallum were two ex-Renton stars, both internationals and described as 'greats of the day'. Willie Groves at centre-forward was a danger; he was capped too and later starred for West Bromwich Albion and Aston Villa. Jimmy McLaren was another to wear the Scotland blue. A wily tactician, he lined up against West End with one of the famous Maley brothers – Tom and Willie – although it is not noted which played on Tyneside. Both were prominent in the rise of Celtic.

The Celts comfortably eased to a 3–1 interval lead in front of a 4,000 crowd at Gallowgate, but West End made the encounter a thrilling one despite a strong wind. After the break the West Enders hit back and Celtic only narrowly won in the end 4–3.

The English Cup runners-up Wolverhampton Wanderers visited Tyneside twice in April and May to meet West End and East End, in the process scoring no fewer than 12 goals. Against West End the visitors fielded just about their strongest line up, including six current or future England internationals. It was a formidable team. Included was the defensive trio of 'keeper Billy Rose with full-backs Dicky Baugh and Charlie Mason, as well as half-backs Harry Allen and Albert Fletcher, with striker Harry Wood up front.

When Preston arrived on Tyneside in 1889 they were the first double holders. Back row, players only, left to right: Drummond, Howarth, Russell, Holmes, Graham, Mills-Roberts. Front: Gordon, Ross, Goodall, Dewhurst, Thompson.

Mason was a founder member of the club and described as being 'in at the start of every facet of Wolves' history', while Fletcher stayed with the club until 1920. Wood scored some 126 goals for Wolves.

The powerful Wanderers demolished West End 9–2 and, despite the heavy defeat, the watching 4,000 locals were thrilled to see football of such quality. Wolves were two goals up in the opening minutes and 5–1 ahead by the break. By the time the referee called for time Wolves had eased off, which was just as well as the scoreline could have easily have reached double-figures.

Thankfully East End performed much better. With Wolves selecting a much weaker line up – only four internationals took to the field this time – the East Enders were actually ahead 2–0 by half-time. James Collins drilled the ball past 'keeper Rose to open the scoring, and then Jock Smith added another. Wolves, though, hit back after the interval and won 3–2.

England forward John Goodall always impressed when he was on Tyneside with the Corinthians, Preston and later Derby County.

The biggest attraction of the season to Tyneside, however, was the visit of Preston North End who faced East End at the end of April 1889. The visitors had lifted the FA Cup and were the very first Football League champions in that season – the first so-called double holders. And they went on to be champions again in 1889–90 and runners-up in 1890–91. Their arrival was the biggest attraction to the region since West Bromwich Albion's appearance the year before. At the time of Preston's visit they had already secured both trophies. Having beaten Aston Villa to the inaugural Football League title during February and then inflicting a 3–0 defeat over another Midland rival in Wolves in the FA Cup Final at the end of March, their appearance in Newcastle was big news.

Preston had been to the city before, of course, in 1883, 1886 and 1888 during their rapid evolution as a major force in the game, but on this occasion they had reached the pinnacle of their early fame. Several of what the future would term the 'Old Invincibles' were on show at Chillingham Road. John Goodall led the attack, and the England striker impressed the Tyneside public as he had done when he faced a Newcastle & District XI three years before. The elder of two footballing brothers, he was top scorer in that title-winning season. An on-field genius, he also captained England. Alongside Goodall were four dynamite Scots: Jack Gordon, Jimmy Ross, George Drummond and Sam Thomson. All moving south to earn a living, they had also excelled previously on Tyneside and repeated the show. Preston's defence was a powerful unit with England's Bob Holmes and Wales 'keeper James Trainer. Scotland international and recent West End favourite Bob Kelso appeared at right-half.

Preston were quickly into their stride on a wet surface, scoring three goals in the first half before a crowd of 3,000. Goodall opened the scoring with a potent drive, and for a long period in the opening 45 minutes East End could hardly get hold of the ball or get it out of their own half. Ross added a second (although some reports credit Russell with the goal) and Goodall the third. The England striker completed his hat-trick after the interval while Collins scored with a 'splendid shot' for the home side's consolation.

In the following two seasons of 1889–90 and 1890–91 both of the Newcastle clubs continued to bring the finest teams and footballers in the country to Tyneside. West End arranged visits by the Corinthians to St James' Park for holiday attractions and in three games played a total of 21 goals were scored – and they were not all registered by the esteemed visitors. Following two defeats, 3–1 and 4–1, West End recorded a resounding triumph, hitting the famed amateurs for eight goals in March 1891.

At first the Corinthians maintained their winning formula on Tyneside. Their two victories meant they had played on five occasions in Newcastle and had won all five, scoring no fewer than 23 goals on their exhibition tours. As was usual, the Corinthians brought with them many celebrated names to Tyneside; Tinsley Lindley returned while fellow England internationals included Leonard Wilkinson, Charles Wreford-Brown and George Brann, as well as Arthur Henfrey, John Veitch and Hugh Stanborough. And that was not all. Tyneside saw Norman Cooper, Anthony Hossack and 6ft 3in powerhouse George Cotterill.

Crowds were decent, between 2,000 and 5,000 for each game, although West End were at first resolutely beaten by the star-studded cast on show. The West Enders soon gained revenge, however. Their eight-goal romp was exceptional; although it has to be noted that the Corinthian line up was not quite as strong – containing only three England footballers – while the visitors did score four goals themselves and indeed were 4–1 ahead at half-time. The goal feast was watched by 3,000, and the crowd was roused by the home team's second-half onslaught. A hat-trick by Roger Patten led the way in the 8–4 victory.

Not content to face the best of amateur English football during 1890 and 1891, West End also faced Renton and Glasgow Rangers from north of the border and then the might of the professional game in Aston Villa, Everton and Preston, who made a quick return visit to Tyneside.

Early January 1890 saw Renton back on Tyneside to attract a crowd of 3,000 to St James' Park where they witnessed a tight encounter which was won narrowly 2–1 by the Scots. It was noted in the press that the visitors 'were attired in dark blue jerseys and in physique they were superior to their opponents; two or three being of massive build'. Despite that perceived handicap, West End challenged well, equalising Renton's opener when Brady set the crowd into 'loud cheers'. The Tynesiders only lost the game in the dying minutes when McColl 'cleverly scored'.

Aston Villa arrived for a Good Friday clash later in the year, and a crowd of between 4,000 and 6,000 turned up at Gallowgate. It was Villa's first time back at the ground since their nine-goal romp over Shankhouse in 1887. This time there was no goal avalanche as West End made them fight all the way. The contest was an even one, and while the visitors did not field three of their biggest names – Devey, Hodgetts and Hunter – they still paraded an impressive side, including five internationals. Scotland's James Cowan was an outstanding half-back while up front Albert Allen was a dangerous England striker. He had scored two of the goals against Shankhouse.

There was surprisingly only a single goal in the contest, and even more surprisingly, perhaps, it was scored by West End. What ended up being the winning strike came early following a Moore cross that was converted by McColl in the box. Dave Whitton in the West End goal was kept busy as Villa searched for a way back, but the Tyneside custodian kept the visitors at bay. The result was a notable one, and not just for West End. It showed that football on Tyneside had perhaps come of age. The Geordies could now beat the best.

When Everton followed Villa to St James' Park the following month, that progress was maintained and illustrated that it was realistic for West End – and for East End – to be thinking about competing in the national Football League. While West End did not beat Everton, they managed to record a respectable 2–1 defeat against a club second only to Preston North End in the League title race that year – and to become Championship winners themselves the following season. Everton included in their ranks a host of internationals; Charlie Parry, Edgar Chadwick, Alf Milward as well as Alex Latta and Andrew Hannah – and also Dan Doyle, briefly with East End.

During the following season of 1890–91, West End tested themselves against both Preston and Rangers but could not maintain their good progress against superior opponents. Preston recorded a trouble-free 4–0 success in front of a bumper crowd in excess of 4,000. The visitors gave an exhibition of 'beautiful passing' at times. Rangers, joint-holders of the Scottish title (the very first), attracted a crowd approaching 5,000 and won comfortably too, 3–0. Scottish international Donald Gow impressed. He scored direct from a free-kick and was soon to join Sunderland.

East End also gave their supporters the chance to see the best in the country and test themselves against top opponents too. They perhaps even got one over the West Enders by bringing Blackburn Rovers to Heaton during September 1889. Up to then Rovers had lifted the FA Cup three times and were to secure the trophy twice more in 1890 and 1891. No other professional club could match that impressive record. Rovers had almost all of their big names on show – eight players who had played international football or who would shortly do so. The leading figure was centre-forward Jack Southworth, a robust and fast striker whose record for Rovers was spectacular. Left-half Jimmy Forrest, the only man to appear in all five of the Lancashire club's FA Cup Finals of the era, was in the side too, as were James Douglas and Billy Townley, two more household names of the game. Douglas was one of several prominent Scots to make the exodus to Blackburn while, in the following season, left-winger Townley became the first player to score a hat-trick in an FA Cup Final.

East End did well against such demanding opponents, just as the West Enders had against Aston Villa and Everton. They showed that since the last occasion Rovers were matched against Geordie opponents – in the FA Cup against Tyne back in 1879 – the standard of local football had improved dramatically, and although East End lost, the 2–1 scoreline was an indication of how close the game had been.

Notts County made a visit to Tyneside as well, and while the Trent club were not in the same bracket as some of the other visitors to Newcastle, they were to be FA Cup runners-up in 1891. The game was played at Jesmond, and the resultant 1–1 draw illustrated East End's progress.

The Heaton side also showed their development was on track with good results over two more advanced clubs during the following 1890–91 season. Sheffield Wednesday, the reigning Football Alliance champions and FA Cup runners-up, as well as Nottingham Forest, Alliance winners in 1891–92, turned up to face East End.

Against the Tykes a goal from Tom McInnes earned a respectable 1–1 draw considering they were facing the likes of Fred Thompson and Jack Dungworth, two of Wednesday's finest early stars. Forest fielded internationals to be, David Russell (Scotland) and Albert Smith (England), and recorded a narrow 2–1 victory in front of around 3,000, a match that saw Jock Sorley charge both the ball and the goalkeeper over the line to earn East End's goal.

As at St James' Park progress was evidently being made in Heaton. But there was still work to do. That was proved when Derby County inflicted a 5–0 defeat on East End during March. Former Preston star John Goodall was back on Tyneside, now as a County man, and he played a significant part in the Rams' triumph. Also in Derby's ranks was goalkeeper Charles Bunyan, who interestingly was Hyde United's 'keeper when Goodall was on the very long score sheet as his Preston team registered that remarkable 26–0 FA Cup victory. Bunyan had something of a bizarre career, later ending up signing for Newcastle United as a reserve custodian.

In those two seasons of 1889 to 1891, both East End and West End had undoubtedly made progress. They may have not won many games – only two, both West End successes against Aston Villa and the Corinthians – but the margin between Tyneside's clubs and their opponents was now much closer. In the 12 games played against what could be termed top opposition, in addition to those two victories, there were two draws and five of the fixtures were close defeats. Only on four occasions were either of the Newcastle clubs well beaten.

By the start of the 1891–92 season, both clubs must have been pleased with their footballing progress. That optimism continued when Wolves and Derby County played fixtures on Tyneside. When Wolves arrived in town to face East End it was reported that they fielded six internationals in their line up. So the Heaton outfit's 3–0 victory was a grand scalp. Inside-forward John Barker started the scoring with a splendid goal – jinking past defenders to strike the ball past goalkeeper Hassall. Barker was on the score sheet again in the second half, and then the popular Tynesider went onto complete his hat-trick in style.

Against Derby County another convincing 4–1 triumph was recorded by East End, in spite of the quality of the opponents, John Goodall et al. And they also took care of Stoke, a club then in the Football League with an acclaimed international defensive triumvirate of William Rowley, Tommy Clare and Alf Underwood. On that occasion the East Enders won 2–0; although Stoke returned a month later and turned the tables, winning 3–2.

However, reality checks resulted when Blackburn Rovers faced both Novocastrian clubs. The Lancashire side were in no mood to be embarrassed by lesser opponents. Despite fielding a weakened side, they swamped West End 7–0 when the Gallowgate club had the temerity to visit Lancashire. With home advantage, East End did better but still lost 3–1 against a side full of international quality. At least the visit of Blackburn set a new ground attendance record at Chillingham Road, with 5,803 spectators paying at the gates.

Preston also made another trip to the North East and reinforced the view that there was still a gap in class between the Tyneside clubs and the very best, albeit one that was narrowing quickly. North End continued their winning streak with a 2–0 success over East End and now had four victories out of four played, in which they scored 16 goals and conceded only two.

There was another friendly challenge with Burnley, not a top bracket side, but East End's 2–1 defeat in Heaton after a very rough game also illustrated that football even in Victorian England had a crowd behaviour problem. There was a complaint in an open letter to the *Daily Journal* which noted that at the bottom end of the Heaton Junction ground the improper language used by the crowd, particularly by 'the young Newcastle rascals' sited on the boundary, was shocking. It was documented that these 'reprobates shouted themselves hoarse, using the worst epithets that could possibly emanate from their mouths and spoiled Newcastle's reputation for generosity and fairness'. The Toon Army had arrived!

Apart from having a policy of bringing the very best clubs football could offer to the view of Tyneside's public, the Newcastle clubs also decided on a strategy of engaging players from out of the region – and several distinguished stars landed in Newcastle. The West Enders were one of several clubs around the country that took advantage of the Football Association's acceptance of the professional ideal in July 1885 – albeit with conditions attached.

Prior to what was a momentous decision in the game's development, players could only receive payment for expenses or lost wages during the time that they played football. But there had been a clandestine payment custom of under-the-counter deals, including where players were sometimes induced to give up their jobs in their home town and move to a new club's community with the guarantee of a job while playing for the side. Even after the 1885 ruling, the Football Association tried to control any excesses in the new professional understanding. There was a controversial residential prerequisite rule for players. Only footballers who were either qualified by birth or by residence during the past two years – within a six-mile area of the club's headquarters – could be permitted to play in FA Cup or local affiliated tournaments. And no professional could play for more than one club in any single season. All paid players also had to be formally registered.

Subsequently there was many a protest over this issue at matches, and in the North East there was no exception. It was no surprise when, in 1889, this legislation was abolished. Clubs then had the pick of any player – money was king, with no maximum wage rule until after the turn of the century.

During the period of professionalism's infancy both East End and West End advertised for players in *Athletic News* and, north of the border, in *Scottish Sport*. Many players from the central regions of Scotland had already migrated south, to Tyne, Wear and Tees before the 1885 rule change due to an uncompromising outlook to professionalism in the north. Matters became so serious in that the Scottish Football Association, fearing the exodus of many of their best players to England, passed a resolution at the end of 1888 to the effect that 'a player who has played under the jurisdiction of any association other than this association, cannot play in any match under our jurisdiction without permission'. This could prohibit international appearances. Of course, a player could come to England and play under a false name (not unheard of) and the Scottish Association would not be any the wiser. It made little difference, however, and a deluge now followed from Scotland.

The arrival of Ralph Aitken on Tyneside during September 1886 meant he was the first Scottish international to land in the whole North East. That move began a flow of top names who settled in the region from Scotland. Aitken was the most famous footballer and the first capped player to appear for any Tyne or Wear club. West End's policy of attracting this level of star player over the coming five years showed they had ambition; although ultimately the buy-in approach failed.

Ralph Allan Aitken was born in Kilbarchan near Paisley and made his name as a member of a fine Dumbarton side. A diminutive outside-left full of tricks on the ball, he was capable of hitting the target too. He first played for Scotland in a 1–1 draw against England at Hampden during March 1886 but headed south over the border for the North East that summer.

The exact circumstances of his arrival in Newcastle are not recorded but, maybe being a Clyde shipyard plater by trade (and still an amateur north of the border), he was on Tyneside for a period connected to the shipbuilding industry and perhaps he was tied up with a job by West End officials. Aitken made his first appearance for the West Enders in

Fact Box

EAST END & WEST END: INTERNATIONAL PLAYERS.

Ralph Aitken:	(West End 1886–87); first capped, Scotland, 1886 (2 app).
Walter Arnott:	(West End 1887–88); first capped, Scotland, 1883 (14 app).
Dan Doyle:	(East End 1888–89); first capped, Scotland, 1892 (8 app).
Bob Kelso:	(West End 1888–89); first capped, Scotland, 1885 (7 app).
James Hannah:	(West End 1888–89); first capped, Scotland, 1889 (1 app).
Tom McInnes:	(East End 1889–90, 90–91); first capped, Scotland, 1889 (1 app).
Bob Calderwood:	(West End 1890–91); first capped, Scotland, 1885 (3 app).
James Gillespie:	(West End 1890–91); first capped, Scotland, 1898 (1 app).

the opening game of the new 1886–87 season in the unlikely setting of Howarth Terrace in Morpeth in front of a few hundred locals. That was a far cry from the 10,000-plus crowd at the England versus Scotland clash.

Ralph clearly stood out as a class-act as West End recorded a 4–1 victory over Morpeth Harriers, apparently their first home defeat for two years. One report credits him with all four goals but others name Angus and Tiffin as scoring two of them. Nevertheless, it was noted that 'the little international' was influential throughout the match and carried 'the ball forward, in a way that called for the highest praise'. His home debut in a local derby with East End attracted a big crowd – it was the first match at West End's new ground of St James' Park. Aitken impressed again by scoring twice in a 3–2 victory, his opener coming after a 'capital dribble'.

The Scot continued to be a threat in attack for West End, scoring frequently. He was a sturdy little forward and the crowd warmed to his wizardry; although he moved back to Dumbarton during January 1887 after only four months on Tyneside. Aitken was soon capped again by his country and scored in a 10–2 rout of Ireland in Belfast. He was also prominent in Dumbarton's run to the Scottish Cup Final where Ralph scored in the 2–1 defeat by Hibs. He was back on Tyneside, though, albeit briefly, when he rejoined West End in 1889–90.

His success in generating interest prompted West End and East End, as well as Sunderland, to engage more top Scottish players in the following seasons. On Wearside, established internationals played for the club such as John Auld, William Dickson and Ted Doig, as well as Donald Gow and James Hannah. Several other Scots went on to win caps after making an impression at Sunderland; Hugh Wilson being one outstanding player. And there were others not to earn a cap but were at the top of the game nevertheless, notably Johnny Campbell, Jimmy Millar and John Harvie. Some of these stars also later played on Tyneside.

On Teesside the same pattern developed, although on a lesser scale. Middlesbrough fielded David Black, capped with Hurlford, while neighbours South Bank paraded James Hutton who had arrived after making a name with St Bernard's. Boro also fielded Irish international full-back Bob Crone and Bob Roberts of Wales.

Back on Tyneside, both East End and West End's committee men brought more distinguished figures south. Two of Scotland's most famous names of the years before the turn of the century, Watty Arnott and Dan Doyle, also had brief stays in Newcastle at this time; although it appears neither had the intension of taking root with either Tyneside club, just making the odd guest appearance, and in Doyle's case even using an alias. Both were formidable players at full-back.

Arnott was an established Queen's Park international when he turned out for West End during December 1887 and appeared at the time for a string of clubs. Capped 14 times for the Scots between 1883 and 1893, few players north of the border were as well known. Sporting an imposing moustache, Watty was only really passing through Newcastle on business when he appeared against Shankhouse – even leaving 20 minutes into the second half to catch a train home. Nevertheless, he did wear West End's red-and-black shirt, and that was a coup for the St James' Park club.

Watty Arnott and Dan Doyle, two notable Scots who pulled on the colours of West End and East End for a brief period.

Dan Doyle was later to be recognised in the 1890s as one of the finest defenders of the era. He won many an honour at Everton and Celtic as well as eight Scotland caps, even being named skipper of his country on occasion. Doyle used a pseudonym when in Heaton with East End – thought to be either McCrindle or McCrinnon – during the later months of 1888, probably in an attempt to avoid sanction by the Scottish Football Association for playing with professional clubs in England. He apparently also had a brief stay with Sunderland.

Just as well known as Arnott and Doyle was Bob Kelso, who spent a much longer period on Tyneside, appearing with distinction for West End. A star player with Renton at half-back and later full-back, he possessed a gritty style. Indeed, Bob was once nicknamed the 'Renton Ruffian' due to his formidable battling qualities on the field. Twice winning the Scottish Cup,

Bob Kelso was another celebrated Scottish international; he was a popular character with West End.

Kelso arrived on Tyneside during the summer of 1888 as an established star, having been capped for the first time three years earlier.

Bob featured in most West End fixtures during the 1888–89 campaign before heading for Preston then Everton, where he had a noted spell for both clubs – winning FA Cup and Football League title medals. Kelso had many admirers in Newcastle, and before he left for Lancashire he was given a testimonial and a memento of his stay at St James' Park – a fine chromograph watch and a silver walking stick. He was also a durable footballer of sure judgement, being recalled by Scotland as captain in 1898, some 13 years after his first appearance for his country.

James Hannah won title medals with Sunderland as part of the 'Team of all the Talents', but he also appeared for West End.

In the same season in which Kelso became a firm favourite of one half of the Newcastle crowd, another admirable Scottish talent, James Hannah, also made a fleeting appearance for West End – and very soon after picked up an international cap. A potent winger on either flank, Hannah was on Tyneside for the beginning of December 1888 and joined Kelso in the West End side. He was once described as a 'veritable box of tricks', but by the end of the season he was back with Third Lanark, winning a Scottish Cup medal and playing for his country against the Welsh at Wrexham. Known as 'Blood' Hannah, he was soon to return to the region when he joined Sunderland Albion in 1890, moving on to Sunderland the following year where he became an important member of the 'Team of all the Talents'.

There were a number of other Scots who did well on Tyneside who never got to wear their country's blue jersey, while there were also many who came and went quickly.

Alex Brady, who appeared up front for West End.

Several also went on to appear for Newcastle United in senior action during the 1890s. East End fielded the likes of Joe McKane, Jock Smith, Bobby Creilly and James Collins, as well as Jimmy Millar, Michael Mulvey and Jock Sorley. There was Joe Wallace and Tom Crate too. West End boasted James Angus, Bob McDermid, James Raylstone and Harry Jeffrey, the latter trio all playing for the East Enders too. Goalkeeper Billy Jardine was also prominent. It was almost a gathering of the clans in Newcastle at this time.

Alex Brady was yet another Scottish footballer who developed into a fine player. An inside-forward from Cathcart in Glasgow and a caulker in the Clyde shipyards – maybe again, the reason why he spent time on Tyneside – Brady was later in his career to win a haul of medals at Celtic, Everton and Sheffield Wednesday. He first appeared for West End in January 1888 and many judges of the time considered that he should have earned a place in the Scottish team, one of the best uncapped forwards around like Johnny Campbell.

While East End chose a somewhat different player acquisition path, mainly finding the less high-profile footballers, they did toy with some leading names of the game. Tom McInnes was another potent winger or inside-forward like Aitken before him. Indeed, he was a rival for the Scotland shirt during his time at Cowlairs. Selected by his country in March 1889 against Ireland, a 7–0 victory at Ibrox in which he scored twice, McInnes had built up a glowing reputation with the Glasgow club.

Tom McInnes became a danger-man in attack for East End. He had played for Scotland.

Tom joined East End for the New Year's Day challenge match with London Casuals in 1890 and goes down in Newcastle United's history as the first player to score a FA Cup hat-trick for the club – when East End defeated Shankhouse the following season in November 1890. At Chillingham Road he rattled in three goals in a 5–0 triumph. His consistently good performances for the East Enders prompted rivals West End to attempt to poach him at the start of the 1891–92 campaign. It was announced that he had signed for them, but he decided to return north instead, joining Clyde; although McInnes did return to appear as a guest for West End in a testimonial match later in the season. Afterwards he headed back to England, signing for Nottingham Forest where he won an FA Cup-winners' medal in 1898 and scored over 50 goals for the Reds.

Jimmy Gillespie turned out for West End, then for both Sunderland and Sunderland Albion.

While East End had McInnes during seasons 1889–90 and 1890–91, their rivals at St James' Park boasted the highly regarded Bob Calderwood. He was capped three times by Scotland in March 1885 when with the Cartvale club of Busby, near Glasgow. In addition,

Sunderland's James Gillespie joined him at Gallowgate and, although he had not yet reached international recognition, the Glaswegian was a highly promising player and would eventually wear his country's blue.

Calderwood made a name for himself with pioneering Scottish clubs Cartvale and Cowlairs. He joined West End for the start of the 1890–91 programme after a spell on Merseyside with Bootle – this after being found guilty of professionalism, being paid north of the border and barred from the game. A winger or centre-forward most of the time, Bob was appointed West End captain and was an experienced footballer. He had been on the field in each of the Home International Championship matches of 1884–85 as the Scots crushed Ireland 8–2, then matched England in a 1–1 draw at the Kennington Oval. Scotland then fired in eight goals for the second time in only nine days when they hammered Wales 8–1 at Wrexham. Bob scored in both of the high-scoring games.

A respected player in Newcastle, Bob was always influential for West End and able to get his name on the scorers' list. It is recorded that when Calderwood was in the region he resided on Wellington Street in Westgate, near to St James' Park, with his wife and four children.

Jimmy Gillespie headed over the border from Morton at the beginning of the 1890–91 season when he joined Sunderland. Described as a wily, goalscoring winger who was versatile enough to feature in any forward position, he pulled on West End's colours from January to March 1891 before returning to Wearside to join the Albion club. He rejoined Sunderland following Albion's demise and earned Football League Championship medals in 1893 and 1895. He returned to Scotland in 1897, joining Third Lanark, and was capped against Wales a year later. Jimmy netted a wonderful hat-trick on his debut for his country, yet never gained a call-up again!

Tyneside's footballing public had revelled in seeing the best clubs and finest players on their own patch. It had aroused further passion for the game of football, and with it the number of supporters attending matches had increased. While the contemporary press only contained estimates of attendances and in many cases stated varying figures for crowds, an assessment over the pioneer years shows a steady growth in the public's support for the sport. Indeed, during 1888 the Newcastle *Daily Chronicle's* correspondent *Captain* wrote: 'The pastime of football in this district has risen in popularity by leaps and bounds till at the present time it is indulged in by almost every youth sound in wind and limb.'

Attendances had increased steadily on Tyneside during the 1880s from around 500 – and often much less – for ordinary challenge matches between local clubs, to the occasional big-match fixture which pushed the gate to 1,000 and over. The best crowd seen at the start of the decade was the 1,300 attendance for the landmark contest with the Scotch-Canadians combination in 1880. Just over 10 years later, in the 1891–92 season, record attendances were set for Chillingham Road, with 5,803 paying at the gate, and at St James' Park where approximately 8,000 watched the Tyneside derby between West End and East End in the FA Cup.

By the 1890–91 season East End and West End could command gates of between 2,000 and 3,000 on a regular basis, with a crowd of 5,000 and more for attractive fixtures. By

ATTENDANCE PROGRESSION ON TYNESIDE 1878–93

(based on contemporary newspaper report estimates)

	'Ordinary' Fixtures	'Big-match' Fixtures
1878–80:	200–300	1,000–1,500
1880–82:	200–300	1,000–1,500
1882–84:	200–300	1,000–1,500
1884–86:	200–300	2,000–4,000
1886–88:	500–1,000	3,000–6,000
1888–90:	1,000–2,000	4,000–7,000
1890–92:	2,000–3,000	5,000–8,000
1893–94*:	3,000–4,000	7,000–10,000

(*based on Newcastle United's first Football League season)

the time East End became Newcastle United and joined the Football League for the 1893–94 season, their League average at St James' Park was around 4,000 with bumper crowds of 10,000 for the League match against Crewe and in the FA Cup with Bolton Wanderers.

On Wearside, Sunderland's – and for a short period, also Sunderland Albion's – advanced development saw larger gates. Almost 10,000 attended the visit of a Canadian touring side in 1888 while anything between 14,000 and 18,000 watched the first local Wearside derby between the two clubs later in the same year. Sunderland's debut in the Football League saw an average of just over 6,000 for games at the Newcastle Road ground, and 21,000 packed into the arena for the FA Cup meeting with Everton that season, by far the largest crowd ever to be recorded in the North East up to then.

As East End developed into Newcastle United, and the city became unified instead of divided in terms of football, attendances at St James' Park quickly caught up their Wearside rivals. The two North East giants over the coming century were to be at the forefront of sustainable support, the Black and Whites creating England's record home crowd average for a single season of over 56,000 in 1947–48, only subsequently beaten by Manchester United and, more recently, by Arsenal.

With support and interest on the up, both West End and East End wanted to join Sunderland in football's elite. While both clubs still had a step to take to match the very best, they were ready to move forward. Turning professional and becoming full-blown business ventures were major steps towards that goal; however, before Tyneside joined the party, that Darwinian theory of survival of the fittest had to be played out.

Chapter 10

UNITING A CITY

'The names of Newcastle, Newcastle City, and Newcastle United were proposed...on the vote being taken, there was a large majority in favour of Newcastle United.'
Daily Journal, 1892

With the appearance in the North East of so many of England's top (and now largely professional) clubs, the two principal teams on Tyneside, East End and West End, began to focus on joining the growing array of football organisations to turn professional and become limited companies. In the years between 1888 and 1895 there was a surge in the game's evolution.

The Football League and FA Cup competitions were highly praised and now fully established. County associations had a grip on the local scene across the regions. Many clubs initially became fully professional and then rapidly developed into business ventures complete with limited company status, including capital investments, shareholders, boards of directors as well as yearly profit and loss accounts and balance sheets. Both East End and West End were to be at the forefront of the game's corporate experiment.

The first of the present-day football clubs in England to try the corporate route in the game was Small Heath (now Birmingham City). In 1888 they incorporated themselves as a limited company, Small Heath Football Club Ltd. It took a few years for the majority of clubs to follow their lead but, in 1890, four clubs took the gamble: Notts County, Grimsby Town and both East End and West End. Several other clubs soon followed in the coming years, including Everton, Liverpool, Preston North End, Bolton Wanderers and West Bromwich Albion. Middlesbrough were another who did so, although Sunderland did not become a limited company until 1906.

On Tyneside, East End were the first to take the plunge. Two meetings were held at Dr Rutherford's Infant School on Shields Road in Byker during January 1890 to make the transformation. Club secretary Charles Tinlin suggested forming a company by issuing 2,000 shares at 10s 0d (50p) each, capital of £1,000. It was noted the cost would 'suit the working classes who are the chief supporters of the institution'. He proposed that extensive changes were needed within the club. Some £150 would have to be raised to put their ground in order and a further £100 to establish a really good team! It was further proposed that a board of management should be appointed, consisting of between eight and 12 members holding at least five shares each.

Within a month, on 17 February, a public meeting was convened at the Leighton Schoolrooms on Heaton Road in a bid to launch the share issue, and the Newcastle East End Football Company Limited formally came into being. Councillor James Birkett chaired the meeting and about 50 shares were sold in the first instance, and by the end of the season the total had risen to 83. There was still a long way to go and, by May, the company was able to hold its first Annual General Meeting when Adam Gilchrist was elected chairman.

Among those first shareholders were, not surprisingly, prominent East Enders. Logged in the surviving original East End share-ledger during that February were Alexander Henry White, James Birkett and John Steel. There was also James Peel as well as John Cameron and family. Joe Bell with Alex Turnbull, whose wider relatives held the largest holding, soon followed. He ran an inn on Chillingham Road near the club's ground. Other notable shareholders were pioneers John Armstrong, ex-Rangers player Walter Dix – one of the quickest to purchase a holding – Matt Hiscock, Walter Golding and John Dixon. David Crawford, another former Rangers man, committed cash as did recent players Peter O'Brien and William Wilson.

East End's first director list, and in essence Newcastle United's first board, was led by Gilchrist and consisted of: Birkett, Peel, White, Hiscock, Dixon, Steel and Armstrong along with William Hudson, Thomas Liddle, William Henry, William Richardson and Bill

One of the early share certificates of Newcastle United FC. William Hudson was a clerk from Byker and purchased five shares in the East End club during March 1890.

An extract from the original East End share-ledger showing Alec White's entry in February 1890; one of the earliest to commit to shares. *(Newcastle United FC archive)*

Woodman. The qualification to become a director was that 'he shall be a shareholder to the amount of £2 10s at least'. Their occupations varied from that of a clerk to a pattern-maker and ironfounder. All resided in the Byker and Heaton area.

Not wanting to be left behind, West End quickly followed suit, and accordingly a meeting at the Bath Lane Hall during February 1890 took place. Then in July at the Clock Restaurant on Clayton Street, the West End Football & Athletic Co Ltd was similarly formed. It was decided to issue 2,000 shares at £1 each to raise capital; although it would be a few months before the wheels would be fully in motion.

William Nesham was elected chairman, with 12 directors voted into office to promote the club. With Nesham at the helm the club's inaugural board was again a lengthy one: G.T. Graham, M. Aynsley, J.J. Eddy, W. Johnson, M. Carverhill, D. MacIntosh, R.A. Scott, J. Robinson, H. Hudson, John Black and Councillor Weidner. It was soon to become a battle for survival between Tyneside's 'big two' clubs.

By the time the new corporate structures had been finalised, East End and West End had both tasted their first season of League football in 1889–90, albeit in the Northern League. There were, of course, three Tyneside teams in the competition for its inaugural season, East End and West End being joined by Elswick Rangers. As has been already related, Rangers found the League too difficult and dropped out after one season (when they finished bottom of the table).

Both of Newcastle's major clubs had strengthened their teams with new signings in anticipation of Northern League action. East End welcomed two players called John Miller, one from Kilmarnock and one from Glasgow. This brought great confusion as the club already had James Miller playing in their first team. It was inevitable that the sporting press would produce a mix-up in reports. The problem was partially overcome by referring to the players as J(ames) Miller(1), J. Miller(2) and J. Miller(3). Some reporters also spelt their names differently, calling them Miller or Millar. There was also equal puzzlement at times on the field identifying which Miller was actually on the pitch! The most prominent recruit for the start of the season, however, was former Everton player Robert Watson, but others were brought on board once the season began.

West End countered by also recruiting new players, the most prominent of which were Alex Brady, formerly of Sunderland and Burnley, and James Angus, a previous West End favourite who had been with Everton.

Ground improvements took place at both clubs. East End erected 'a large and comfortable stand' at Chillingham Road, and the St James' Park side would have done likewise, but problems over the lease of the ground prevented them from doing so. Nevertheless, as 30 gentlemen had donated £5 each to improve the club, West End erected a press box on the Leazes Terrace side of the ground and placed footboards around the pitch to keep the spectators' feet dry.

The Northern League began on Saturday 7 September 1889, and East End played one of the very first games. There were 10 clubs in the competition, but not all of them played at the same time. Indeed, on the first day there were only three fixtures.

A decent crowd, variously reported as between 1,500 and 3,000, turned up at Chillingham Road to watch what was, effectively, Newcastle United's first-ever League match. However, they had to wait 45 minutes for the game to start because Darlington arrived late. They were rewarded with a victory, John Miller(3) scoring the first goal after 25 minutes play with John Miller – Miller(2) – adding a second soon afterwards. Tommy Hutchinson netted a consolation goal for the visitors before half-time, but that ended the scoring and East End collected their first League points. The teams for this historic match lined up as follows:

East End: Henderson, Miller(1), Sawers, Creilly, McCurdie, Broughton, Collins, Watson, Miller(2), Mulvey, Miller(3).

V

Darlington: Auld, Withington, Davison, McCrimmond, Waites, Soulsby, Cleghorn, Carling, Hutchinson, Brown, Devey.

West End began their Northern League campaign a week later when East End visited St James' Park. The game was a big attraction with between 4,000 and 5,000 cramming into the Gallowgate enclosure. Meetings between these rivals in the past had been marred by over-exuberant, rough play. This game went one step further when violence erupted on the field as both sides tried to kick their opponents into submission. The first players to be sent off for either side in a competitive game were dismissed by referee Fred Hardisty when James Miller, the East End captain, and West End's John Barker were given their marching orders following a 'scuffle'. Dismissing players was a rare occurrence in the days when it was legal for half-a-dozen players to charge a goalkeeper over the goalline. West End won the match 2–0, thanks to first-half goals by J. McDonald and T. McKay.

The teams for this somewhat notorious first League derby were as follows:

West End: Whitton, Jeffrey, Swinburne, Raylstone, Kirkham, McKay (G.), Barker, Brady, McColl, McDonald, McKay (T.).

V

East End: Henderson, Miller(1), Sawers, Creilly, McCurdie, Broughton, Collins, Watson, Miller(2), Mulvey, Miller(3).

Both East End and West End recorded comfortable League wins away from home in their next fixtures, the former thrashing Elswick Rangers 5–0 at Mill Lane while the West Enders did almost as well, winning 4–1 at South Bank.

Then, to end off the month, they both chalked up comfortable home victories a week later. Middlesbrough visited Chillingham Road and left suitably chastised 3–1, while Darlington St Augustine's provided the opposition at St James' Park where the crowd witnessed an exciting game with West End battling back from a two goal deficit to win 3–2. With the benefit of hindsight, this was an excellent result as St Augustine's went on to lift the Northern League title.

An insight into the cost of football can be gained with those last games. West End charged 6d (2½p) for admission plus another 3d (1p) for entry into the special reserve area. Ladies were admitted free. East End reduced their prices for the Middlesbrough contest, charging 3d (1p) for admission to the ground plus (like West End) a further 3d (1p) for entry to the reserved enclosure. However, it cost 6d (2½p) to go into the new stand.

Both clubs were well placed at the end of September with East End lying third, having picked up six points from their opening four fixtures. They were behind second placed West End on goal average, however, with the St James' Park club able to boast a 100 per cent record so far.

There was a break from Northern League football early in October, with both clubs embarking on the FA Cup trail. In the first qualifying round, East End inflicted the first defeat of the season on the Northern Association Cup holders, Shankhouse Black Watch, winning 4–0, and West End romped home 9–1 against Teesside minnows Port Clarence; both J. McDonald and T. McKay scored hat-tricks in that game.

Back in the Northern League, East End soon lost their unbeaten home record when they succumbed to St Augustine's 2–1. But West End continued on their peerless way by playing an 'away' fixture against Birtley at St James' Park and winning comfortably 3–1. They were by now (in mid-October) top of the League, one point ahead of Darlington and two in front of Stockton, East End and St Augustine's.

The repercussions of the West End versus East End derby flare-up were now felt as both John Barker and James Miller were suspended. James Collins took over East End's captaincy as his side, in an attempt to strengthen their team, signed Matthew Scott, the Elswick Rangers and Northumberland goalkeeper. John Miller(3) left the club – which eased some of the confusion – while other new recruits came in – Lytleton Wood from Science & Art and Scots McLaughlin and Calder, the latter a former Sunderland reserve player from Albion Rovers.

Matt Scott made his debut for his new club in the FA Cup second qualifying round game at St Augustine's Chestnut Grove pitch, but he could not prevent East End from bowing out of the competition, although they were apparently very unlucky. Turning around with a 2–0 half-time deficit, they applied sustained pressure on the home defence but only had one goal to show for their efforts, Gibbon striking. Reportedly, Scott only touched the ball once during the entire second half. West End had better luck, making progress by winning 2–1 in a clash at Birtley.

West End's unblemished record in the Northern League came to an end at the beginning of November when they dropped a point to Auckland Town at St James' Park; however, they still remained two points clear at the top of the League. On the other side of the city, though, all was not well at Chillingham Road where rival factions had emerged within the East End camp. There was even talk of a break-away club being set up, as had happened at Sunderland. Even a similar name was proposed – East End Albion. In the end, however, the schism was healed.

East End lost narrowly 1–0 away to Darlington St Augustine's, in a game that received the plaudits of the spectators who were delighted with the splendid play of both sides. Defeat, however, left East End down in fifth position, well adrift of their arch rivals across the city who consolidated the leadership of the Northern League with an excellent single-goal victory at unbeaten Stockton. The game attracted a very healthy crowd of 7,000 in Cleveland, with lucrative gate receipts of £77.

The East Enders were also more than satisfied with gate receipts of over £60 from the visit of Sunderland to Chillingham Road for a friendly match. The Wearsiders had now become one of the best teams in the country and won easily 4–0. Interestingly, East End Swifts had a fixture arranged against Sunderland Reserves on the same day, but only seven of the East End side turned up on Wearside, the rest preferring to watch the first team play. Sunderland had to refund entrance fees to the 1,500 spectators who had gathered to see the reserve match.

But East End had more important things to worry about. Their landlords, the North Eastern Railway Company, notified them that their Heaton ground would be required for development and gave them notice to quit the premises within three months. By February 1890 they would need to find a new HQ.

West End, safely ensconced in St James' Park, had no such worries. They were more concerned with progressing in the FA Cup. They did so in the third qualifying round at the expense of South Bank but in rather unusual circumstances. Amazingly only nine West End men turned up in time for the kick-off at St James' Park, and the visitors raced into a two-goal lead before the home side reached a full complement. The leeway was soon made up, and a comfortable 5–2 win ensued, which included a hat-trick by Tom Nicholson. They won again in the next tie, 1–0 at Stockton, Nicholson once more on target, to become the first of the Tyne rivals to reach the FA Cup proper.

Back in the Northern League, East End picked up two points by winning 2–1 at Birtley but ended the game with 10 men as William Coldwell was carried off seriously injured. West End also gained two points when they romped home 8–1 against Elswick Rangers at St James' Park in a rough match which characterised meetings between the two clubs.

West End around 1890, showing their hooped red-and-black shirts and badge, 'WEFC'. Unfortunately the players are not named.

East End had not started their first League season well and were now in the doldrums. A goalless draw at home to Elswick Rangers during mid-December left them languishing in mid-table while West End won 4–2 at Bishop Auckland and were clear at the top of the table. There was no doubt which club was the premier team in Newcastle now.

East End tried to bridge the gap when they visited Bishop Auckland in their next fixture. Alec White had temporarily returned to the team to help them out and the Heaton side returned to Tyneside with a 2–2 draw but were unfortunate not to pick up both points. They had two goals disallowed and were so incensed at one of the decisions that they walked off the field in protest but were persuaded to return and complete the game.

Despite the introduction of competitive League football, the Christmas Day friendly at St James' Park between West End and East End was eagerly anticipated within the city. West End were obviously favourites, although East End had enlisted the services of Willie Thompson, the Shankhouse forward, to strengthen their side. He was soon to establish himself and become an integral part of the club as it developed into Newcastle United.

Both teams were reminded that this was only a friendly and were instructed not to be too rough, dirty play having spoiled earlier encounters. Whoever gave the advice may as well have been talking to the proverbial brick wall as, once again, both sides proceeded to produce a feisty and tempestuous contest. Within 15 minutes, the dark blues of East End were reduced to 10 men when Raylstone kicked the visitors' centre-half, McLaughlin, in the ribs and forced him to withdraw. West End won comfortably 3–0, each player earning himself a £1 bonus for beating their arch-rivals. They had received a similar bonus payment for taking care of Stockton in the FA Cup. The overall wages for Northern League games paled in comparison – 10s 0d (50p) for a win or a draw and 7s 6d (37½p) for a defeat.

On the last Saturday of the year, East End travelled to Stockton and were once again cursed with ill luck when their left-half, Broughton, was carried off injured after only a quarter of an hour's play. The home team were also reduced to 10 men early in the second half but by this time they were 3–0 ahead and that remained the final score. On the same day West End defeated Elswick Rangers 2–0 at Mill Lane to consolidate their place as leaders.

East End lay in fifth position, seven points adrift. West End had a hope of becoming the very first Northern League champions, and during the remainder of the programme they were to contest the title to the very end with Stockton and St Augustine's – and, for a time, a resurgent East End.

By the turn of the year, though, serious doubt had arisen about the financial viability and effectiveness of the Northern League. Quite a few of the participating clubs felt that the League fixtures were preventing them from meeting more attractive clubs from other parts of the country and there was a consensus of opinion that the League could fold at the end of the season. Thankfully it did not, and local competitive League action was allowed to develop from its infancy.

Meanwhile the Heaton club, under a threat of having their ground lease terminated, had been looking for a new venue. East End believed that they had found it when they identified five acres of land not far from their Chillingham Road home close to the Byker Tramcar Terminus in Millers Lonning near the top of the Fosse Way. They expressed their hope to enclose the ground and move there during early February. In the event, the railway company decided not to develop their land immediately, so the relocation did not take place. Another more significant move would soon materialise, however.

East End, with new signing Tom McInnes – a Scottish international – in the ranks, completed their first Northern League double in January when they defeated Darlington 2–1 at Feethams. On the same day West End lost their unbeaten League record when Middlesbrough visited St James' Park and also won 2–1.

A week later Grimsby Town of the Football Alliance arrived on Tyneside to play West End in the first round of the FA Cup proper. In pouring rain, 3,000 spectators saw the home team dominate the game only for questionable shooting in front of goal to let them down. The decisive goal for Grimsby in their eventual 2–1 victory was hotly disputed. Most contemporary reports agree that Scotland-capped David Black, the scorer, was offside but nevertheless his goal was allowed and West End were eliminated.

On the same day, Auckland Town were East End's Northern League opponents at Chillingham Road. Alec White was playing quite regularly for the Heaton club at that point, and the veteran scored the first goal for his team as well as having another effort disallowed for offside in a match that ended 2–2. McLaughlin scored East End's other goal.

The next visitors in League action at Chillingham Road were none other than West End. Bobby Creilly opened the scoring for the East Enders after McLaughlin had seen an earlier effort disallowed for hands. Creilly had steadily emerged as a quality performer, and a number of teams had tried to entice him away from Heaton, but he had remained loyal to the club. As the game went on, West End gradually gained control, and it came as no surprise when Bill Swinburne levelled the scores before half-time. But it was East End who exerted pressure in the second half, and eventually McLaughlin managed to score the winner.

The East End management were so delighted in the derby victory that they gave their players a sovereign each as a bonus. West End, however, were subjected to intense criticism in the press. They had been undefeated in the Northern League and FA Cup up to the turn of the year but had now lost five consecutive games, including friendlies. It was noted that there were 13 members on the team selection committee and that nine different team line ups were proposed for the local derby. That was hardly a way to lift the Northern League title.

Two visits to Teesside followed for East End during early February. The first was a friendly fixture against Ironopolis, a game which saw East End, naming no fewer than eight Scots in their team, play the first 20 minutes with only 10 men but still win 2–1.

Remarkably, a week later, the Heaton club started the Northern League game at Middlesbrough's Linthorpe Road with only 10 men on the field again. Comically, two of the travelling party noticed the shortage and both changed independently, eager to get on the pitch. They both went on separately, and for a few minutes East End had 12 players on the field before someone noticed that they now had too many! Muir retired, leaving the teams on equal terms, but Middlesbrough went on to win comfortably, 6–2.

Meanwhile, matters were slowly improving for West End, although this recovery came after a series of controversial incidents. The Gallowgate club suspended their belligerent centre-half James Raylstone following a fracas with a Northumberland FA official, and he missed a friendly fixture at home to Gainsborough Trinity, which West End won 4–2. But this game was to have serious repercussions with an FA Commission of Inquiry

EAST-WEST UNION I

September 1890:	Northern League commences, first games for East & West End.
January 1890:	Proposal that East End becomes a limited company.
February 1890:	East End share issue launched.
February 1890:	West End similarly decide to become a limited company.
April 1890:	West End win Northumberland Challenge Cup v Rendel (5–0 replay).
April 1890:	East End win Tyne Charity Shield v Elswick Rangers (6–2).
June 1890:	West End renew lease on St James' Park (14 years).
June 1891:	West End fold but are reformed.

Fact Box

investigating alleged malpractice involving certain Trinity players and one of the umpires. The Commission ruled that they had interfered with the duties of the referee. The umpire, W. Croft, was suspended for the rest of the season while two of the players, Petrie and Brown, were suspended for 14 days.

Apart from the Northern League and FA Cup tournaments, both of Newcastle's major clubs had Northumberland Challenge Cup games to play, although they were now exempt from the early rounds. In the semi-finals East End were drawn against Rendel, the amateur side who had not been considered good enough to join the Northern League. The Heaton club were forced to field a weak team as some of their normal first-choice players were ineligible to play in the local tournament. Nevertheless, it came as a shock when, in pouring rain, they were held to a 1–1 draw at Chillingham Road. West End, however, comfortably defeated Elswick Rangers 3–1 in the other semi-final.

East End continued to pick up League points by virtue of home wins over South Bank (3–0) and Birtley (3–1) but suffered a shock when Rendel knocked them out of the Northumberland Challenge Cup in the replayed semi-final. The 4–2 result was greeted with disbelief when it filtered through from Benwell to Heaton and Byker. Supporters expressed their anger at the team, but fortunately their side soon had the chance to redeem themselves, with League leaders Stockton being the next visitors to Chillingham Road. A 2–1 victory quickly made supporters forget the shock Cup exit. Indeed, East End's Northern League form had improved noticeably from the opening months of the new competition.

Meanwhile, West End had collected both points from a home fixture against Birtley, although by the only goal of the match, and they then gained a creditable draw, 1–1 away to Middlesbrough. These latest results meant that West End were still on course with a very good chance of lifting the inaugural Northern League title. They were in second place, only one point behind Stockton and one ahead of East End who were now third. But West End still had four games to play, while both Stockton and East End only had one. No one was taking much notice of St Augustine's, who were back in fifth place, four points behind West End but with a game in hand.

There was dissension in the West End camp, however, and this did little to help their title chances. Their players were far from happy because they were now being paid less than their rivals across the city in Heaton. Both teams had similar basic wages, but the Heaton players received an extra shilling (5p) for every goal scored, and thereafter slight, but important, differences in the wage structures of East End and West End developed.

The Final of the Northumberland Challenge Cup was staged in Jesmond at the end of March 1890 and a big crowd turned up to see if amateurs Rendel could pull off another shock victory. They nearly did so, leading West End 3–0 at half-time. But the second half saw a dramatic change in fortunes, and the St James' Park side were able to claw their way back into the game and force a replay, the game ending 3–3. In the rematch West End made no mistake, romping home 5–0.

A spate of friendly games were played over the Easter holidays. Some of the more important matches included a draw for East End away to Sunderland Albion and a victory for West End at home to Aston Villa. The most important game, however, was the

West-East local derby at St James' Park where both teams once again indulged in unnecessary violence in a goalless draw.

The Northern League Championship came to a conclusion at the beginning of May, although East End took little interest. They entertained Sheffield United in a friendly encounter at Chillingham Road and won 2–0, although the club had to fulfil their final League fixture away to South Bank on that same date. Such was the low esteem in which the Northern League was held that the Heaton club had no hesitation in fielding a reserve side on Teesside. They lost 3–1.

West End, with the League trophy virtually in their grasp, slipped up badly, losing two of their last three fixtures, both in south Durham: 4–1 at St Augustine's and 3–0 at Darlington. They even failed to field a full complement of players at Feethams, only playing with 10 men. The 6–2 success on Tyneside against South Bank between these defeats was of little consequence because dropping four points, coupled with a very good run-in by St Augustine's who won four of their last five games, saw the Darlington club win the title from West End on goal average.

West End's failure did not confine itself to the League. Fielding six guests, five from Sunderland Albion and one from Elswick Rangers, they lost 2–1 at home in a friendly to Everton. But their fall from grace was not restricted to games against renowned teams like the Merseysiders. They were also surprisingly knocked out of the Tyne Charity Shield after a 3–0 defeat by Elswick Rangers in a semi-final replay at Chillingham Road.

In contrast, East End went on to win the Charity Shield, defeating Rendel 6–0 in the semi-final and Elswick Rangers 6–2 in the Final. Both games were staged at St James' Park. The season had ended well for the Heaton club, and they believed that the following campaign would see them emerge as Newcastle's premier team. They were right, although neither club was to set the Tyne on fire.

With the first season of Northern League football completed, both East End and West End relied on a core of players. As far as the Heaton club was concerned, the first team was composed of Bobby Creilly, James Collins, Michael Mulvey, Alec McCurdie, James Miller and Matt Scott. James Miller – Miller(1) – was a solid full-back who hailed from Scotland, eventually appearing in Newcastle United's first Football League programme. James was, however, a touch temperamental and once refused to turn up for action. The club suspended him, and he never played senior football for Newcastle again, soon heading over the border.

At the time, football was still regarded as a team game, so too much stress was not placed on the identity of goalscorers. Indeed, various match reports differ in the names of the scorers and, on a few occasions, do not even bother to record them. For this season, however, it would appear that John Miller(3), Gibbon and Tom McInnes were joint top scorers with five goals apiece (Northern League and FA Cup only). If the Northumberland Challenge Cup and Tyne Charity Shield games are taken into consideration, McInnes emerges as clear top scorer with eight goals.

West End similarly relied on key players for the season with Harry Jeffrey, Dave Whitton, James Raylstone, Bill Swinburne, Tom Nicholson and John Barker to the fore. Their top scorers for the campaign were Tom Nicholson with 13 goals and John

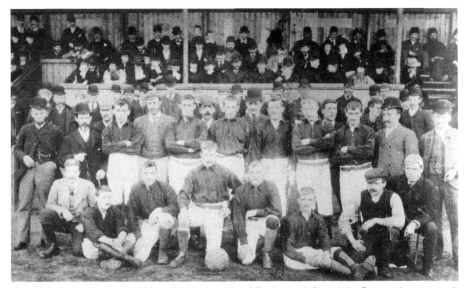

East End pictured in April 1892 at Chillingham Road. Back row, left to right: Forster (committee), Cameron (committee), Jeffrey (behind), Creilly, Hardisty (referee), Watson, Scott, Golding (behind with a bowler hat), Wilson, Miller, McKane, Bell (committee), Turnbull (committee). Front row: unknown, Barker, Crate, Thompson, Sorley, Wallace, Bayles (trainer), Peel.

McDonald with 10 (Northern League and FA Cup only) which increased to 14 and 12 respectively when the Northumberland Cup and Tyne Charity Shield were taken into consideration.

There was one final game worthy of note at the end of the 1889–90 season. It took place at St James' Park in late May and was an 'international' game of sorts; an England versus Scotland match staged to raise funds for the Northumberland FA to enable the association to form a Minor Cup competition. The unusual thing about the game was that both sides were made up from local players, one side Englishmen (although Forfarshire-born Alec White played for England) and the other Scotsmen. The contest gives an insight into the number of Scots who were plying their trade on Tyneside.

England: Scott (East End), McCoull (Ovingham), Jeffrey (West End), Wardropper (Rendel), White (East End), Carnelly (West End), Thompson (East End), Dixon (West End), Jefferson (Rendel), Wood (Science & Art), Barker (West End).
V
Scotland: Jardine (West End), Knox (Elswick Rangers), Miller(1) (East End), McIntyre (Elswick Rangers), Robertson (West End), McKane (East End), Stewart (Elswick Rangers), Collins (East End), McLucas (Elswick Rangers), McInnes (East End), Kennedy (West End).

Interestingly, the English team played in black-and-white vertical stripes, while the Scots turned out in all-white shirts lent to them by West End. England won 3–0 thanks to a Willie Thompson hat-trick.

The summer of 1890 saw development behind the scenes for East End to move grounds, and they entered into an agreement with Newcastle Corporation to take a lease for five acres of ground in Walker. The lease was to be back-dated to March and was to last five years at £12 10s 0d (£12 50p) a year. In the event the club, once again, did not move to these new premises, yet they were to find a new home as events on Tyneside unfolded.

Changes in the playing staff took place at both East End and West End. At Chillingham Road a number of new signings arrived, but few stayed long enough to make an impact. Notable exceptions were Will Young (who had turned out for the club a couple of seasons earlier) and W. Wilson, formerly of Vale of Leven, Greenock Morton and Renton but who had played for West End the previous season. The other important change was the appointment of Walter Heathcote Golding as secretary in place of John Steel who only had a short term in office. Golding was a solicitor's clerk and was named after a certain Colonel Heathcote who had saved the life of his father during the Crimean war.

West End, meanwhile, underwent a massive upheaval. Clearly unhappy at the decline in fortunes on the playing field in the closing stages of the previous season, the club management decided on radical changes in the playing staff. Only three first-team regulars from the previous term were retained: David Whitton, Harry Jeffrey and John Barker. Even then, Barker hardly played in the coming season. Strangely, in due course, all three of these players were eventually to join East End. Otherwise it was all change at St James' Park. Some of the more notable players went to other clubs. Raylstone joined Rotherham Town, Moore went to Grimsby, Nicholson to Heywood Central (Manchester) and some remained local. Swinburne, for instance, joined Newcastle Pelicans.

Virtually all of West End's replacement players in the summer of 1890 were Scots: Patrick Dowling (ex-Celtic and Third Lanark), D. Walker (Our Boys), J. Ross (Heart of Midlothian), Dugald McKellor (Dumbarton) and Robert Calderwood (Cowlairs). Calderwood was by far the best known of the new recruits, being a Scottish international. Other players signed as well, but few remained at Gallowgate long enough to make a telling impression.

Walter Golding became secretary of East End and guided the club through several decisive moments as the 1890s opened.

West End also made progress behind the scenes by renewing their lease on St James' Park from the Freemen of the City for another 14 years. The cost was £10 2s 6d (£10 12½p) an acre per annum with a total of 5.25 acres leased. Sadly the club was not to last anywhere near 14 years. But the lease was a valuable and attractive asset as St James' Park's location was clearly the most appealing in Newcastle.

There were also significant changes in the management at Gallowgate. Bill Tiffin, generally regarded as the founding father of West End, left to take over as honorary secretary of the Northumberland FA and was succeeded at club level by Robert Spittle.

There were also changes on the administrative front in the region. The Northern League was effectively disbanded and reformed. The four bottom clubs from the inaugural season, Elswick Rangers, Birtley, Auckland Town and South Bank, all resigned from the League; although new recruits were found in Middlesbrough Ironopolis and Sunderland Albion. With only eight teams in the League, this meant a significant reduction on the number of League games from 18 to 14.

Both of the Newcastle clubs began the new 1890–91 season by welcoming distinguished guests to Tyneside. West End turned out in their new strip of maroon-and-light-blue vertical stripes and played hosts to the reigning Football League Champions, Preston North End, and easily attracted the bigger crowd, with 4,000-plus turning up at St James' Park despite atrocious weather to see the illustrious Lancastrians beat the local side 4–0. The gate receipts of over £50 were suitable compensation to the West End management. Sheffield Wednesday were the visitors to Chillingham Road and a 1–1 draw took place, although the poor weather meant that the crowd of 1,500 was somewhat disappointing and East End lost money on the game. The Chillingham Road club also sported slightly different colours for this season, switching to Cambridge blue.

West End made the perfect start to their Northern League campaign by trouncing the reigning champions, Darlington St Augustine's, 5–1 at St James' Park. The Gallowgate club were not to know that their visitors were to be nowhere near the force that they had been the previous season and were to fail to win a single League game this term, finishing bottom of the table.

East End were to do even better with their first League contest a week later, thrashing Darlington 6–0 at Chillingham Road. The result was even more impressive than it sounds because the East Enders played over half of the game with only 10 men, Creilly having left the field injured when the score was 3–0.

But both of the Tyneside teams were soon brought back down to earth when they faced Northern League newcomers Middlesbrough Ironopolis. West End were the first to feel the Teessiders' scoring power when they crashed 5–1 at their Paradise ground. A week later, East End suffered their biggest League defeat so far when the Washers, as Ironopolis were nicknamed, leading only 1–0 with half-an-hour to go, slammed in another seven goals in the remaining 30 minutes. Wally McReddie scored four of them.

Yet only a week later East End, still smarting from their humiliation on Teesside, took revenge on their next opponents by chalking up their biggest League victory to date. West End were the hapless victims and visitors in a game that was surrounded by sickness and injuries. To begin with, McLaughlin, the East End centre-half, took ill just before the kick-off, and veteran stalwart Alec White stepped in to fill the breach again. As usual, the encounter between these arch-rivals was violent and rough in the extreme, and no quarter was either asked or given. Bobby Creilly gave the home team the lead before he was carried off injured. He resumed, and by half-time East End were leading 2–1. Unfortunately, during the interval, Paddy Dowling, West End's full-back, then became unwell and did not appear for the second half. East End piled on the pressure and scored another five goals without reply, winning the game 7–1. The ailments did not end with the final whistle because Kennedy, the visitors' centre-half, took ill in the horse-drawn brake taking the team back across the city. It was discovered that he had broken some of his ribs in the first half but had played on in pain.

West End began their quest for FA Cup honours at the first qualifying stage at the beginning of October when they were paired away to Elswick Rangers. Initially they were made to struggle and 20 minutes from the final whistle were trailing 2–1. But four goals in the final quarter of the match saw the West Enders progress. Elswick also visited Chillingham Road for a friendly match but were trounced 9–1, with Thompson scoring four. East End also had four goals disallowed, two of which looked valid. Rangers were also to concede 10 goals against East End in the Northumberland Challenge Cup later in the season. The results showed the widening gap in football status on Tyneside.

With so few Northern League games to play, there were a lot of friendly matches during the season. In fact, the only League game involving a Tyneside team during October was West End's home game against Middlesbrough. Both teams shared the points as a result of the 1–1 draw. The attendance of between 3,500 and 4,000 for this match was good and was significantly bigger than the 1,500 for West End's FA Cup second qualifying round game against Southwick at St James' Park. The 8–1 win for the home side shows that they were hardly stretched in that tie. The same could not be said about East End, who were drawn away to Bishop Auckland. They won 2–1, but the game was as close as the scoreline suggests.

The next round of the FA Cup was played in mid-November. At the time, the qualifying rounds of the tournament were arranged on a divisional basis to minimise travel. The third qualifying round was regarded as a divisional semi-final, and it paired East End with those renowned local Cup heroes of yesteryear, Shankhouse, while West End were paired with Sunderland Albion. Both of the Newcastle teams had home advantage.

The Heaton side had no problems at Chillingham Road. Former Shankhouse star Willie Thompson gave the East Enders an early lead and, before half-time, Tom McInnes had added two more. McInnes completed his hat-trick in the second half, and Thompson added another to give East End a comfortable 5–0 win.

At St James' Park, West End were not as fortunate as they crashed 3–0 to the Wearsiders, James Hannah scoring two of the goals. However, the home team submitted a protest on the grounds that one of Albion's players, Wardrop, was ineligible. But it was to no avail and they were eliminated.

Back in the League, East End welcomed Middlesbrough to Heaton and easily defeated the Teessiders 4–1, Thompson scoring a brace. Most press reports gave the result as 5–1, but an own-goal conceded by Boro was actually disallowed, although many reporters did not notice it. On the same day West End crashed 5–0 at Stockton. This was largely due to the fact that the Newcastle side played throughout with only 10 men, Dempsey having missed his train connection at Chester-le-Street.

The FA Cup Divisional Final qualifying round between East End and Sunderland Albion was played at Chillingham Road in front of a substantial crowd of 5,000 early during December. A very close and exciting game was played out. James Collins gave the home team the lead, but Boyd equalised before half-time. In the second period Hannah then put the visitors ahead, although Michael Mulvey managed to equalise with a deflection. The scores were still level at the end of 90 minutes, so extra-time was started, although it was evident that the game would not be completed due to darkness setting in. This proved to be the case and the match was eventually abandoned after an additional seven minutes' play.

There would have to be a replay. Perhaps strangely, it was to be staged once again at Chillingham Road. The attendance at the replay was variously reported as 3,000, 4,000 and 5,000. Whatever it was, they were entertained to another enthralling game. The Tynesiders exerted most of the pressure in the first half, but the best that they could muster for their superiority was an effort that came back off the crossbar. There was still no score with a quarter of an hour to go, but Albion managed to score twice in the closing stages through McLellan and Boyd to reach the last 32 in the competition.

The traditional Christmas Day friendly contest between West End and East End at St James' Park once again drew a huge crowd (for the era) of 6,000. Gate receipts were a very lucrative £115, but that was about all West End had to celebrate as they were comfortably beaten 5–0. The money was welcome, and the receipts set a record for a West End fixture at their ground. The only higher receipts had been for the historic Shankhouse Black Watch FA Cup encounter with Aston Villa in 1887.

West End's fortunes were on a downward spiral, and there was trouble brewing behind the scenes. The shareholders were not only dissatisfied with the performance of the team but also with the attitude of certain directors, who regularly failed to attend meetings. A special shareholders' meeting was convened to discuss the situation.

The comparative weakness of the West End team can be gauged by East End's next two results. They were quickly brought down to earth by two heavy League defeats – 7–0 at Sunderland Albion and 6–0 at Middlesbrough. One of the East End players, McLaughlin, failed to turn up for the latter fixture, prompting the club to declare that he would not play for them again.

East End signed two new Scottish players from Newmilns at the end of 1890 – Peter Watson, a full-back, and Joseph Wallace, a forward. They both made their East End debuts in the 4–1 win over Burnley on New Year's Eve. Wallace in particular proved a worthwhile acquisition from Ayrshire. He quickly became a firm favourite of the crowd and could operate in any forward position. Joe became one of the mainstays of Newcastle United's first Football League season and was top scorer with 15 goals during that historic opening campaign.

James Collins and Tom McInnes, two of East End's best known forwards, were approached by West End who asked them to sign for them. The Heaton outfit protested to the St James' Park club, complaining about their poaching. Nevertheless, East End eventually agreed to let them go, providing that reasonable transfer remuneration could be agreed. It was to be the end of the season before they moved.

Meanwhile East End signed another new recruit from Newmilns in Ayrshire, hot on the heels of Watson and Wallace. Jock Sorley, a forward, was eventually to become captain of East End and Newcastle United. He was another popular Scot. When on form, few defenders could cope with his darting runs and eye for goal.

West End blotted their copybook with the Northumberland FA when the Gallowgate club belatedly decided to withdraw from the Northumberland Challenge Cup after being drawn to play Rendel. Indeed, the decision to pull out of the competition was met with loud protests and criticism locally. The fact was, however, that both West End and East End had probably grown too big to participate in the county tournament – at least at first-team level. The East Enders were drawn away to Elswick Rangers, but on the day that the tie was due to be played they also had to fulfil a League fixture at Stockton. They had no hesitation in fielding a reserve team against Elswick. While the first team were being soundly beaten 5–0 on Teesside, a team primarily comprising amateurs of the old school played Rangers. Star players of East End's recent past once again turned out with the likes of Alec White, Tommy Hoban, Joseph Coupe, Charles Tinlin (who scored a hat-trick) and Andrew Muir taking to the field. Sadly, interest in the old competition was now waning, and a crowd of only 300 turned out to watch a one-sided and poor game, a 10–2 win for East End amply illustrating the superiority of the veterans.

On the last day in January the two major Tyneside clubs fared badly in the League against Teesside opposition. Ironopolis visited Chillingham Road and defeated East End 2–0 in a game that saw Sorley make his debut for his new club. West End, meanwhile, travelled to Middlesbrough and lost by a single goal to the current League leaders. The two Teesside clubs were to dominate the opening years of the Northern League Championship.

East End had to fulfil two fixtures on the same day during mid-January. The majority of the first team travelled to Middlesbrough to play in a charity match held for the widows and orphans of the crew of a ship, the SS *Bear*, which had sunk recently while a side that was virtually the reserve team met Shankhouse in the semi-final of the Northumberland Challenge Cup where, despite leading 2–1 at half-time, they were eliminated 5–2. The first team also lost the charity match.

The replayed League encounter between West End and East End, which had been postponed in January, was scheduled to take place at St James' Park in mid-March, but before the kick-off both teams protested at the state of the ground so the game was reclassified as another friendly game. East End won again, this time 2–0.

A week later, East End defeated St Augustine's 2–0 in the Northern League programme at Chillingham Road. This was followed by the usual spate of Easter friendly games. On Good Friday, East End again trounced West End 4–0 in Heaton, a game that saw a very good crowd of 4,000 pay £76 which, after expenses, meant that each club received £35.

It was to be easily the most lucrative fixture over Easter for either club. Other home games at Chillingham Road over the holiday weekend consisted of matches against Nottingham Forest (a splendid game which Forest won 2–1) and Derby County (when the home team were outclassed 5–0). Meanwhile, West End played hosts to London Caledonians (a 3–0 victory in front a meagre crowd of 400), Burnley (won 3–1) and the Corinthians. The latter drew 3,000 to St James' Park and an amazing game was played out with the amateurs in front 4–1 at half-time but eventually losing 8–4.

East End travelled to Feethams and lost their Northern League clash with Darlington, 4–1, at the beginning of April. On the same day, West End drew at home (2–2) to the eventual Northern League champions, Middlesbrough Ironopolis. This was a contentious day because Harry Jeffrey, normally right-back for West End, was chosen to play at right-half but refused to do so.

Both of the Tyneside clubs struggled in the League during that 1890–91 season, and Sunderland Albion must have been confident when they visited both grounds to fulfil League fixtures during mid-April. Their confidence was justified when they comfortably defeated West End at St James' Park 4–1, but when they visited Chillingham Road they received a bit of a surprise, going down to the only goal of the match, scored by Joe Wallace in the first half. An indication of the levels of support for the Newcastle clubs can be appreciated by the attendances at these games. The crowd at St James' Park was a mere 2,000, while at Chillingham Road it was 4,000.

The decline in West End's support was giving cause for concern, and the club were gradually falling into financial difficulties. East End were bearing up better, and their success against Albion saw them leap-frog West End in the League table, climbing to the dizzy heights of sixth (out of eight). St Augustine's were well adrift in bottom place. But East End were also encountering financial problems. It seemed as if the city could not support two clubs.

A draw against St Augustine's (2–2) in Darlington consolidated East End in sixth position, especially when West End lost 3–1 to Sunderland Albion at the Blue House Field. When the long-awaited final League fixture, the twice-postponed game between West End and East End at St James' Park, was played at the end of April, both teams were happy to see the end of the Northern League campaign with the resultant 2–2 draw. Their record in the competition left a lot to be desired, with both clubs finishing in the bottom three above St Augustine's.

The last three clubs had to apply for re-election to the League, an ignominious task for teams that had pretensions of greater things. Both East End and West End were successful but St Augustine's dropped out, with South Bank returning to the League and Sheffield United also joining the fray – even though they were a considerable distance from the mainstream in the North East.

A taste of the potential crowds and income on Tyneside outside the Northern League was gained when Sunderland, now established as a Football League team, visited Tyneside for a double friendly encounter. They attracted a gate of between 5,000 and 6,000 to St James' Park for a benefit game for John Barker which ended 1–1, and also 3,000 to Chillingham Road for a game against East End which the Wearsiders won comfortably 3–0.

The season was virtually over. All that was left to play for was the comparatively unimportant Tyne Charity Shield. East End defeated the Science & Art School 4–3 at St James' Park in a semi-final replay after an initial goalless draw but West End dropped out, withdrawing from the tournament after a 1–1 stalemate with Willington Athletic at Chillingham Road. West End only fielded a reserve side in this match and claimed that they could not raise a team to contest a replay. Willington went on to win the trophy, defeating East End by the only goal of the match at St James' Park in a game that was played over two periods of 30 minutes.

So the season ended with a defeat. Indeed, the entire season had been one of disappointment for the two Newcastle clubs, although East End could boast they had won five of the six meetings between the city rivals. The only bright spot had been East End's FA Cup run and, even then, they had failed to reach the first round proper.

East End had relied largely on a nucleus of regular players: Matt Scott, W. Wilson, James Miller and Joe McKane as well as James Collins, Tom McInnes, Alec McCurdie, Michael Mulvey, Bobby Creilly and centre-forward Willie Thompson. No one had been prolific as a goalscorer during the season. McInnes had scored the most in Northern League and FA Cup games with nine goals, while Collins and Thompson weighed in with six and five respectively.

West End used more players, a considerably higher figure of 31 in only 17 Northern League and FA Cup fixtures. A number of new recruits had been enlisted at various times during the season as the club tried to find a winning combination but to no avail. Former Cowlairs forward W. Dempsey arrived early in the programme, one of a number of Scots who were tried out. More locally, during the season amateur forward James Gillespie came from Sunderland but was to return to Wearside, joining Albion a few months later and becoming quite a star. Two of Rendel's top players, Joseph Wardopper and Sam Wood, were enlisted later in the campaign and Roger Patton notably emerged from the reserves to become a first-team regular. The Ryders, Joseph and William, also graduated into the first team, William taking over from Dave Whitton in goal in the latter part of the season after the regular 'keeper was badly injured.

The mainstays of the team were Robert Calderwood, Paddy Dowling, Harry Jeffrey, Roger Patton and Dave Whitton and their goalscorers in competitive games were not exactly prolific, with Calderwood managing to top the charts with six goals followed by Dempsey (5) and Patton (4). Patton also managed to score three in the Tyne Charity Shield games and Calderwood one, so they reached a magnificent seven apiece.

There was a lack of stability within the West End club and a clear indication of this can be gained when it is considered how the captaincy was passed from one player to another. It started with Calderwood, then to Dempsey, on to Jeffrey and finally to McCann. There was no evident leadership on the pitch, and West End were a team in turmoil. Matters were no better off the field. The West Enders had to find a way of reviving their fortunes – but they never did. Indeed, the West End company collapsed. During June 1891 it was recorded that West End 'had been wound up voluntarily and that it was now to be managed on the old lines'. Four enthusiastic directors took over the club, thought to be Nesham, Black, John Graham and secretary Bennett. They decided to run it as a private enterprise.

John Graham was a West End man, but he joined East End's camp and became Newcastle United chairman.

East End were in a touch better shape and held their Annual General Meeting in Turnbull's Assembly Rooms in Heaton during mid-June. Most of the influential players were retained for the following season, but the match and financial secretaries, Alec White and Charles Tinlin, regrettably decided that they could not continue with their duties. Walter Golding, however, was able to continue as club secretary.

The club announced the full playing record for last season, including Northern League, Cup and friendly games: P40 W21 D6 L13 F101 A76. But most people were more interested in the finances, and this was reported in detail. The balance sheet makes interesting reading. The principal items of expenditure included wages of £524, guarantees paid to visiting teams of £296 and expenses of £119. On the income side, gate receipts were substantially up by £528 to £1,134, and these did not include season-ticket sales of just over £45. Unfortunately, miscellaneous costs resulted in a net loss for the year of almost £100. This was obviously a major concern and was exacerbated by the landlords, the North Eastern Railway Company, announcing that they were going to increase the ground rent to £50 per annum. Although the club had not been evicted (which had been a real threat earlier in the season), it was highly doubtful that they could afford the increased rent. Things were looking bleak, although not as dire as at St James' Park. East End were supported through this difficult period by their directors.

In retrospect, it seems obvious that Newcastle could not support two 'major' teams. One would have to go to the wall. The following season of 1891–92 would be decisive; one club would prosper and develop, the other fade and collapse.

Both sets of players reported for pre-season training in August. In East End's case, this meant two evenings a week (Tuesday and Thursday) under the watchful eyes of new trainer William Bayles, a former athlete of note who joined the Chillingham Road set-up for a salary of 10 shillings (50p) a week. He soon combined his fitness duties with that of groundsman. As usual there were some new player recruits as well. They included J. Connelly, a winger from Stockton, half-back John Spence from Sunderland, the tricky Harry Reay from Shankhouse and, notably, Tom Crate, a Scottish forward from New Cumnock. Tom was to carve his name in Newcastle United's history by scoring the first-ever Football League goal for Newcastle United against Arsenal in September 1893 (although some sources credit William Graham with the goal after a 'scrimmage' in the box). Two of East End's players completed their move across the city to join West End – James Collins and Tom McInnes.

East End formed an amateur second XI (East End Amateurs) which consisted of a number of former amateur players. This team had different colours to the first team, who now played in red shirts. The Amateurs adopted black-and-white stripes as their colours – which may have been an indicator of why in August 1894 East End, as Newcastle United, those now famous colours were selected. Towards the end of the summer, season-tickets were offered for sale – priced at 6s 0d (30p).

For the second season in a row, West End opted for a radical clear out of their playing staff. The only regulars retained from the previous year were full-backs Jeffrey and Dowling, although a number of fringe players were kept on. They acquired a significant number of new players, including McLeod (Glasgow Northern), Ferguson (Vale

Wanderers) and Willie Knox (Elswick Rangers). McNichol (Darlington), Gilmour (Benburb) and Hutchinson (Whitefield) arrived too. Some were to stay and establish themselves, but others were to move on swiftly, none quicker than McInnes who only played in the pre-season practice matches before eventually joining Nottingham Forest. McNichol and McLeod did not stay long either.

There were also significant changes made to St James' Park. The pitch was moved 40 yards to the north and returfed. This had a levelling effect, although there was still a considerable slope. The club had also planned to build a grandstand, but permission had not yet been received from the City Corporation – an ongoing theme which was to thwart stadium development for the century that followed.

West End made a disastrous start to the season when, in their opening game, they crashed 8–1 to a rampant Sunderland in a friendly game at Gallowgate. This was merely a foretaste of what was to come. In their next fixture, a Northern League encounter on Tyneside against Middlesbrough Ironopolis, they received another hiding, this time to the tune of 5–0. And rivals East End were to inflict five agonising defeats on the West End fold. They eventually conceded over 100 goals in all games. West End were on an irretrievable slide.

At Chillingham Road, East End, resplendent in their brand new red strip, were having a much happier time of it. Their season began with three home friendlies and they won them all. London Casuals, an amateur team, were crushed 4–0, the next Football League champions, Sunderland, were shocked to fall 2–0 and Queen of the South Wanderers were heavily defeated 6–3, Connelly scoring four goals for the Tyneside club.

Both of the Newcastle teams had League visits to Darlington on successive Saturdays in the middle of September, West End winning 4–2 (their only away League victory of the season) and East End recording a creditable 1–1 scoreline. East End's draw is notable because, for the first time, a Newcastle goalkeeper had to face a penalty-kick, which had been introduced that season. The invidious task fell to Matt Scott, but he had nothing to worry about because McNally, the Darlington inside-forward, sent his shot over the bar. But there was a different kind of penalty to pay for another East End player in this game. Connelly, their centre-forward, was sent off for striking Waites, the home centre-half. He never played for East End again.

Although West End succumbed 5–1 to Sunderland Albion on Wearside in League combat, they romped home 6–0 against Northern League newcomers South Bank at St James' Park in their next match and ended the day as competition leaders. This result raised hopes of a recovery among the Gallowgate faithful. But it was a false dawn. West End were only top because they had played the most games, and it was downhill virtually all of the way from that point onwards.

West End's decline began with a 6–1 defeat at Middlesbrough, and they slipped to fourth in the table as September came to an end. East End had only played one League fixture (to West End's five) and were second-bottom of the pack in eighth position.

The first qualifying round of the FA Cup arrived at the beginning of October and East End were drawn to travel to face Tow Law. The consensus of opinion was that the County Durham amateurs had no chance against the Tyneside professionals, and the Heaton management offered the Lawers a 'substantial inducement' to scratch from the competition. This offer was quite legal at time, but Tow Law proudly rejected it and were rewarded when a very healthy crowd of 1,000 turned out to see the tie. In the event, East End won easily enough 5–1, with Harry Reay scoring a hat-trick, but the game was a shot in the arm for the north Durham club. East End's reward was a second-stage tie with West End, who had received a bye through the first round.

Before the Cup clash, both sides met in a League encounter at Gallowgate. Football supporters of both persuasions eagerly awaited this game, and both teams underwent special preparations. Despite incessant rain, a good crowd of 5,000 turned out to see a contest played at a fast pace. East End emerged victorious 2–0, with strikes from Joe Wallace and Willie Thompson.

A week later East End picked up two more points in League action by recording a 3–1 victory at Stockton. They now moved up to third place in the table behind Sheffield United and Middlesbrough Ironopolis, passing West End as they did so.

The big FA Cup clash took place at St James' Park on 24 October. This time 8,000 supporters paid almost £169 to cram into the enclosure and witness another game played at pace. West End suffered the agony of having two goals disallowed and losing wing-half McCrory with a cut eye before Jock Sorley broke the deadlock for the visitors. The injured man returned for the second half, but by then East End had the measure of their hosts and soon increased their lead with further goals by Sorley and Spence to win comfortably 3–0.

The last day of October saw East End visit South Bank and share the spoils in a 3–3 draw, while West End completed their only League double of the season by virtue of a 2–1 win over Darlington. Sadly many of their supporters were becoming disillusioned following two home defeats by East End, and only 2,000 turned up for the Darlington fixture.

EAST-WEST UNION 2

March 1892:	West End Reserves win Northumberland Challenge Cup v Rendel (2–1).
May 1892:	West End fold and are disbanded.
May 1892:	East End take over lease of St James' Park.
May 1892:	East End fail in bid to join Football League.
September 1892:	East End's first home game at St James' Park v Celtic (0–1).
December 1892:	East End change name to Newcastle United.
December 1892:	First game as Newcastle United v Middlesbrough (h) (2–1).
May 1893:	Newcastle United elected into Football League (Division 2).
September 1893:	First Football League game v Woolwich Arsenal (a) (2–2).

Fact Box

So far in the League programme East End had played four games, all away from Heaton, and remained unbeaten. They staged their first home League contest at the beginning of November and proved themselves vastly superior to visitors Darlington, winning at a canter 4–0, with Sorley striking a hat-trick. On the same day West End travelled to Teesside to face the mighty Ironopolis, the eventual champions. The Washers were only to lose one League fixture all season, and this clearly was not it as they rattled in six goals without reply.

The divisional semi-final of the FA Cup (third qualifying round) now arrived and East End welcomed their old Northumberland rivals Shankhouse to Chillingham Road. The amateurs shocked the big-city professionals by racing into a two-goal lead during the first 10 minutes of the match, with goals by inside-forwards Auld and Willis. East End battled to restore their pride, but the pitmen doggedly held on and a great Cup tie followed. It was not until the 60th minute that Wallace managed to breach the visitors' defence to give East End hope. It was still 2–1 with 15 minutes to go, and it seemed as if Shankhouse were going to inflict a shock defeat on the Heaton club when the visitors were reduced to 10 men. Their left winger, Scott, was injured and had to leave the field. East End had two former Shankhouse players in their team, Willie Thompson and Harry Reay, and it was they who sank their former teammates. No sooner had Scott left the field than Thompson grabbed the equaliser, and Reay registered the winner a mere three minutes from time to give East End a narrow win. But it had been a rousing Cup tie, and Shankhouse went home with their pride intact.

The Divisional Final of the FA Cup now approached. East End received a home draw against Bishop Auckland, and judges noted they were clear favourites to reach the first round proper. That view was well justified. The game was very one-sided as East End continuously attacked the visitors' goal, and only the Bishop's goalkeeper Strachan kept the score respectable in the first half. Although the home side held a one-goal advantage at the interval, an avalanche of goals after the break saw them eventually win 7–0, Thompson scoring a hat-trick. By now the dashing striker was fast becoming East End's danger-man. He grabbed another three goals in a League match with South Bank which was won 4–0.

West End, meanwhile, went steadily downhill. A League visit to Sheffield United saw them receive another hiding 5–1, and in their traditional Christmas Day friendly at home to East End they succumbed again, this time 3–0. There appeared to be no way out of their downward spiral. At the end of 1891, John Barker, West End's long-serving forward who was now usually to be found in their reserves side, moved across the city to join the Chillingham Road club. There he was to receive a new lease of life.

The customary friendly matches took place at the beginning of the new year of 1892. East End welcomed both of the Sunderland teams to Heaton, comfortably beating Albion 3–1 and losing an amazing match against the other half of Wearside – and prospective champions of the Football League. Played in a snowstorm before 5,000 spectators, the Northern League side stunned the mighty Wearsiders when Crate, Thompson and Reay scored early goals. Campbell reduced the arrears for Sunderland, but Thompson scored another before half-time to restore the three-goal advantage. After the turn-around it was a different game entirely as Sunderland, probably with the elements in their favour, came into their own and rattled in no fewer than five goals to win 6–4. Their prolific centre-forward Johnny Campbell, later to play for Newcastle United, scored three in that game.

During mid-January East End travelled to Nottingham to play Forest, champions of the Football Alliance that season, in the first round proper of the FA Cup. Both teams usually played in red so East End had to change colours. They opted for the black-and-white-striped shirts of both their amateur side and the Northumberland County team so, for the first time in the competition in which they were to gain so much fame, they became 'the Magpies'.

The crowd of around 7,000 received good value for money at Forest's old Town Ground near the River Trent. East End excelled themselves and turned out a performance on par with high-calibre opponents who were to join the Football League that summer and who included Tinsley Lindley in their line up. Forest scored through another notable name, their former Scottish international centre-forward Sandy Higgins, after 21 minutes, but the Tynesiders held out until half-time. East End pressed forward in the second period and Brown, the Forest 'keeper, deflected the ball into his own net following a Reay corner to make the scoreline all square. Higgins soon grabbed a second goal to restore Forest's lead, but East End were not finished yet. They had a goal disallowed for offside and only trailed 2–1 at the final whistle. Even then, the visitors submitted a protest against the eligibility of one of the Forest stars, Scottish international Jock McPherson, who was supposed to have played football in the close-season contrary to regulations. The protest was not upheld so East End headed out of the FA Cup.

A week later the Heaton team went to Middlesbrough to play a friendly game. They won 1–0, and the match was not particularly memorable except for the fact that the winning strike was scored by Willie Thompson from the penalty spot – the very first penalty scored by the club. Meanwhile, West End also visited Teesside to play a Northern League fixture against Stockton. They lost 10–0 but protested against the state of the pitch before the kick-off, and their objection was sustained. The fixture would have to be replayed.

Changes were taking place on Tyneside as January came to a close. Two East End players, McCurdie and Connelly, were transferred to West End. But ground improvements at the Chillingham Road site received just as much publicity, especially as it benefitted the press. The club built a new press-box and included a luxury of sorts – a stove for heating. This was loudly acclaimed by the reporters, although any alterations to the ground seem strange in retrospect as it was common knowledge that the lease on the arena could be terminated at any moment.

The new signings strengthened the West End team just in time for the Northern League derby against East End at Chillingham Road early in February. East End were forced to field a weakened team due to injury and suspension, but they were still far too good for their rivals. West End flattered to deceive when Gilmour gave them an early advantage, but once Jock Sorley equalised there was only one team in it. By half-time, East End had built up an unassailable 5–1 lead. Two more goals in the second half made the final score 7–1, and West End's humiliation was complete. It must have been particularly galling when their former player John Barker scored two of East End's goals.

There was no doubt that East End were the top Northumberland club by far. A suggestion was made in the press that the two Newcastle clubs should amalgamate because, although East End had a good team, they had a poor ground which they could lose at any time. The reverse applied for West End – a good ground but a poor team. Both of the clubs' secretaries, Golding of East End and Bennett of West End, refuted the merger suggestion. But perhaps a seed of an idea had been planted.

When East End played their home League match against Stockton, the visitors were late in arriving and the game kicked-off half an hour behind schedule; although delayed starts were not an uncommon practice at the time. This particular fixture was notable for the fact that an East End player, for the first occasion, missed a penalty-kick (although the miss was not critical). It occurred early in the contest before either team had scored. Sorley took the spot-kick but goalkeeper McLachlan parried his shot. Fortunately for Sorley he managed to put away the rebound so he scored in any event. He later became the hero of the match in the second half when, after Stockton had fought back to level the scores after being two goals in arrears, he fired home the winning goal.

West End won their last-ever trophy early in March when their reserve side lifted the Northumberland Challenge Cup. Sympathy, at the time, was felt for the losers, Rendel, who were appearing in their third successive Final but had lost them all. Cattell and Grierson scored for West End Reserves in the first half and, although Price managed to reduce the leeway for Rendel in the second period, they were not able to equalise.

Meanwhile, East End travelled to Wearside to meet Sunderland Albion in a Northern League match. A splendid contest took place as the Tynesiders were cheered on by a large

West End's final trophy-winning side just before folding; holders of the Northumberland Challenge Cup in 1893. Back row, left to right: Dixon (secretary), Redding, Queen, Ward, Bell, Nesham (committee), Black (committee), Pears (trainer). Middle row: Cattell, Anderson, Fitzgerald, Wilde, Atteridge, Dodds. Front: Grierson, Dixon, Simms.

contingent of supporters from Albion's rivals, Sunderland's Football League club. Albion played at the Blue House ground in Hendon, south of the Wear, and every time East End visited them the Heaton club always had plenty of support from Albion's adversaries. Local rivalry on Wearside was more volatile than that between Wear and Tyne. East End emerged as comfortable 3–0 winners.

A special award was made to Peter Watson, the East End full-back, by the Ouseburn Division of the Newcastle Constabulary. Peter had played at Sunderland in that match against Albion, and on the following day, Sunday 6 March, he was walking in the vicinity of Byker Bank when he saw a local policeman, PC Walton, being set upon by a gang of roughs. Peter immediately went to the policeman's assistance and, after a struggle, the assailants were arrested. PC Walton himself presented Peter with a silver-mounted briar pipe as a mark of appreciation on behalf of the local division.

Former West End player Tom Nicholson was transferred back to St James' Park from West Manchester, and he scored in his first game on his return against Sunderland Albion at Gallowgate. Unfortunately for West End their dismal season continued as the Wearsiders won the League fixture 7–1.

Other notable players were brought in to try and stop the West End rot, with the likes of Alec McCurdie, Connelly, the Ryder brothers, William Simms and James Wardropper (Joseph's brother) turning out at various times with varying degrees of success and failure. With Dave Whitton still injured for the early months of the season, William Ryder was the regular goalkeeper. But once Dave returned in November, he re-established himself between the posts.

When East End invited top-draw Wolverhampton Wanderers to Heaton during mid-March 1892, a crowd of 5,000 turned up. West End could only attract 1,000 to St James' for a Northern League encounter. They lost 1–0 to Stockton and found themselves stuck in second-bottom place in the League. Meanwhile East End defeated their famous visitors 3–0, with former West End player John Barker scoring all of the goals.

As West End tottered on the brink of collapse, East End were fired with ambition. They were informed that they would be exempt from the preliminary qualifying rounds of the FA Cup the following season and decided to boldly apply for membership of the Football League in the summer. The contrast between the two Tyneside rivals was stark.

Both East End and West End showed a social conscience by playing a benefit match at Heaton in aid of labourers who had been thrown out of work owing to an engineers' strike. East End cruised to a 4–0 success which meant that they had won all five games against their Newcastle rivals in the current season, scoring 19 goals against West End's one.

The East Enders completed a League double over Sunderland Albion at the beginning of April by virtue of a 1–0 victory at Chillingham Road, but their crowds were being affected by local strikes which were leaving many supporters short of cash. This did not prevent the club from arranging prestigious friendly games against well-known clubs, however. But East End were not too worried about losing money at the gate; the object was to impress upon the teams of higher status that they were good enough for the Football League.

The Northern League campaign was coming to a close. West End played their last-ever League fixture at St James' Park on 9 April against Middlesbrough. This was the restaging of the game played during February that West End had won 5–4. This time they lost 3–0. East End had a poor end to their League season too, but they ended on a high. They visited Teesside and lost to unbeaten Northern League champions Ironopolis 3–0, and then they also fell by the same score at Bramall Lane against Sheffield United.

East End's next League fixture was a return against Ironopolis, and the visit of the new champions attracted 6,000 spectators to Chillingham Road, the biggest attendance of the season there. The home team shocked the Washers by taking the lead through Harry Reay's header and, although Coupar equalised for the visitors, Sorley restored the home lead from a corner before half-time. Further goals by Thompson and Langley (an own-goal) gave East End a surprise 4–1 victory. This reverse was the only defeat suffered by Ironopolis in League action during the whole season.

East End and West End both completed their League campaigns with defeats against Teesside opposition. West End lost their last-ever League fixture with a single-goal defeat at Stockton while East End fell by the same margin at home to Middlesbrough; however, many regarded East End as unfortunate in this encounter as they had a goal disallowed and also hit the bar.

Those results meant that East End finished fourth in the table behind Ironopolis, Middlesbrough and Sheffield United while West End finished their League career in second-last position, only one point ahead of wooden spoonists Darlington. West End had only gathered eight points from 16 games.

Not surprisingly, East End had a much more stable set-up, using only 16 players in their 21 Northern League and FA Cup matches. Compare this with West End, who fielded no fewer than 33 players in their 17 competitive games.

For the Heaton club, Matt Scott, Joe McKane and Harry Reay were ever presents with Bobby Creilly, Tom Crate, Joe Wallace, Willie Thompson as well as W. Wilson, James Miller, John Spence and Jock Sorley missing little of the action. Two players had weighed in with the bulk of the goals, with Sorley topping the goalscoring charts with 18 goals and Thompson with 13.

If stability had proved successful for East End, instability had done the opposite for West End. James Collins was the mainstay, missing only one competitive game while W. McFarlane only missed two. A few others reached double figures: Dowling, Ferguson, Jeffrey, McCrory, Gilmour and Joseph Wardropper. Most players, though, only turned out a handful of times as the club desperately, and unsuccessfully, tried to find a winning combination.

The season had been an unmitigated disaster for the West Enders. They only managed to win one Northern League contest after the end of October and had failed to score in eight of their 17 competitive matches. They had conceded 56 goals in those games, scoring only 21 in reply. Gilmour was their top scorer with a mere seven goals.

Enough was enough, and the West End management gave up the struggle for survival early in May 1892 and the club folded. West End's William Nesham and John

Black approached their counterparts from the other side of the city. They explained their dire position and offered their East End rivals over the last decade the pick of their playing staff and other assets, including the possibility of taking over the lease of St James' Park which still had some 12 years to run. A few of the players, notably Dave Whitton, Harry Jeffrey and James Collins, joined East End.

The demise of West End resulted in a special meeting being called by East End's directors on 8 May 1892, and a further gathering was held soon after at the home of Joseph Bell on Rothbury Terrace in Heaton between officials of his club and those of West End to discuss events and also finalise a move to St James' Park.

In attendance at that historic summit were Alex Turnbull, T. Carmichael, John Cameron, James Neylon and Bell from East End. West End were represented by Nesham and Black with George Milne, James Telford, George McConachie, John Graham and William Bramwell. All were to become directors of Newcastle United at one time or another in the coming years.

As the future of the Chillingham Road ground was still uncertain, the prospect of moving to a permanent location near to the city-centre was very attractive. Agreement was soon reached between the various officials, and some of the West End directors joined the East End board.

East End's Alex Turnbull was the club's figurehead in those early days, and he also resided in Rothbury Terrace, a neighbour of the host. Bell himself ran a grocer's business at the time. He was later known as 'Uncle Joe' as Newcastle United reached the ascendancy of the English game. Bell also became chairman of the club in the Edwardian era.

Like Bell, several of the attendees became prominent as East End turned into Newcastle United and rose to glory over the next two decades, including two men from the West End camp. James Telford, a bank clerk who also ran a drapery business, was noted as one of the individuals responsible for taking the club to the next stage of its development as the century turned. He was a Scot of dominating personality. John Graham was another clerk and remained connected with Newcastle United for over 40 years. He was another future chairman of the club.

The local press recorded what was to be a key historical point in Newcastle United's annals:

'For the last two seasons Newcastle West End has had anything but a prosperous career and a heavy financial loss has been incurred. Dr Neasham and Mr John Black, who have had control of affairs, have done everything in their power for the success of the venture, but they have had the worst of luck and now announce their intention of severing their connection with the club. In sportsmanlike manner, however, they have made known their intentions to the executive of the East End club, whose directors have accepted the offer of the lease of the West End field. We regretfully, therefore, bid farewell to West End. We shall only have the East End as our representative club in Newcastle. The East Enders will take possession of the St James Park having a team of the strongest possible description and we look forward to an eventful season.'

Joseph Bell was a supporter of East End; it was at his home in Heaton that the club decided to move to St James' Park.

SHOOTING.

MATCH NEAR NORTH BIDDICK.—A great shooting match was decided yesterday morning between "Tavern" of North Biddick and "Scamp" of Washington, who shot at a 4-inch ring, 40 yards off, single guns, 1¼oz shot, for a tenner. Result:— Tavern, 6 marks; Scamp, 5.

FOOTBALL.

ASSOCIATION.

GOODBYE TO WEST END.—We are informed that the Newcastle West End Club has now ceased to exist, and on the invitation of Messrs W Neasham and J Black, the executive of the East End club will become the occupiers of St. James' Park. With the change of grounds, and the increased strength of their eleven for next season, East End should attract big gates in the future, and the financial pressure which has formerly been known should become a thing of the past.

ATHLETICS.

FIVE MILES WALKING MATCH AT MIDDLESBROUGH.—Yesterday a

Farewell to West End. A newspaper editorial on the club's demise in May 1892.

Just about at the same time as West End's closure, coincidentally some 12 miles away on Wearside, Sunderland Albion also came to an end. During the summer of 1892 both communities ended up with sole clubs: Newcastle East End and Sunderland. As it turned out, that proved a defining point in the game's development in the North East.

The announcement that, in future, East End would play their home games at St James' Park was met with considerable alarm among many East End supporters, who objected to the move. The club was in a potential quandary. Although the rivalry between East End and West End had never reached the virulent levels of that between, say, Sunderland and Sunderland Albion on Wearside, it was still intense. It was an anathema for some of the patrons of Chillingham Road to switch their allegiance to St James' Park. Little could be done about that. But something could be done to address the concerns of the erstwhile West End supporters who, on principle, would refuse to support East End. In addition, other sections of the public pointed out that as East End no longer played in that area of the city, their name was a misnomer. A name change could resolve this conundrum. Suggestions for a new club name poured into the press: Newcastle City, Newcastle, Tyne, Newcastle Rangers and Northumbria were initially the main suggestions.

Meanwhile, on 13 May, at the Annual Meeting of the Football League held in the Queen's Hotel in Fawcett Street, Sunderland (in honour of the Wearsiders winning the title), East End submitted their application to join the Football League. At that time there was only one division of the competition consisting of 14 clubs, the bottom four of whom had to apply for re-election. It was intended to extend the tournament to accommodate 16 clubs that year so there were six vacancies; however, as West Bromwich Albion had

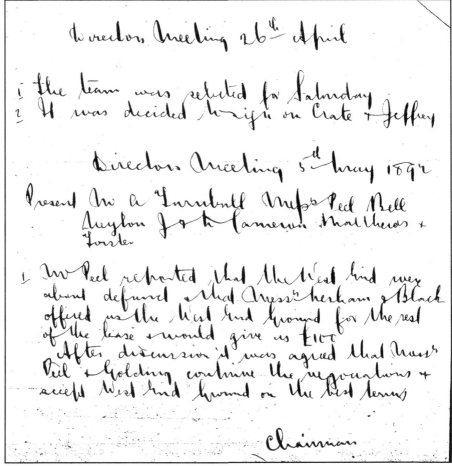

East End switched to St James' Park during the summer of 1892; the official club minute recording the move. *(Newcastle United FC archive)*

won the FA Cup that season, it was unanimously decided to re-admit them. Therefore only five places were to be filled.

Several clubs had issued applications to join the competition, so it was decided to allow each club to appoint an advocate to argue their case for election. The problem was that they were only allotted three minutes to do so. Alex Turnbull stated East End's case. He argued that, with the demise of West End, East End were now the only professional club in Newcastle. In addition, he impressed that the city was easily accessible by train and that their new ground was centrally located.

The voting resulted in the following teams being elected: Sheffield Wednesday (10 votes), Nottingham Forest (nine votes), Accrington (seven votes), Stoke and Newton Heath (Manchester United) (six votes). Only Darwen, of those seeking re-election, failed to gain enough votes. East End polled only one vote, along with Middlesbrough Ironopolis, who had submitted a joint application with Middlesbrough with the aim of amalgamating if successful. However, it was decided to form a new Second Division of the Football League for the 1892–93 season, and both the North East applicants were invited to join, yet both asked to be excused from doing so because, as the official Football League history noted, 'on account of the great expense incurred in travelling'. They had doubts as to whether it would be financially viable. Another season of Northern League football beckoned.

East End held their own Annual General Meeting during mid-June, and club secretary Walter Golding explained the reasoning behind the move to St James' Park. He also reported a financial loss on the year of £50 but did not regard this as serious. He also explained that the club had received an application from West End Reserves, who had secured the Northumberland Challenge Cup last season, to join the East End band. This application had been viewed with favour, and the team would play under the banner of East End A.

The summer of 1892 had been quite a momentous one in the development of football on Tyneside. West End were no more, and East End now reigned supreme. The coming 1892–93 season was to be equally notable. The East Enders would consolidate their position locally, change their name and join Sunderland on the national stage.

The players reported for pre-season training under William Bayles at the beginning of August and, by the end of the month, crowds of 2,000 were turning out to see their practice games. A significant new recruit during the close-season (apart from those

joining from West End) was Willie Graham, formerly of Preston North End and New Cumnock, a player who was really to stamp his authority in Newcastle United's team in the forthcoming years. A tireless worker in the middle of the park and an inspiration on the field, Graham totalled over 100 games for Newcastle United in the coming period. He hailed from a footballing family, his more famous brother, John, also appearing for Preston and for Scotland.

East End played in red shirts and red shorts during the 1892–93 season, although at times during this period they also may have occasionally pulled on red-and-white striped shirts, and they changed to black-and-white colours in 1894. Their first game

Willie Graham was a resolute player for East End and for Newcastle United as they joined the Football League.

at the new St James' Park HQ was played on 3 September when Celtic travelled from Glasgow to provide the opposition. At the time the public entrance to the ground was at the Leazes Park end, although season-ticket holders could enter at both Leazes and Strawberry Lane ends. Ladies were admitted free.

An excellent crowd of between 6,000 and 7,000 turned up to see the friendly encounter with the Scottish Cup holders, and they witnessed the use of goal nets for the first time. The Scots won the game thanks to a controversial Campbell goal (although at least one report credited McMahon) when the home 'keeper Whitton was bundled over the line rugby-style. The star of the game was East End's new Scottish centre-half, Willie Graham. He was just giving a foretaste of the service that he was to render in the future. The teams in this historic game lined up as follows:

East End: Whitton, Jeffrey, Miller (James), Creilly, Graham, McKane, Collins, Crate, Thompson, Sorley, Wallace.
V
Celtic: Cullen, Dunbar, Doyle, Maley, Kelly, Clifford, Murray, Blessington, Madden, McMahon, Campbell.

Sunderland, champions of the Football League, were the next visitors to St James'. There were still no changing facilities at the ground, so while East End changed in the Lord Hill pub nearby on Pitt Street, just off Barrack Road, the visitors changed at the Clock Restaurant on Clayton Street and travelled to the ground by horse-drawn brake. East End took the lead twice against their illustrious visitors through Tom Crate and Joe Wallace, but Sunderland equalised each time with David Hannah and James Gillespie finding the net. Most of the 4,000 crowd were well satisfied with the 2–2 draw.

A double header, home and away, in friendly matches against the Northern League champions Middlesbrough Ironopolis followed and augured well for the new season, although League fixtures were to be few and far between, with the Northern League reduced to a mere six clubs for 1892–93. West End, obviously, had gone but Sunderland Albion had also folded and South Bank had decided to return to amateur status and joined the local Teesside League. Fortunately Sheffield United decided to take part again, although they had also joined the Second Division of the Football League, yet played in both competitions.

But any confidence that the Tyneside supporters had about the new League campaign quickly evaporated when East End visited Sheffield United for their first League fixture. The match started well for East End, with Jock Sorley giving them a half-time advantage, but the Blades swamped them in the second 45 minutes when all five forwards scored in an eventual 5–1 home victory.

The only League match in October took place at the very beginning of the month when Middlesbrough visited Tyneside. East End, minus the injured Sorley and Creilly, were disappointing but still managed to win 3–1. Two first-half goals by Joe Wallace, playing up the hill, gave East End an interval lead and, although Abraham reduced the arrears for the Boro, Willie Thompson later restored the home advantage and gave East End their first points of the season.

There was a six-week wait before East End's next Northern League fixture when Darlington visited Tyneside. They were sent packing at the wrong end of a 5–0 scoreline. A much more difficult League fixture followed a week later when East End visited the unbeaten leaders Middlesbrough Ironopolis. An outstanding game saw the lead change hands as first the Washers led through Seymour but then East End fought back to take the lead thanks to a Thompson brace. But Ironopolis were not top of the table for nothing. They also struck back to equalise through Hughes and then clinch victory with a scrambled goal.

That was a much better game than the one East End played towards the end of the month when they completed a notable League double over the Quakers. They won 7–0 at Feethams, Joe Wallace netting a hat-trick. November ended with the Gallowgate club second only to Ironopolis after five fixtures (which meant the halfway stage in the competition).

A comfortable 5–1 victory over Stockton early in December saw East End consolidate their position in the table, but most interest in Newcastle was focused on a forthcoming meeting which was to be held to decide on a new name for the club. The possibility of a new title had already been mooted between officials of East End and West End when the judgement was made to switch to St James' Park. Now it was decision time, and it was important to gain public approval.

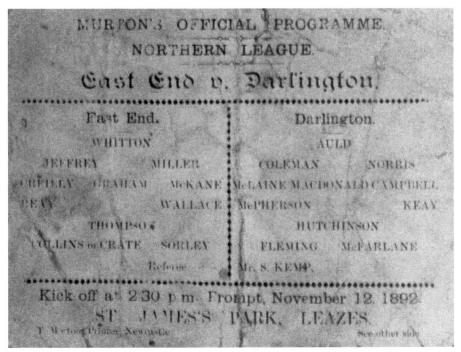

An official 'match card' from the Northern League contest between East End and Darlington in November 1892, won 5–0 by the Tynesiders. (*T. Fiddes collection*)

THE EAST END FOOTBALL CLUB.
THE NAME CHANGED.

Last night a meeting of persons interested in Association football in Newcastle and district was held in the Bath Lane Hall, Newcastle, for the purpose of considering the advisability of changing the name of the East End Football Club, which succeeded West End this season at St. James's Park. Mr A. Turnbull presided, and there was a large attendance.

The Chairman expressed his pleasure at seeing so large an audience, and said it augured well for Association football in the future. They would all be aware that they were met to consider the question of changing the name of the East End Football Club. He believed that there was a certain amount of jealousy existing amongst some people regarding the present title of the club, and it was considered that a more general and representative name should be chosen for it. (Hear, hear.) He might tell them that it was understood between the management of East End and West End when the former changed their quarters that the name of the club should be altered at the end of the season, but it had been conveyed to them that the change should be made at once if they wished to obtain the unanimous support of the public. The directorate were quite willing to accede to this request, for all they wanted was a first class team, and to see the game played as it ought to be, and they all knew that to secure a team to do honour to the city they must have the unanimous support of the public. Amongst the new titles that had been suggested were Newcastle, Newcastle United, Newcastle City, and City of Newcastle. It was for them to decide which it should be, and, whichever one they chose, he hoped they would be unanimous upon it. (Hear, hear.)

Councillor Henderson said he attended that meeting to show that he was still in sympathy with one of their manliest sports, and he was glad to see such a large audience, for it proved that the interest in Association football, so far as Newcastle was concerned, was not diminishing. (Hear, hear.) They all regretted the West End Club was extinct, but that was no reason why they should withhold their influence and support from the club which had come to take its place with the best of intentions. (Hear, hear.) He believed the chief desire of the directorate was to place the best team on the field they could, in order to attract the people to witness the game played as it ought to be. (Hear, hear.) The supporters of the East End and the old West End would have to sink any little jealousies they had, and be united. (Hear, hear.) With the support of the whole of the Newcastle sporting public, they ought to have a team second to none in the country. It might be said the ground was not suitable, but if they brought their influence to bear upon the powers that be, they might then make it as they would like to see it. (Hear, hear.) The East End Club was to be complimented on the excellence of their present combination, and he was sure that, if they got rid of their old jealousies, the team would have a prosperous career. (Hear, hear.)

The names of Newcastle, Newcastle City, and Newcastle United were proposed as new titles for the club, and, on the vote being taken, there was a large majority in favour of Newcastle United, and when the latter was put in the form of a substantial motion it was carried with only three dissentients.

The Chairman said the English Association would meet on Monday next, and they would bring the new name of the club before that body.

A vote of thanks to the chairman concluded the proceedings.

RUGBY.

How the *Daily Journal* reported the historic meeting in December 1892 that confirmed Newcastle United as the new title of the club.

The meeting was held on 9 December 1892 in the Bath Lane Hall near to St James' Park, with Alexander Turnbull in the chair on behalf of the East End executive. Initially, five suggestions were made, but only three were proposed and seconded, thus eliminating any ideas of calling the club Newcastle Central or City of Newcastle. The meeting was asked to vote on the remaining three. The *Daily Journal* reported: 'The names of Newcastle, Newcastle City, and Newcastle United were proposed…on the vote being taken, there was a large majority in favour of Newcastle United.' The *Daily Journal* added the comment: 'The club certainly deserves better support than it is at present receiving and if a change in name will have the effect of bringing up the public, by all means let us have it.'

The club wrote to the Football Association to have the name changed to Newcastle United, but before notification was received back from the FA that the change had been agreed East End played two more League matches. On an icy St James' Park pitch, they lost 2–1 to an unbeaten Ironopolis side, a protest by East End to have the game rescheduled as a friendly fixture being rejected, and they then won comfortably 5–2 against Stockton on Teesside. This was the last fixture played under the East End banner.

Just before Christmas, the Football Association notified East End that the change of name had been accepted, and so the Newcastle United Football Company Limited came into being; although the legal corporate paperwork was not completed until sometime later, not until late in 1895.

The draw for the first round of the FA Cup paired the newly branded Newcastle club at home to Middlesbrough. The Teessiders offered a £20 inducement to switch the match to their ground, but this offer was refused. The first game ever played under the title of Newcastle United was a Christmas Eve friendly against Middlesbrough at St James' Park – a contest which had added significance in view of the forthcoming Cup tie, although the crowd was only between 2,500 and 3,000. United's first goal was scored by J. McIntosh, a new signing from Dundee who was making his debut for the club. Harry Reay had found the net before this but had seen his effort disallowed for a foul. Boro equalised through McManus in the second half, but Reay later scored a valid goal to give United victory. The teams lined up as follows:

Newcastle United: Whitton, Jeffrey, Miller (James), Creilly, Graham, McKane, Reay, Collins, Thompson, Sorley, McIntosh.
V
Middlesbrough: Fall, Crone, McManus, Bates, Stobbs, Taggart, Cronshaw, Blythe, McCabe, Lewis, Black.

For a while the club were still referred to as East End in various media publications around the country, while an amusing incident occurred when Walter Golding, Newcastle's secretary, tried to register McIntosh as a Newcastle player with the Football Association. The FA notified Golding that they were unable to enlist the player as they had never heard of Newcastle United! They had only agreed to the change a couple of days earlier. McIntosh eventually changed his mind and returned to Dundee, after playing one other game for Newcastle, a controversial fixture at home to the Corinthians on New Year's Eve. The famous amateurs had defeated mighty Sunderland a few weeks earlier so great things were expected of them. In the event, the game was a travesty. The visitors could do nothing against the combination and skill of the Novocastrians. Willie Thompson scored a hat-trick and Harry Reay a couple in United's 8–1 victory. In addition, Newcastle had a goal disallowed and also hit the woodwork in a ridiculously one-sided game. In consequence, the St James' Park management refused to pay the Corinthians their £50 guarantee, claiming that they had fielded a weak team.

The new year of 1893 began with visits from well-known clubs for friendly matches. Former West End favourite Bob Kelso was in the Everton team that lost 4–2 and Newcastle scored another four goals, this time without reply, when Glasgow Rangers visited St James' Park. Next came Bolton Wanderers, and they were also sent packing after a 3–1 win.

Newcastle played their last Northern League contest at Gallowgate against Sheffield United in mid-January. This match was notable for the over-enthusiastic play of both sides. In fact, the referee had to stop the action at one stage and call the players together to tell them not to be too rough. The match ended as a 1–1 draw, with two own-goals.

The first-round FA Cup tie against Middlesbrough now took place, and in front of 8,000 it turned out to be one of the most controversial games in Newcastle United's early history. With home advantage, United started briskly and quickly stormed into an early lead, Thompson scoring after only 10 minutes' play. Within a further minute, Harry Reay had made it 2–0, charging goalkeeper Joe Fall over the line. But from this point, the game took a dramatic turn. Blythe reduced the lead before half-time (at least one report credited it to John McKnight), and further goals for the visitors by McKnight and Lewis in the second half gave them a 3–2 victory.

This result would, ostensibly, have been the end of the matter, but notorious repercussions were in store. After the game it was noticed that someone had appeared to have tampered with the Newcastle players' boots. A number of nails (an early stud), commonly inserted back then to help the players keep their feet on the slippery surface, were missing. Allegations and rumours abounded to the effect that certain United men had been placing bets on their team to lose and that the nails had been loosened.

The seriousness of the affair was apparent to everyone when, three days after the match, the directors convened a special meeting at the Viaduct Inn in Byker to consider the drastic action of winding up the club. Club chairman Alexander Turnbull, secretary Walter Golding and treasurer Joseph Bell were shocked and disgusted that some of their own footballers could have connived to throw the game, and the three officials all tendered their resignations. They were prevailed upon to withhold them to allow the matter to be investigated and to make no final decision until after another meeting had taken place a week later when more evidence would be available. When the next gathering was held, the directors threatened to take legal action against the guilty parties (although the latter were not named in the press). Messrs Turnbull and Bell were persuaded to withdraw their resignations, but Walter Golding adamantly refused to remain as first-team secretary. He exchanged places with Mr Dixon, the A-team secretary, although this was to be a temporary expedient. It was only after further evidence was uncovered, possibly completely clearing him, that Golding took over the first-team secretary's role again.

James Miller, the former East End captain, was incensed at the slanderous comments surrounding him and requested that his personal circumstances should be specifically investigated. The club was remarkably secretive about naming names, but they did at least publicly exonerate Miller. He was totally cleared of any misdemeanours, although the club committee investigating the affair could not discover the name of the person who had instigated the slanders against him.

In the end the official inquiry concluded that bribery of some kind had taken place but announced that no suspicion rested on any of their players. Nevertheless, they sacked one of their trainers and also one of their players (who was not in the Cup team) and suspended another. None were named. It was an unsavoury end to the FA Cup campaign.

United played a couple of friendlies against Stockton before their last-ever Northern League fixture against Middlesbrough at Linthorpe Road. Joe McKane missed the train to Teesside so United were forced to play with only 10 men. The team also arrived at the ground late and the contest started an hour behind time. United played well and held the home team at bay for 70 minutes but tired badly in the closing stages and conceded four goals. This was the only League game in the season when they had failed to score.

They ended the term as runners-up in the Northern League, eight points adrift of champions Ironopolis and one ahead of third placed Sheffield United. The club had fielded remarkably consistent line ups in competitive football, fielding only 14 players in the Northern League and FA Cup. Dave Whitton, James Miller, Willie Graham and James Collins were ever presents, with Bobby Creilly and Harry Reay only missing a single outing. Other regulars were Tom Crate, Willie Thompson, Jock Sorley, Joe Wallace, Harry Jeffrey and Joe McKane. Peter Watson and John Barker helped out when needed too. These footballers could well be termed the pioneer players of Newcastle United. Sorley and Thompson topped the goal charts with seven goals apiece.

There were also many friendly matches in the programme that the club played, and there were some notable fixtures among them. One was an encounter against the Football League champions and neighbours Sunderland, who did United no favours when they demanded (and received) an expensive guarantee of £60 to visit St James' Park. United were no match for the polished performance of the Wearsiders, who won easily 6–1, despite playing most of the game with 10 men. The 'Team of all the Talents' was in its prime.

A number of other sides arrived at Gallowgate to take part in friendly games. Stoke proved popular, winning a high-scoring thriller 4–3, but Newcastle proved too strong for Derby County (3–1) and Nottingham Forest (4–1). Among others, Liverpool paid their first visit to St James' and played out a goalless draw, but West Bromwich Albion shipped no fewer than seven goals on their visit (7–2) and Accrington five (5–0).

Until the closing stages of the season, United had only lost a single home friendly match by more than one goal – the 6–1 thrashing by Sunderland. The local players were convinced that they could do better against the famous Wearside combination if they had another chance. So the 'Team of all the Talents' were invited again; and they came and saw and conquered – to the tune of 4–0. But at least the Tyneside players had fulfilled their promise of producing an improved performance.

In total, Newcastle played 35 friendly games during that 1892–93 season (compared to only 10 Northern League fixtures) and, of these, 27 were at home, including a nostalgic trip to their old East End ground at Chillingham Road. This was to play in a benefit match for Alec McCurdie, the erstwhile East End and West End player. United defeated a District Team 5–3. There was one other game against Bedlington Wednesday, but the club did not regard this as a first-class outing.

Although a few games were away from Gallowgate, only a single fixture took place out of the North East. United visited Everton, and not only did Newcastle lose the match 5–2 but they also returned home without their free-scoring winger Harry Reay, who was transferred to their Merseyside opponents during the visit!

The season ended with a visit from Preston North End who were well beaten. This match rounded off a successful season. Second place in the Northern League was satisfactory, and the club had acquitted themselves well in most of their friendly matches – and against Football League opposition. They had certainly raised the profile of Newcastle United. The less said about the FA Cup competition, though, the better it would be for the club's reputation. The playing record of the first season under the banner of Newcastle United was:

Northern League:	P10	W5	D1	L4
FA Cup:	P1	W0	D0	L1
Others:	P35	W23	D4	L8
Total:	P46	W28	D5	L13

Financially, however, the first season at St James' Park was not a success. Large guarantees had attracted quality opposition and had promoted the club nationally but limited attendances had resulted in a loss of £200. This state of affairs could not be allowed to continue. The club needed support from the wider community on Tyneside, and it took two to three years before that was fully achieved and financial security maintained.

On 18 May 1893 a meeting was called at the Northumberland Hall on High Friar Street to consider means of placing the club on a more successful basis. Alex Turnbull was in the chair, and he explained the present situation and outlined proposals to raise fresh capital. He also revealed that the club was, once again, to apply for membership of the Football League, preferably to the First Division but, failing that, to the competition's second tier.

The Annual General Meeting of the Football League was held in Manchester at the end of May, and a Grimsby Town proposal to extend the Second Division was accepted. It was increased from 12 to 16 teams. All four clubs seeking re-election to the Second Division (Lincoln City, Crewe Alexandra, Burslem Port Vale and Walsall Town Swifts) were successful, but Accrington dropped out of the competition from the First Division. This

NEWCASTLE UNITED AFC
1893 - 1894

W. GOLDING   J. WILLIS   H. JEFFREY   W. LOWERY   T. RODGERS   J. PEARCE   J. GRAHAM
R. CREILLY   W. GRAHAM   J. McKANE
C. QUINN   T. CRATE   W. THOMPSON   J. WALLACE   J. LAW

Newcastle United ready for their Football League debut in September 1893. Back row, left to right: Golding (secretary), Willis, Jeffrey, Lowery, Rodgers, Pearce (trainer), Graham (J.) (director). Middle: Creilly, Graham (W.), McKane. Front: Quinn, Crate, Thompson, Wallace, Law.

left four vacancies in the Second Division, and Newcastle United were at the front of the queue. They were duly elected, along with Rotherham Town and (later) Woolwich Arsenal and Liverpool. Another vacancy arose during the close-season when Bootle resigned from the competition. Their place was subsequently taken by another North East club, Middlesbrough Ironopolis.

The North East now had three clubs in the Football League, and the region eagerly anticipated the start of the 1893–94 season. As far as Newcastle United were concerned when they headed for London, to Plumstead, south of the Thames on 2 September to face fellow newcomers Woolwich Arsenal in both clubs' first-ever Football League fixture, it was a momentous day. At the Manor Ground, the historic match was to end with honours even, 2–2, and a new era had begun. The trailblazing days of football were well and truly over.

The Pioneers of the North had done their job. It was time to hand over the reins of football to others. Sunderland had already become Football League champions, and Newcastle United were soon to follow. By the outbreak of World War One both clubs had become part of the game's elite, winning eight Football League titles and reaching six FA Cup Finals between them. Crowds of 50,000 and more would soon pack into Roker Park and St James' Park. Those Victorian pioneers of Tyne Association and Rangers, and the likes of Corbridge, Rendel and Shankhouse Black Watch, had created a true Hotbed of Football.

APPENDIX

The principal competitions in the North East during the pioneering era, 1880–93

Northumberland & Durham Challenge Cup Finals

1880–81 Rangers 1 Haughton-le-Skerne 0

1881–82 Rangers 2 Corbridge 0 (after 1–1 draw)

1882–83 Tyne 2 Sunderland 0

Northumberland Challenge Cup Finals

1883–84 Tyne 4 Rangers 1

1884–85 East End 1 Sleekburn Wanderers 0

1885–86 Shankhouse Black Watch 3 West End 2 (shared with Morpeth Harriers)

1886–87 Shankhouse Black Watch 5 West End 1

1887–88 West End 6 Shankhouse Black Watch 3

1888–89 East End 3 Elswick Rangers 2 (after 0–0, 1–2 protest)

1889–90 West End 5 Rendel 0 (after 3–3)

1890–91 Shankhouse Black Watch 1 Rendel 0 (after 0–0, 2–2)

1891–92 West End Reserves 2 Rendel 1

1892–93 Shankhouse Black Watch v Rendel (Rendel failed to turn up after 1–1 draw)

Durham Challenge Cup Finals

1883–84 Sunderland 2 Darlington 0 (after 4–2 protest)

1884–85 Darlington 3 Sunderland 0

1885–86 Bishop Auckland Church Institute 3 Birtley 1

1886–87 Sunderland 1 Darlington 0

1887–88 Sunderland 2 Bishop Auckland Church Institute 1

1888–89 Sunderland Albion 3 Birtley 0 (after abandoned game)

1889–90 Sunderland 2 Darlington 0

1890–91 Darlington 8 Bishop Auckland 1

1891–92 Bishop Auckland 2 Darlington 1

1892–93 Darlington 2 Bishop Auckland 1 (after 0–0, 3–3)

Northumberland v Durham Inter-County Challenge

1884–85   Darlington 1 East End 0

1885–86   Morpeth Harriers 0 Bishop Auckland Church Institute 3

1886–87   Sunderland 0 Shankhouse Black Watch 0

1887–88   West End 0 Sunderland 2

1888–89   Sunderland Albion 0 East End 1

1889–90   West End 1 Sunderland 4

As far as can be ascertained, no trophy was awarded for the Inter-County contest, and it appears the challenge match died out after 1890.

Cleveland Challenge Cup Finals (later North Riding Challenge Cup)

1881–82   Middlesbrough 2 Redcar 1 (after 3–3)

1882–83   Middlesbrough 3 Redcar/Coatham 2

1883–84   Middlesbrough 3 Redcar 0

1884–85   Middlesbrough 3 Redcar 0

1885–86   Middlesbrough 8 Redcar 1 (after 0–0)

1886–87   Darlington 4 St Augustine's 1

1887–88   Middlesbrough 3 Stockton 0

1888–89   St Augustine's 5 Redcar 1

1889–90   Middlesbrough 1 Stockton 0

1890–91   Stockton 1 Darlington 0

1891–92   Ironopolis 4 Middlesbrough 0

1892–93   Darlington v Stockton (Darlington awarded Cup)

Northumberland Minor Cup Finals

1888–89   Heaton Wanderers 2 Trafalgar 0

1889–90   Science & Art 2 Alnwick 1

1890–91   Mickley 3 Willington Athletic 2

1891–92   Berwick Rangers 6 Godfrey 2

1892–93   Newcastle North Eastern 5 Alnwick 3

Northumberland Junior Cup Finals

1882–83   All Saints' Juniors 1 Elswick Leather Works 0

1883–84   Elswick Leather Works 3 St Cuthbert's 0

1884–85   Elswick Leather Works 2 Bedlington Burdon 1 (after two draws)

1885–86   Elswick Leather Works 1 Cheviot 0

1886–87   Weetslade 1 Science & Art 0 (after 1–1)

1887–88   Morpeth Grammar School 2 Weetslade 1

1888–89   Science & Art 2 Morpeth Grammar School 1

1889–90   Science & Art 2 Mickley 1

1890–91   Science & Art 6 Mickley 1

1891–92   Science & Art 4 St Lukes' Juniors 0

1892–93   Science & Art 3 St Lukes' Juniors 0 (after 0–0)

Northumberland/Tyne Charity Shield Finals

1883–84   Tyne 3 Newcastle FA 2 (after 1–1)

1884–85   East End 10 Newcastle FA 0

1885–86   East End 2 Morpeth Harriers 1

1886–87   Shankhouse Black Watch 2 Elswick Rangers 0

1887–88   West End 3 Shankhouse Black Watch 0

1888–89   East End v Elswick Rangers (Rangers scratched)

1889–90   East End 6 Elswick Rangers 2

1890–91   Willington Athletic 1 East End 0

1891–92   Willington Athletic 5 Rendel 0 (after 1–1)

1892–93   Shankhouse Black Watch 2 Trafalgar 0

Northumberland Challenge Bowl: Winners

1884–85   East End

1885–86   East End

1886–87   Shankhouse Black Watch

1887–88   West End

1888–89   East End

1889–90   East End

1890–91   Willington Athletic

1891–92   Willington Athletic

1892–93   Shankhouse Black Watch

Northern League Championship

1889–90   St Augustine's (champions) West End (runners-up)

1890–91   Ironopolis (champions) Middlesbrough (runners-up)

1891–92   Ironopolis (champions) Middlesbrough (runners-up)

1892–93   Ironopolis (champions) East End/Newcastle United (runners-up)

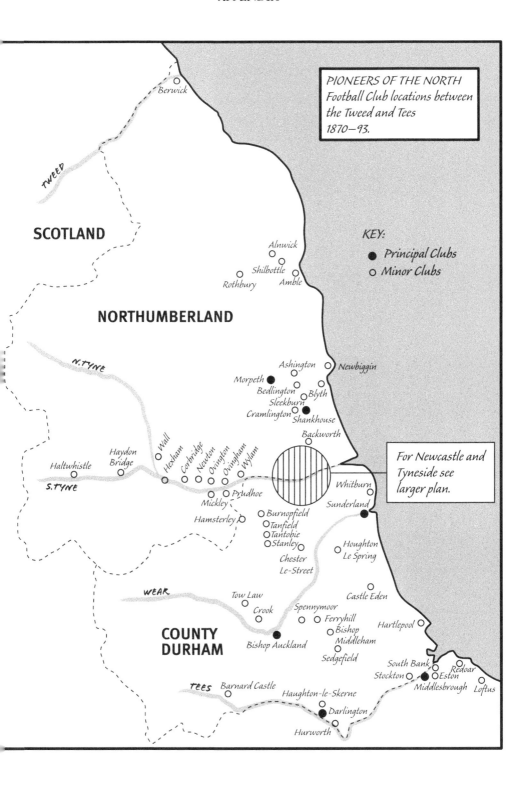

PIONEERS OF THE NORTH
Football Club locations between
the Tweed and Tees
1870–93.

KEY:
● Principal Clubs
○ Minor Clubs

SCOTLAND

NORTHUMBERLAND

For Newcastle and
Tyneside see
larger plan.

COUNTY
DURHAM

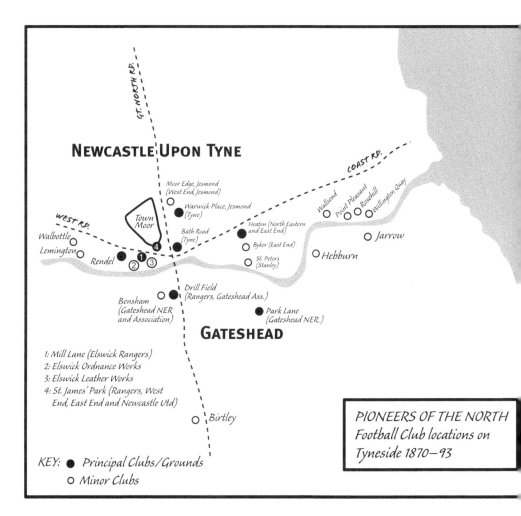

NEWCASTLE UPON TYNE

GT. NORTH RD.

COAST RD.

WEST RD.

Town Moor

Moor Edge, Jesmond
(West End, Jesmond)

Warwick Place, Jesmond
(Tyne)

Bath Road
(Tyne)

Heaton (North Eastern
and East End)

Byker (East End)

St. Peters
(Stanley)

Wallsend

Point Pleasant

Rosehill

Willington Quay

Jarrow

Hebburn

Walbottle

Lemington

Rendel

Drill Field
(Rangers, Gateshead Ass.)

Bensham
(Gateshead NER
and Association)

Park Lane
(Gateshead NER.)

GATESHEAD

1: Mill Lane (Elswick Rangers)
2: Elswick Ordnance Works
3: Elswick Leather Works
4: St. James' Park (Rangers, West
   End, East End and Newcastle Utd)

Birtley

KEY: ● Principal Clubs/Grounds
     ○ Minor Clubs

PIONEERS OF THE NORTH
Football Club locations on
Tyneside 1870–93

ND - #0257 - 270225 - C0 - 234/156/19 - PB - 9781780914077 - Gloss Lamination